JACK THE RIPPER
Truth, Lies, and Conspiracy

by
Daniel Johnson

GW00976113

Acknowledgements;

I owe thanks to Christer Holmgren for allowing me to proceed with a discussion of the case of Charles Lechmere, as well as the information he has provided me. Thanks to the folk at **casebook.org** and **jtrforums.com** for their hospitality, continued support and good nature, and their bottomless knowledge of the case and resources to boot. Acknowledgement to Ordinance Survey and the National Archives for their assistance also. I am indebted to Twisted Saw Media for their wonderful cover design. Thanks to Kirstie and co., for your generosity and your support for me and my "second job!" I'd most like to thank Louise and the ladies at my counselling course for helping me find my way back to where I want to be.
Map credits: Ordinance Survey
Picture credits: All photos used are in the public domain in the United Kingdom and have been sourced from Wikimedia Commons or Wikipedia

Dedicated To

My mother, as always xx

JACK THE RIPPER

JACK THE RIPPER:
Truth, Lies, and Conspiracy

by
Daniel Johnson

Table of Contents

Map of Whitechapel and the Canonical Five Murders

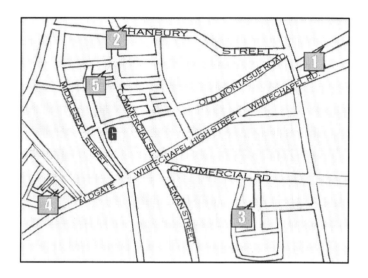

1. Mary Ann "Polly" Nichols, Buck's Row, 31st August 1888
2. Annie Chapman, 29 Hanbury Street, 8th September 1888
3. Elizabeth Stride, Dutfield's Yard, 30th September 1888
4. Catharine Eddowes, Mitre Square, 30th September 1888
5. Mary Jane Kelly, 13 Miller's Court, 9th November 1888
6. "G" – the Goulston Street Graffiti.

INTRODUCTION

In the 129 years since the series of murders committed by the serial killer nicknamed "Jack the Ripper," there have been countless attempts to solve the mystery. Innumerable books, documentaries, and movies, each touting new suspects, are pushed to the public riddled with misinformation and mythology. I have written this book because I was sick of hearing the same tired canards, the same theories and the same myths, trotted out time and again. With this book I do not intend to stick to the script and toe the party line with these untruths.

Not in this book. Just the facts, ma'am.

I intend to take you back to these facts using the original documents, the original witnesses, and an open-minded analysis of what really happened. In doing so I will explore several aspects of this most notorious serial murder case; an examination and discussion of the crimes themselves; a detailed study of the police's pet theory of who the Ripper was; and an intensive exploration of the killer's private world and his psychopathology.

I will begin by going over the crimes in detail, filtering out the myths and the misconceptions and presenting only what the witnesses saw and only what the official documents of the time reported. Unfortunately, many official documents are missing, and I've had to rely upon press reports for some details, including transcripts of some of the inquests. Nevertheless, I examine the facts of the case and come to some truly astonishing conclusions which raise serious questions about the "story" of the Ripper crimes we have accepted for more than a century. Who the victims were, how and why they were targeted, what the killer did and the consequences of these crimes on the community – these elements are up for debate like never before.

Then I will move onto the aftermath of the case, and the deeper political wheels which were always turning behind the scenes. The Metropolitan Police's top brass – Sir Robert Anderson, Donald Swanson and Melville Macnaghten – would in the years following the end of the Whitechapel Murders, claim that the real killer had been detained in an asylum, claiming he was a poor Polish Jew who succumbed to madness. However, the story is far from straightforward, and the truth complex and disturbing. It is a story of prejudice, social unrest, immigration and integration, police hubris, corruption and cover-up that exposes only that the politics of policing can undermine the purpose of the job. Moreover, their unreliable and clashing recollections in their memoirs suggests there was a lot of wishful remembering in how they were written; the post-truth approach to autobiography. It would be funny if it wasn't so terrifying, given that these people were entrusted to investigate, report and testify to things that got people hanged

Then, I move onto a deeper analysis of the crimes themselves, from a criminological and psychological perspective. When it comes to exploring the killer's psychology, and his motivations, I am privileged to have the benefit of generations of criminological and psychological analysis of the phenomenon of serial murder preceding me. In 1888, they'd never encountered a killer like Jack the Ripper. In fact, even now, killers quite like Jack are rare, but examples do exist that can be compared to the man and which allow us to deduce aspects of his motivation. Back then, they had no idea, and it is something of an admirable stroke of genius to see observations made by, for example, Dr. Frederick Gordon Brown about the lack of sexual activity on the body of Catherine Eddowes, or the psychological profile made by Dr. Thomas Bond following the final murder at Miller's Court. Now such observations are commonplace. Most laymen who watch popular crime shows on TV would ask similar questions of a crime scene nowadays without barely a flicker. However, that works both ways – in a time of ubiquitous serial murder, a latter-day psychopath has a collective unconscious to draw upon when developing his fantasies and planning his crimes. What did Jack have? What was his reference for his fantasies, his actions? I tackle these questions and more. Ultimately though any profile on Jack must draw on the facts and upon knowledge and reason, and not make any unjustified assumptions – some recent writers make astounding leaps of faith that would win the Olympic gold for conclusion jumping. I do not intend to shoehorn in any such irrationality.

Finally, I put all of this together and make my case for suspecting a man whose name crops up in every history of the Jack the Ripper crimes, and one who has been named as a viable suspect multiple times in the past. In my analysis, I draw together a profile of the killer which my suspect matches to a tee. I did not seek this suspect for my book, my analysis took me to him. It was one of many shocks this project brought me.

On a personal note, I am truly horrified that vulnerable women's lives are reduced to scribbled notes, gathered from myriad dog-eared books devoted to their murderer bookmarked where I can scrape together information about their personal lives, childhood, work life, their vulnerabilities and their flaws, their mistakes and their hard work. A woman's private life is now public property. They struggled and suffered in a life they probably found painfully mundane, a life they clearly pushed through with a will that was stubborn but insufficient to keep the wolf from the door, with drink and desperation never far behind. And I know that there will be certain Ripperologists who will be going through my book line by line to check the facts are right, not because they necessarily care about the victims, but because they're too keen to give an approving nod when the "canon" is correct or sneer with a jabbing finger if I made a mistake. For the sake of the victims I'd ask those same Ripperologists to try and remember that these are people, these were real events, and with reality comes a degree of humility. I'm offering theories, interpretations of the evidence – maybe I'm correct, maybe not. It is our job to work towards the truth together.

In the spirit of truth, I found myself on numerous occasions staring quite shocked at my computer screen, presented with evidence I couldn't possibly ignore, coming to conclusions I railed against. I had my own preconceptions, and some of them are dying hard. These are the words of a changed man, who is sharing with you a labour of love that offends my beliefs as much as it enriches them. So long after the events, the truth of the Ripper case is still bogged down by the fog of time. However, I think that by swallowing my pride and following the evidence, hopefully I have shed some light in the gloom.

Don't be put off when I stray into slang, or share my personal opinion, while we go through this case together. My tone in this book is supposed to be conversational, because being po-faced about it isn't going to bring back the dead. We're having a chat about things that happened, and I'll do my very best to get the facts right. But this is Polly's story, Annie's story, Elizabeth's story, Catherine's story and Mary's story. It isn't pleasant, dignified or even particularly special – it just is. I want to bring their stories to you as best I can.

I hope you will take away from this book one simple fact. This is an account of real events. The myths and legends around the Ripper crimes are steeped in ideas that are often from the least reputable sources. The idea of the Ripper being a royal, or a doctor, or a "toff" in a top hat was put about by tabloids who sell to the poor. The idea he was a poor Polish Jew was put about by the rich, terrified of the immigrant populations of the East End. I implore you to look at the original documents, all accessible on **casebook.org**, and make your own mind up, and to take every theory – even the ones I report here – with a spoonful of salt, and never stop following the evidence.

Thank you.

DANIEL JOHNSON

PART ONE: Jack the Ripper

The Canonical Five

In the field of Ripperology, the term "the Canonical Five" refers to the five murders attributed to Jack the Ripper by the broad consensus of experts. This hard-and-fast definition was being more or less employed as far back as the 1890s, although there are in fact a total of 11 murders at one time or another considered potential Ripper murders.

The Canonical Five murders are those of; Mary Ann "Polly" Nichols (31/8/1888), Annie Chapman (8/9/1888), Elizabeth Stride (30/9/1888), Catharine Eddowes (30/9/1888), and Mary Jane Kelly (9/11/1888). In this section I will present an overview of these five murders, provide additional details and explore congruent topics and discuss various myths, theories and even suspects. I will also analyse the crimes to some extent, although deeper analysis into the crimes shall be explored later in the book.

Mary Anne "Polly" Nichols

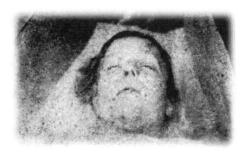

Illustration 1 Mary Ann Nichols' Mortuary Photo

Polly Nichols was like so many other souls caught up in
this tale. Poor, alcoholic, desperate. My instinct
immediately is not to roll out the old, "she was a product
of her time" rubbish, but instead to point out that Mary
Ann "Polly" Nichols was a flesh-and-blood person, with a
childhood, memories, wishes, ambitions, pain and
heartbreak and needs and flaws, like all the victims. Her
desperation, her vagrant lifestyle, her drinking and her
prostitution were symptoms not of the "social conditions"
but of the fallout when a person is left behind by other
people. This was the time of the workhouse, the time of

slums, the time of rampant unchecked immigration, social decay and crime in the darkest corners of the East End, a place referred to by some writers as "the Abyss." But that is not to say it was a time long past. In 2017 the poor, homeless, vulnerable, and plenty of sex workers, continue to suffer violence and exploitation at the hands of those with even the slightest advantage in society. If you think those days are gone, think again.

Polly was born Mary Ann Walker on 26th August 1845 in London, and she married William Nichols aged 19. Five children and a series of moves around London later and the relationship began to go downhill. Between 1877 and 1880 Polly descended into alcoholism and the marriage broke down. She was paid maintenance by William until, in 1882, he was able to prove she was living by "immoral earnings" when she took him to court and lost. Sadly, that was when things took a downward step for her.

In and out of doss houses and workhouses, Polly slept rough and struggled through despite her drinking. Eventually, on 12th May 1888, she would obtain employment with the Cowdry family in Wandsworth as a domestic servant, which seemed to be a shard of light in the darkness. In a letter to her father she wrote of how her life seemed to be on the up;

> "I just right to say you will be glad to know that
> I am settled in my new place, and going all
> right up to now. My people went out yesterday
> and have not returned, so I am left in charge. It
> is a grand place inside, with trees and gardens
> back and front. All has been newly done up.
> They are teetotalers and religious so I ought to
> get on. They are very nice people, and I have

not too much to do. I hope you are all right and
the boy has work. So good bye for the present.
from yours truly,
Polly
Answer soon, please, and let me know how you
are

However, she would be sacked for theft, and was
back in the same position as she was before, which would
be her last spiral into desperation and poverty. She ended
up living first at 18 Thrawl Street between the 2nd August
1888 and 24th August 1888, where she shared a bed with a
woman named Ellen Holland, and lastly at the so-called
White House, 56 Flower and Dean Street from 24th August
1888 until 31st August 1888.

Both doss houses sat within the notorious "Wicked
Quarter-Mile," an area which, even within the "Abyss" of
the East End was considered the most dangerous few
streets in the district, the main area where criminals and
prostitutes took lodging and plied their trade. Thrawl
Street, Flower and Dean Street and Fashion Street lay at
the heart of it. Attempts to clear the slums by the
construction of Commercial Street during the mid-1800s
had been unsuccessful, and only concentrated the slum-
dwelling population into a string of locales including the
quarter-mile. A homeless encampment nicknamed "Itchy
Park" also lay along the stretch. The fact that all the
Ripper victims had, at one time or another, lived within
this area is an indication of the desperate situation many
people in the East End endured. Unemployment,
unintegrated migrant communities and criminal gangs
made the East End an inner-city sinkhole of transient
populations and poor residents, all staving off destitution
and starvation however they could. Partly, this is what

makes the "Gentleman Jack" theories, that the Ripper was a doctor, or a Royal, or some other high-class educated man, so laughable; such a person would stand out a mile among the residents of the place acclaimed writer Jack London nicknamed "the Abyss." It is a fiction, and a silly one at that, which needs to be nipped in the bud.

Last Movements

Mary Ann Nichols was seen on Whitechapel Road at 11:30pm according to a police report, signed by Inspector Joseph Helson. In the same report, he detailed her other known movements. At 12:30 she was seen leaving the Frying Pan pub on Brick Lane, and was again seen at 1:20am the doss house at 18 Thrawl Street, where Mary Ann had lived until the 24th August when she took lodging at 56 Flower and Dean Street, also known as "the White House."

While visiting Thrawl Street, she was asked by the deputy keeper for her 4d doss money, but had none, claiming she was going to go back out and earn it, her words quoted as being, "I'll soon get my doss money, what a jolly bonnet I've got now!" The next recorded sighting of Mary Ann was the last. Ellen Holland, with whom Mary Ann had shared a bed at Thrawl Street for six weeks until a week or so prior to Mary's death, testified that she met Mary Ann, very drunk by now, at the corner of Osborne Street and Whitechapel Road at 2:30am on 31st August. Dejected that she was apparently not allowed back to her doss at the White House until she could pay the 4d for a bed, she claimed to have earned, and drank, the money twice already that night at the Frying Pan pub. The striking clock at St Mary's church gave Mrs Holland the time of the meeting.

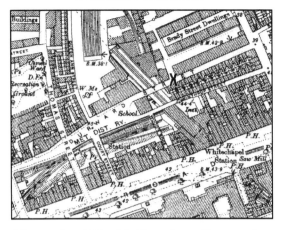

Illustration 2 Buck's Row (now Durward Street)

Now, Ellen Holland's testimony about meeting Mary Ann would segue into the alibi for an important figure who would play a key part in the cover-up to come; John Pizer, a boot-finisher, was arrested on 10th September 1888 by Sgt William Thick as a prime suspect for being a local menace known as "Leather Apron," a man accused of harassing and blackmailing prostitutes with menaces, using a knife and the threat to "rip up" the girls who didn't pay. More on this man later, but let's focus on his relevance to the Polly Nichols case. According to his testimony, Pizer claimed that, like Mrs Holland, he had been down to Seven Sisters Road to witness a huge fire at the docks – and he conversed with a policeman whilst there. This occurred at around 1:30am, several miles from Whitechapel, and took place at the dockside premises of Messrs Gibbs and Co at Shadwell Dry Docks. The inferno raged until morning, eating through hundreds of tons of coal as the flames spread, lighting up the night sky with an orange glow. This fire, and the chance encounters that took place as a result, both clears Pizer and places Mary

JACK THE RIPPER

Ann Nichols heading east along Whitechapel Road for the express purpose of obtaining her doss money.

Somewhere between the corner of Osborn Street and Buck's Row, where she met her death, she encountered her killer. In terms of the timeline, this last sighting at 2:30 was one hour and ten minutes before her freshly-killed body was found at 3:40am, plenty of time for her to have seen several clients and earned the 4d doss money, however, when she was found, she was penniless. Moreover, the circumstances of her discovery invite more questions than answers.

At 3:40am, according to his testimony, carman Charles Cross was walking from his home in Doveton Street, Cambridge Heath Road, Bethnal Green to his place of work for over twenty years, Messrs. Pickford and Co. in Broad Street, when he noticed what he claimed he mistook for a tarpaulin lying next to the locked gates of Brown's Stable Yard on the southern side of Buck's Row. To get an idea of the geography of Buck's Row, it was a narrow and dark straight road with towering buildings on either side, and it included a railway bridge about half-way. Almost concurrently to finding the body, Cross heard the footsteps of another man – Robert Paul, who was similarly on his way from home, 30 Foster Street, Whitechapel, to his workplace at Corbett's Court on the corner of Hanbury Street and Commercial Street. Drawing Paul's attention to the sight, they went over to investigate.

Mary Ann was barely dead when she was found, and Paul would later claim, incorrectly, possibly still breathing. He had felt her temperature and found her to be cold to the touch with no sign of breath, but thought he felt her chest rise and fall when he accidentally brushed her breast with his hand whilst replacing her dress. She lay on her back lengthways across the pavement, her head facing east towards Brady Street, and her right arm laid beside her with her left touching the doors of the stable yard. In the darkness of the street, neither man apparently saw the blood on or near the body. Her dress was dishevelled but otherwise, hid the injuries to her torso, a contrast to the Ripper's other victims, who were put on display quite deliberately. This dishevelment apparently made the men think she may have been raped, and whilst Cross suggested they try to preserve what life she may have left by propping her up, Paul refused and instead suggested that, since they were both already late for work, they continue to work and accost the first policeman they see and report their findings. Paul agreed, and they headed towards Hanbury Street, on their respective routes to work.

As they left, Police Constable John Neil turned into Buck's Row and headed eastwards, probably missing Cross and Paul by an instant. This discovery Neil timed at 3:45am. Aided by a lantern, PC Neil instantly saw the body and the blood and signalled to a fellow officer who was passing the top of Buck's Row along Brady Street. That officer, PC John Thain, joined Neil at the murder site. Neil had previously patrolled the same route at 3:15am, giving the killer a window of only about twenty-five minutes to take Mary Ann into Buck's Row, kill her and mutilate her before apparently fleeing at the sight of Charles Cross entering from Brady Street at the top of Buck's Row. If Cross did indeed disturb the killer, as seems likely, then the killer must have escaped with only moments to spare – had Cross not disturbed him by appearing as a speck on the horizon all the way at the top of Buck's Row, then a policeman's lantern would have been shone in his face right with little or no warning within minutes.

27

JACK THE RIPPER

Neil and Thain agreed that Neil would stay with the body and Thain would run and get the doctor, Dr Rees Ralph Llewellyn, to see the body. At roughly the same time, Constable Jonas Mizen arrived to tell Neil that two men, unnamed but later identified as Cross and Paul, had stopped him and told him of the murder whilst he was patrolling along Hanbury Street. Neil told him to bring assistant and an ambulance from Bethnal Green Police Station. Alone, Neil decided to start knocking on doors, joined later by a Sgt Kerby who aided him. The homes of Walter Purkiss and Emma Green, opposite and next to the scene respectively, were disturbed but neither occupant or their families heard a thing.

At around about 4am Dr Llewellyn arrived and pronounced her dead, suggesting she had probably been dead since for about half-an-hour. At that time, the bodily mutilations were still hidden by her dress, but the throat injuries were apparent in the lantern-light. By the time the body was moved to the Old Montague Street mortuary, alongside Mizen, Kirby and Neil, the residents were waking up and a crowd had gathered. As an aside, but interesting for the purposes of establishing a timeline of events, consider the testimony of Henry Tomkins, James Mumford and Charles Brittain, who worked at a nearby knacker's yard, would contradict PC Thain. The men claimed Thain visited them to tell them of the murder and left his cape there, picking it up later. He denied this, but nevertheless they claim to have heard nothing, despite being a mere 150 yards from the scene with their gates open, and said that at around 4:15am they'd visited the scene to find the doctor and several policemen surrounding the body. As the body was removed, Thain remained and was joined at 4:30am by Inspector John Spratling, who was just in time to see the bloody pavement being washed clean by Emma Green, the nearest resident.

Dr Llewellyn had left after pronouncing death, but was recalled at the mortuary a short time later after the body had been taken after a shocked Inspector Spratling made a horrible discovery. Spratling arrived to find the ambulance sitting outside and the mortuary locked. The mortuary keeper, Robert Mann, was on his way to open up. In the interim he began taking down details of the victim's appearance, and continued whilst the body was eventually being moved inside. Examining her clothes for evidence, Spratling was the first to discover the mutilations inflicted on the body. Deep slashes exposing her intestines ran down her abdomen, causing Spratling to immediate recall Dr Llewellyn. He remarked to the press on the case, "I have seen many terrible cases but never such a brutal affair as this." He would recount the full extent of her injuries in his inquest testimony (see below).

She was described as looking younger than her years, being 44 at the time of her murder. He had greying hair, grey eyes and delicate features, and stood at around 5 feet 2 inches tall. She carried little on her when she was found. As previously mentioned, despite having more than an hour to find more punters to pay for her 4d doss money, she carried no money when she was found. In his haste, it is unlikely the Ripper stole it, but it shouldn't be ruled out. So, there was no money but there was a handkerchief, a small mirror and a comb. She wore a burgundy coat, a woollen frock, two petticoats, a flannel, stays, black ribbed stockings, side-fastening shoes and a black straw bonnet trimmed with black velvet. On one of the petticoats was a label indicating it originated in Lambeth Workhouse. Indeed, Mary Ann had been resident at the workhouse on and off for years. A fellow inmate, Mary Ann Monk, as well as Mary Ann's bed mate Ellen Holland, both came forward to identify Mary Ann after her description, and details of the crime, spread through the community. It was at 7:30pm that Ms Monk formally identified her and soon Mary Ann Nichols' family was traced. The following day, the inquest opened into her death.

Inquest
(Source: The Daily Telegraph, 3rd, 4th, 18th, 24th September 1888 and The Evening News, 3rd September 1888)

The inquest opened on 1st September 1888 at 9:00am, presided over by Coroner Wynne Baxter at the Working Lad's Institute, Whitechapel Road, and coincidentally, was also the same day in which Dr (later Sir) Robert Anderson would become Assistant Commissioner of the Metropolitan Police's CID. However, he was burnt out, and upon doctor's orders went on holiday immediately to Switzerland. He placed Chief Inspector Donald Swanson in charge of the Mary Ann Nichols murder, and he would remain in charge until Anderson returned in October.

The inquest began with the testimony of Mary Ann Nichols' father, Edward Walker. He recounted Mary Ann's recent history, at least what he knew of it. He confirmed her identity and recounted the last time they had seen one another, but aside from these personal details, nothing substantive to the investigation was offered. Next was the testimony of PC John Neil. This is far more interesting, as the line of questioning addresses several key pieces of information; the nature of the deposition site and the Ripper's escape route.

John Neil, police-constable, 97J, said:
Yesterday morning I was proceeding down
Buck's-row, Whitechapel, going towards
Brady-street. There was not a soul about. I had
been round there half an hour previously, and I
saw no one then. I was on the right-hand side
of the street, when I noticed a figure lying in
the street. It was dark at the time, though there
was a street lamp shining at the end of the row.
I went across and found deceased lying outside
a gateway, her head towards the east. The
gateway was closed. It was about nine or ten
feet high, and led to some stables. There were
houses from the gateway eastward, and the
School Board school occupies the westward.
On the opposite side of the road is Essex
Wharf. Deceased was lying lengthways along
the street, her left hand touching the gate. I
examined the body by the aid of my lamp, and
noticed blood oozing from a wound in the
throat. She was lying on her back, with her
clothes disarranged. I felt her arm, which was
quite warm from the joints upwards. Her eyes
were wide open. Her bonnet was off and lying
at her side, close to the left hand. I heard a
constable passing Brady-street, so I called him.
I did not whistle. I said to him, "Run at once for
Dr. Llewellyn," and, seeing another constable
in Baker's-row, I sent him for the ambulance.
The doctor arrived in a very short time. I had,
in the meantime, rung the bell at Essex Wharf,
and asked if any disturbance had been heard.
The reply was "No." Sergeant Kirby came after,
and he knocked. The doctor looked at the
woman and then said, "Move her to the
mortuary. She is dead, and I will make a further

31

examination of her." We placed her on the ambulance, and moved her there. Inspector Spratley came to the mortuary, and while taking a description of the deceased turned up her clothes, and found that she was disembowelled. This had not been noticed by any of them before. On the body was found a piece of comb and a bit of looking-glass. No money was found, but an unmarked white handkerchief was found in her pocket.

Coroner: Did you notice any blood where she was found?

Neil: There was a pool of blood just where her neck was lying. It was running from the wound in her neck.

Coroner: Did you hear any noise that night?

Neil: No; I heard nothing. The farthest I had been that night was just through the Whitechapel-road and up Baker's-row. I was never far away from the spot.

Coroner: Whitechapel-road is busy in the early morning, I believe. Could anybody have escaped that way?

Neil: Oh yes, sir. I saw a number of women in the main road going home. At that time any one could have got away.

Coroner: Some one searched the ground, I believe?

Neil: Yes; I examined it while the doctor was being sent for. Inspector Spratley: I examined the road, sir, in daylight.

A Juryman (to witness): Did you see a trap in the road at all?

Neil: No.

A Juryman: Knowing that the body was warm, did it not strike you that it might just have been laid there, and that the woman was killed elsewhere?

Neil: I examined the road, but did not see the mark of wheels. The first to arrive on the scene after I had discovered the body were two men who work at a slaughterhouse opposite. They said they knew nothing of the affair, and that they had not heard any screams. I had previously seen the men at work. That would be about a quarter-past three, or half an hour before I found the body.

Neil's testimony is striking because it addresses the question of whether the body had been dumped there rather than the victim having been killed on the spot. He replies that there was no evidence of marks left by wheels and no witnesses nearby had seen or heard anything. Clearly the juror is puzzled by the killer's ability to seemingly vanish despite having freshly murdered his victim. Two policemen, Thain and Neil, patrolled Buck's Row at either end, leaving a twenty-five-minute window for the killer to get in and out, and it is already clear he barely made it out. The coroner asks Neil if it is possible the killer could have escaped via the busy early-morning rush of Whitechapel Road, and he concurs, suggesting Inspector Spratley conducted a search by eye of the road after the discovery. It would certainly make sense for the killer to slip into the throng of people on Whitechapel Road and head back into the district, unseen and with little blood staining him. Even then, depending upon his profession, he may be able to get away with even that, as the Coroner notes in his summing-up that the preponderance of slaughterhouses in the area would make bloodstained clothing a common sight.

JACK THE RIPPER

Next comes the crucial testimony from Dr Llewellyn on the results of the post-mortem examination of Mary Ann Nichols.

Henry Llewellyn, surgeon: On Friday morning I was called to Buck's-row about four o'clock. The constable told me what I was wanted for. On reaching Buck's-row I found the deceased woman lying flat on her back in the pathway, her legs extended. I found she was dead, and that she had severe injuries to her throat. Her hands and wrists were cold, but the body and lower extremities were warm. I examined her chest and felt the heart. It was dark at the time. I believe she had not been dead more than half-an-hour. I am quite certain that the injuries to her neck were not self-inflicted. There was very little blood round the neck. There were no marks of any struggle or of blood, as if the body had been dragged. I told the police to take her to the mortuary, and I would make another examination. About an hour later I was sent for by the Inspector to see the injuries he had discovered on the body. I went, and saw that the abdomen was cut very extensively. I have this morning made a post-mortem examination of the body. I found it to be that of a female about forty or forty-five years. Five of the teeth are missing, and there is a slight laceration of the tongue. On the right side of the face there is a bruise running along the lower part of the jaw. It might have been caused by a blow with the fist or pressure by the thumb. On the left side of the face there was a circular bruise, which also might have been done by the pressure of the fingers. On the left side of the neck, about an inch below the jaw, there was an incision about four inches long and running from a point immediately below the ear. An inch below on the same side, and commencing about an inch in front of it, was a circular incision terminating at a point about three inches below the right jaw. This incision completely severs all the tissues down to the vertebrae. The large vessels of the neck on both sides were severed. The incision is about eight inches long. These cuts must have been caused with a long-bladed knife, moderately sharp, and used with great violence. No blood at all was found on the breast either of the body or clothes. There were no injuries about the body till just about the lower part of the abdomen. Two or three inches from the left side was a wound running in a jagged manner. It was a very deep wound, and the tissues were cut through. There were several incisions running across the abdomen. On the right side there were also three or four similar cuts running downwards. All these had been caused by a knife, which had been used violently and been used downwards. The wounds were from left to right, and might have been done by a left-handed person. All the injuries had been done by the same instrument.

Dr Llewellyn's remarks give us the first indication of the killer's modus operandi and signature. Bruising to the face and jaw, caused either by a blow or "pressure of the fingers," i.e., strangulation, came first while the victim was still alive. The missing teeth may be related to this, but I see no further evidence of tooth loss due to violence in any of the reports of the scene or her injuries, so I doubt it. Either way, rendered insensible, the victim was then laid on the floor, with the killer by her right side. This can be determined by what occurred next. The killer cut her throat, with two long, deep cuts commencing on the far left of her throat and terminating below the jaw on the right. The initial incision appears to have been aimed at the main arteries in the left-hand-side of the victim's throat so that any blood spraying out was directed away from the killer, a fact confirmed – along with the suggestion that the killer lay her down to cut her throat – by the lack of blood on her chest as reported by the doctor. After this cut, he cut again, this time running the blade through the neck wholesale, cutting through all the tissue and vessels on both sides. This double-cutting technique is important to understanding what the killer was trying to do, and why, and will be developed as we go on, sufficed to say his motives and methods become clearer with each murder.

The presence, or absence, of blood is often a contentious factor in the Ripper murders. In this case, blood was indeed seen "oozing" from the neck wound by PC Neil, whilst Inspector Spratling commented that he saw some of Mary Ann's clothing stained with blood and he witnessed Emma Green washing blood away from the scene when he arrived. The apparent disparity between Dr Llewellyn's testimony and that of Spratling's could simply be that Dr Llewellyn specifically noted the breast as being devoid of blood whilst Spratling wasn't so clear – and judging by the blood on the pavement he clearly meant the back of the body. Nevertheless, it is clear that the killer's method, violently severing the side of the throat opposite himself, shows a desire to rapidly seize control of his victim and kill her in as efficient a manner as possible, whilst trying to keep himself clean of blood. This could be for both sanitary reasons as well as trying to avoid incriminating himself to onlookers, family or friends. It is an odd quirk of serial murder that often, little evidence ever comes to light of killers captured or suspected due to the presence of blood on their person. Peter Sutcliffe, the Yorkshire Ripper, reported in his statement to police that he sometimes found spots of blood on his shoes, and that's about it. Certainly, there are no reports of Sutcliffe being reported by people who suspected him because of bloodstains. Similarly, in the case of Jack the Ripper, the killer quite deliberately avoided getting blood on himself, and probably succeeded

After cutting the victims' throat he commenced with the abdominal mutilations. Considering the subsequent murders, these are rather tame injuries. A single long, deep cut exposing the intestines on the left-hand side, and a handful of cuts running downwards and across on the right. They appear similar to those inflicted on the Miller's Court victim – a series of cuts rather than the single gutting injury seen in Chapman and Eddows. In this case, rather than being far more violent, as with the final victim, these cuts are far less violent. Dr Llewellyn commented that they were carried out "with great violence," but in fairness, he hadn't seen anything yet. As the following crimes unfolded the killers' ability and the depth of his depravity would put this first murder into context. It appears here that the killer made a single deep cut, found it to be taking too long given his exposed position in the street, and contented himself to a series of slashes in the flesh, the exact sort of repeated activity seen in offenders with picquerism in their profiles.

CRIMINAL MIND

Picquerism is a paraphilia (an abnormal sexual desire) associated with stabbing or cutting. Sexually-motivated serial killers who repeatedly stab their victims are often displaying this behaviour, as are killers who mutilate or dismember, and they get their thrill from performing on these actions. This is not to be confused with killers who use knives as substitute penises, as those killers are either impotent or are sexually dominating their victims, rather than deriving pleasure from the act of mutilation itself. Another important aspect of the Ripper murders is that the killer is carrying his mutilations out on a dead victim rather than a live one, the technical term being **necrosadism,** or the derivation of pleasure from mutilation of the dead.

The next important, and strange, piece of inquest testimony worth detailing here is that related to Charles Cross, Robert Paul and PC Mizen. At this early stage of the book, we meet our first person of interest, Charles Cross.

Charles Cross, aka Charles Allan Lechmere

Perhaps the first man named in any account of the Ripper murders is the man who discovered the first victim's body, carman Charles Cross. In most accounts, this is where we leave him, and but for the work of Christopher Holmgren, who analysed Cross testimony and found glaring holes in his story, as well as evidence of deceit towards the police and courts that cast serious suspicion over him, his candidacy as a suspect would have been ignored.

The case against Charles Cross is largely based upon his involvement with the Mary Ann Nichols case and little else, and is in my opinion an extremely important set of observations, but the theory that this evidence carries over to Cross being the killer is a little far-fetched. I am including the basics of this theory here, with Mr Holmgren likely to set his theory out in full in his own writings at some later time, and I hope it illustrates to the reader that 129 years later, there are myriad theories that can be posited with convincing evidence, with no definitive way of knowing one way or another whether they come close to the truth. In this case, the claim made by Holmgren's analysis of the evidence is startling; that Charles Cross lied about his identity, that he can be placed near each crime scene at around the times of the murders, and that he can be placed with Mary Ann Nichols at the exact time of death. Let us examine the evidence.

First, read the testimony of PC Mizen;

> **Police-constable Mizen** said that at a quarter to four o'clock on Friday morning he was at the crossing, Hanbury-street, Baker's-row, when a carman who passed in company with another man informed him that he was wanted by a policeman in Buck's-row, where a woman was lying. When he arrived there Constable Neil sent him for the ambulance. At that time nobody but Neil was with the body.

Mizen claims that the carman and another man, certainly Charles Cross and Robert Paul, informed him that a policeman was waiting for him at Buck's Row, where "a woman was lying." They were then apparently allowed to leave. PC Neil would discover Mary Ann's body at almost the same time as Cross and Paul left the scene, but they did not meet. Neil instead signalled Thain, who fetched

39

the doctor. When questioned, Cross denied having seen a policeman.

Charles Cross, carman, said he had been in the employment of Messrs. Pickford and Co. for over twenty years. About half-past three on Friday he left his home to go to work, and he passed through Buck's-row. He discerned on the opposite side something lying against the gateway, but he could not at once make out what it was. He thought it was a tarpaulin sheet. He walked into the middle of the road, and saw that it was the figure of a woman. He then heard the footsteps of a man going up Buck's-row, about forty yards away, in the direction that he himself had come from. When he came up witness said to him, "Come and look over here; there is a woman lying on the pavement." They both crossed over to the body, and witness took hold of the woman's hands, which were cold and limp. Witness said, "I believe she is dead." He touched her face, which felt warm. The other man, placing his hand on her heart, said "I think she is breathing, but very little if she is." Witness suggested that they should give her a prop, but his companion refused to touch her. Just then they heard a policeman coming. Witness did not notice that her throat was cut, the night being very dark. He and the other man left the deceased, and in Baker's-row they met the last witness, whom they informed that they had seen a woman lying in Buck's-row. Witness said, "She looks to me to be either dead or drunk; but for my part I think she is dead." The policeman said,

"All right," and then walked on. The other man left witness soon after. Witness had never seen him before.

[...]

[Cross] denied having seen Police-constable Neil in Buck's-row. There was nobody there when he and the other man left. In his opinion deceased looked as if she had been outraged and gone off in a swoon; but he had no idea that there were any serious injuries.

Coroner: Did the other man tell you who he was?

Cross: No, sir; he merely said that he would have fetched a policeman, only he was behind time. I was behind time myself.

A Juryman: Did you tell Constable Mizen that another constable wanted him in Buck's-row?

Cross: No, because I did not see a policeman in Buck's-row.

Compare with Robert Paul's testimony:

Robert Paul, 30, Forster-street, Whitechapel, carman, said as he was going to work at Cobbett's-court, Spitalfields, he saw in Buck's-row a man standing in the middle of the road. As witness drew closer he walked towards the pavement, and he (Paul) stepped in the roadway to pass him. The man touched witness on the shoulder and asked him to look at the woman, who was lying across the gateway. He felt her hands and face, and they were cold. The clothes were disarranged, and he helped to pull them down. Before he did so he detected a slight movement as of breathing, but very faint.

JACK THE RIPPER

The man walked with him to Montague-street, and there they saw a policeman. Not more than four minutes had elapsed from the time he first saw the woman. Before he reached Buck's-row he had seen no one running away.

The Evening News (3rd September 1888) reported his testimony in far greater detail;

Robert Paul, a carman, has made the following remarkable statement: He says: It was exactly a quarter to four when I passed up Buck's Row to my work as a carman for Covent Garden market. It was dark, and I was hurrying along, when I saw a man standing where the woman was. He came a little towards me, but as I knew the dangerous character of the locality I tried to give him a wide berth. Few people like to come up and down here without being on their guard, for there are such terrible gangs about. There have been many knocked down and robbed at that spot. The man, however, came towards me and said, "Come and look at this woman." I went and found the woman lying on her back. I laid hold of her wrist and found that she was dead and the hands cold. It was too dark to see the blood about her. I thought that she had been outraged, and had died in the struggle. I was obliged to be punctual at my work, so I went on and told the other man I would send the first policeman I saw. I saw one in Church Row, just at the top of Buck's Row, who was going round calling people up, and I told him what I had seen, and I asked him to come, but he did not say whether he should come or not. He continued calling the people up, which I thought was a great shame, after I had told him the woman was dead. The woman was so cold that she must have been dead some time, and either she had been lying there, left to die, or she must have been murdered somewhere else and carried there. If she had been lying there long enough to get so cold as she was when I saw her, it shows that no policeman on the test had been down there for a long time. If a policeman had been there he must have seen here, for she was plain enough to see. Her bonnet was lying about two feet from her head.

Cross denied seeing a policeman in Buck's Row, but claims in the same deposition that he and Paul heard a policeman coming when they decided to leave Buck's Row to get to work, yet also appears to have decided to seek out a policeman on their way to direct them to the body – rather than just wait momentarily for the approaching cop to find them. Apparently in justification of this, he claims both he and Paul were "behind time." This must mean late in getting out of the house, as he only lived around the corner at Doveton Street, Bethnal Green. Paul doesn't mention the policeman Cross alleges they heard coming towards Buck's Row in his testimony. Mizen claims it was around 3:45am when he was accosted by the men, whilst the discovery of the victim is placed at around 3:40am, and Paul suggests around four minutes had passed since he met Cross and left Buck's Row. The timings appear correct, until you look deeper into Cross' testimony.

In a nutshell, newspaper reports of his story are contradictory and his timings, when examined, do not add up. He claimed to have left home late at 3:30am, ten minutes later than usual, and found the body at 3:40am, then left the scene with Robert Paul at around 3:45am to head for his workplace at Pickford's and Co. (a firm for which Cross worked carrying meat around the district). When examined, there are chunks of time unaccounted for in Cross' timeline that raise serious questions These discrepancies are just part of the tapestry of circumstantial evidence which present Cross as a person of interest in the murders. For now, we will discuss the discrepancies in his timings for the Mary Ann Nichols murder.

To start with, walking times between his home at 22 Doveton Street and Pickford's at Broad Street were at the time around 40 minutes. Between his home and Buck's Row, an easy five or six minutes. Cross claims to have left his home late, at 3:30am, and found the body at 3:40am. Robert Paul claims he encountered Cross at 3:45am in Buck's Row, and they left only to encounter PC Mizen along the way. PC Mizen places this meeting at 3:45am also, while Paul suggests around four minutes elapsed between his seeing the body and encountering the policeman. I am inclined to believe that Paul, who also claimed to be late for work, would be more keenly aware of the true time in this circumstance, and that an officer on the beat may not be as accurate. However, interpret that detail how you will.

Now to state the facts drawn from the testimony of the key individuals involved in order to make my point. The body was never alone once Neil found it at 3:45am; he stayed with it and signalled PC Thain, who sent for the doctor, then Mizen arrived and was sent to get the ambulance by Neil. If Mizen is correct and he was accosted at 3:45am, Neil must have missed Cross and Paul by moments as Paul reports that it took a total of four minutes or so between his seeing Cross and the body, and reaching PC Mizen at the corner of Old Montague Street and Hanbury Street. Recall, Cross claimed to have heard a policeman approaching. Paul places his discovery of Cross and the body at 3:45am. Cross puts his discovery of the body at 3:40am, and claims to have left his home at 3:30am. It is a six-minute walk between his home and the murder scene, and yet even shaving off ten minutes by claiming to have been late, Cross doesn't account for nine minutes of time, between 3:36am and 3:45am. The attack on Mary Ann had taken place immediately prior to her discovery – she was still warm. Dr Llewellyn, after a cursory examination at the scene, suggested she had died within half-an-hour of his examination at 4am, an earliest time of death of 3:30am. That is only if his examination did take place at 4am.

Two newspapers, The Daily News and The Evening News, reported Dr Llewellyn as saying he was called at "five to four [on the morning of the murder]," whilst the East London Advertiser suggested he took "ten minutes" to get there. Thain's and horse slaughterer employee Henry Tomkins' testimony suggests PC Thain passed by telling them of the murder prior to fetching Dr Llewellyn. Thain claims that "ten minutes after I fetched the surgeon, I saw two workmen standing with Neil." Tomkins claims he and his colleagues went to see the body at twenty minutes past four rather than head home after their shift. This puts Thain and the Doctor's arrival at the scene at 4:10am.

So, if Dr Llewellyn made his claim that the victim had been killed within half-an-hour of his examination at 4:10am, it means the murder took place, at the earliest, at 3:40am. This is the exact time Cross claims to have found the body, and slap-bang in the middle of the nine-minute window of missing time in his testimony. Given that Cross lives a mere five or six minutes away on foot, and claims to have left home at 3:30am, found the body at 3:40am, but is only placed at the scene independently by Robert Paul's testimony at 3:45am, that leaves Cross 15 minutes in total, the latter nine completely unaccounted for, the final few moments all that would have been needed for him to have killed Mary Ann Nichols. He could have encountered Mary Ann on his way to work and doubled back, to where he assumed the doors of Brown's Stable Yard would be unlocked, which it wasn't, made a hash of the killing and was disturbed by Robert Paul. Faced with either running, and drawing attention to his guilt, or simply walking away and hoping Paul paid no attention to Mary Ann's body, he decided instead to think on his feet and accost Paul, showing concern for a woman he claimed may have simply been drunk or fainted.

The timings are one thing, but his identity is another. At the inquest, he gave his name as Charles Cross and his address as 22 Doveton Street. A quick check of the census for 1891 shows that living at 22 Doveton Street, Bethnal Green was actually a man named Charles Allen Lechmere. Cross had been the name of one of the man's many "stepfathers." Lechmere was 39, lived with his wife and twelve children, and had worked for Pickford's carting meat around the district to and from butchers and slaughterhouses for twenty years. His early life was unsettled – he continually moved around the district with his mother, who would fall in and out of relationships with men who would repeatedly abandon Lechmere and his mother. In June 1888, he moved away from his mother to live with his wife in Bethnal Green, having previously clung to her for emotional and financial support, but when he left he also left his own eldest daughter behind.

As we shall explore a in more detail later, these aspects of his life play into another telling clue – the geographical profile of the killer. For example, tracing the shortest routes between his home and workplace takes him by several of the crime scenes at around the times of the crimes taking place. Finally, his job, carting raw meat around the district, would allow him to move around covered in blood with relatively little suspicion.

However, the problems with Lechmere's candidacy comes with the fact that so many details are missing after so many decades. It is hard to believe that the police did not spend the time between 1888 and 1892, when the case was closed, investigating the murders without noticing and following up on the glaring timeline errors with Lechmere's story – a single amended statement explaining the timeline would clear this up, and if such documentation existed then, it probably is lost to us now. There is also no real issue with the man using his stepfather's name, and nevertheless, he did provide his correct address and occupation for the police and courts. Finally, Christopher Holmgren's theory includes the claim that Lechmere did not come forwards until Robert Paul did – but this is untrue, as it was in fact Robert Paul who did not come forwards until later. That said, the existence of very questionable evidence pointing a finger of suspicion at a suspect cannot be ignored and I hope in future additional effort is made by commentators to explore Lechmere's candidacy as a Ripper suspect.

*   *   *

The inquest went on to speak to several witnesses from Buck's Row who saw, and heard, nothing. The somewhat comical testimony of mortuary workers Robert Mann and James Hatfield came next, with their uncertain memories of even basic details of the night providing little to help the investigation. Some have suggested that Mann's patchy testimony makes him a suspect himself, but, there's little to single him out. Finally, the inquest closed on 22nd September 1888, with a verdict of wilful murder against person or persons unknown.

Mary Ann Nichols was buried at Ilford Cemetery on 6th September 1888.

Annie Chapman

Illustration 3 Annie Chapman's Mortuary Photo

Born Eliza Ann Smith in 1841 in Paddington, Annie married her husband John Chapman at the age of 27. Hers was a story not free of heartache. Of their three children, one son was born disabled and her daughter died very young. The marriage subsequently broke down, reportedly because of Annie's "drinking and immorality," although John continued to pay Annie 10 shillings per week as maintenance. When John died in 1886, this income ended, leaving Annie penniless – and which prompted her to resort to prostitution to survive. The loss of income was not the worst consequence of his death though; Annie went downhill from then on, evidently upset and depressed whenever she spoke of him. Prior to John's death, Annie had moved to 30 Dorset Street and met a man named John Sivvey, but they parted once Annie's maintenance stopped. Between 1886 and 1888 she moved between doss houses in Whitechapel, ending up at 35 Dorset Street, Crossingham's Lodging House in mid-1888. This was her home at the time of her murder.

Last Movements

Annie Chapman was seen by the deputy manager at Crossingham's Lodging House (35 Dorset Street) at 11:30am on 7th September 1888, when he let her into the kitchen. She was seen 40 minutes later at 12:10am 8th September by witness William Stevens, who said she looked drunk. His testimony also explained a piece of otherwise out-of-place evidence found on her person after her murder; an envelope baring the crest of the Sussex Regiment that contained pills. It also bore the date and location "London, 28 August 1888," and the letter M, all in a man's handwriting. Rather than being some smoking gun as to the killer's identity, it was in fact lying around on the floor of the doss house while Annie was there, and she picked it up to use when a pill box she owned broke, something Stevens witnessed. So much for mysterious clues. However, in his inquest testimony, Stevens, and another acquaintance Eliza Cooper, did confirm that Annie was wearing three brass rings on her finger. They were missing when her body was found.

By 1:35am she had left and come back, and was

now sitting eating a baked potato. Again, she was seen by Stevens, and by Donovan, who asked for her 4d doss money. By now quite drunk, she said she did not have it. "I don't have it. I'm weak and ill and I've been to the Infirmary." No records support this visit to the infirmary. On her way out, she asked Donovan to keep her bed, and she'll return with the doss money, repeating her intentions to John Evans, the·night watchman. Unfortunately, her movements from then become cloudy. Reports of her being seen in the Ten Bells pub were made and turned out be incorrect. What is known is that at 5:30am on the 8th September 1888, Mrs Elizabeth Darrell witnessed a woman she later identified as Annie Chapman standing with a man – taller than Annie, shabby-genteel, "foreign-looking," and wearing a deer-stalker hat – at the entrance to 29 Hanbury Street. She heard the man ask, "Will you?" and Annie reply, "Yes."

To clarify the circumstances of the discovery of Annie's body, the layout of 29 Hanbury Street needs to be addressed. Eddleston (2010, p.26-27) provides an excellent guide here; the building was a three-storey lodging house, with a cat's meat shop facing the street, a flat in the back, and two flats in each of the next two floors. Access to the shop was by one door, and access to the rest of the properties was via a passageway leading from another door next to the shop entrance and terminating in the backyard, which was the scene of the murder. The yard was down three stone steps and surrounded entirely by tall fences, and there was also a basement entrance there used by one of the residents, Amelia Richardson of the back-ground-floor flat as part of her packing-case business. Often homeless people needed to be moved on from the passageway and the back yard by the residents, meaning access to the

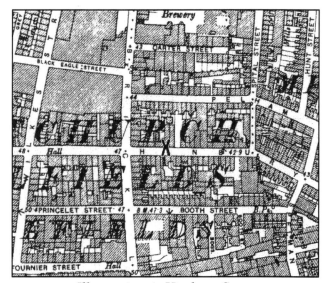

Illustration 4: Hanbury Street

passageway and the back yard was obviously quite public and unmonitored. This passageway entrance was the door Annie was seen with a man at 5:30am, a man who was certainly her killer.

At about the same time, neighbour Albert Cadoche, who lived next door at number 27 Hanbury Street, was out in his back yard, adjacent to the murder scene, and heard a woman's voice say, "No," then within minutes heard something fall heavily against the fence. All he would have needed to do was peek over the fence, and he would have certainly seen the Ripper at work on Annie's body. It can be reasonably assumed that after she exclaimed "No" the killer struck, strangling her into submission Once she was docile she probably went limp in his arms and he lowered her head-first into the recess between the steps into the house and the fence. Cadoche left for work at Spitalfields Market and passed Spitalfields church at around 5:32am. That places the Ripper's attack on Annie at precisely 5:30am, give or take a few minutes either way in both Mrs Darrell's and Cadoche's timings.

John Davis, an elderly carman who worked at Leadenhall Market, left for work just before 6:00am after rising at 5:45am. He lived with his family in the front third floor room and had lived there just weeks. On that day he left for work and noticed the front door to the passageway was wide open – witness John Richardson was the last to leave the building before 5.00am, and insisted he had shut both doors. Curious, Davis pushed open the back door to check for dossers, and found the remains of Annie Chapman.

Unlike Mary Ann Nichols, she had been put on display. Lying with her head in the recess between the steps and the fence, her left hand lay across her breast and her legs were lying open, her feet flat on the floor and her dress pulled up to expose her abdomen and genitals. A red handkerchief masked the extensive throat injuries but her abdominal mutilations were plain; her intestines had been entirely cut out and dumped on her right shoulder, whilst her uterus, minus a portion of the vagina and two-thirds of the bladder, were missing (Dr Phillips' full notes are given below). Large flaps of skin removed from her abdomen lay above her left side along with a quantity of blood. The killer had not covered the body this time, and he had not limited himself to a series of slashes, although the progression is clear; instead of several small slashes, he has made several deep incisions to remove portions of skin and expose the abdominal cavity, removing the flesh and organs and dumping them either side of the victim's head. Presumably he placed those parts there to get them out of his way, his intention to expose the abdominal and genitals regions.

JACK THE RIPPER

Davis panicked and ran into the street, calling out to whoever was within range. Shouting, "Men, come here!" to two workers – James Kent and James Green - from nearby Bayley's packing case business at 23a Hanbury Street, and attracting the attention of Henry John Holland who was also on his way to work, as well as Inspector Joseph Chandler, who was on the corner of Commercial Street and Hanbury Street. They rushed to the scene, with Holland first heading in to see the body, and immediately rushing off to fetch an officer (unaware, it seems, that Chandler was on his way). James Kent, after steadying his nerves with brandy, went to his workplace nearby to fetch a canvas with which to cover the body. Chandler was next in, taking a look at the body, and then sending for backup from the police station, an ambulance, and Dr George Bagster Phillips, who arrived some twenty minutes later at 6:30am. He pronounced death, and the body was moved to the Mortuary for further examination while Inspector Chandler conducted a search of the yard.

RIPPER MYTH
"MASONIC PATTERNS"

Chandler's search is the focus of at least two areas of interest to Ripper research, one of them being the allegation that the Ripper created elaborate arrangements of coins, rings and whatever else he could get his hands on at the murder scenes. Masonic symbolism seems to be the popular choice for the conspiracy crowd, however, no such symbolism was present. Inspector Chandler found some muslin and a couple of combs on the ground near where the victim had lain, as well as the aforementioned envelope. No special patterns were really found at this or any scene, and there is no mystery.

Chandler also reported a substantial quantity of blood at the scene. It stained the ground where the entrails had been laid, and there was spatter on the wall behind Annie's head and smears around a foot or so above the ground on the fence next to her. Recall, she lay parallel to the fence with her head in the recess between the fence and the steps into the building. The killer, from Cadoche's witness statement, seems to have encountered a little resistance from Annie before silencing her in his customary manner, strangulation, before cutting her throat. The way I interpret the evidence, she was facing the fence for a rear-end encounter, when he said or did something to unsettle her. She goes to turn around, utters "No," and he grabs her, throttling her. She struggles, and he finally feels her going limp. Aware she could, in an excited state reawaken quickly and call out, or possibly be faking her faint, cuts her throat as he's lowering her to the ground – accounting for the spatter on the wall. This awkward action could mean he lost his grip and she fell against the wall, smearing it, before he settled her onto the floor in the recess. This would also account for the sound of "something heavy" falling against the fence heard by Cadoche. He then set to work on her abdomen. Between entering the yard at around 5:30am and her body being found shortly before six, say at 5:55am, he had 25 minutes to work, as in the Mary Ann Nichols case. Neither Kent nor Green saw the killer come or go it seems, neither did any of the police officers on patrol nearby report anything, despite the killer having to have fled Hanbury Street to escape, quite possibly bloodstained.

One additional discovery Inspector Chandler did make that impacted upon the investigation was a leather apron lying in the yard. This was at the height of the aforementioned "Leather Apron" scare, which was now on the verge of triggering race riots and lynch mobs. The press had already linked him to the murders of Emma Smith, Martha Tabram and Mary Ann Nichols. However, the apron was soon identified as belonging to one of the residents, John Richardson, and had nothing to do with the killing. However, the finding was not without consequence, as we'll see later in the book.

After his inspection of the back yard, Chandler went to the mortuary to write up a description of the victim which eventually lead to her identification. Amelia Palmer (or Farmer) and Timothy Donovan, the deputy manager at 35 Dorset Street, both identified her. Her family were traced, and the inquest could begin, but only after a tumultuous couple of days as the news of the discovery of the leather apron went around.

Inquest
(Source: The Daily Telegraph, 11th, 13th, 14th, 20th, 27th September 1888)

The inquest opened on 10th September 1888 at the Working Lad's Club, presided over by Coroner Wynne Edwin Baxter. Because the inquest into Mary Ann Nichol's death continued until 22nd September, the inquests overlapped, and the Annie Chapman murder had an impact upon it, with Dr Llewellyn being recalled to account for all of Mary Ann's viscera considering the removal of organs in the Annie Chapman case.

John Davis testified first, recalling the circumstances of his discovery of Annie's body, whilst the other occupants of 29 Hanbury Street each told the same story – not seeing or hearing anything. The Ripper was nothing if not quiet in his work. The testimony explained bruises Annie had on her chest as coming from a series of fights she had with a woman over a man called "Harry the Hawker" over the last week of her life, and established that she was generally ill and a drinker. The key testimony, however, comes from only a handful of people.

First, John Pizer, who'd been arrested as "Leather Apron" the same day as the inquest opened. Concurrent with the Nichols inquest, his testimony was intended to quell the scare and prevent the police's worst fears of race riots in the East End coming true. The scare did not die quite as quickly as they'd have liked, and would in fact have far-reaching consequences for the case for years to come, but his testimony nonetheless is evidence of the police's willingness to throw someone under the bus for political reasons;

> **John Pizer**: I live at 22, Mulberry-street, Commercial- road East. I am a shoemaker.
> **Coroner** Are you known by the nickname of "Leather Apron?" -
> **Pizer**: Yes, sir.
> **Coroner** Where were you on Friday night last?
> **Pizer**: I was at 22, Mulberry-street. On Thursday, the 6th inst. I arrived there.
> **Coroner** From where?
> **Pizer**: From the west end of town.
> **Coroner**: I am afraid we shall have to have a better address than that presently.
> **Coroner** What time did you reach 22, Mulberry-street?
> **Pizer**: Shortly before eleven p.m.
> **Coroner** Who lives at 22, Mulberry-street?
> **Pizer**: My brother and sister-in-law and my stepmother. I remained indoors there.
> **Coroner** Until when?

Pizer: Until I was arrested by Sergeant Thicke, on Monday last at nine a.m.

Coroner You say you never left the house during that time?

Pizer: I never left the house.

Coroner Why were you remaining indoors?

Pizer: Because my brother advised me.

Coroner You were the subject of suspicion?

Pizer: I was the object of a false suspicion.

Coroner You remained on the advice of your friends?

Pizer: Yes; I am telling you what I did.

Coroner: It was not the best advice that you could have had. You have been released, and are not now in custody?

Pizer: I am not. I wish to vindicate my character to the world at large.

Coroner: I have called you in your own interests, partly with the object of giving you an opportunity of doing so.

Coroner Can you tell us where you were on Thursday, Aug. 30?

Pizer (after considering): In the Holloway-road.

Coroner You had better say exactly where you were. It is important to account for your time from that Thursday to the Friday morning.

Pizer: What time, may I ask?

Coroner: It was the week before you came to Mulberry-street.

Pizer: I was staying at a common lodging-house called the Round House, in the Holloway-road.

Coroner Did you sleep the night there?

Pizer: Yes.

Coroner: At what time did you go in?

Pizer: On the night of the London Dock fire I went in about two or a quarter-past. It was on the Friday morning.

Coroner When did you leave the lodging-house?

Pizer: At eleven a.m. on the same day. I saw on the placards, "Another Horrible Murder."

Coroner: Where were you before two o'clock on Friday morning?

Pizer: At eleven p.m. on Thursday I had my supper at the Round House.

Coroner Did you go out?

Pizer: Yes, as far as the Seven Sisters-road, and then returned towards Highgate way, down the Holloway-road. Turning, I saw the reflection of a fire. Coming as far as the church in the Holloway-road I saw two constables and the lodging-housekeeper talking together. There might have been one or two constables, I cannot say which. I asked a constable where the fire was, and he said it was a long way off. I asked him where he thought it was, and he replied: "Down by the Albert Docks." It was then about half-past one, to the best of my recollection. I went as far as Highbury Railway Station on the same side of the way, returned, and then went into the lodging house.

Coroner Did any one speak to you about being so late?

Pizer: No: I paid the night watchman. I asked him if my bed was let, and he said: "They are let by eleven o'clock. You don't think they are to let to this hour." I paid him 4d for another bed. I stayed up smoking on the form of the kitchen, on the right hand side near the fireplace, and then went to bed.

Coroner You got up at eleven o'clock?

Pizer: Yes. The day man came, and told us to get up, as he wanted to make the bed. I got up and dressed, and went down into the kitchen.

Coroner Is there anything else you want to say?

Pizer: Nothing.

Coroner When you said the West-end of town did you mean Holloway?

Pizer: No; another lodging house in Peter-street, Westminster.

Coroner (addressing Sgt William Thicke): It is only fair to say that the witness's statements can be corroborated.

Sgt William Thicke: Knowing that "Leather Apron" was suspected of being concerned in the murder, on Monday morning I arrested Piser at 22, Mulberry-street. I have known him by the name of "Leather Apron" for many years.

Coroner When people in the neighbourhood speak of the "Leather Apron" do they mean Pizer?

Thicke: They do.

Coroner He has been released from custody?

Thicke: He was released last night at 9.30.

It is made clear that Pizer has only been called in to exonerate him, but it is not made plain that Pizer is apparently admitting to being Leather Apron despite a complete absence of evidence. Nobody who could have confirmed his identity did so – such as the many streetwalkers who claimed to know Leather Apron by sight – and his identification by DS Thick is unquestioned. Pizer states he was the victim of "false suspicion" in his testimony, which is odd since the only suspicion he reports outside the courtroom that he was aware of was his out-of-the-blue arrest by Thick as Leather Apron. The only identification came from a man deemed so unreliable he was dropped from the inquest – a man named Emmanuel Violenia, who claimed to have seen Pizer at Hanbury Street arguing with Annie Chapman...but it turned out his desire to testify came from a morbid intention to see Annie's body. This testimony, nor that of Sgt Thicke, is corroborated by any of his family, who it is claimed warned him off the streets. Otherwise, his clipped responses, and the somewhat leading tit-for-tat between Baxter and Pizer makes one wonder if this whole exchange was in some way arranged by the police, terrified of the fallout if the scare were to continue. There is no evidence for this, however – Pizer never claimed to have been in on a deal to rig his testimony and seemed genuinely incensed by the accusations against him. Nevertheless, he came and went and was neatly exonerated. The Leather Apron scare died down, for now at least.

Inspector Chandler's testimony is next, describing the scene as he found it;

Joseph Chandler, **Inspector H Division Metropolitan Police, deposed**: On Saturday morning, at ten minutes past six, I was on duty in Commercial-street. At the corner of Hanbury-street I saw several men running. I beckoned to them. One of them said, "Another woman has been murdered." I at once went with him to 29, Hanbury-street, and through the passage into the yard. There was no one in the yard. I saw the body of a woman lying on the

61

ground on her back. Her head was towards the back wall of the house, nearly two feet from the wall, at the bottom of the steps, but six or nine inches away from them. The face was turned to the right side, and the left arm was resting on the left breast. The right hand was lying down the right side. Deceased's legs were drawn up, and the clothing was above the knees. A portion of the intestines, still connected with the body, were lying above the right shoulder, with some pieces of skin. There were also some pieces of skin on the left shoulder. The body was lying parallel with the fencing dividing the two yards. I remained there and sent for the divisional surgeon, Mr. Phillips, and to the police-station for the ambulance and for further assistance. When the constables arrived I cleared the passage of people, and saw that no one touched the body until the doctor arrived. I obtained some sacking to cover it before the arrival of the surgeon, who came at about half-past six o'clock, and he, having examined the body, directed that it should be removed to the mortuary. After the body had been taken away I examined the yard, and found a piece of coarse muslin, a small tooth comb, and a pocket hair comb in a case. They were lying near the feet of the woman. A portion of an envelope was found near her head, which contained two pills. [...]

Coroner Was there any appearance of a struggle there?

Chandler: No.

Coroner Are the palings strongly erected?

Chandler: No; to the contrary.

Coroner Could they support the weight of a

man getting over them?

Chandler: No doubt they might.

Coroner Is there any evidence of anybody having got over them?

Chandler: No. Some of them in the adjoining yard have been broken since. They were not broken then.

Coroner You have examined the adjoining yard?

Chandler: Yes.

Coroner Was there any staining as of blood on any of the palings?

Chandler: Yes, near the body.

Coroner Was it on any of the other yards?

Chandler: No.

Coroner Were there no other marks?

Chandler: There were marks discovered on the wall of No. 25. They were noticed on Tuesday afternoon. They have been seen by Dr. Phillips.

Coroner Were there any drops of blood outside the yard of No. 29?

Chandler: No; every possible examination has been made, but we could find no trace of them. The blood-stains at No. 29 were in the immediate neighbourhood of the body only. There were also a few spots of blood on the back wall, near the head of the deceased, 2ft from the ground. The largest spot was of the size of a sixpence. They were all close together. I assisted in the preparation of the plan produced, which is correct.

Coroner Did you search the body?

Chandler: I searched the clothing at the mortuary. The outside jacket - a long black one, which came down to the knees - had bloodstains round the neck, both upon the

inside and out, and two or three spots on the
left arm. The jacket was hooked at the top, and
buttoned down the front. By the appearance of
the garment there did not seem to have been
any struggle. A large pocket was worn under
the skirt (attached by strings), which I produce.
It was torn down the front and also at the side,
and it was empty. Deceased wore a black skirt.
There was a little blood on the outside. The two
petticoats were stained very little; the two
bodices were stained with blood round the
neck, but they had not been damaged. There
was no cut in the clothing at all. The boots were
on the feet of deceased. They were old. No part
of the clothing was torn. The stockings were
not bloodstained.

The important thing here is, as I've mentioned, the
presence of lots of blood compared to the Mary Ann
Nichols case. The killer may well have been bloodstained,
and that seems to have led to the questions over whether
the killer tried to escape over the fence, although that
seems unlikely. The scene is described here for the first
time also; this time the killer has cut sections of flesh off
the abdomen of his victim and cut out the intestines,
leaving the flesh and the entrails on the shoulders of his
victim. The level of mutilation and the methods the killer
used have raised several questions, mainly whether the
killer had any medical experience. Dr Phillips' testimony is
controversial in this respect. I have reproduced Dr Phillips'
testimony here mostly in full;

Mr. George Baxter Phillips: On Saturday last
I was called by the police at 6.20 a.m. to 29,
Hanbury-street, and arrived at half-past six. I

found the body of the deceased lying in the
yard on her back, on the left hand of the steps
that lead from the passage. The head was about
6in in front of the level of the bottom step, and
the feet were towards a shed at the end of the
yard. The left arm was across the left breast,
and the legs were drawn up, the feet resting on
the ground, and the knees turned outwards. The
face was swollen and turned on the right side,
and the tongue protruded between the front
teeth, but not beyond the lips; it was much
swollen. The small intestines and other portions
were lying on the right side of the body on the
ground above the right shoulder, but attached.
There was a large quantity of blood, with a part
of the stomach above the left shoulder. I
searched the yard and found a small piece of
coarse muslin, a small-tooth comb, and a
pocket-comb, in a paper case, near the railing.
They had apparently been arranged there. I also
discovered various other articles, which I
handed to the police. The body was cold,
except that there was a certain remaining heat,
under the intestines, in the body. Stiffness of
the limbs was not marked, but it was
commencing. The throat was dissevered deeply.
I noticed that the incision of the skin was
jagged, and reached right round the neck. On
the back wall of the house, between the steps
and the palings, on the left side, about 18in
from the ground, there were about six patches
of blood, varying in size from a sixpenny piece
to a small point, and on the wooden fence there
were smears of blood, corresponding to where
the head of the deceased laid, and immediately
above the part where the blood had mainly

flowed from the neck, which was well clotted. Having received instructions soon after two o'clock on Saturday afternoon, I went to the labour- yard of the Whitechapel Union for the purpose of further examining the body and making the usual post-mortem investigation. I was surprised to find that the body had been stripped and was laying ready on the table. It was under great disadvantage I made my examination. As on many occasions I have met with the same difficulty, I now raise my protest, as I have before, that members of my profession should be called upon to perform their duties under these inadequate circumstances.

[...]

The body had been attended to since its removal to the mortuary, and probably partially washed. I noticed a bruise over the right temple. There was a bruise under the clavicle, and there were two distinct bruises, each the size of a man's thumb, on the fore part of the chest. The stiffness of the limbs was then well-marked. The finger nails were turgid. There was an old scar of long standing on the left of the frontal bone. On the left side the stiffness was more noticeable, and especially in the fingers, which were partly closed. There was an abrasion over the bend of the first joint of the ring finger, and there were distinct markings of a ring or rings - probably the latter. There were small sores on the fingers. The head being opened showed that the membranes of the brain were opaque and the veins loaded with blood of a dark character. There was a large quantity of fluid between the membranes and the substance of the brain. The brain substance was unusually firm, and its cavities also contained a large amount of fluid. The throat had been severed. The incisions of the skin indicated that they had been made from the left side of the neck on a line with the angle of the jaw, carried entirely round and again in front of the neck, and ending at a point about midway between the jaw and the sternum or breast bone on the right hand. There were two distinct clean cuts on the body of the vertebrae on the left side of the spine. They were parallel to each other, and separated by about half an inch. The muscular structures between the side processes of bone of the vertebrae had an appearance as if an attempt had been made to separate the bones of the neck. There are various other mutilations of the body, but I am of opinion that they occurred subsequently to the death of the woman and to the large escape of blood from the neck.

[...]

Phillips: From these appearances I am of opinion that the breathing was interfered with previous to death, and that death arose from syncope, or failure of the heart's action, in consequence of the loss of blood caused by the severance of the throat.

Coroner: Was the instrument used at the throat the same as that used at the abdomen?

Phillips: Very probably. It must have been a very sharp knife, probably with a thin, narrow blade, and at least six to eight inches in length, and perhaps longer.

[...]

Coroner: Would any instrument that slaughterers employ have caused the injuries?

Phillips: Yes; well ground down.

Coroner: Would the knife of a cobbler or of any person in the leather trades have done?

Phillips: I think the knife used in those trades would not be long enough in the blade.

Coroner: Was there any anatomical knowledge displayed?

Philips: I think there was. There were indications of it. My own impression is that that anatomical knowledge was only less displayed or indicated in consequence of haste. The person evidently was hindered from making a more complete dissection in consequence of the haste.

Coroner: Was the whole of the body there?

Phillips: No; the absent portions being from the abdomen.

Coroner: Are those portions such as would require anatomical knowledge to extract?

Phillips: I think the mode in which they were extracted did show some anatomical knowledge.

[...]

Coroner: Was the bruising you mentioned recent?

Phillips: The marks on the face were recent, especially about the chin and sides of the jaw. The bruise upon the temple and the bruises in front of the chest were of longer standing, probably of days. I am of opinion that the person who cut the deceased's throat took hold of her by the chin, and then commenced the incision from left to right.

Coroner: Could that be done so instantaneously that a person could not cry out?

Phillips: By pressure on the throat no doubt it

would be possible.
Foreman of the Jury:: There would probably
be suffocation.
Coroner: The thickening of the tongue would
be one of the signs of suffocation?
Phillips: Yes. My impression is that she was
partially strangled.

Despite protestations, Dr Phillips returned to the inquest
and delivered more information on the mutilations carried
out upon Annie's body.

Dr Phillips: The abdomen had been entirely
laid open. The intestines, severed from their
mesenteric attachments, had been lifted out of
the body and placed on the shoulder of the
corpse; whilst from the pelvis, the uterus and
its appendages, with the upper portion of the
vagina and the posterior two-thirds of the
bladder had been entirely removed. No trace of
these parts could be found and the incisions
were cleanly cut, avoiding the rectum,and
dividing the vagina low enough to avoid injury
to the cervix uteri. Obviously the work was that
of an expert – of one, at least, who had such
knowledge of anatomical or pathological
examinations as to be enabled to secure the
pelvic organs with one sweep of the knife,
which must therefore have been five or six
inches in length, probably more.

Crucial information is discussed here, and information
about the killer's MO and signature also come to light.
Most of the detail is lost in the fog of media
sensationalism, which is ironic given that the reality is far

more interesting than the fiction. First is the scene itself –
as with the Mary Ann Nichols case, the body is on its back,
head turned to the side, with evidence of suffocation or
strangulation, a point that is made throughout Dr Phillips'
testimony. Again, the throat is "deeply dissevered," and
again there are abdominal mutilations. Now, in order to
get an idea of what the killer was doing and why, we need
to picture the scene. The doctor describes the flaps of
abdominal flesh, small intestines, "other portions," and
part of the stomach as lying on the ground above both
shoulders. He also notes that there are still intestines
inside the body when discussing body temperature and
time of death, suggesting the killer's removal of the
intestines was not complete. This, it seems, was not due
to interruption but deliberation; he appears to have
opened the abdomen and simply cut and slung whatever
he could get his hands on, placing them out of the way of
his immediate line of sight – much like how he moved the
victims' face away from him. Once he has opened the
abdomen and cut material out of the cavity, he moves on
to removal of the uterus. He suggests this occurred "with
one sweep of the knife." Not quite – the killer divided the
vagina and took away most of the bladder in his haste,
hardly a single sweeping motion.

    Much is made of the killers' anatomical
knowledge, and Dr Phillips is largely to blame for this.
There are two reasons to cast doubt on his assertion; one,
it is still possible that the parts removed were actually
removed post-mortem en route to the mortuary not by
the killer, but by some opportunistic hand intent on selling
them. Not a theory I subscribe to, but nonetheless
plausible. Two, cases like this were unheard of in this day
and age – the idea of any common man carrying out
mutilations like this would be hard to accept without

assuming they were medically trained or at least had some professional knowledge of the human body. This ignores the far more plausible and likely scenario, that the Ripper showed no skill in this regard and even if he did, it could be from previous experience with unknown earlier victims, and/or a morbid fascination with human anatomy which has a lot to do with his unhealthy sexual deviance. In the absence of this insight, the removal of organs, rather than written off as a snatch-and-grab, is elevated to the level of a professional operation, because that seems the only rational scenario in which organ removal could occur.

Another point made by Dr Phillips is the killer's attempt to decapitate Annie Chapman. Rather than the commonly held belief that the killer simply slit his victim's throat to kill them, here we have evidence that the throat-cutting had another purpose – to depersonalise the victim. He did cut their throats to kill them but also to try and sever the victims' head, which he failed at. This is evidence of the killer attempting something he is entirely unskilled at, and it is telling in that regard. More crucially, it is important because it is a sign of the killer's perception of his victims. He is removing their identity.

Furthermore, the doctor points to the bruising to the victim's fingers where her rings had ostensibly been stripped from her hands. They were not found at the scene, where the contents of Annie's pockets lay at her feet in disarray, and the presumption was that these base metal rings had been stolen by the killer. This is certainly the solution offered by the situation but, like the uterus, there is also the possibility that thieves stole the rings between the body's discovery and the autopsy.

In what time period did this occur? Let us look at the inquest evidence of Albert Cadoche and Elizabeth

Darrell;

Albert Cadoche: I live at 27, Hanbury-street, and am a carpenter. 27 is next door to 29, Hanbury-street. On Saturday, Sept. 8, I got up about a quarter past five in the morning, and went into the yard. It was then about twenty minutes past five, I should think. As I returned towards the back door I heard a voice say "No" just as I was going through the door. It was not in our yard, but I should think it came from the yard of No. 29. I, however, cannot say on which side it came from. I went indoors, but returned to the yard about three or four minutes afterwards. While coming back I heard a sort of a fall against the fence which divides my yard from that of 29. It seemed as if something touched the fence suddenly.

Coroner: Did you look to see what it was?
Cadoche: No.
Coroner: Had you heard any noise while you were at the end of your yard?
Cadoche: No.
Coroner: Any rustling of clothes?
Cadoche: No. I then went into the house, and from there into the street to go to my work. It was about two minutes after half-past five as I passed Spitalfields Church.
Coroner: Do you ever hear people in these yards?
Cadoche: Now and then, but not often.
The Foreman: What height are the palings?
Cadoche: About 5 ft. 6 in. to 6 ft. high.
Coroner: And you had not the curiosity to look over? **Cadoche:** No, I had not.
Coroner: It is not usual to hear thumps against

the palings?

Cadoche: They are packing-case makers, and now and then there is a great case goes up against the palings. I was thinking about my work, and not that there was anything the matter, otherwise most likely I would have been curious enough to look over.

The Foreman of the Jury: It's a pity you did not.

Cadoche: I did not see any man and woman in the street when I went out.

*　　*　　*

Mrs. Elizabeth Darrell (or Long): I live in Church-row, Whitechapel, and my husband, James Long, is a cart minder. On Saturday, Sept. 8, about half past five o'clock in the morning, I was passing down Hanbury-street, from home, on my way to Spitalfields Market. I knew the time, because I heard the brewer's clock strike half-past five just before I got to the street. I passed 29, Hanbury-street. On the right-hand side, the same side as the house, I saw a man and a woman standing on the pavement talking. The man's back was turned towards Brick-lane, and the woman's was towards the market. They were standing only a few yards nearer Brick-lane from 29, Hanbury-street. I saw the woman's face. Have seen the deceased in the mortuary, and I am sure the woman that I saw in Hanbury-street was the deceased. I did not see the man's face, but I noticed that he was dark. He was wearing a brown low-crowned felt hat. I think he had on a dark coat, though I am not certain. By the look of him he seemed to me a man over forty years of age. He appeared to me to be a little taller than the deceased.

Coroner Did he look like a working man, or what?

Darrell: He looked like a foreigner.

Coroner: Did he look like a dock labourer, or a workman, or what?

Darrell: I should say he looked like what I should call shabby-genteel.

Coroner: Were they talking loudly?

Darrell: They were talking pretty loudly. I overheard him say to her "Will you?" and she replied, "Yes." That is all I heard, and I heard this as I passed. I left them standing there, and I did not look back, so I cannot say where they went to.

Coroner: Did they appear to be sober?

Darrell: I saw nothing to indicate that either of them was the worse for drink.

Coroner: Was it not an unusual thing to see a man and a woman standing there talking?

Darrell: Oh no. I see lots of them standing there in the morning.

Coroner: At that hour of the day?

Darrell: Yes; that is why I did not take much notice of them.

Coroner: You are certain about the time?

Darrell: Quite.

Coroner: What time did you leave home?

Darrell: I got out about five o'clock, and I reached the Spitalfields Market a few minutes after half-past five.

The Foreman of the jury: What brewer's clock did you hear strike half-past five?

Darrell: The brewer's in Brick-lane.

These are extremely revealing pieces of testimony. First, we have Cadoche explaining that he heard "No" uttered minutes before hearing the thud against the palings, and providing evidence to nail the timeline down, claiming he heard the commotion between 5:20am and 5:30am. Second, we have the testimony of Elizabeth Darrell (or Long), who provides corroborating evidence suggesting she saw Annie Chapman (she in fact identified the body afterwards as the woman she'd seen), with a man at 5:30am. Also, Darrell provides the first eyewitness description of a suspect – in his 40s, dark complexion, "shabby-genteel," with a low-crowned felt hat, coat and a "foreign appearance," and taller than Annie Chapman. The timings and descriptions are invaluable.

We can place Annie Chapman and her killer entering 29 Hanbury Street at 5:30am, and the body being discovered at about 6:00am. Unlike the Mary Ann Nichols case, where a time of death can confidently be established, this case is complicated by Dr Phillips' assertion that the victim died two hours or more before being examined – placing her death sometime around 4:20am. As we have seen, witness testimony from Elizabeth Darrell and Alfred Cadoche place the time of death at 5:30am. Dr Phillips is demonstrably off by an hour. I suspect the degree of disembowelment may have cooled the body quickly, and I doubt Dr Phillips, or any doctor of the day had seen a case similar to this one. I suspect therefore that going by the cooling of the body as a measure of time of death with little basis for comparison could have confused the doctor. Either way, we know the killer had about half an hour in which to work. Accounting for his leaving and being quite out of sight of the property by 6:00am, we'll give him a five-minute head start and call it 25 minutes. That is certainly enough time to have carried out these mutilations. Killing Annie took seconds, so he took nearly all the time with the mutilations.

This inquest was complicated by the minutiae of Annie Chapman's social circle. Bruising to her body caused by fights over "Harry the Hawker," her acquaintance with a man called Ted Stanley, who may or may not have been a man nicknamed "the pensioner," clouded the issue. In the end, it is what the killer did and how he did it that interests us. As we proceed, we will re-examine the details of this case and the others to paint a picture of the Ripper's methods and motivations, but suffice to say that here we can at least summarise what we know;

The killer stood and chatted with Annie Chapman, apparently calmly and non-threateningly, outside 29 Hanbury Street, before asking her into the back of the building – which was regularly used for dossing and for "immoral purposes" - by asking her "will you?" She accepted and followed him in. Now, judging by Cadoche's testimony, and the crime scene and autopsy details provided in the testimony of Chandler and Phillips, we can tentatively figure out what happened. The killer somehow caught Annie's attention and she protested, "No." At this point he grabs and strangles her. Minutes pass, as they do when strangling a person, before she falls limp against the fence. Placing, or dropping her, into the recess between the fence and the steps – running the risk of discovery at any moment, it must be said – the killer then slashed her throat twice on the left side, away from himself. The first slash was probably to kill her, and the second was part of an effort to remove her head. Unsuccessful, he gave up and simply went to work on her abdomen. Pulling her skirting up and drawing her legs into a "stirrups" position, he subjected her to several long, deep cuts, removed the flesh of the lower abdomen and cut out and removed sections of intestine. Then, in the dark light of dawn, he groped around and found the uterus, cutting the whole organ out with a few imprecise cuts (despite Dr. Phillips' assertion that the killer must have had anatomical knowledge).

Caution must be given here – there is still the possibility that the organs were stolen after the fact for profit by opportunists, and not the killer. However, I do not believe this. That said, I do not believe the killer necessarily had significant anatomical knowledge either – I think he was simply aiming for the sexual organs and cut out what he found. Thinking of the action as the "removal of organs" takes away from the symbolism of the removal or destruction of sexuality – the killer wasn't a surgeon performing an operation, but a psychopath cutting a woman open for his own gratification. And if that gratification was sexual in nature, then that gives great context to the attack upon and removal of this particular organ.

Anyway, after about 25 minutes, probably less, he leaves the body posed in the doorway – legs asunder, organs splayed, and the left hand across the breast (take note of the position of the body – *legs apart, left hand across the breast.* It is yet another aspect of the Ripper's signature) – and flees.

One final aspect to be considered is the fact that missing from Annie's body was a scarf, reportedly worn by her in the testimony of Timothy Donovan;

Coroner: You have seen that handkerchief?
Donovan: I recognise it as one which the

77

deceased used to wear. She bought it of a
lodger, and she was wearing it when she left the
lodging-house. She was wearing it three-corner
ways, placed round her neck, with a black
woollen scarf underneath. It was tied in front
with one knot.

And yet when Annie's body was found, this item
was missing from the inventory of clothing and items
found with her. This will not the last occasion where items
are taken from the scene presumably by the killer, and
this will be discussed later. But for now, it is worth
considering if the Ripper used the scarf to transport the
organ he removed from Annie.

The inquest concluded on 26th September, with an
extensive summary by the coroner. The verdict was
murder by person or persons unknown. Annie had been
buried already on the 14th September 1888 at a ceremony
attended by her family. In the wider community, fear was
rising. The killings of Annie Chapman and Polly Nichols
had been connected but also, the earlier murders of
Martha Tabram and Emma Smith were being lumped in
there, too.

It raises an interesting chicken-and-egg question
about the Ripper crimes; whilst Emma Smith's murder is
nowadays never seriously linked to the others, and the
Tabram case is still up for debate, the evidence linking
four of the Whitechapel Murders is conclusive. There was
definitely a serial killer murdering the women of
Whitechapel between August and November 1888. But
the press seems to have got the jump on the killer by
putting about the terror of a serial killer weeks early!
Following the Nichols murder the press were genuinely
suggesting that hers was murder number three, when it

most certainly wasn't. In particular, *The Star* newspaper (unrelated to the modern newspaper) was seemingly responsible for capitalising on, and sensationalising, the case. One wonders if the real killer himself capitalised on the fear in the district of a series of murders of women and engaged in a public campaign of slaughter when he saw the effect it had on society. That suggests that prior to the first murder he had no concept of the serial murder of women in public as a vehicle for satisfying his craving for public outrage (which, given the posing of his victims in public, he clearly had). This may seem hard to conceptualise for you, reader, because you and I have grown up in a world of Peter Sutcliffes, Ted Bundys and Jeffrey Dahmers. I hesitate to suggest that the press gave him the idea for a public killing spree because he couldn't think of doing it himself, because it conflicts with common sense in the 21st Century. However, it must be pointed out that the Ripper was unique in many ways – he was the first public, modern-style serial murderer.

An example to provide context is the case of the Columbine school massacre. The killers in that case planned not to shoot up the school, but to bomb it. They idolised the Oklahoma bomber Timothy McVeigh and intended to carry out a massacre in the same vein. However, their bombs did not detonate, and they resorted to Plan B. Subsequently, however, they became poster-boys for school shootings and inspired twenty years of copycat attacks. In the case of Jack the Ripper, he was possibly influenced by the newspaper stories of a killer leaving mutilated victims in public and he would have witnessed the impact such actions were having on those around him.

This is, of course, speculation. And back to the premise of this book, the only facts here are that the press were linking murders together, before murders which can reasonably *be* linked together actually occurred, such was the case with the so-called "Double Event."

Elizabeth Stride

Illustration 5: Elizabeth Stride, mortuary photo

Elizabeth Stride was born in Sweden on 27th November 1843 as Elizabeth Gustafsdotter, in the town of Torslanda near Gothenburg. She would begin her working life in domestic services at the age of 17, and that would be where she made her legitimate living for most of the rest of her life. However, over a similar time evidence of a disordered and troubled life also emerged. Between 1865 and 1866 she suffered a stillbirth of a daughter, was treated repeatedly for sexually-transmitted diseases and was recorded by police as a prostitute.

Her life seemed to turn around when she moved to London in 1866. Again working in domestic services, she met and married carpenter John Thomas Stride, and the two of them owned and ran a coffee shop in Poplar between 1870-1874. This is where things get a little murky. No records appear to exist anywhere for John Thomas Stride between 1874 and 24th October 1884, when he died in Bromley Sick House. At that time his address is listed as Poplar Workhouse, and it would appear that Elizabeth and John's marriage had broken down years earlier. Incredibly, Elizabeth would later invent a somewhat more interesting explanation for her husband's death – she claimed he'd died, along with their two children, in a famous maritime accident that occurred years earlier, the sinking of the pleasure cruiser *Princess Alice.* The ship collided with a coal vessel on the Thames and sank on 3rd September 1878, killing 527 people. John Stride was not on board. Many people who knew "Long Liz" later in life recounted the story she told as fact.

Elizabeth had in fact been in Popular Workhouse in 1877 and would later drift around Whitechapel, dossing at 32 Flower and Dean Street in the Wicked Quarter-Mile, cleaning and doing for Jewish residents whilst possibly also working the streets. Indeed, between 1882-1888, Elizabeth's life was again patchy and troubled. In the last year of her life alone, she would be convicted as many as eight times of drunkenness, and despite starting a relationship with Michael Kidney in 1885, and living with him at Devonshire Street, their relationship was tumultuous, and she often left him for periods only to return later – Kidney suggested she was absent for around five months out of the past three years of their relationship. She even had him charged with assault in

April 1887, but the case fell through when she failed to attend court. This, however, is a pattern of behaviour for Kidney; it would later be claimed that he tried to lock her in the house to prevent her leaving and going drinking (this is very much in dispute; there are various versions given for the testimony he gave in relation to this detail. Certainly, a padlock key found on Elizabeth's body suggests the existence of a padlock but also that it was probably their front-door lock, rather than some kind of shackle). He is no saint; a drunk himself, he would eventually be treated for syphilis in 1889, begging the question about just what motivated Elizabeth's absences and drinking sprees besides alcoholism. On the day of the murder, Elizabeth had told people she and Kidney had had an argument, and she'd stormed out. He, however, denied having seen her at all for five days and denied any argument took place.

In the context of this unsettled and desperate life (applications for financial support in 1886 testify to that), Elizabeth Stride was one of the more vulnerable and troubled individuals of the Jack the Ripper story. It is clear that her invention of the *Princess Alice* story was simply an effort to cover up the sad truth that her failed marriage ended with her destitute husband dying in a workhouse. She had worked her whole life – domestic service, running a coffee shop, even doing domestic work whilst dossing at 32 Flower and Dean Street. She attempted to form a working partnership, first with John Stride and then Michael Kidney, but her drinking, temper and, as Kidney later put it, "immoral" behaviour, were a curse on her pursuit of happiness and in the end her lifestyle made her vulnerable to violence on the streets of Whitechapel. Sadly, Elizabeth's is a familiar tale and the victims of the Ripper are as much victims of this downward spiral.

Last Movements

On 29th September 1888 she was seen at her on-off lodging house at 32 Flower and Dean Street by Elizabeth Tanner. Elizabeth had been lodging there since the 26th, after commenting to resident Catherine Lane that she'd argued with Michael Kidney. Incredibly, Dr Barnardo, the philanthropist, would visit the lodging house as part of an outreach project and later identified her body as one of the women he'd encountered there.

She was paid 6d for her service and left to go drinking at the Queen's Head pub at 6:30pm. There she drank with Mrs Tanner and returned with her to the lodging house. She left again to go drinking at 8pm and would next be seen at 11pm in the company of a well-dressed Englishman by two men, J. Best and John Gardner, at the Bricklayer's Arms heading in the direction of Commercial Road and Berner Street around 11pm. The men would joke to Elizabeth as she passed that "Leather Apron's gotten 'round you!"

Time for an important digression. At the time, a detail often overlooked, is that the murders were being blamed on Leather Apron, the menacing figure the press were keen to magnify to sell their copy. The name "Jack the Ripper" would be popularised with the publication of the so-called "Dear Boss" letter, published by *The Daily News* on 3rd October 1888, the day after the double-event. The letter was dated the 25th September 1888, and had been received by the Central News Agency on the 27th. Scotland Yard were forwarded the letter two days later. I will discuss the letters later, but for now this is an interesting detail not least because the saga of this first letter to use the name "Jack the Ripper" was unfolding whilst Elizabeth Stride and Catherine Eddowes were living out their final days.

Back to the timeline, and the next sequence of events is a little murky. William Marshall was the next witness to Elizabeth Stride's movements with the mysterious Englishman, seeing them near Dutfield's Yard, where she would be killed, and Matthew Packer's greengrocer's, at around 11:45pm. The issue seems to be that the subsequent timings, according to the approximations of the witnesses, do not seem to make sense. Eddleston (2010, p. 86-88) dives into these issues and rethinks the timeline and I encourage you to pick up his book and take a glance at his reasoning. Essentially, the issue is that at least two witnesses gave timing inconsistent with that of others, creating impossible inconsistencies in the timeline, whilst only two individuals used timepieces to fix their times – Louis Diemshütz, who found the body, and Dr Frederick William Blackwell. I will use Eddleston's revised timeline here, but given the inconsistencies of the timings, feel free to draw your own conclusions based on the evidence.

Grocer Matthew Packer, who claimed to have seen Elizabeth earlier, shut his shop about 12:30am in the first hour of 30th September 1888. At about the same time, a man by the name of Joseph Lave went out for some fresh air into Dutfield's Yard, which he described as being in pitch darkness. At the time nobody else was around, and he returned to the adjacent International Working-man's Club. A moment or so later, a woman by the name of Fanny Mortimer spent about six minutes at her front door, until around 12.42am.

**RIPPER MYTH
"GENTLEMAN JACK"**

Fanny Mortimer's evidence is fascinating, because her sighting of a character with a shiny black bag walking down the street would go down in history. She wasn't called to give evidence at the inquest because the man was identified and eliminated. Leon Goldberg was an ordinary guy on his way home after having a cuppa at a cafe in Spectacle Alley. When Fanny's evidence was reported, he called into Leman Street Police Station and explained himself. Inside the shiny bag were empty cigar boxes, rather than some macabre bloodstained medical kit as Hollywood would like you to believe.

The grocer, Matthew Packer, claimed initially not to have seen anything that night. He would later put about the story that he'd sold grapes to Elizabeth Stride and the man she was with. The officer he'd spoken to initially, Sgt Stephen White, picked him up and interrogated him. In the time to come he proved to a useless witness full of hot air, perpetually altering his story to police. As a result, he is absent from the inquests. Thanks to him, there is now a pervasive myth about grapes being found clutched in the hands of the victims, a straight-up lie. Of course, as you may guess, those who buy into the idea of a well-dressed, well-groomed millionaire or royal family member gliding into the East End apparently unseen to kill prostitutes love this idea. But it's fiction, and Matthew Packer was a fantasist.

Let me clarify this for you; the idea of a gentleman killer with a shiny black bag came entirely from this one witness statement, and the man was identified. He was an ordinary bloke, coming home after having a cup of coffee. It is a myth.

According to Eddleston's timeline, the earliest

time of death for Elizabeth Stride is around 12:44am, and the latest is 12:54am. Within this ten-minute window, there is perhaps one of the most crucial incidents in the whole Ripper saga; the sighting by witness Israel Schwartz of Elizabeth Stride and a drunken assailant fighting at Dutfield's Yard. A Hungarian Jew, unable to speak a word of English, Schwartz reported via an interpreter that at around 12:45am he was going down Berner Street and as he passed the entrance to Dutfield's Yard, he saw Elizabeth Stride be accosted by a drunken man who had been stumbling down the street ahead of him towards Dutfield's Yard. This man spoke to Elizabeth, then threw her to the ground. Bruising on her body corroborates this. It seems the man had tried to push her into the street initially, before throwing her to the ground into the yard. Schwartz, not wanting to get involved, crossed the road where another man stood, lighting a pipe. At that moment, the assailant pointed to Schwartz, yelled the pejorative phrase "Lipski!", and the other man began to follow Schwartz, who legged it.

Schwartz would later identify Elizabeth Stride in the mortuary as the woman he'd seen. He described the attacker as around 30, around 5 feet 5 inches, fair hair and a dark moustache, well-built and dressed darkly with a peaked cap. The other man he described as around 35, 5 feet 11 inches, fair hair and complexion, wearing a dark overcoat, a hard, wide-brimmed hat, and carrying a clay pipe. The reference to Lipski has been debated over the years but it seems to have been an anti-Semitic jibe intended to instruct the man with the pipe to go after the Jewish Schwartz – Israel Lipski being a man convicted of murder on Berner Street itself some time earlier. The name was bandied around as a racist insult ever since.

Unsurprisingly, the plucky reporters of that bastion

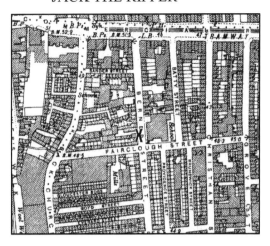

Illustration 6: Berner Street, site of Dutfield's Yard, circa 1894

of prolefeed, *The Star,* tracked Schwartz down and took a garbled translation of his story, which they ran on 1st October 1888. They got several details wrong, writing that the police did not take the sighting seriously. Chief Inspector Donald Swanson wrote in a report that, "if Schwartz is to be believed, and the police report of his statement casts no doubt on it, it follows [that] the man Schwartz saw and described is [more probably] the murderer." *The Star* ran instead with the line, "the truth of the man's statement is not wholly accepted." Also, despite no records existing of Schwartz testifying at Elizabeth's inquest, Dr Robert Anderson, who would lead the Whitechapel investigation from 6th October onwards, wrote in a series of memos that Schwartz did indeed provide evidence at the inquest. Since original documents relating to the inquests of Polly, Annie and Elizabeth are lost, and press reports are the only source left, there is a distinct possibility that he did testify but for some reason the journalists missed it. Possibly he provided witness statements or was cross-examined separately, and the evidence was provided to the jury on paper. Who knows.

Moving on. At 1am on 30th September 1888, local salesman Louis Diemschütz was returning to the International Workingman's Club where he lived with his wife. On his cart was unsold stock from his market stall. As he turned the cart into Dutfield's Yard, which to recap was an enclosure between two buildings accessible via a narrow entrance alleyway, his horse reacted to something on the ground near the gate. Louis disembarked to examine the mass, which he could barely see in the darkness. Striking a match, he found the mass to be a woman's body. Fearful it was his own wife he checked to find her in the club, before he and a friend, Isaac Kozebrodsky, ran to fetch the police. They returned with a man named Edward Spooner and another club man, Morris Eagle, who brought officers Constable Lamb and Reserve Constable Collins.

Spooner would later testify that when he got there, within minutes of the finding of the body, blood still flowed from the injury to the woman's throat. A stream of it ran across the yard, in fact. This is in stark contrast to the other Ripper murders, where the victims' blood was restricted to (a) spatter from the infliction of injuries, including the cutting of the throat itself and (b) the residual blood left behind by the removed flesh and organs as they are left on the ground. No flowing blood or substantial pools; in the previous cases, blood was found to be under the body having flowed much more slowly, and having soaked into the clothes of the victims. This was because the killer strangled the other victims first, substantially lowering the victims' blood pressure, before rapidly cutting the throat right to the bone. In the case of Elizabeth Stride, her killer simply threw her to the ground, slashed her throat once and left her to bleed out.

Once at the scene, Constable Lamb sent Constable Collins to fetch the doctor. By 1:13am Dr. Frederick William Blackwell arrived and pronounced death. He noted that the body was still warm, but that the blood had stopped flowing from the wound in her neck. The body's position was also noted; she lay on her left side, with her knees together and facing the club to the right of the yard, almost touching the wall. Her right hand was bloodstained and lay on her chest, and the left hand was clasping cachous (small sweets intended to freshen the breath for smokers) in a small packet, some of which had fallen out. There were signs of a struggle; she'd been wearing a bonnet that now lay on the floor near her head, and her silk scarf was pulled tightly as if someone had grabbed it and pulled. The scarf was also cut from the same action that made the injury to the neck. That said, the injury was relatively shallow, cutting deeply along the left-hand-side but still not dividing deeper than the windpipe. The opinion of Dr George Bagster Phillips, who attended within half-an-hour of Dr Blackwell, was that she would have taken several minutes to die from the wound.

On 1st October 1888, the same day as Schwartz's interview with *The Star* was printed, within days of the name "Jack the Ripper" first appearing in the press, Elizabeth Stride's inquest opened, after some difficulty identifying her.

Inquest
(Source: The Daily Telegraph 2nd and 3rd October 1888)

The inquest opened on 1st October under Coroner Wynne Edwin Baxter at the Vestry Hall, Cable Street.

The first witness who testified was William West,

who worked at a socialist newspaper whose officers were adjacent to the club and Dutfield's Yard. He saw and heard nothing. Next came Morris Eagle with his testimony, followed by Louis Diemshütz. His testimony is important for several reasons. Lengthy as it is, it describes the scene as it appeared freshly discovered, and it addresses a number of important questions, as we shall see.

> **Louis Diemshütz:** I reside at No. 40 Berner-street, and am steward of the International Workmen's Club. I am married, and my wife lives at the club too, and assists in the management. On Saturday I left home about half-past eleven in the morning, and returned exactly at one o'clock on Sunday morning. I noticed the time at the baker's shop at the corner of Berner-street. I had been to the market near the Crystal Palace, and had a barrow like a costermonger's, drawn by a pony, which I keep in George-yard Cable-street. I drove home to leave my goods. I drove into the yard, both gates being wide open. It was rather dark there. All at once my pony shied at some object on the right. I looked to see what the object was, and observed that there was something unusual, but could not tell what. It was a dark object. I put my whip handle to it, and tried to lift it up, but as I did not succeed I jumped down from my barrow and struck a match. It was rather windy, and I could only get sufficient light to see that there was some figure there. I could tell from the dress that it was the figure of a woman.
> **Coroner:** You did not disturb it?
> **Diemshütz:** No. I went into the club and asked

JACK THE RIPPER

where my wife was. I found her in the front room on the ground floor.

Coroner: What did you do with the pony?

Diemshütz: I left it in the yard by itself, just outside the club door. There were several members in the front room of the club, and I told them all that there was a woman lying in the yard, though I could not say whether she was drunk or dead. I then got a candle and went into the yard, where I could see blood before I reached the body.

Coroner: Did you touch the body?

Diemshütz: No, I ran off at once for the police. I could not find a constable in the direction which I took, so I shouted out "Police!" as loudly as I could. A man whom I met in Grove-street returned with me, and when we reached the yard he took hold of the head of the deceased. As he lifted it up I saw the wound in the throat.

Coroner: Had the constables arrived then?

Diemshütz: At the very same moment Eagle and the constables arrived.

Coroner: Did you notice anything unusual when you were approaching the club?

Diemshütz: No.

Coroner: You saw nothing suspicious?

Diemshütz: Not at all.

Coroner: How soon afterwards did a doctor arrive?

Diemshütz: About twenty minutes after the constables came up. No one was allowed by the police to leave the club until they were searched, and then they had to give their names and addresses.

Coroner: Did you notice whether the clothes

92

of the deceased were in order?

Diemshütz: They were in perfect order.

Coroner: How was she lying?

Diemshütz: On her left side, with her face towards the club wall.

Coroner: Was the whole of the body resting on the side?

Diemshütz: No, I should say only her face. I cannot say how much of the body was sideways. I did not notice what position her hands were in, but when the police came I observed that her bodice was unbuttoned near the neck. The doctor said the body was quite warm.

Coroner: What quantity of blood should you think had flowed from the body?

Diemshütz: I should say quite two quarts.

Coroner: In what direction had it run?

Diemshütz: Up the yard from the street. The body was about one foot from the club wall. The gutter of the yard is paved with large stones, and the centre with smaller irregular stones.

Coroner: Have you ever seen men and women together in the yard?

Diemshütz: Never.

Coroner: Nor heard of such a thing?

Diemshütz: No.

A Juror: Could you in going up the yard have passed the body without touching it?

Diemshütz: Oh, yes.

Coroner: Any person going up the centre of the yard might have passed without noticing it?

Diemshütz: I, perhaps, should not have noticed it if my pony had not shied. I had passed it when I got down from my barrow.

Coroner: How far did the blood run?

Diemshütz: As far as the kitchen door of the club.

Coroner: Was any person left with the body while you ran for the police?

Diemshütz: Some members of the club remained; at all events, when I came back they were there. I cannot say whether any of them touched the body.

Inspector Reid (interposing): When the murder was discovered the members of the club were detained on the premises, and I searched them, whilst Dr. Phillips examined them.

A Juror: Was it possible for anybody to leave the yard between the discovery of the body and the arrival of the police?

Diemshütz: Oh, yes - or, rather, it would have been possible before I informed the members of the club, not afterwards.

Coroner: When you entered the yard, if any person had run out you would have seen them in the dark?

Diemshütz: Oh, yes, it was light enough for that. It was dark in the gateway, but not so dark further in the yard.

So here we have Louis Diemshütz testifying that the body's clothes were in perfect order, which doesn't apply to the rest of the Ripper victims, that the victim had bled out considerably and the flow reached the kitchen door of the club quite a way away, and that he had never heard of the Yard being used for what can be interpreted as "immoral purposes." This contrasts with the other murders; Annie Chapman and the Miller's Court victim were killed in areas used by prostitutes, and Mitre Square was immediately next to "Prostitute Island," the notorious prostitution amnesty area police demarcated as the area surrounding St Botolph's in Aldgate. Polly Nichols is an exception, it seems, as Buck's Row had little association with prostitution. However, it does appear the killer chanced upon her as she plied her trade in that area as witnesses place her heading in that direction on the night of her killing. The same could be said for Elizabeth, were it not for the specifics of the crime and the context of what we know about the attack.

Next to testify was Constable Henry Lamb, when the inquest resumed the following day. He claimed that there were "no signs of a struggle" and discussed the possibility of the killer having still been in the Yard as the body was found;

> **Coroner:** Were her clothes disturbed?
> **Lamb:** No.
> **Coroner:** Only her boots visible?
> **Lamb:** Yes, and only the soles of them. There were no signs of a struggle. Some of the blood was in a liquid state, and had run towards the kitchen door of the club. A little - that nearest to her on the ground - was slightly congealed. I can hardly say whether any was still flowing from the throat. Dr. Blackwell was the first doctor to arrive; he came ten or twelve minutes after myself, but I had no watch with me.
> **Coroner:** Did any one of the crowd say whether the body had been touched before your arrival?
> **Lamb:** No. Dr. Blackwell examined the body and its surroundings. Dr. Phillips came ten minutes later. Inspector Pinhorn arrived directly

after Dr. Blackwell. When I blew my whistle other constables came, and I had the entrance of the yard closed. This was while Dr. Blackwell was looking at the body. Before that the doors were wide open. The feet of the deceased extended just to the swing of the gate, so that the barrier could be closed without disturbing the body. I entered the club and left a constable at the gate to prevent any one passing in or out. I examined the hands and clothes of all the members of the club. There were from fifteen to twenty present, and they were on the ground floor.

Coroner: Did you discover traces of blood anywhere in the club?

Lamb: No.

Coroner: Was the steward present?

Lamb: Yes.

Coroner: Did you ask him to lock the front door?

Lamb: I did not. There was a great deal of commotion. That was done afterwards.

Coroner: But time is the essence of the thing.

Lamb: I did not see any person leave. I did not try the front door of the club to see if it was locked. I afterwards went over the cottages, the occupants of which were in bed. I was admitted by men, who came down partly dressed; all the other people were undressed. As to the waterclosets in the yard, one was locked and the other unlocked, but no one was there. There is a recess near the dust-bin.

Coroner: Did you go there?

Lamb: Yes, afterwards, with Dr. Phillips.

Coroner: But I am speaking of at the time.

Lamb: I did it subsequently. I do not recollect

looking over the wooden partition. I, however, examined the store belonging to Messrs. Hindley, sack manufacturers, but I saw nothing there.

Coroner: How long were the cottagers in opening their doors?

Lamb: Only a few minutes, and they seemed frightened. When I returned Dr. Phillips and Chief Inspector West had arrived.

Coroner: Was there anything to prevent a man escaping while you were examining the body?

Lamb: Several people were inside and outside the gates, and I should think that they would be sure to observe a man who had marks of blood.

Coroner: But supposing he had no marks of blood?

Lamb: It was quite possible, of course, for a person to escape while I was examining the corpse. Every one was more or less looking towards the body. There was much confusion.

Coroner: Do you think that a person might have got away before you arrived?

Lamb: I think he is more likely to have escaped before than after.

Detective Inspector Reid: How long before had you passed this place?

Lamb: I am not on the Berner-street beat, but I passed the end of the street in Commercial-road six or seven minutes before.

Coroner: When you were found what direction were you going in?

Lamb: I was coming towards Berner-street. A constable named Smith was on the Berner-street beat. He did not accompany me, but the constable who was on fixed-point duty between Grove-street and Christian-street in

Commercial-road. Constables at fixed-points leave duty at one in the morning. I believe that is the practice nearly all over London.

Coroner: I think this is important. The Hanbury-street murder was discovered just as the night police were going off duty. Did you see anything suspicious?

Lamb: I did not at any time. There were squabbles and rows in the streets, but nothing more.

The Foreman: Was there light sufficient to enable you to see, as you were going down Berner-street, whether any person was running away from No. 40?

Lamb: It was rather dark, but I think there was light enough for that, though the person would be somewhat indistinct from Commercial-road.

The Foreman: Some of the papers state that Berner-street is badly lighted; but there are six lamps within 700 feet, and I do not think that is very bad.

Coroner: The parish plan shows that there are four lamps within 350 feet, from Commercial-road to Fairclough-street.

Lamb: There are three, if not four, lamps in Berner-street between Commercial- road and Fairclough-street. Berner-street is about as well lighted as other side streets. Most of them are rather dark, but more lamps have been erected lately.

Coroner: I do not think that London altogether is as well lighted as some capitals are.

Lamb: There are no public-house lights in Berner-street. I was engaged in the yard and at the mortuary all the night afterwards.

Constable Lamb suggests there was no sign of a struggle. Later testimony from Dr Blackwell and Dr Phillips will probably cast doubt on this, both from the details about the scene and the autopsy report. However, of far greater importance is the officer's questioning about whether a man could have escaped after the body's discovery. Certainly, Elizabeth had been attacked within minutes of the discovery of her body, blood flowing from her still-warm torso. They discuss the number and quality of lights in Berner Street and conclude it "isn't that bad" compared to what the newspapers are reporting. One interesting detail here is Lamb's suggestion that although he witnessed nothing suspicious, there were "squabbles and rows" in the streets. Recall Israel Schwartz? Seeing such a quarrel in the street at the murder scene? Given Lamb's indifferent attitude to this observance, such fights in the street were likely a common occurrence, particularly in areas like Berner Street where clubs full of drunken folk would produce regular disturbances. However, there's nothing to suggest that he's referring to particular incidents in Berner Street at the time, and certainly nothing to link his comments directly to the Stride murder. But the link, considering Schwartz's observations, is interesting.

Next comes the testimony of Edward Spooner, whose comments add nothing to what we have already learned. After this was Mary Malcolm, a woman who insisted the victim was her sister Elizabeth Watts. She was a timewaster and you would probably throw this book at me for wasting your time by reproducing her testimony – visit **casebook.org** to see it if you wish, sufficed to say the woman's "dead" sister appeared publicly to confirm she was alive and well sometime later.

Next was another crucial witness, Dr Blackwell:

Mr. Frederick William Blackwell: I reside at No. 100, Commercial-road, and am a physician and surgeon. On Sunday morning last, at ten minutes past one o'clock, I was called to Berner-street by a policeman. My assistant, Mr. Johnston, went back with the constable, and I followed immediately I was dressed. I consulted my watch on my arrival, and it was 1.16 a.m. The deceased was lying on her left side obliquely across the passage, her face looking towards the right wall. Her legs were drawn up, her feet close against the wall of the right side of the passage. Her head was resting beyond the carriage-wheel rut, the neck lying over the rut. Her feet were three yards from the gateway. Her dress was unfastened at the neck. The neck and chest were quite warm, as were also the legs, and the face was slightly warm. The hands were cold. The right hand was open and on the chest, and was smeared with blood. The left hand, lying on the ground, was partially closed, and contained a small packet of cachous wrapped in tissue paper. There were no rings, nor marks of rings, on her hands. The appearance of the face was quite placid. The mouth was slightly open. The deceased had round her neck a check silk scarf, the bow of which was turned to the left and pulled very tight. In the neck there was a long incision which exactly corresponded with the lower border of the scarf. The border was slightly frayed, as if by a sharp knife. The incision in the neck commenced on the left side, 2 inches below the angle of the jaw, and almost in a direct line with it, nearly severing the vessels on that side, cutting the windpipe completely in two, and terminating on the opposite side 1 inch below the angle of the right jaw, but without severing the vessels on that side. I could not ascertain whether the bloody hand had been moved. The blood was running down the gutter into the drain in the opposite direction from the feet. There was about 1lb of clotted blood close by the body, and a stream all the way from there to the back door of the club.

Coroner: Were there no spots of blood about?

Blackwell: No; only some marks of blood which had been trodden in.

Coroner: Was there any blood on the soles of the deceased's boots?

Blackwell: No.

Coroner: No splashing of blood on the wall?

Blackwell: No, it was very dark, and what I saw was by the aid of a policeman's lantern. I have not examined the place since. I examined the clothes, but found no blood on any part of them. The bonnet of the deceased was lying on the ground a few inches from the head. Her dress was unbuttoned at the top.

Coroner: Can you say whether the injuries could have been self-inflicted?

Blackwell: It is impossible that they could have been.

Coroner: Did you form any opinion as to how long the deceased had been dead?

Blackwell: From twenty minutes to half an hour when I arrived. The clothes were not wet with rain. She would have bled to death comparatively slowly on account of vessels on one side only of the neck being cut and the artery not completely severed.

Coroner: After the infliction of the injuries was there any possibility of any cry being uttered by the deceased?

Blackwell: None whatever. Dr. Phillips came about twenty minutes to half an hour after my arrival. The double doors of the yard were closed when I arrived, so that the previous witness must have made a mistake on that point.

A Juror: Can you say whether the throat was cut before or after the deceased fell to the ground?

Blackwell: I formed the opinion that the murderer probably caught hold of the silk scarf, which was tight and knotted, and pulled the deceased backwards, cutting her throat in that way. The throat might have been cut as she was falling, or when she was on the ground. The blood would have spurted about if the act had been committed while she was standing up.

Coroner: Was the silk scarf tight enough to prevent her calling out?

Blackwell: I could not say that.

Coroner: A hand might have been put on her nose and mouth?

Blackwell: Yes, and the cut on the throat was probably instantaneous.

Blackwell's observations are interesting as it provides an interpretation of the attack that took Elizabeth's life. The doctor suggests that the killer grabbed her scarf and pulled her back, cutting her throat as she fell. This ties in with the reports of a struggle seen by Schwartz. Intriguingly, he suggests he cannot tell if the body was moved. I interpret this in a different way, too – that he couldn't tell if the body had been posed. Annie Chapman's body had been posed, with her legs drawn up and feet flat on the ground, whilst Polly Nichols had been covered up after her wounds were inflicted. With Elizabeth Stride, she was apparently left dumped in a heap where she fell. As the final comments suggest, it is possible that the killer was fumbling – the scarf may not have stopped her crying out but a hand over her mouth may have.

By comparing these observations with Schwartz's statement, we can imagine the scene; a drunken killer grabbing his victim, dragging her around by her scarf, and eventually having her fall into the Yard, trying to silence her with his hand whilst also slashing at her throat quite feebly. Blood on her hand suggests she grabbed at her wound as she died, falling and bleeding out onto the pavement, the blood running into the gutter. Hardly the swift and effective silencing the Ripper is credited with in the other cases.

Next up at the inquest was Elizabeth Tanner. She confirmed that she had seen Elizabeth at the Queen's Head that night, and that she was definitely the same woman as the one in the morgue. Two pieces of information come out here of interest; she reports Elizabeth as being "sober", a marked contrast to the other victims who are reported as being quite intoxicated on the nights they died. The next witness, Catherine Lane, similarly confirmed that she was sober on the night of her death. Also, Tanner reported that she was being paid for her cleaning services by Tanner herself, but also by "at work among the Jews." Other than that, she reports that she was unaware of any other money Elizabeth Stride had coming in. This begs the question of just to what extent Elizabeth was engaging in prostitution. We know, because of several witnesses, that she was in the presence of an Englishman the night of her murder, but by no means are we given a definitive narrative that says she was an active and well-known prostitute. So, she was sober, she was possibly engaging in prostitution very casually and not full-time, and she was in a stormy and abusive relationship with her boyfriend Michael Kidney. The clues, as they say, are there.

Speak of the devil and here he is. Michael Kidney's testimony is the next crucial event in the inquest. It is worth reproducing his evidence in full;

Michael Kidney: I live at No. 38, Dorset-street, Spitalfields, and am a waterside labourer. I have seen the body of the deceased at the mortuary.
Coroner: Is it the woman you have been living with?
Kidney: Yes.
Coroner: You have no doubt about it?
Kidney: No doubt whatever.
Coroner: What was her name?
Kidney: Elizabeth Stride.
Coroner: How long have you known her?
Kidney: About three years.
Coroner: How long has she been living with you?
Kidney: Nearly all that time.
Coroner: What was her age?
Kidney: Between thirty-six and thirty-eight years.
Coroner: Was she a Swede?
Kidney: She told me that she was a Swede, and I have no doubt she was. She said she was born three miles from Stockholm, that her father was

a farmer, and that she first came to England for the purpose of seeing the country; but I have grave doubts about that. She afterwards told me that she came to England in a situation with a family.

Coroner: Had she got any relatives in England?

Kidney: When I met her she told me she was a widow, and that her husband had been a ship's carpenter at Sheerness.

Coroner: Did he ever keep a coffee-house?

Kidney: She told me that he had.

Coroner: Where?

Kidney: In Chrisp-street, Poplar.

Coroner: Did she say when he died?

Kidney: She informed me that he was drowned in the Princess Alice disaster.

Coroner: Was the roof of her mouth defective?

Kidney: Yes.

Coroner: You had a quarrel with her on Thursday?

Kidney: I did not see her on Thursday.

Coroner: When did you last see her?

Kidney: On the Tuesday, and I then left her on friendly terms in Commercial- street. That was between nine and ten o'clock at night, as I was coming from work.

Coroner: Did you expect her home?

Kidney: I expected her home half an hour afterwards. I subsequently ascertained that she had been in and had gone out again, and I did not see her again alive.

Coroner: Can you account for her sudden disappearance? Was she the worse for drink when you last saw her?

Kidney: She was perfectly sober.

Coroner: You can assign no reason whatever for her going away so suddenly?

Kidney: She would occasionally go away.

Coroner: Oh, she has left you before?

Kidney: During the three years I have known her she has been away from me about five months altogether.

Coroner: Without any reason?

Kidney: Not to my knowledge. I treated her the same as I would a wife.

Coroner: Do you know whether she had picked up with any one?

Kidney: I have seen the address of the brother of the gentleman with whom she lived as a servant, somewhere near Hyde Park, but I cannot find it now.

Coroner: Did she have any reason for going away?

Kidney: It was drink that made her go on previous occasions. She always came back again. I think she liked me better than any other man. I do not believe she left me on Tuesday to take up with any other man.

Coroner: Had she any money?

Kidney: I do not think she was without a shilling when she left me. From what I used to give her I fancy she must either have had money or spent it in drink.

Coroner: You know of nobody whom she was likely to have complications with or fall foul of?

Kidney: No, but I think the police authorities are very much to blame, or they would have got the man who murdered her. At Leman-street Police-station, on Monday night, I asked for a detective to give information to get the man.

DANIEL JOHNSON

Coroner: What information had you?

Kidney: I could give information that would enable the detectives to discover the man at any time.

Coroner: Then will you give us your information now?

Kidney: I told the inspector on duty at the police-station that I could give information provided he would let me have a young, strange detective to act on it, and he would not give me one.

Coroner: What do you think should be inquired into?

Kidney: I might have given information that would have led to a great deal if I had been provided with a strange young detective.

Inspector Reid: When you went to Leman-street and saw the inspector on duty, were you intoxicated?

Kidney: Yes; I asked for a young detective, and he would not let me have one, and I told him that he was uncivil. (Laughter.)

Coroner: You have been in the army, and I believe have a good pension?

Kidney: Only the reserve.

A Juror: Have you got any information for a detective?

Kidney: I am a great lover of discipline, sir. (Laughter.)

Coroner: Had you any information that required the service of a detective?

Kidney: Yes. I thought that if I had one, privately, he could get more information than I could myself. The parties I obtained my information from knew me, and I thought someone else would be able to derive more from them.

Inspector Reid: Will you give me the information directly, if you will not give it to the coroner?

Kidney: I believe I could catch the man if I had a detective under my command.

Coroner: You cannot expect that. I have had over a hundred letters making suggestions, and I dare say all the writers would like to have a detective at their service. (Laughter.)

Kidney: I have information which I think might be of use to the police.

Coroner: You had better give it, then.

Kidney: I believe that, if I could place the policeman myself, the man would be captured.

Coroner: You must know that the police would not be placed at the disposal of a man the worse for drink.

Kidney: If I were at liberty to place 100 men about this city the murderer would be caught in the act.

Inspector Reid: But you have no information to give to the police?

Kidney: No, I will keep it to myself.

A Juror: Do you know of any sister who gave money to the deceased?

Kidney: No. On Monday I saw Mrs. Malcolm, who said the deceased was her sister. She is very like the deceased.

Coroner: Did the deceased have a child by you?

Kidney: No.

Coroner: Or by a policeman?

Kidney: She told me that a policeman used to court her when she was at Hyde Park, before she was married to Stride. Stride and the policeman courted her at the same time, but I never heard of her having a child by the policeman. She said she was the mother of nine children, two of whom were drowned with her husband in the Princess Alice, and the remainder were either in a school belonging to the Swedish Church on the other side of London Bridge, or with the husband's friends. I thought she was telling the truth when she spoke of Swedish people. I understood that the deceased and her husband were employed on the Princess Alice.

Where to start with this evidence?

In my opinion, Michael Kidney's tone in this evidence, given days after his partner of three years has been brutally murdered, is casual, self-serving, egotistical and even whimsical. His demand to have policemen at his personal disposal to "catch the man in the act" because of the information he claims to have – and refuses to share – is borderline comedic. His joking, laughter, wry and sarcastic tone, his laid-back attitude, all point to a man enjoying the spotlight and barely bothered by his common-law wife's death.

In fact, he remarks that she always came back to him because he thinks "she likes me better than any other man," and that he didn't believe that she was shacking up with anybody else for that reason. Maybe he was in denial that his wife occasionally engaged in prostitution, or maybe – just maybe – he's telling the truth. It is hard to tell given that he also states that he did not see her and did not quarrel with Elizabeth despite witness evidence from Catherine Lane that Stride "had words with" the man she lived with on the previous Thursday and was stopping at the doss house in the meantime. The truth is a slippery customer here. Nevertheless, it is his tone here and the claims he makes, real and false, that offer comment on his character.

Kidney would be recalled once for a brief statement but that would be it for now. However, his quite frankly cold and sardonic attitude at the inquest offers an insight into the man's relationship with Elizabeth, which we shall explore in more detail later.

The next witnesses, Thomas Coram and Constable Joseph Drage, testified to a bloodstained knife found on the doorstep at an address nearby, 253 Whitechapel Road. The knife was actually found before Elizabeth's murder, so is of no relevance anyway. However, later it may become more important.

The next key evidence comes from Dr. George Bagster Phillips;

George Baxter Phillips: I live at No. 2, Spital-square, and am surgeon of the H Division of police. I was called on Sunday morning last at twenty past one to Leman-street Police-station, and was sent on to Berner-street, to a yard at the side of what proved to be a club-house. I found Inspector Pinhorn and Acting-Superintendent West in possession of a body, which had already been seen by Dr. Blackwell, who had arrived some time before me. The body was lying on its left side, the face being turned towards the wall, the head towards the yard, and the feet toward the street. The left arm was extended from elbow, and a packet of cachous was in the hand. Similar ones were in the gutter. I took them from the hand and gave them to Dr. Blackwell. The right arm was lying

110

over the body, and the back of the hand and wrist had on them clotted blood. The legs were drawn up, feet close to wall, body still warm, face warm, hands cold, legs quite warm, silk handkerchief round throat, slightly torn (so is my note, but I since find it is cut). I produce the handkerchief. This corresponded to the right angle of the jaw. The throat was deeply gashed, and there was an abrasion of the skin, about an inch and a quarter in diameter, under the right clavicle. On Oct. 1, at three p.m., at St. George's Mortuary, present Dr. Blackwell and for part of the time Dr. Reigate and Dr. Blackwell's assistant; temperature being about 55 degrees, Dr. Blackwell and I made a post-mortem examination, Dr. Blackwell kindly consenting to make the dissection, and I took the following note: "Rigor mortis still firmly marked. Mud on face and left side of the head. Matted on the hair and left side. We removed the clothes. We found the body fairly nourished. Over both shoulders, especially the right, from the front aspect under colar bones and in front of chest there is a bluish discolouration which I have watched and seen on two occasions since. On neck, from left to right, there is a clean cut incision six inches in length; incision commencing two and a half inches in a straight line below the angle of the jaw. Three-quarters of an inch over undivided muscle, then becoming deeper, about an inch dividing sheath and the vessels, ascending a little, and then grazing the muscle outside the cartilages on the left side of the neck. The carotid artery on the left side and the other vessels contained in the sheath were all cut through, save the posterior portion of the carotid, to a line about 1-12th of an inch in extent, which prevented the separation of the upper and lower portion of the artery. The cut through the tissues on the right side of the cartilages is more superficial, and tails off to about two inches below the right angle of the jaw. It is evident that the haemorrhage which produced death was caused through the partial severance of the left carotid artery. There is a deformity in the lower fifth of the bones of the right leg, which are not straight, but bow forward; there is a thickening above the left ankle. The bones are here straighter. No recent external injury save to neck. The lower lobe of the ear was torn, as if by the forcible removing or wearing through of an earring, but it was thoroughly healed. The right ear was pierced for an earring, but had not been so injured, and the earring was wanting. On removing the scalp there was no sign of bruising or extravasation of blood between it and the skull-cap. The skull was about one-sixth of an inch in thickness, and dense in texture. The brain was fairly normal. Both lungs were unusually pale. The heart was small; left ventricle firmly contracted, right less so. Right ventricle full of dark clot; left absolutely empty. Partly digested food, apparently consisting of cheese, potato, and farinaceous edibles. Teeth on left lower jaw absent." On Tuesday, at the mortuary, I found the total circumference of the neck 12« inches. I found in the pocket of the underskirt of the deceased a key, as of a padlock, a small piece of lead pencil, a comb, a broken piece of comb, a metal spoon, half a dozen large and one small button, a hook, as if off a dress, a piece of muslin, and one or two small pieces of paper. Examining her jacket I found that although there was a slight amount of mud on the right side, the left was well plastered with mud.

A Juror: You have not mentioned anything about the roof of the mouth. One witness said part of the roof of the mouth was gone.

Phillips: That was not noticed.

Coroner: What was the cause of death?

Phillips: Undoubtedly the loss of blood from the left carotid artery and the division of the windpipe.

Coroner: Did you examine the blood at Berner-street carefully, as to its direction and so forth?

Phillips: Yes.

Coroner: The blood near to the neck and a few inches to the left side was well clotted, and it had run down the waterway to within a few inches of the side entrance to the club-house.

Coroner: Were there any spots of blood anywhere else?

Phillips: I could trace none except that which I considered had been transplanted - if I may use the term - from the original flow from the neck. Roughly estimating it, I should say there was an unusual flow of blood, considering the stature and the nourishment of the body.

A Juror: I did notice a black mark on one of the legs of the deceased, but could not say that it was due to an adder bite.

A few things can be learned from this testimony. Probably most striking is, of course, the fact that Elizabeth was spared the mutilations inflicted on the other victims, and as testified by Louis Diemshütz, her clothes were not in any way disturbed, meaning her killer did not bother to even try and inflict injuries – even though the Ripper certainly had a go with Polly, despite the huge risk and exposed position. Considering he could have inflicted the injuries within seconds, even the moving of clothing or the lifting of her dress would have suggested an intention to do so. Similarly, there was zero evidence of strangulation or asphyxia as there is with the others. This killer simply manhandled Elizabeth and slashed her throat quite superficially. This struggle is in evidence with Elizabeth's body being matted with mud on the left side, mostly, and the bruising on the upper portions of the body. This seems to correspond, as other commentators have pointed out, with the observations made my Israel Schwartz of Elizabeth being pushed to the ground by her attacker.

Both Drs. Phillips and Blackwell return for further illuminating evidence the following day;

> **Dr. Phillips (recalled)**: On the last occasion I was requested to make a re-examination of the body of the deceased, especially with regard to the palate, and I have since done so at the mortuary, along with Dr. Blackwell and Dr. Gordon Brown. I did not find any injury to, or absence of, any part of either the hard or the soft palate. The Coroner also desired me to examine the two handkerchiefs which were found on the deceased. I did not discover any blood on them, and I believe that the stains on the larger handkerchief are those of fruit. Neither on the hands nor about the body of the

deceased did I find grapes, or connection with them. I am convinced that the deceased had not swallowed either the skin or seed of a grape within many hours of her death. I have stated that the neckerchief which she had on was not torn, but cut. The abrasion which I spoke of on the right side of the neck was only apparently an abrasion, for on washing it it was removed, and the skin found to be uninjured. The knife produced on the last occasion was delivered to me, properly secured, by a constable, and on examination I found it to be such a knife as is used in a chandler's shop, and is called a slicing knife. It has blood upon it, which has characteristics similar to the blood of a human being. It has been recently blunted, and its edge apparently turned by rubbing on a stone such as a kerbstone. It evidently was before a very sharp knife.

Coroner: Is it such as knife as could have caused the injuries which were inflicted upon the deceased?

Phillips: Such a knife could have produced the incision and injuries to the neck, but it is not such a weapon as I should have fixed upon as having caused the injuries in this case; and if my opinion as regards the position of the body is correct, the knife in question would become an improbable instrument as having caused the incision.

Coroner: What is your idea as to the position the body was in when the crime was committed?

Phillips: I have come to a conclusion as to the position of both the murderer and the victim, and I opine that the latter was seized by the shoulders and placed on the ground, and that the murderer was on her right side when he inflicted the cut. I am of opinion that the cut was made from the left to the right side of the deceased, and taking into account the position of the incision it is unlikely that such a long knife inflicted the wound in the neck.

Coroner: The knife produced on the last occasion was not sharp pointed, was it?

Phillips: No, it was rounded at the tip, which was about an inch across. The blade was wider at the base.

Coroner: Was there anything to indicate that the cut on the neck of the deceased was made with a pointed knife?

Phillips: Nothing.

Coroner: Have you formed any opinion as to the manner in which the deceased's right hand became stained with blood?

Phillips: It is a mystery. There were small oblong clots on the back of the hand. I may say that I am taking it as a fact that after death the hand always remained in the position in which I found it - across the body.

Coroner: How long had the woman been dead when you arrived at the scene of the murder, do you think?

Phillips: Within an hour she had been alive.

Coroner: Would the injury take long to inflict?

Phillips: Only a few seconds - it might be done in two seconds.

Coroner: Does the presence of the cachous in the left hand indicate that the murder was committed very suddenly and without any struggle?

Phillips: Some of the cachous were scattered

about the yard.

The Foreman: Do you not think that the woman would have dropped the packet of cachous altogether if she had been thrown to the ground before the injuries were inflicted?

Phillips: That is an inference which the jury would be perfectly entitled to draw.

Coroner: I assume that the injuries were not self-inflicted?

Phillips: I have seen several self-inflicted wounds more extensive than this one, but then they have not usually involved the carotid artery. In this case, as in some others, there seems to have been some knowledge where to cut the throat to cause a fatal result.

Coroner: Is there any similarity between this case and Annie Chapman's case?

Phillips: There is very great dissimilarity between the two. In Chapman's case the neck was severed all round down to the vertebral column, the vertebral bones being marked with two sharp cuts, and there had been an evident attempt to separate the bones.

Coroner: From the position you assume the perpetrator to have been in, would he have been likely to get bloodstained?

Phillips: Not necessarily, for the commencement of the wound and the injury to the vessels would be away from him, and the stream of blood - for stream it was - would be directed away from him, and towards the gutter in the yard.

Coroner: Was there any appearance of an opiate or any smell of chloroform?

Phillips: There was no perceptible trace of any anaesthetic or narcotic. The absence of noise is

117

a difficult question under the circumstances of this case to account for, but it must not be taken for granted that there was not any noise. If there was an absence of noise I cannot account for it.

The Foreman: That means that the woman might cry out after the cut?

Phillips: Not after the cut.

Coroner: But why did she not cry out while she was being put on the ground?

Phillips: She was in a yard, and in a locality where she might cry out very loudly and no notice be taken of her. It was possible for the woman to draw up her legs after the wound, but she could not have turned over. The wound was inflicted by drawing the knife across the throat. A short knife, such as a shoemaker's well-ground knife, would do the same thing. My reason for believing that deceased was injured when on the ground was partly on account of the absence of blood anywhere on the left side of the body and between it and the wall.

A Juror: Was there any trace of malt liquor in the stomach?

Phillips: There was no trace.

***

Dr. Blackwell (recalled): I can confirm Dr. Phillips as to the appearances at the mortuary. I may add that I removed the cachous from the left hand of the deceased, which was nearly open. The packet was lodged between the thumb and the first finger, and was partially hidden from view. It was I who spilt them in removing them from the hand. My impression is that the hand gradually relaxed while the woman was dying, she dying in a fainting condition from the loss of blood. I do not think that I made myself quite clear as to whether it was possible for this to have been a case of suicide. What I meant to say was that, taking all the facts into consideration, more especially the absence of any instrument in the hand, it was impossible to have been a suicide. I have myself seen many equally severe wounds self-inflicted. With respect to the knife which was found, I should like to say that I concur with Dr. Phillips in his opinion that, although it might possibly have inflicted the injury, it is an extremely unlikely instrument to have been used. It appears to me that a murderer, in using a round-pointed instrument, would seriously handicap himself, as he would be only able to use it in one particular way. I am told that slaughterers always use a sharp- pointed instrument.

Coroner: No one has suggested that this crime was committed by a slaughterer.

Blackwell: I simply intended to point out the inconvenience that might arise from using a blunt-pointed weapon.

The Foreman: Did you notice any marks or bruises about the shoulders?

Blackwell: They were what we call pressure marks. At first they were very obscure, but subsequently they became very evident. They were not what are ordinarily called bruises; neither is there any abrasion. Each shoulder was about equally marked.

A Juror: How recently might the marks have been caused?

Blackwell: That is rather difficult to say.
Coroner: Did you perceive any grapes near the body in the yard?
Blackwell: No.
Coroner: Did you hear any person say that they had seen grapes there?
Blackwell: I did not.

There is quite a lot to take in here. Let us break it down.

In Phillips' recalled testimony, backed-up by Blackwell, we dispense with the myth of grapes being anywhere near the scene. Matthew Packer's story was disproved, and there is no evidence of grapes in the vicinity of the Elizabeth Stride murder. No grape stalks, seeds, skins, juice or even stomach contents including grapes.

This is interesting for a second reason; in his analysis of Elizabeth's stomach contents, another thing is absent; alcohol. In concordance with the testimony of several witnesses who saw Elizabeth that night, and the unreliable testimony of Michael Kidney who claimed not to have seen her in days, admittedly, she is described generally as sober and specifically as sober on that night. The other victims up until now were described as being drunk, as I pointed out previously, and here we have evidence that she was probably either sober or she had had very little to drink some time before her death. Neither, it seems, was there any evidence of narcotics or chloroform. It seems, like modern commentators, the contemporary authorities were at a loss to explain the absence of any cries or sound during the murders. However, referring again to both the testimonies of Schwartz but also Lamb, not only was Elizabeth seen and heard to cry out, but such cries were not exactly uncommon. So really, it is a moot point, made more moot by Phillips' suggestion that the killing itself could have taken a mere two seconds to carry out.

This brings us on to the knife. Now, the knife continually mentioned in this inquest was found bloody and wrapped in cloth on the doorstep of an address in Whitechapel Road at around 12:30am, 30th September 1888. It is already clear that, timings-wise, this cannot be the knife used in either murder that night. However, it is still produced and debated in the inquest – which allows for discussion of the type of knife that may have been used. Blackwell cheekily slips in the suggestion that slaughtermen use sharp-pointed knives, rather than the blunt knife found on the night, only to be slapped down by the coroner who reminds him that nobody suggested the killer is a slaughterman. Further, Phillips explains that a shorter knife, not necessarily pointed, was probably used and that the longer bladed knife that was found was "unlikely" to be the weapon he would fixate on as being responsible for the wounds.

As if the lack of strangulation, lack of disturbance of clothing, lack of posing of the body, difference in knife being used (Annie and Polly's murders; long-bladed, sharp, pointed knives; in Elizabeth's murder, a shorter, round-tipped knife), and distinct difference in the victim's precrime behaviour (being apparently sober), wasn't enough to present a great deal of doubt in the minds of the reader that Elizabeth Stride's murder was committed by the same serial killer as had murdered Polly Nichols and Annie Chapman, Phillips then states in plain English that the crime is "greatly dissimilar" to those previous crimes. Crucially, he draws attention to the fact that in the Annie Chapman case, effort had been made to decapitate the victim;

In Chapman's case the neck was severed all round down to the vertebral column, the vertebral bones being marked with two sharp cuts, and there had been an evident attempt to separate the bones.

Phillips has pointed out that the killer's cutting of the victims' throat was part of a bigger plan – decapitation. With Elizabeth Stride, he simply slashed her throat, not particularly deeply, and left her to bleed. This is important in understanding the methods and implied motives of the killer, and why this murder is substantially different from the rest, as will be discussed later in the book.

To round off the inquest testimony, the final two witnesses of note are Constable William Smith, James Brown, and William Marshall. Constable Smith reported seeing a man and woman (who he thought may have been Elizabeth), whilst on his beat around Berner Street at around 10pm. He reports seeing the woman in the company of a man of around 5 feet 7 inches, about 28-years-old, respectable-looking, with a dark cutaway coat, dark felt deerstalker hat, clean-shaven and carrying a parcel about 18 inches long. They apparently stood talking on the opposite side of the street to the murder scene when he saw them.

William Marshall saw a similar man with a woman he positively identified as the deceased at around 11:45pm on Berner Street. The pair were kissing, and the man remarked, in an apparently well-heeled voice, "You'd say anything but your prayers." To this, Elizabeth laughed. He described the man as wearing dark trousers, a dark cutaway coat, and a peaked cap. He appeared to be middle-aged, although the witness admitted he didn't get a good enough look to see if he was shaven or not. He estimated the man as being around 5 feet 6 inches tall, and respectably dressed and presented, like a clerk rather than a labourer.

Finally, James Brown saw Elizabeth at around 12:45am with a man in dark clothing at the corner of Fairclough Street and Berner Street (mere yards from the murder scene, and minutes before the murder). Again, he stated the man to be about 5 feet 7 inches all, and neither appeared drunk. Moments after his sighting, Israel Schwartz would witness a different, drunken man approach the lone Elizabeth Stride and attack her.

So, if these witnesses are correct, this man was with Elizabeth between 10pm and 12:45am, and for some reason she was persistently in the vicinity of Berner Street, the murder scene, around two-and-a-quarter-hours before her death. She was dossing at 32 Flower and Dean Street, quite a way to the north, whilst she and Michael Kidney lived in Devonshire Street, far nearer to Buck's Row, in fact, than Berner Street. What was she doing there? Going by the prostitute narrative, she could have been there fishing for clients, except we have her in the company of just one man described as respectable and "clerk" like in appearance between 10pm and 12:45pm. J Best and John Gardner, who did not testify at the inquest, also reported seeing her around the same time – 11pm – at a pub in Settle Street, just north of Berner Street. This is not a woman hooking up with a client, this is a woman on a date. She spends all night with the well-dressed man, publicly and openly chatting, kissing, going for drinks in pubs – but not on the lash, as it were. Again, there is nothing to suggest she was drunk and nothing to suggest she'd drunken any great quantity of alcohol.

In the Elizabeth Stride murder, this individual is important. A man around his late 20s – early 30s, clean-shaven, well-spoken, dressed in dark clothes, apparently a cutaway coat and a peaked cap or deerstalker, in the company of the victim for over two hours, right up until the moments preceding her murder. They were witnessed clearly by several individuals, right up until the murder itself. At that moment, we have Schwartz's report. By now Elizabeth was alone, and the drunken man approached her, placing his hand on her shoulder and pushing her to the ground. Schwartz crossed the road because, as *The Star*'s article says, he didn't want to get "mixed up in quarrels."

I think this is time to sum up the evidence in this case, and I think the conclusion should be obvious.

The Murder of Elizabeth Stride

In the clear majority of cases, people are murdered by people they know. Even when a serial killer is stalking the streets, these commonplace murders still happen. In the case of Elizabeth Stride, there is, as Dr. Phillips testified in the inquest suggested, "great dissimilarity" between her murder and those of Mary Ann "Polly" Nichols and Annie Chapman. We can simply list these dissimilarities, and the aspects of the crime that appear the most salient. To begin with, let's recap the events leading up to the murder.

27th September 1888: Elizabeth sees Michael Kidney for the last time on Thursday prior, and according to testimony by Elizabeth Tanner, she'd "had words" with him. Kidney denies seeing her, denies an argument occurred, suggests he expected her to be home as usual with no ill-feelings. He also insists that Elizabeth is unlikely to have seen other men besides him.

27th September - 29th September 1888: She dosses at 32 Flower and Dean Street whilst away from him. She was working for Elizabeth Tanner at the doss house whilst also working for local Jews in domestic service, as she has done all her life.

29th-30th September 1888: No less than five witnesses (J Best, John Gardner, James Brown, William Marshall, and Constable Smith) place Elizabeth Stride in the company of a well-dressed, well-spoken, clerk-like man for at least two-and-a-quarter-hours between 10pm on the 29th and 12:45am on the 30th. He is described as around 28 or older, clean-shaven, 5 feet 7 inches tall, wearing dark clothing and a peaked cap of some sort. They are seen mostly near the murder scene. They appear to have met in Settle Street at the Bricklayer's Arms, and ended their night opposite Dutfield's Yard minutes before the murder.

30/9/88, 12:47am: Israel Schwartz walks behind a drunken man along Berner Street, and witnesses the man assault a lone Elizabeth Stride outside Dutfield's Yard. A second man makes an appearance, either as a bystander who leaves at the same time as Schwartz, as an accomplice to the attacker, or as a man who tries to intervene in the attack upon Stride, the details are misreported and open to interpretation. The official police report simply states that the man left and followed Schwartz away from the scene. There was also a cry of "Lipski," apparently a racial slur, but again this is attributed both in meaning and origin differently.

1am: About 12 minutes later, Louis Diemshütz finds the body of Elizabeth Stride in Dutfield's Yard.

Now for the murder itself, and the ways it differs from the others;

- The victim was apparently sober, or at least in no way incapacitated by alcohol. *The other victims had all been very drunk on the night of their deaths.*
- The victim in this case had been subject to a violent attack, having her scarf yanked tightly around her neck probably during a struggle, or to pull her towards the killer. She is missing teeth but

125

that is unlikely to be a consequence of contemporaneous violence. *The other victims had been rapidly seized, strangled and suffered incidental violence, not instrumental violence.*

- She is not strangled, and no effort is otherwise made to incapacitate her. *The other victims had been strangled first, which both incapacitated the victim but also lowered their blood pressure and reduced the amount of blood that escaped the body.*

- Her throat is slashed superficially, allowing her to apparently spill blood on her hand and bleed out quite effusively onto the pavement, the blood even clotting in a pool near her head. According to medical evidence, she died slowly. *The other victims would have died very quickly from the extremely deep slashes to their throats.*

- The body is not posed in any way – she simply lies in a twisted heap, muddy from her fall to the ground. *The other victims had been posed.*

- Despite potentially having a minute or two to commence an attack, no effort is made at all by the killer to disturb the victim's clothing. *Even in the totally exposed position he was in with the Nichols murder, the killer still inflicted wounds upon the body, covering them quickly and apparently escaping just as the body was found.*

- The killer uses a shorter knife, possibly something well-ground-down. *The other murders were committed with a long, sharp bladed knife.*

The murder takes place a mere 35 minutes before the second. This murder was extremely haphazard, disorganised, deeply out of character for the killer of the

126

previous victims and of Eddowes, deeply different in modus operandi and signature. Are we to seriously believe that the same man went on, within the space of about 40 minutes, to take a 15-minute walk to Mitre Square, pick up another victim, and despite being spotted by witnesses there, carry out a textbook Jack the Ripper murder vastly different to the one he apparently committed minutes prior?

The conclusion I draw is that Elizabeth Stride was not killed by Jack the Ripper. Here is my preferred theory.

I find it far more likely that, during a drinking "bender," a jealous and angry Michael Kidney, determined to track down his missing girlfriend, finds her in the company of the well-dressed man. That man bids her goodnight after their night out, or he enters the club, momentarily leaving her outside. Kidney stumbles down the street ahead of Israel Schwartz, and accosts Elizabeth, attacking her and pushing her to the ground. Seeing Israel Schwartz, he spits out the racist jibe, "Lipski!" and Schwartz flees. The second man appears and flees along with Schwartz. Eddleston (2010, p.88) suggests Elizabeth's latest time of death would be around 12:54am. Schwartz's sighting took place around 12:47am. That's a seven-minute period. Enough time for Elizabeth and Kidney to argue, and Kidney to murder her. He flees, and continues to drink.

Kidney then appears at Leman Street Police Station the following day, drunken, and insisting that he knew Elizabeth was the victim, and that he could catch the killer if he was gifted 100 police officers. This is the killer piece of evidence. It was not until 3rd October 1888 that Elizabeth Stride was positively identified by Elizabeth Tanner and Catherine Lane. Although tentative identification had been made, on day one of the inquest was the testimony of time-waster Mary Malcolm, who unhesitatingly identified the victim as her sister Elizabeth Watts. Here is a comment by the Coroner to the jury during the inquest on day one;

> **Coroner:** The body has not yet been identified?
> [...]
> **The Foreman:** I do not quite understand that. I thought the inquest had been opened on the body of one Elizabeth Stride.
> **Coroner:** That was a mistake. Something is known of the deceased, but she has not been fully identified. It would be better at present to describe her as a woman unknown. She has been partially identified. It is known where she lived. It was thought at the beginning of the inquest that she had been identified by a relative, but that turns out to have been a mistake.

Mary Malcolm would come down to identify the victim but initially said it was not her sister Elizabeth Watts. Later she insisted it was, and sobbed bitterly in court as she was cross-examined, stating she was now convinced utterly that the body was of her sister. The name of Elizabeth Stride was still doing the rounds, but at that time, nobody had identified her as such. It wouldn't be until later, when Elizabeth Tanner and Catherine Lane saw her at the mortuary that she was positively identified. In fact, the mystery of Mary Malcolm took until the end of the inquest, with Elizabeth Watts herself appearing to testify that she was alive and well, that the issue was truly resolved.

DANIEL JOHNSON

Crucially, Michael Kidney stormed down to the police station well before any of this, and demanded to be given police officers at his disposal to single-handedly catch the killer. It was later that he would identify her body in the morgue for himself. Somehow, he knew instantly that Elizabeth Stride had been murdered in Dutfield's Yard, and he inserted himself into the investigation immediately, before stringing along a self-serving story about his secret knowledge of the killer, and laughing and joking in court amidst the lies. This insistence, hours after the event, that Elizabeth was the victim also seems to contrast with his suggestion at the inquest that they had spent lengthy times apart when he did not know where she was or what she was doing – how did he know this time that she was indeed the victim of the murder, and not simply on one of her constitutionals? Did he present himself at Leman Street each time if Elizabeth happened to be out for a few hours at the same time? I think not.

Michael Kidney ended his days in the depressing slum of Thrawl Street, receiving treatment for syphilis and other ailments during 1889, probably received from his continued liaisons with sex workers in the East End.

RIPPER MYTH
"THE DOUBLE EVENT"

I have a message at the end of this literary prosecution of Michael Kidney for the murder of his common-law wife, Elizabeth Stride. The myth of the double-event in Ripperology is a powerful, persistent and attractive one. People want to believe it, they want to imagine a bloodthirsty killer unsatisfied with a botched kill, stalking the streets for a second victim. They love the idea, and they are keen to cling on to it as part of Ripper lore. It is demonstrably false, however. Never in the annals of serial murder has there been a similar case of a murderer botching one attack, despite killing the victim, and within 30 minutes, moving on to a second. And there is a crucial logical error in assuming that a killer's state of mind can cause him to so terribly mess up a kill, ignoring his own methods and abandoning his signature behaviours, yet apparently change on a sixpence half-an-hour later and allow him to expediently carry out a textbook signature murder. It is irrational and silly. It is time to let the idea go and move on.

The inquest ended on 24th October 1888, with a finding of wilful murder against person or persons unknown. Elizabeth Stride was buried in a pauper's grave on the 6th October in East London Cemetery.

Catharine Eddowes

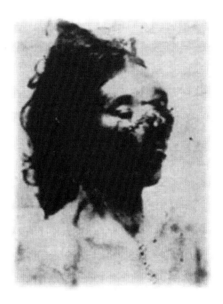

Illustration 7: Catharine Eddowes, mortuary photo

Catharine Eddowes was born on the 14th April 1842 in Wolverhampton. Her family moved to Bermondsey in London when she was two, and when she was six, her mother died. Thereafter, her siblings went into the workhouse and she was sent to live with her aunt back in Wolverhampton. She received an education, though, which is more than can be said for many of her time, going to St Johns Charity School and Dowgate Charity School respectively. Nevertheless, at the age of roughly 19-20 she started a relationship with a pensioner called Thomas Conway. They were close enough that Catharine had Conway's initials tattooed on her arm.

The pair stayed together until 1880, producing three children, including a daughter named Annie. Upon the pair's separation (they claimed to be married, but no documentary evidence exists to support this), Catharine took custody of Annie while the two sons were taken by Conway. It is interesting to note that Conway appears to have joined the Royal Fusiliers at one time under the name Quinn, apparently to avoid contact with a previous partner! Not a particularly trustworthy bloke in my opinion.

In 1881, Catharine met an Irish porter by the name of John Kelly and they began living at Cooney's Lodging House (55 Flower and Dean Street, in the heart of the "wicked quarter-mile"). It appears Catharine spent the rest of her days there with Kelly, occasionally seeking out her daughter Annie and tapping her for money and things. The daughter would later blame her mother for the breakdown of her family, blaming drink and her frequent absences, although others pointed the finger at Conway. The turbulent relationship surely lead to Catharine's downfall into the life she would end up leading.

Before we get on to the last movements of Catharine Eddowes, and interesting segue must be made. Two days before her murder, the 28th September 1888, Catharine apparently visited either Shoe Lane or Mile End Workhouse and spoke to the superintendent there, claiming she knew the identity of the killer. She reportedly told him, "I have come back to earn the reward for the apprehension of the Whitechapel murderer. I think I know him." This sounds to me like jest, and the fact that she would be murdered by the Ripper days later speaks volumes I think. One is reminded of the haunting television interview with Paula Clennell in 2006 during the Suffolk serial murders, when the hooded and then-unidentified figure admitted she needed the money and couldn't just stop working the streets. Nevertheless, the killer was able to murder five times and was caught not because a plucky investigator or a suspicious prostitute tracked him down, but because his DNA was on the bodies. The point I'm making is that regardless of the desperation of the girls, nobody walks willingly into a death trap. Catharine claims to some random bloke that she knows the killer and will collect a small fortune, for her at least, and is murdered by him days later – and witnessed with her killer, quite happy, moments prior. Clearly, this claim that she knew the killer can be dismissed by common sense and logic.

Last Movements

Back to Catharine's last movements. Early on the 29th September 1888, Catharine and John Kelly were moved on from Shoe Lane and headed for Cooney's Lodging House. On the way they pawned a pair of boots and were able to pay for their breakfast. Their money ran out quickly and by mid-afternoon they separated, Catharine reportedly on a mission to tap her daughter Annie up for more cash. She never got there, but when she was next seen she'd evidently gotten money from somewhere as she was arrested for being drunk and causing a scene on Aldgate High Street at around 8pm that day. Two officers, PC Louis Robinson and PC George Simmons, found her reportedly "imitating a fire engine" (Begg, *et al*, 1991, p.130) and trying to sleep in the middle of the pavement. Evidently, she was drunk. At Bishopsgate Police Station she gave her name to Station Sergeant Byfield as "nothing," and was locked in the drunk tank to sober up.

She was inspected regularly until 1am, having protested her detention and singing to herself in the meantime. Then-on-duty PC George Hutt released her and their interactions here are worth reproducing as the only recorded last words of a Ripper victim;

> HUTT: Too late for you to get any more drink.
> CATHARINE: I shall get a damn fine hiding when I get home.
> HUTT: And serve you right. You've no right to get drunk.
> [...]
> HUTT: This way, missus. [guiding her to the exit]
> CATHARINE: All right, good night, old cock.

These would be the last words anyone reported hearing her say. She'd given her name as Mary Ann Kelly and her address as 6 Fashion Street, and was allowed to go into the night.

Fifteen minutes or so earlier, Israel Schwartz had witnessed the attack on Elizabeth Stride. As we have seen, at about the time Catharine was being released from the police station, around 1am, Elizabeth's killer had struck and was now fleeing the scene. Whether you believe the two women were murdered by the same man or not, this fact is worth adding in for context.

Next come the most important witnesses in the whole Ripper story. These witnesses were considered of such crucial importance to the police at the time that their description of a suspect was withheld from the public and key figures would later claim that their prime suspect was identified and detained in an asylum based on their evidence. These witnesses may hold the key to the identity of the Ripper, although interpretations of the truth have varied across the years. I will attempt to lay out the details as accurately as I possibly can for you.

At around 1:30am on the 30th September 1888, three men, Joseph Lawende, Joseph Hyam Levy and Harry Harris, left the Imperial Club at 16-17 Duke's Place. They'd apparently stayed back to allow the rain to stop before leaving. At 1:35am according to Lawende's estimations, the trio spotted a man and a woman – who Lawende later identified as Catharine Eddowes – speaking at the entrance to Church Passage. This narrow cut lead from Duke Street into Mitre Square, and the pair were seen at the Duke Street entrance. Lawende and Levy both got a look at the pair, describing the man in general terms as "shabby," "rough-looking," with a cloth-cap, and standing a few inches taller than Catharine. They appeared to be amicably engaged, with Catharine's hand placed on his chest as to initiate a sexual encounter. Levy would comment that he believed the pair were "up to no good" at such a late hour. He was right, it seems. However, the story does not end with Levy, whose behaviour and comments during the following investigation raise many questions.

Lawende, who saw the man face-on, later commented he probably wouldn't recognise the man again. Nevertheless, he did furnish police with a description, which was withheld from the inquest (but which did leak to the press); he described a man in his 30s, around 5 feet 7-9 inches tall, fair complexion, moustache, medium build, a "salt-and-pepper" loose jacket, grey cloth peaked cap and a red neckerchief. He commented that the man looked shabby and a bit like a sailor. This could well be the only accurate eyewitness description of the Ripper worth taking real note of. Hidden in there are clues to the Ripper's lifestyle, his employment, his background. Most telling is probably the fact that Lawende considered the man so utterly unremarkable that he would struggle to recognise him twice. Once this sighting was made, Levy apparently warned his friends to move on because of the undesirable sorts around there, and they left. Again, this was around 1:35am.

Only five minutes later, PC James Harvey patrolled down Church Passage and back out, not entering Mitre Square. He saw nothing.

At 1:45am, PC Edward Watkins entered the Square on his beat and found the body. It was positioned in the darkest spot, in the southwest corner, lying across the path with the head nearest the wall. Dr. Brown would give details of the sight later; her body was lying with her arms by her sides, head turned to the left, and clothing raised, exposing her thighs and the savage mutilations carried out upon her. Her intestines had been cut out and dumped on her left side, with a section cut away and laid between her left arm and her body, seemingly on purpose. Her face had also been slashed and stabbed in a frenzy, and her throat was deeply cut to the bone. Dr Brown reported that there was no sign of blood spatter or staining to the front or the bottom half of the body, and neither did he spot any ejaculate from the killer (a keen and prescient observation for his time), but that there was a quantity of drying blood beneath the left side and a flow from the body down the slope of the pavement. Death had occurred within a short time of the body's discovery.

PC Watkins had previously entered the square at around 1:30am and his beat took him on a circuit of the surrounding streets, including Duke Lane, Creechurch Lane, Mitre Street, Leadenhall Street and St James' Place took around a quarter of an hour or less according to Begg *et al* (1991, p.489). The sighting of the suspect with Catharine in Church Passage had been at 1:35am and the body found at around 1:45am. Ten minutes to get in, kill Catharine, and leave without being seen by any more passers-by or the police officers of regular patrols in the surrounding streets, particularly when at the same time, news was spreading of the murder of Elizabeth Stride a mere fifteen-minute jog away in Dutfield's Yard.

Illustration 8: Mitre Square, circa 1894

The killer clearly had a practised knowledge of the streets, the alleyways but also the local police patrols. This speaks of a man not only local, but who knows the minutiae of the urban landscape well enough to slip around anywhere. I doubt any regular Joe would have such a knowledge unless their lived immediately in the vicinity of the crime, within a street or so, or if some aspect of their lifestyle or employment lent itself to such an intimate knowledge. More evidence for the killer's geographical prowess will come later. For now, we return to the discovery of the body of Catharine Eddowes.

On the opposite side of the square to the murder scene, occupying the corner buildings, was the imposing facade of Kearley and Tonge's Workhouse. At 1:45am that night, the watchman George Morris was disturbed not by the usual patter of policeman's footsteps from his routine patrols – which he claims were the only sound he heard all night – but by the arrival of PC Watkins. "For God's sake, mate, come to assist me!" The PC cried out. Taking a lantern with him to aid the distressed copper, Morris asked what was wrong. Watkins replied, "Oh dear, here's another woman cut to pieces." Morris fled to Aldgate to bring the aforementioned PC Harvey and another, PC Holland. Holland then went to Jewry Street to bring Dr George William Sequeira to the scene.

Thus, began a circus of police activity – Station Inspector Collard at Bishopsgate (2:03am), Dr. F. Gordon Brown (2:18am, the man who would carry out the autopsy, and for whom Dr. Sequeira waited without further examining the body *in situ*), arrived and were joined by others, including three plain-clothed officers. As another testament to the killer's ability to elude capture, Sgt Robert Outram, PC. Daniel Halse and PC Edward Marriott arrived within fifteen minutes of the discovery

138

and fled in opposite directions to catch the killer, *having been summoned from their respective patrols nearby where they were actively hunting the killer anyway.* It is quite astonishing that the killer was able to slip in and out unseen like this. Eventually the bombastic Major Smith would arrive, but not before the discovery of a crucial clue.

For the second time that night police whistles pierced the night and flustered officers ran in all directions fitfully combing the area street by street for the killer they were sure was on foot and hurrying back to his hideout. News spread of a second murder as the tragedy in Dutfield's Yard a stone's throw away was still unfolding. Throwing jurisdiction out the window, the City Police followed their noses deep into Met ground and at 2:55am, just over an hour after the murder was discovered, Constable Alfred Long came across a crucial clue at the door of 108-119 Wentworth's Model Dwellings, at the corner of Wentworth Street and Goulston Street, just a few streets over. Marked as "G" on the main map at the front of this book, is the Goulston Street graffito.

By this time Catharine's body had been moved to the City Mortuary on the orders of Dr. Brown, and the police were dragging the area for the killer. So, the discovery of a piece of evidence unequivocally from the murder scene was of the utmost importance. Two things were found, only one of which really deserves any credible attention in my opinion; first, a piece of anti-Semitic graffiti, important not for the reasons usually ascribed it (anything from a complex anagram left by the killer, to some kind of Masonic warning. I usually interpret the message as being instructions for constructing a tinfoil hat), and secondly and most critically, a scrap of apron cut from the body of Catharine Eddowes. It was messy with blood and faeces, and may have been dropped there by her killer.

The scrap, found on the floor of the doorway into the dwellings and directly beneath the graffiti, is the only known item of evidence from a Ripper victim found in a secondary location to the body itself. What happened to the scrap after the inquest is anyone's guess, despite it being almost certainly the only item in existence from which we could reasonably hope to extract the Ripper's DNA even after a century and a half. It was almost certainly lost as time progressed and police evidence outstays its need to be retained. A tragic shame.

Long took the apron to a nearby police station whilst Detective Constable Baxter Hunt reported the discovery to Inspector McWilliam at Mitre Square. He ordered the graffiti be photographed but it would not be. In fact, what occurred next is a key part of the story of the police's key suspect and the cover-up that would define the legacy of the Ripper crimes.

The wording of the writing varies according to who is reporting it, including several people who didn't even see it first-hand. Eddleston (2010, p.171) lists the most commonly-cited variations;

- Sir Charles Warren: "The Juwes are The men That Will not be Blamed for nothing."
- PC Long, Superintendent Arnold and even the chief Rabbi Dr Hermann Adler, writing of the graffiti to Warren, all agree except for the spelling of "Juwes."
- Chief Inspector Swanson claimed the text read, "The Juwes are the men who will not be blamed for nothing.

- Dr Robert Anderson: "The Jewes are not the men to be blamed for nothing."
- Sir Melville Macnaghten: "The Jews are the men who will not be blamed for nothing."
- PC Daniel Halse: "The Juwes are not the men that will not be blamed for nothing."
- Inspector McWilliam: "The Jewes are the men that will not be blamed for nothing."
- Major Henry Smith: "The Jews are the men who won't be blamed for nothing."

As Eddleston comments (p. 171), neither Smith, Macnaghten or Anderson actually saw the writing. However, the message is clear – the writer was plastering a hate message on a black wall in white chalk that Jews are like Teflon and they won't be blamed for anything they do. It's an old and tired anti-Semitic jibe that Jews have a special privilege that protects them in a way in doesn't protect Gentiles. The likely explanation for this vandalism is that a disgruntled Gentile wrote this a few streets from the Great Synagogue, on the corner of Wentworth Street – the greatest concentration of Jews in the city – clearly with the intent of fuelling anti-Semitic hatred and fanning the flames of the dreaded ethnic disorder the police were already taking ridiculous steps to thwart. It was a lazy hate message, a political statement, a sociological curiosity...but it has nothing to do with the murder of Catharine Eddowes. Even if the murders, attributed to the Jewish spectre of Leather Apron, was partly the reason for the message being left, it was still not a clue to the killer himself. Instead, in supreme irony, it could be that the killer stopped to muse over it and in that moment dropped the slice of apron. He may well have had similar thoughts about the message as we do, but there's nothing to say he wrote it. Chief Inspector Walter Dew – the man who caught Dr Crippen – remarked that such vandalism was common in the East End, and dismissed it. I'm inclined to agree with him.

At 5:30am the writing, having not been photographed, was washed away at the orders of none other than Sir Charles Warren, the Commissioner of the Metropolitan Police. PC Daniel Halse had strongly protested this, and insisted that officers photograph only part of the message to avoid the offending word "Juwes." He was overruled in a move Dr Robert Anderson would later call "crass stupidity" (*Daily Chronicle*, 1st September 1908). The police were terrified by the idea of the ethnic melting pot of the East End erupting into racial rioting, evidenced by their framing of John Pizer as Leather Apron just to kill off the panic surrounding the figure (fanned by *The Star* among other rags). Wiping this away was just another of their questionable decisions here.

The level of blind panic and denial, but also tacit collaboration with community leaders to keep the lid on the simmering pot of Whitechapel is evidenced in Warren's communications with Chief Rabbi Adler and his subsequent statement that "Juwes" meant "Jews" in no known language. Admitting a connection but teaching of the difference is a step forward – but what Warren did, and what the modern authorities do, is the equivalent of sticking their fingers in their ears and singing la-la-la. I think such panicked ignorance makes things worse.

By the start of the working day the graffiti was gone. The body of Catharine Eddowes was at the mortuary undergoing examination. Police were sweeping out from two murder scenes within minutes of each other and the city was waking to the news of the so-called

DANIEL JOHNSON

"Double Event."

Inquest
(Source: The Daily Telegraph, 5th and 12th October 1888)

The Inquest into Catharine Eddowes' death opened on 4th October 1888 at the Golden Lane Mortuary, presided over by Coroner Samuel Frederick Langham, and was adjourned and concluded on the 11th October 1888.

The first witness was an upset Eliza Gold, Catharine's sister. She confirmed that Catharine had been living with John Kelly at 55 Flower and Dean Street (Cooney's Lodging House), but that she had seen her sister only a few times across several months. The following witness, Kelly himself, confirmed this and neither knew if Thomas Conway, Catharine's previous partner, was alive or dead. Kelly recounted, in his muddled manner, their movements the previous few days to the murder and their sleeping arrangements. The only real parts to note in his testimony, again, are those relating to their financial situation – specifically, that Catharine did not seem to be bringing in extra money from sleeping around. Again, we see doubt that the victim was a prostitute. Multiple witnesses would deny her "immoral living" and testified to her good nature. We will explore this a little more as time progresses.

Next, we have the testimony of the deputy of Cooney's Lodging House, Frederick William Wilkinson. He reiterated that the suggestion of Catharine being a prostitute was alien to him;

> **Frederick William Wilkinson**: I am deputy of the lodging-house at Flower and Dean-street. I have known the deceased and Kelly during the

143

last seven years. They passed as man and wife, and lived on very good terms. They had a quarrel now and then, but not violent. They sometimes had a few words when Kate was in drink, but they were not serious. I believe she got her living by hawking about the streets and cleaning amongst the Jews in Whitechapel. Kelly paid me pretty regularly. Kate was not often in drink. She was a very jolly woman, always singing. Kelly was not in the habit of drinking, and I never saw him the worse for drink. During the week the first time I saw the deceased at the lodging-house was on Friday afternoon. Kelly was not with her then. She went out and did not return until Saturday morning, when I saw her and Kelly in the kitchen together having breakfast. I did not see her go out, and I do not know whether Kelly went with her. I never saw her again.

Coroner: Did you know she was in the habit of walking the streets at night?

Wilkinson: No; she generally used to return between nine and ten o'clock. I never knew her to be intimate with any particular individual except Kelly; and never heard of such a thing. She use to say she was married to Conway; that her name was bought and paid for - meaning that she was married. She was not at variance with any one that I know of. When I saw her last, on Saturday morning, between ten and eleven, she was quite sober. I first heard from Kelly on Saturday night that Kate was locked up, and he said he wanted a single bed. That was about 7.30 in the evening. A single bed is 4d, and a double 8d.

A Juryman: I don't take the names of the

lodgers, but I know my "regulars." If a man comes and takes a bed I put the number of the bed down in my book, but not his name. Of course I know the names of my regular customers.

She worked, cleaning for local Jews, she "hawked" on the streets, and she claimed she was married to Thomas Conway, even keeping his name, it seems. Later, of course, she would give her name as "Mary Ann Kelly" at Bishopsgate Police Station upon her release and apparently nailed her loyalty colours to the mast. There were no other lovers, no sign of any income from immoral purposes, and she was not a drunkard either. Moreover, Catharine Eddowes and John Kelly appeared to have a happy, healthy relationship.

At this point in the researching and writing of this book I am beginning to seriously doubt the pegging of Ripper victims as prostitutes. But, that said, I am also seriously questioning if, in the depths of the East End with all its desperation and deprivation, one can draw a distinction between a prostitute and a poverty-stricken woman trying to make ends meet. Let us not forget that "prostitute" is a value-laden term, a patriarchal judgement, and that it is a way of conveniently sweeping women under the carpet, a linguistic hand-wave, an act of semantic genocide. The only salient, and relevant, fact to take away from this is that they were vulnerable women being exploited.

The next witness was PC Watkins, who found the body;

Edward Watkins, No. 881 of the City Police:
I was on duty at Mitre-square on Saturday

night. I have been in the force seventeen years. I went on duty at 9.45 upon my regular beat. That extends from Duke-street, Aldgate, through Heneage-lane, a portion of Bury-street, through Cree-lane, into Leadenhall-street, along eastward into Mitre-street, then into Mitre-square, round the square again into Mitre-street, then into King-street to St. James's-place, round the place, then into Duke-street, where I started from. That beat takes twelve or fourteen minutes. I had been patrolling the beat continually from ten o'clock at night until one o'clock on Sunday morning.

Coroner: Had anything excited your attention during those hours?

Watkins: No.

Coroner: Or any person?

Watkins: No. I passed through Mitre-square at 1.30 on the Sunday morning. I had my lantern alight and on - fixed to my belt. According to my usual practice, I looked at the different passages and corners.

Coroner: At half-past one did anything excite your attention?

Watkins: No.

Coroner: Did you see anyone about?

Watkins: No.

Coroner: Could any people have been about that portion of the square without your seeing them?

Watkins: No. I next came into Mitre-square at 1.44, when I discovered the body lying on the right as I entered the square. The woman was on her back, with her feet towards the square. Her clothes were thrown up. I saw her throat was cut and the stomach ripped open. She was lying in a pool of blood. I did not touch the body. I ran across to Kearley and Long's warehouse. The door was ajar, and I pushed it open, and called on the watchman Morris, who was inside. He came out. I remained with the body until the arrival of Police-constable Holland. No one else was there before that but myself. Holland was followed by Dr. Sequeira. Inspector Collard arrived about two o'clock, and also Dr. Brown, surgeon to the police force.

Coroner: When you first saw the body did you hear any footsteps as if anybody were running away?

Watkins: No. The door of the warehouse to which I went was ajar, because the watchman was working about. It was no unusual thing for the door to be ajar at that hour of the morning. I was continually patrolling my beat from ten o'clock up to half-past one. I noticed nothing unusual up till 1.44, when I saw the body.

So Watkins entered the Square from the Mitre Street entrance, right beside the body, and crossed the Square to the opposite side to the Kearley and Tonge's. There really is no realistic way the killer was hiding in some dark corner – the body was indeed in the darkest corner of the Square! Given that Lawende and co. saw Eddowes with a man at 1:35am, and the body was found a mere nine minutes later, the killer must have fled down Church Passage very shortly before the body was found. It is conceivable that as Watkins entered the Square, the killer was still in the passage effecting his escape, I suppose, but either way, this is yet another occasion where the killer almost had a policeman's lantern in his face before he could so much as get to his feet. The Polly Nichols murder saw him almost caught red-handed – apparently fleeing as Cross and Paul entered the street one by one, and missing a police officer by moments, too. The murder of Annie Chapman was less risky, but this third crime was again an exercise in either brazen nerve or disorganisation. I tend towards the idea that the Ripper made a calculated risk rather than a reckless one, and that this again speaks to his motivations.

Inspector Collard spoke next, and was the first to testify to the apron fragment found on Goulston Street;

Inspector Collard: At five minutes before two o'clock on Sunday morning last I received information at Bishopsgate-street Police-station that a woman had been murdered in Mitre-square. Information was at once telegraphed to headquarters. I dispatched a constable to Dr. Gordon Brown, informing him, and proceeded myself to Mitre-square, arriving there about two or three minutes past two. I there found Dr. Sequeira, two or three police officers, and the deceased person lying in the south-west corner of the square, in the position described by Constable Watkins. The body was not touched until the arrival shortly afterwards of Dr. Brown. The medical gentlemen examined the body, and in my presence Sergeant Jones picked up from the foot way by the left side of the deceased three small black buttons, such as are generally used for boots, a small metal button, a common metal thimble, and a small penny mustard tin containing two pawn-tickets. They were handed to me. The doctors remained until the arrival of the ambulance, and saw the body placed in the conveyance. It was then taken to the mortuary, and stripped by Mr. Davis, the mortuary keeper, in presence of the two doctors and myself. I have a list of articles of clothing more or less stained with blood and cut.

Coroner: Was there any money about her?

Collard: No; no money whatever was found. A piece of cloth was found in Goulston-street, corresponding with the apron worn by the deceased. When I got to the square I took immediate steps to have the neighbourhood searched for the person who committed the murder. Mr. M'Williams, chief of the Detective Department, on arriving shortly afterwards sent men to search in all directions in Spitalfields, both in streets and lodging-houses. Several men were stopped and searched in the streets, without any good result. I have had a house-to-house inquiry made in the vicinity of Mitre-square as to any noises or whether persons were seen in the place; but I have not been able to find any beyond the witnesses who saw a man and woman talking together.

Coroner: When you arrived was the deceased in a pool of blood?

Collard: The head, neck, and, I imagine, the shoulders were lying in a pool of blood when she was first found, but there was no blood in front. I did not touch the body myself, but the doctor said it was warm.

Coroner: Was there any sign of a struggle having taken place?

Collard: None whatever. I made a careful inspection of the ground all round. There was no trace whatever of any struggle. There was nothing in the appearance of the woman, or of the clothes, to lead to the idea that there had been any struggle. From the fact that the blood was in a liquid state I conjectured that the murder had not been long previously committed. In my opinion the body had not been there more than a quarter of an hour. I endeavoured to trace footsteps, but could find no trace whatever. The backs of the empty houses adjoining were searched, but nothing was found.

She was found penniless and her belongings on the floor beside her. It is possible the Ripper robbed her, but it is equally possible she was spent up from her night drinking and her items simply fell as she did onto the floor. Nevertheless, the story is familiar and helps us build a picture; her body was deeply bloodstained on the back and the shoulders, but there was no blood on the front of the body. Pooling around the neck and around the body supports the idea that her throat was cut as she lay on the ground, just as with Annie Chapman. Indeed, this is the opinion of Dr. F. Gordon Brown, whose crucial testimony comes next, including a detailed explanation of the injuries sustained by Catharine;

Dr. Frederick Gordon Brown: I am surgeon to the City of London Police. I was called shortly after two o'clock on Sunday morning, and reached the place of the murder about twenty minutes past two. My attention was directed to the body of the deceased. It was lying in the position described by Watkins, on its back, the head turned to the left shoulder, the arms by the side of the body, as if they had fallen there. Both palms were upwards, the

150

fingers slightly bent. A thimble was lying near. The clothes were thrown up. The bonnet was at the back of the head. There was great disfigurement of the face. The throat was cut across. Below the cut was a neckerchief. The upper part of the dress had been torn open. The body had been mutilated, and was quite warm - no rigor mortis. The crime must have been committed within half an hour, or certainly within forty minutes from the time when I saw the body. There were no stains of blood on the bricks or pavement around. There was no blood on the front of the clothes. There was not a speck of blood on the front of the jacket. Before we removed the body Dr. Phillips was sent for, as I wished him to see the wounds, he having been engaged in a case of a similar kind previously. He saw the body at the mortuary. The clothes were removed from the deceased carefully. I made a post-mortem examination on Sunday afternoon. There was a bruise on the back of the left hand, and one on the right shin, but this had nothing to do with the crime. There were no bruises on the elbows or the back of the head. The face was very much mutilated, the eyelids, the nose, the jaw, the cheeks, the lips, and the mouth all bore cuts. There were abrasions under the left ear. The throat was cut across to the extent of six or seven inches.

Coroner: Can you tell us what was the cause of death?

Brown: The cause of death was haemorrhage from the throat. Death must have been immediate.

Coroner: There were other wounds on the lower part of the body?

Brown: Yes; deep wounds, which were inflicted after death.

Here, Dr. Brown outlined the injuries sustained by Catharine, as well as other details about how the body was found. His full report is given here;

"The body was on its back, the head turned to left shoulder. The arms by the side of the body as if they had fallen there. Both palms upwards, the fingers slightly bent. The left leg extended in a line with the body. The abdomen was exposed. Right leg bent at the thigh and knee. The throat cut across.

The intestines were drawn out to a large extent and placed over the right shoulder -- they were smeared over with some feculent matter. A piece of about two feet was quite detached from the body and placed between the body and the left arm, apparently by design. The lobe and auricle of the right ear were cut obliquely through.

There was a quantity of clotted blood on the pavement on the left side of the neck round the shoulder and upper part of arm, and fluid blood-coloured serum which had flowed under the neck to the right shoulder, the pavement sloping in that direction.

Body was quite warm. No death stiffening had taken place. She must have been dead most likely within the half hour. We looked for superficial bruises and saw none. No blood on the skin of the abdomen or secretion of any kind on the thighs. No spurting of blood on the bricks or pavement around. No marks of blood below the middle of the body. Several buttons were found in the clotted blood after the body was removed. There was no blood on the front of the clothes. There were no traces of recent connexion.

When the body arrived at Golden Lane, some of the blood was dispersed through the removal of the body to the mortuary. The clothes were taken off carefully from the body. A piece of deceased's ear dropped from the clothing.

I made a post mortem examination at half past two on Sunday afternoon. Rigor mortis was well marked; body not quite cold. Green discoloration over the abdomen.

After washing the left hand carefully, a bruise the size of a sixpence, recent and red, was discovered on the back of the left hand between the thumb and first finger. A few small bruises on right shin of older date. The hands and arms were bronzed. No bruises on the scalp, the back of the body, or the elbows.

The face was very much mutilated. There was a cut about a quarter of an inch through the lower left eyelid, dividing the structures completely through. The upper eyelid on that side, there was a scratch through the skin on the left upper eyelid, near to the angle of the nose. The right eyelid was cut through to about half an inch.

There was a deep cut over the bridge of the

nose, extending from the left border of the nasal bone down near the angle of the jaw on the right side of the cheek. This cut went into the bone and divided all the structures of the cheek except the mucous membrane of the mouth.

The tip of the nose was quite detached by an oblique cut from the bottom of the nasal bone to where the wings of the nose join on to the face. A cut from this divided the upper lip and extended through the substance of the gum over the right upper lateral incisor tooth.

About half an inch from the top of the nose was another oblique cut. There was a cut on the right angle of the mouth as if the cut of a point of a knife. The cut extended an inch and a half, parallel with the lower lip.

There was on each side of cheek a cut which peeled up the skin, forming a triangular flap about an inch and a half. On the left cheek there were two abrasions of the epithelium under the left ear.

The throat was cut across to the extent of about six or seven inches. A superficial cut commenced about an inch and a half below the lobe below, and about two and a half inches behind the left ear, and extended across the throat to about three inches below the lobe of the right ear.

DANIEL JOHNSON

The big muscle across the throat was divided through on the left side. The large vessels on the left side of the neck were severed. The

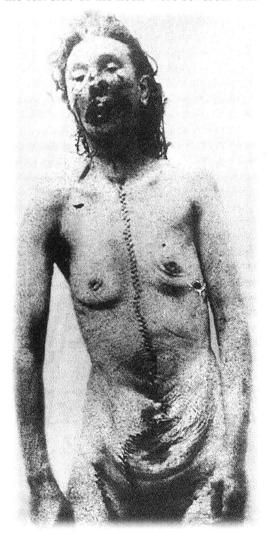

Illustration 9 Catharine Eddowes Mortuary Photo

larynx was severed below the vocal chord. All

the deep structures were severed to the bone, the knife marking intervertebral cartilages. The sheath of the vessels on the right side was just opened.

The carotid artery had a fine hole opening, the internal jugular vein was opened about an inch and a half -- not divided. The blood vessels contained clot. All these injuries were performed by a sharp instrument like a knife, and pointed.

The cause of death was haemorrhage from the left common carotid artery. The death was immediate and the mutilations were inflicted after death.

We examined the abdomen. The front walls were laid open from the breast bones to the pubes. The cut commenced opposite the enciform cartilage. The incision went upwards, not penetrating the skin that was over the sternum. It then divided the enciform cartilage. The knife must have cut obliquely at the expense of that cartilage.

Behind this, the liver was stabbed as if by the point of a sharp instrument. Below this was another incision into the liver of about two and a half inches, and below this the left lobe of the liver was slit through by a vertical cut. Two cuts were shewn by a jagging of the skin on the left side.

The abdominal walls were divided in the middle line to within a quarter of an inch of the navel. The cut then took a horizontal course for two inches and a half towards the right side. It then divided round the navel on the left side, and made a parallel incision to the former horizontal incision, leaving the navel on a tongue of skin. Attached to the navel was two and a half inches of the lower part of the rectus muscle on the left side of the abdomen. The incision then took an oblique direction to the right and was shelving. The incision went down the right side of the vagina and rectum for half an inch behind the rectum.

There was a stab of about an inch on the left groin. This was done by a pointed instrument. Below this was a cut of three inches going through all tissues making a wound of the peritoneum about the same extent.

An inch below the crease of the thigh was a cut extending from the anterior spine of the ilium obliquely down the inner side of the left thigh and separating the left labium, forming a flap of skin up to the groin. The left rectus muscle was not detached.

There was a flap of skin formed by the right thigh, attaching the right labium, and extending up to the spine of the ilium. The muscles on the right side inserted into the frontal ligaments were cut through.

The skin was retracted through the whole of the cut through the abdomen, but the vessels were not clotted. Nor had there been any appreciable bleeding from the vessels. I draw the conclusion that the act was made after death, and there would not have been much blood on the murderer. The cut was made by someone on the right side of the body, kneeling below the middle of the body.

I removed the content of the stomach and placed it in a jar for further examination. There seemed very little in it in the way of food or fluid, but from the cut end partly digested farinaceous food escaped.

The intestines had been detached to a large extent from the mesentery. About two feet of the colon was cut away. The sigmoid flexure was invaginated into the rectum very tightly.

Right kidney was pale, bloodless with slight congestion of the base of the pyramids.

There was a cut from the upper part of the slit on the under surface of the liver to the left side, and another cut at right angles to this, which were about an inch and a half deep and two and a half inches long. Liver itself was healthy.

The gall bladder contained bile. The pancreas was cut, but not through, on the left side of the spinal column. Three and a half inches of the lower border of the spleen by half an inch was attached only to the peritoneum.

The peritoneal lining was cut through on the left side and the left kidney carefully taken out and removed. The left renal artery was cut through. I would say that someone who knew the position of the kidney must have done it.

The lining membrane over the uterus was cut
through. The womb was cut through
horizontally, leaving a stump of three quarters
of an inch. The rest of the womb had been
taken away with some of the ligaments. The
vagina and cervix of the womb was uninjured.

The bladder was healthy and uninjured, and
contained three or four ounces of water. There
was a tongue-like cut through the anterior wall
of the abdominal aorta. The other organs were
healthy. There were no indications of
connexion.

I believe the wound in the throat was first
inflicted. I believe she must have been lying on
the ground.

The wounds on the face and abdomen prove
that they were inflicted by a sharp, pointed
knife, and that in the abdomen by one six
inches or longer.

I believe the perpetrator of the act must have
had considerable knowledge of the position of
the organs in the abdominal cavity and the way
of removing them. It required a great deal of
medical knowledge to have removed the kidney
and to know where it was placed. The parts
removed would be of no use for any
professional purpose.

I think the perpetrator of this act had sufficient
time, or he would not have nicked the lower

eyelids. It would take at least five minutes.

I cannot assign any reason for the parts being taken away. I feel sure that there was no struggle, and believe it was the act of one person.

The throat had been so instantly severed that no noise could have been emitted. I should not expect much blood to have been found on the person who had inflicted these wounds. The wounds could not have been self-inflicted

Now we return to the Inquest testimony. When pushed on his suggestion that the killer may have anatomical knowledge, Dr. Brown confirms a butcher, or someone acquainted with dissecting animals may have the necessary anatomical knowledge;

Coroner: Would such a knowledge be likely to be possessed by some one accustomed to cutting up animals?
Brown: Yes.
Coroner: Have you been able to form any opinion as to whether the perpetrator of this act was disturbed?
Brown: I think he had sufficient time, but it was in all probability done in a hurry.
Coroner: How long would it take to make the wounds?
Brown: It might be done in five minutes. It might take him longer; but that is the least time it could be done in.
Coroner: Can you, as a professional man, ascribe any reason for the taking away of the

parts you have mentioned?

Brown: I cannot give any reason whatever.

Coroner: Have you any doubt in your own mind whether there was a struggle?

Brown: I feel sure there was no struggle. I see no reason to doubt that it was the work of one man.

Coroner: Would any noise be heard, do you think?

Brown: I presume the throat was instantly severed, in which case there would not be time to emit any sound.

Coroner: Does it surprise you that no sound was heard?

Brown: No.

Coroner: Would you expect to find much blood on the person inflicting these wounds?

Brown: No, I should not. I should say that the abdominal wounds were inflicted by a person kneeling at the right side of the body. The wounds could not possibly have been self-inflicted.

Coroner: Was your attention called to the portion of the apron that was found in Goulston Street?

Brown: Yes. I fitted that portion which was spotted with blood to the remaining portion, which was still attached by the strings to the body.

Coroner: Have you formed any opinion as to the motive for the mutilation of the face?

Brown: It was to disfigure the corpse, I should imagine.

A Juror: Was there any evidence of a drug having been used?

Brown: I have not examined the stomach as to

that. The contents of the stomach have been
preserved for analysis.

As usual, the testimony of the pathologist is the most
enlightening. We learn several things here;

- Dr. Brown had the presence of mind to call in Dr.
  Phillips, who'd worked on the case of Annie
  Chapman, to examine the body, noting the
  "similar case[s]."
- The cause of death was an instantly fatal wound to
  the throat, which again dissected all structures
  down to the bone, and was no simple throat-
  cutting action.
- The time of death was estimated to be around
  half-an-hour prior to the Doctor's arrival and
  examination of the body *in situ* – that makes it
  around the time Eddowes was spotted with a man
  in Church Passage. She must have been murdered
  within minutes of this sighting.
- There was no sign of sexual activity in the form of
  semen on or around the body.
- Catharine's face was extensively mutilated in what
  appear to be precise and specific ways, however
  there are other interpretations as to the nature of
  the wounds.
- Her abdominal mutilations consisted of a series of
  frenzied stabbing and hacking motions – she had
  been cut open in a rough, upwards series of
  slashes, leaving jagged and haphazard wounds
  extending from her breastbone all the way down
  to her anus. Her killer had inflicted stab wounds
  and slashes to her body all the way, too, including

onto her genitals.

- According to Dr. Brown, the killer would not have had much blood on him, as the wounds were inflicted post-mortem. Also, he suggests the killer sat at her right side to inflict the injuries – and this makes sense I think. He would have wished to be facing the entrance to the Square to react quickly to any oncoming people. Not only that, but her face was turned to the left, away from where the killer would have been sitting – a clue to his psychopathology.
- Catharine's organs were otherwise healthy, besides the wounds inflicted by the killer.
- The left kidney and the uterus were cut out, and were missing. Interestingly, Dr. Brown suggests that the kidney was removed "carefully," but that the uterus was almost hacked away, leaving a chunk behind and "some" appendages.
- The killer possessed anatomical knowledge in Dr. Brown's opinion, and had to know the location and anatomy of the parts he was removing to do what he did – but he claims the parts have no professional value.

The attack on Catharine Eddowes was a vicious, rapid and frenzied one. After appearing perfectly friendly with her when witnessed in Church Passage, he turned on a sixpence and within minutes had lured her into the darkest corner of Mitre Square, subdued her and cut her throat all the way to the bone to instantly silence and kill her.

He then launched his assault on the poor woman's face, hacking and slashing and slabbing at it to render her almost unrecognisable, before turning what would have been a bloody and ragged face away from him. This is a key escalation – whilst in the Annie Chapman case he attempted decapitation, here he cut the victim's throat to the bone in a similar way but opted this time to disfigure her and physically turn her face away from where he sat at her right side. The message here is clear – attacking the eyes, slashing the face, rendering the common features unrecognisable, and acting to face the victim the other way – he was not so much removing her identity as putting it out of his sight. The theme of depersonalisation will be discussed later in this book, and as we will learn this murder marks a very telling insight into the killer's motives.

Then he pulled up her clothes and commenced his primary assault. In a series of violent hacks and cuts, he literally ripped her open and tore out her intestines, all the time stabbing and slashing at her. This was not quite as clean-cut as the previous two murders, those of Mary Ann Nichols and Annie Chapman, even if the actions were similar, instead this was an emotional outpouring. Finally, he appears to have removed organs again, most prominently the uterus.

Now, the missing organ which seems to be most in keeping with this style of attack is indeed the missing uterus. It wasn't carefully removed – he cut through the organ as he removed it and "some" of its appendages. The uterus of course was the organ closest to the focus of his mutilations – the lower abdomen and genitals. The kidneys are quite a distance away from here, and harder to reach (not that the uterus exactly lends itself to an easy grab). Moreover, it is described as having been "carefully" removed. The fact that a sexually-motivated killer who rips his victim up in a frenzy has the presence of mind to calm down and methodically cut away a particular organ with no sexual associations attached is a little questionable. Whoever removed it also cut through its surrounding membrane, and that surely required at least basic human anatomical knowledge and possibly even some experience. Of course, we're not finished with this kidney yet, and neither are we finished with the expert testimony.

The picture painted by Dr. Brown is of a horrendous attack that bares all the hallmarks of the Annie Chapman murder, only through a filter of exaggerated fury. Again, he kills in an enclosed space, albeit a more public one, and again his method is of rapid assassination and a focus on the almost gleeful destruction of his victim through, firstly, the efforts at depersonalisation, and second, disembowelment.

The second source of medical testimony came from Dr. Sequeira, who arrived before Dr. Brown and pronounced death, and the medical officer for health for the City, Mr William Sedgwick Saunders;

> **Dr. G. W. Sequeira:** On the morning of Sept. 30 I was called to Mitre-square, and I arrived at five minutes to two o'clock, being the first medical man on the scene of the murder. I saw the position of the body, and I entirely agree with the evidence of Dr. Gordon Brown in that respect.I am well acquainted with the locality and the position of the lamps in the square. Where the murder was committed was probably the darkest part of the square, but there was sufficient light to enable the miscreant to perpetrate the deed. I think that the murderer had no design on any particular organ

165

of the body. He was not possessed of any great anatomical skill.

Coroner: Can you account for the absence of noise?

Sequeira: The death must have been instantaneous after the severance of the windpipe and the blood-vessels.

Coroner: Would you have expected the murderer to be bespattered with blood?

Sequeira: Not necessarily.

Coroner: How long do you believe life had been extinct when you arrived?

Sequeira: Very few minutes - probably not more than a quarter of an hour.

**   *

Mr. William Sedgwick Saunders: I received the stomach of the deceased from Dr. Gordon Brown, carefully sealed, and I made an analysis of the contents, which had not been interfered with in any way. I looked more particularly for poisons of the narcotic class, but with negative results, there being not the faintest trace of any of those or any other poisons

Dr. Sequeira disputed Dr. Brown's insistence that the killer was "possessed of anatomical skill." I think he is correct – the killer was not necessarily trained or experienced in any sort of dissection. We can summarise the evidence in this regard briefly here;

- The killer tried and failed to decapitate Annie Chapman. Basic anatomical knowledge and/or basic butchery skills would have been sufficient to

166

have accomplished the deed.

- The knife he used was estimated to be, according to all medical evidence thus far, a six-inch, moderately sharp, pointed weapon, such as that used by a cobbler or if "well-ground down," a slaughterman (according to Dr. Phillips' testimony on the Annie Chapman case). Not a tool for use in making anything like clean cuts in flesh.

- The killer's cuts in the Catharine Eddowes case were jagged, rough, and violent. Not clean precise incisions – he cut Catharine open groin to sternum and simply pulled and cut the intestines out, apparently scattering them and dumping them where he pleased, as he also appears to have done with Annie.

- His organ of choice in both cases was a poorly-extracted uterus; he sliced through the vagina and bladder when removing it from Annie and he almost cut the thing in half when removing it from Catharine. How he knew it was there at all is the question, as there is no doubt in his total lack of skill in adequately locating and removing it.

Another interesting note on the scene is an interview Dr. Brown gave in the immediate aftermath of the murder, to Lloyd's Weekly Newspaper on the day of the crime;

> [Dr. Sequeira and Dr. Brown] made a minute examination of the body, Dr. Gordon Brown taking a pencil sketch of the exact position in which it was found. This he most kindly showed to the representative of Lloyd's, when subsequently explaining the frightful injuries inflicted upon the body of the deceased. The

throat had been cut from the left side, the knife
severing the carotid artery and other parts of
the neck. The weapon had then apparently been
stabbed into the upper part of the abdomen, and
cut completely down. Besides the fearful
wound on the face the tops of both of the thighs
were cut across. **The intestines, which had
been torn from the body, were found twisted
into the gaping wound on the right side of
the murdered woman's neck.** *(Lloyds Weekly
Newspaper - 30 September 1888)* [Author's
emphasis added]

The intestines that the killer removed from Catharine's
body had been shoved into her throat wound by her killer.
This is another example of the killer posing the body,
setting the scene. Disassembling and reorganising the
disarticulated body parts of a fellow human for shock
value, sexual arousal, or both. This provides a truly
fascinating, and horrifying, look into the killer's psyche.
The killer's removal of the intestines can be understood a
little clearer when taken into this context – he was clearly
revelling in the destruction of a human body, playing
around and acting out fantasies that he intended to
horrify those who found the body.

Next in the inquest came a handful of witnesses,
including Annie Phillips, the daughter of Catharine
Eddowes, who commented on Catharine's background or
on the circumstances of the crime's discovery. But the
most important testimony came towards the conclusion
of the inquest – the testimonies of Joseph Lawende,
Joseph Hyam Levy, and the various testimonies relating
to the chalk message and apron found at Goulston Street.

Joseph Lawende: I reside at No. 45, Norfolk-road, Dalston, and am a commercial traveller. On the night of Sept. 29, I was at the Imperial Club, Duke-street, together with Mr. Joseph Levy and Mr. Harry Harris. It was raining, and we sat in the club till half-past one o'clock, when we left. I observed a man and woman together at the corner of Church-passage, Duke-street, leading to Mitre-square.

Coroner: Were they talking?

Lawende: The woman was standing with her face towards the man, and I only saw her back. She had one hand on his breast. He was the taller. She had on a black jacket and bonnet. I have seen the articles at the police-station, and believe them to be those the deceased was wearing.

Coroner: What sort of man was this?

Lawende: He had on a cloth cap with a peak of the same.

Mr. Crawford [Lawyer for the City]: Unless the jury wish it, I do not think further particulars should be given as to the appearance of this man.

The Foreman: The jury do not desire it.

Crawford: You have given a description of the man to the police?

Lawende: Yes.

Coroner: Would you know him again?

Lawende: I doubt it. The man and woman were about nine or ten feet away from me. I have no doubt it was half-past one o'clock when we rose to leave the club, so that it would be twenty-five minutes to two o'clock when we passed the man and woman.

Coroner: Did you overhear anything that

either said?

Lawende: No.

Coroner: Did either appear in an angry mood?

Lawende: No.

Coroner: Did anything about their movements attract your attention?

Lawende: No. The man looked rather rough and shabby.

Coroner: When the woman placed her hand on the man's breast, did she do it as if to push him away?

Lawende: No; it was done very quietly.

Coroner: You were not curious enough to look back and see where they went.

Lawende: No.

** *   *

Mr. Joseph Hyam Levy: I was with the last witness at the Imperial Club on Saturday night, Sept. 29. We got up to leave at half-past one on Sunday morning, and came out three or four minutes later. I saw a man and woman standing at the corner of Church-passage, but I did not take any notice of them. I passed on, thinking they were up to no good at so late an hour.

Coroner: What height was the man?

Levy: I should think he was three inches taller than the woman, who was, perhaps, 5ft high. I cannot give any further description of them. I went down Duke-street into Aldgate, leaving them still talking together.

The Jury: The point in the passage where the man and woman were standing was not well lighted. On the contrary, I think it was badly lighted then, but the light is much better now.

DANIEL JOHNSON

Levy: Nothing in what I saw excited my suspicion as to the intentions of the man. I did not hear a word that he uttered to the woman.
Coroner: Your fear was rather about yourself?
Levy: Not exactly. (Laughter.)

The Daily News (12th October 1888) reports that Levy made comments to the effect that Mitre Square should be watched with such people out at such late an hour, whilst the *Evening News* (9th October 1888), following an interview with Levy, claimed he was afraid to testify, refused to answer questions, and seemed to know more than he was letting on. So, while Lawende provided a description of such importance that it was withheld from the inquest, Levy appears to be just as interesting a character.

Perhaps the most telling thing about Lawende's testimony is the apparent placidity of the suspect. For a man about to erupt in rage-filled homicidal violence, ripping and disembowelling the woman in front of him, the suspect is apparently calm and good-natured. Despite common sense telling us that he is clearly a maniac who will flip in a second and rip apart the first person he sees, this instead speaks of a man demonstrating supreme self-control. His actions at the crime scene – a swift assassination followed by a methodical, if horrendously violent and emotionally-charged, series of mutilations – speak of fantasy fulfilment, the venting of pent-up aggression, the use of the victim as a bloody canvass to express his deepest pathological desires. But despite this he manages to kill silently, apparently avoid getting blood on himself, and in the Annie Chapman and Miller's Court cases, pose the body and the scene for his liking, and slip away unseen and without alerting a soul to his presence.

JACK THE RIPPER

An interesting note about the crime scene here, too – the presence of quantities of faeces. According to Dr. Brown's description of the crime scene, as given above, the intestines that were removed were smeared with "feculent matter." These had been placed upon the shoulder of the victim and stuck into her throat. Given the ferocity of the injuries inflicted, it is more than likely the killer perforated her bowel and spilled the contents, and quite late on in the attack, too. Within moments Catharine's body would be found by PC Watkins. And we know this was late in the attack by going by the pattern established by the previous murders; throat cutting whilst the victim lies prone, perform abdominal mutilations, remove organs, pose the body and leave. The pose we saw with Annie Chapman, and that we'd see repeated with the final murder, was of the legs posed wide open and the left hand draped across her torso. This posing wasn't present with Catharine Eddowes, but the organs were indeed missing. In fact, that's another reason to suspect the Ripper did not take the missing kidney – the cuts he made to remove the uterus likely were the ones to puncture the bowel, ending his assault and forcing him to flee. It is likely that he would have removed the Kidney second, since it is a new behaviour compared to the removal of the uterus. Thus, it is still highly debatable whether the Ripper did remove the kidney, and I cannot be certain myself. The apron piece found at Goulston Street similarly had stains of blood and faeces. There are five possible explanations as to the existence of this piece of Catharine's apron.

First, the medical evidence suggested that the killer likely did not get blood on himself as he killed his victim. And after the throat-cutting killed her, allowing blood to escape onto the ground as reported at the scene,

172

the internal bodily environment would have been less likely to spray him with blood and fluids either. However, the evidence lends itself to the suggestion that he was sprayed with bodily fluids, and thus the possibility that he cut away part of the apron to clean himself is supported. This, in turn, could provide us with a clue to his escape route; north, via Goulston Street.

Secondly, it is possible he used it to wipe his knife. PC Long, as we will see, described it as "wet with blood." And if he had left shortly after spraying the scene with faeces, his knife of course would have been soiled too. This would explain why he simply dropped the item after using it, but it doesn't explain where he dropped it, or the fact that the apron was found at 2:55am, an hour and ten minutes after the body was found (which was minutes after the murder itself).

The third option, that he used the apron fragment to transport the organ(s) he removed from A to B, raises the same timing question as the second, and raises more questions than it answers – could it be the killer lived in the building the apron was found, or could he have disposed of the organ on the way? Why else would the item be discarded where it was, if not because either he'd reached his final destination or for some reason he no longer wished to carry any incriminating items around in public? That would certainly make sense given the police dragnet sweeping across the district from two separate murder scenes. But that raises the question of where the organ(s) ended up. Nevertheless, there is precedence for items of clothing to be missing from the scenes of these murders; recall, Annie Chapman's scarf was missing when her body was found. It is entirely possible that the killer again used the victim's clothing to transport his trophies.

A fourth option is that the killer used the apron to

patch up a wound on himself sustained during the messy work of his mutilations. Despite managing to kill his victim without much in the way of blood spatter, the act of cutting his victim open groin to sternum and eviscerating her not only released blood and other internal fluids, but we know also produced faeces, as discussed above. He could have easily found his hands becoming slick with the mess and cut himself with his own knife – which would have left him vulnerable to infection. In his haste, he may have cut away a slice of apron and clutched his wounded hand. This means anyone who can find that apron, as unlikely as it would be 129 years later, could potentially provide a sample of the Ripper's DNA from it to be tested against present-day relatives via familial profiling. This is a very unlikely scenario, as the apron was almost certainly discarded or lost in the years since, and that's without considering the damage wrought by the Second World War (in which the City archives were all destroyed). This explanation for the presence of the apron accounts for it being left in the street, which the third option does not.

Trevor Marriott, the acclaimed crime writer, proposes a final option that he regrets may not be seriously accepted by purist Ripperologists; that the apron was used by Catharine Eddowes as a sanitary towel, and that she simply discarded it in Goulston Street prior to heading to Mitre Square where she met her killer. I have to say this option makes a darn sight more sense than most of the others. In his book, *Jack the Ripper: The 21st Century Investigation* (2005, p. 165), Marriott argues that there were two things lacking in 19th Century London; sanitary products and public toilets. He proposes that Catharine used the scrap of cotton to clean up after using a side-street to relieve herself. The rank ordinariness of this idea inclines me to believe it over the more elaborate, although muddier, theories presented here. That said, I'd like to believe the killer's own blood is on the scrap, and I'd love to believe it'll turn up in some dusty old box in a retired policeman's attic one day, left there by his great-grandfather alongside missing files that fill in the gaps in our knowledge of the case!

Let us delve into the testimony regarding the Goulston Street discovery;

Constable Alfred Long: I was on duty in Goulston-street, Whitechapel, on Sunday morning, Sept. 30, and about five minutes to three o'clock I found a portion of a white apron (produced). There were recent stains of blood on it. The apron was lying in the passage leading to the staircase of Nos. 106 to 119, a model dwelling-house. Above on the wall was written in chalk, "The Jews are the men that will not be blamed for nothing." I at once searched the staircase and areas of the building, but did not find anything else. I took the apron to Commercial-road Police-station and reported to the inspector on duty.

Coroner: Had you been past that spot previously to your discovering the apron?

Long: I passed about twenty minutes past two o'clock.

Coroner: Are you able to say whether the apron was there then?

Long: It was not.

Crawford: As to the writing on the wall, have you not put a "not" in the wrong place? Were not the words, "The Jews are not the men that will be blamed for nothing"?

Long: I believe the words were as I have stated.

Coroner: Was not the word "Jews" spelt "Juwes?"

Long: It may have been.

Coroner: Yet you did not tell us that in the first place. Did you make an entry of the words at the time?

Long: Yes, in my pocket-book.

Coroner: Is it possible that you have put the "not" in the wrong place?

Long: It is possible, but I do not think that I have.

Coroner: Which did you notice first - the piece of apron or the writing on the wall?

Long: The piece of apron, one corner of which was wet with blood.

Coroner: How came you to observe the writing on the wall?

Long: I saw it while trying to discover whether there were any marks of blood about.

Coroner: Did the writing appear to have been recently done?

Long: I could not form an opinion.

Coroner: Do I understand that you made a search in the model dwelling-house?

Long: I went into the staircases.

Coroner: Did you not make inquiries in the house itself?

Long: No.

The Foreman: Where is the pocket-book in which you made the entry of the writing?

Long: At Westminster.

Coroner: Is it possible to get it at once?

Long: I dare say.

Crawford: I will ask the coroner to direct that

the book be fetched.
Coroner: Let that be done.

**   *

Detective Daniel Halse: On Saturday, Sept. 29, pursuant to instructions received at the central office in Old Jewry, I directed a number of police in plain clothes to patrol the streets of the City all night. At two minutes to two o'clock on the Sunday morning, when near Aldgate Church, in company with Detectives Outram and Marriott, I heard that a woman had been found murdered in Mitre-square. We ran to the spot, and I at once gave instructions for the neighbourhood to be searched and every man stopped and examined. I myself went by way of Middlesex-street into Wentworth-street, where I stopped two men, who, however, gave a satisfactory account of themselves. I came through Goulston-street about twenty minutes past two, and then returned to Mitre-square, subsequently going to the mortuary. I saw the deceased, and noticed that a portion of her apron was missing. I accompanied Major Smith back to Mitre-square, when we heard that a piece of apron had been found in Goulston-street. After visiting Leman-street police-station, I proceeded to Goulston-street, where I saw some chalk-writing on the black facia of the wall. Instructions were given to have the writing photographed, but before it could be done the Metropolitan police stated that they thought the writing might cause a riot or outbreak against the Jews, and it was decided to have it rubbed out, as the people were already bringing out their stalls into the street. When Detective Hunt returned inquiry was made at every door of every tenement of the model dwelling-house, but we gained no tidings of any one who was likely to have been the murderer. At twenty minutes past two o'clock I passed over the spot where the piece of apron was found, but did not notice anything then. I should not necessarily have seen the piece of apron.

Coroner: As to the writing on the wall, did you hear anybody suggest that the word "Jews" should be rubbed out and the other words left?

Halse: I did. The fear on the part of the Metropolitan police that the writing might cause riot was the sole reason why it was rubbed out. I took a copy of it, and what I wrote down was as follows: "The Juwes are not the men who will be blamed for nothing."

Coroner: Did the writing have the appearance of having been recently done?

Halse: Yes. It was written with white chalk on a black facia.

The Foreman: Why was the writing really rubbed out?

Halse: The Metropolitan police said it might create a riot, and it was their ground.

Crawford: I am obliged to ask this question. Did you protest against the writing being rubbed out?

Halse: I did. I asked that it might, at all events, be allowed to remain until Major Smith had seen it.

Crawford: Why do you say that it seemed to have been recently written?

Halse: It looked fresh, and if it had been done

long before it would have been rubbed out by the people passing. I did not notice whether there was any powdered chalk on the ground, though I did look about to see if a knife could be found. There were three lines of writing in a good schoolboy's round hand. The size of the capital letters would be about 3/4 in, and the other letters were in proportion. The writing was on the black bricks, which formed a kind of dado, the bricks above being white.

Mr. Crawford: With the exception of a few questions to Long, the Metropolitan constable, that is the whole of the evidence I have to offer at the present moment on the part of the City police. But if any point occurs to the coroner or the jury I shall be happy to endeavour to have it cleared up.

A Juror: It seems surprising that a policeman should have found the piece of apron in the passage of the buildings, and yet made no inquiries in the buildings themselves. There was a clue up to that point, and then it was altogether lost.

Crawford: As to the premises being searched, I have in court members of the City police who did make diligent search in every part of the tenements the moment the matter came to their knowledge. But unfortunately it did not come to their knowledge until two hours after. There was thus delay, and the man who discovered the piece of apron is a member of the Metropolitan police.

A Juror: It is the man belonging to the Metropolitan police that I am complaining of. (PC Long returns with his pocketbook)
Crawford: What is the entry?

179

Long: The words are, "The Jews are the men that will not be blamed for nothing."

Coroner: Both here and in your inspector's report the word "Jews" is spelt correctly?

Long: Yes; but the inspector remarked that the word was spelt "Juwes."

Coroner: Why did you write "Jews" then?

Long: I made my entry before the inspector made the remark.

Coroner: But why did the inspector write "Jews"?

Long: I cannot say.

Coroner: At all events, there is a discrepancy?

Long: It would seem so.

Coroner: What did you do when you found the piece of apron?

Long: I at once searched the staircases leading to the buildings.

Coroner: Did you make inquiry in any of the tenements of the buildings?

Long: No.

Coroner: How many staircases are there?

Long: Six or seven.

Coroner: And you searched every staircase?

Long: Every staircase to the top.

Coroner: You found no trace of blood or of recent footmarks?

Long: No.

Coroner: About what time was that?

Long: Three o'clock.

Coroner: Having examined the staircases, what did you next do?

Long: I proceeded to the station.

Coroner: Before going did you hear that a murder had been committed?

Long: Yes. It is common knowledge that two

180

murders have been perpetrated.

Coroner: Which did you hear of?

Long: I heard of the murder in the City. There were rumours of another, but not certain.

Coroner: When you went away did you leave anybody in charge?

Long: Yes; the constable on the next beat - 190, H Division - but I do not know his name.

Coroner: Did you give him instructions as to what he was to do?

Long: I told him to keep observation on the dwelling house, and see if any one entered or left.

Coroner: When did you return?

Long: About five o'clock.

Coroner: Had the writing been rubbed out then?

Long: No; it was rubbed out in my presence at half-past five.

Coroner: Did you hear any one object to its being rubbed out?

Long: No. It was nearly daylight when it was rubbed out.

A Juror: Having examined the apron and the writing, did it not occur to you that it would be wise to search the dwelling?

Long: I did what I thought was right under the circumstances.

The Juror: I do not wish to say anything to reflect upon you, because I consider that altogether the evidence of the police redounds to their credit; but it does seem strange that this clue was not followed up.

Long: I thought the best thing to do was to proceed to the station and report to the inspector on duty.

JACK THE RIPPER

The Juror: I am sure you did what you deemed best.
Crawford: I suppose you thought it more likely to find the body there than the murderer?
Long: Yes, and I felt that the inspector would be better able to deal with the matter than I was.
The Foreman: Was there any possibility of a stranger escaping from the house?
Long: Not from the front.
Coroner: Did you not know about the back?
Long: No, that was the first time I had been on duty there

Here we have the story behind the graffiti.

Det. Halse recounts that he patrolled the area at 2:20am and saw no graffiti, but says he would not have noticed the apron in the doorway anyway. Reasonable, I suppose, it being dark. Then at 2:55am the apron was discovered by PC Long, and the graffiti nearby. After this discovery, Long searched the staircases of the Wentworth's Model Dwellings building, but not the actual flats within – that would be done hours later by Detective Hunt. Long then proceeded to Leman Street police station, leaving another PC at the scene. Returning at five o'clock, PC Long then was party to the Metropolitan Police nervously watching day breaking and stall-holders setting up in the adjoining Wentworth Street, a busy commercial area. Terrified of a race riot, and despite protestations by Detective Halse to at least photograph the text minus the word "Jews," the words were washed away. This would be at the command of Police Superintendent Thomas Arnold, at the behest of Sir Charles Warren, the commissioner of the Met.

DANIEL JOHNSON

Repeatedly in this testimony is the insistence that fear of race rioting was the sole reason for the destruction of the text. This is potentially crucial evidence from the killer himself – although, as I've said, I doubt it and there's no actual evidence to link it to the killer other than the happenstance of the apron being nearby. Nevertheless, it would have needed to be recorded but instead it was deliberately erased for political reasons; the Met were too busy keeping the peace in the East End to prioritise the recording of evidence, even the correct pursuit of suspects (harking back to the John Pizer incident), in a serial murder investigation.

What amazes me the most about something of a top-level conspiracy, is the sheer ineptitude of the whole thing. Lawende's description of the suspect was withheld from the public, but leaked to the press anyway; the text of this graffiti of course, ended up in local papers thanks to reporting of the public inquests; and despite fearing for his life, John Pizer was not lynched in the streets as Leather Apron, quite probably because the public – still referring to the killer in this manner up until the Double Event – didn't believe he was either the real Leather Apron nor the killer.

Let us hear from Superintendent Arnold (quoted in Evans and Skinner, 2000, pp.213-4) and Sir Charles Warren in their own words regarding this matter;

Report by Superintendent Thomas Arnold:
"I beg to report that on the morning of 30th Sept. last my attention was called to some writing on the wall of the entrance to some dwellings No.108 Goulston Street Whitechapel which consisted of the following words "The Juews are not [the word 'not' deleted] the men

183

that will not be blamed for nothing", and knowing that in consequence of a suspicion having fallen upon a Jew named 'John Pizer' alias 'Leather Apron' having comitted a murder in Hanbury Street a short time previously a strong feeling ['ag' deleted] existed against the Jews generally and as the buildings upon which the writing was found was situated in the midst of a locality inhabited principally by that sect. I was apprehensive that if the writing were left it would be the means of causing a riot and therefore considered it desirable that it should be removed having in view the fact that it was in such a position that it would have been rubbed by the shoulders of persons passing in & out of the building. Had only a portion of the writing been removed the context would have remained. An Inspector was present by my directions with a sponge for the purpose of removing the writing when the Commissioner arrived on the scene"

Report by Sir Charles Warren: "A discussion took place whether the writing could be left covered up or otherwise or whether any portion of it could be left for an hour until it could be photographed; but after taking into consideration the excited state of the population in London generally at the time, the strong feeling which had been excited against the Jews, and the fact that in a short time there would be a large concourse of the people in the streets, and having before me the Report that if it was left there the house was likely to be wrecked (in which from my own observation I entirely concurred) I considered it desirable to

obliterate the writing at once, having taken a
copy of which I enclose a duplicate.

After having been to the scene of the murder, I
went on to the City Police Office and informed
the Chief Superintendant of the reason why the
writing had been obliterated.

I may mention that so great was the feeling
with regard to the Jews that on the 13th ulto.
the Acting Chief Rabbi wrote to me on the
subject of the spelling of the word "Jewes" on
account of a newspaper asserting that this was
Jewish spelling in the Yiddish dialect. He added
"in the present state of excitement it is
dangerous to the safety of the poor Jews in the
East [End] to allow such an assertion to remain
uncontradicted. My community keenly
appreciates your humane and vigilant action
during this critical time.

It may be realised therefore if the safety of the
Jews in Whitechapel could be considered to be
jeopardised 13 days after the murder by the
question of the spelling of the word Jews, what
might have happened to the Jews in that quarter
had that writing been left intact.

I do not hesitate myself to say that if that
writing had been left there would have have
been an onslaught upon the Jews, property
would have been wrecked, and lives would
probably have been lost; and I was much
gratified with the prompitude with which
Superintendent Arnold was prepared to act in
the matter if I had not been there."

Note how Sir Charles speaks of contact with then-chief
rabbi Adler, who gently suggests the spelling of "Jewes"

was from a Yiddish dialect, and that allowing this "uncontradicted" information to be public knowledge could prompt anti-Semitic outpourings. This lead to the occasion when Warren goes to lengths to argue that the word does not mean "Jews" in any language. Also, note how Thomas Arnold casually throws Pizer under the bus again, despite his exoneration at the Annie Chapman inquest.

These people are living in a fantasy world in my opinion – one of murderous, shifty Jews and violent angry thugs ready to riot. But I reiterate; all of these "suppressed" things got out anyway. Lawende's description. The graffiti. Even Pizer walked free and safe, dying of ill health many years later and even successfully suing for false arrest and slander. There were no riots, even if there were angry scenes, demonstrations, an upsurge in racist crimes. Notwithstanding, Sir Charles Warren and every rank of officer below him seemed to be more concerned with this imaginary tsunami of violence, an oncoming storm of racial warfare, than actually solving the crime. They prioritised politics and community relations rather than policing and investigation. Consequently, maybe the safety and integrity of the community was preserved, I'm not saying they failed in that task – but consequently, the investigation floundered.

We're seeing the bare bones of a rather moronic conspiracy – to suppress the "Jewish connection" to these crimes in order to prevent an imagined racial apocalypse in the East End. A conspiracy where all the secrets leak immediately. One where the people you'd predict are behind it, are. And worse, the media and the police and Jewish leaders are indeed all part of it, but in the stupidest way possible – the press are trying to sell copy by playing to racial stereotypes, fear and hate (like they do today), and they do very well out of it by plugging away with this Leather Apron bullshit. The community leaders obviously wish to protect the members of their community, a poor and downtrodden mass in the middle of a slum district, so they appeal to the fears of the police. Sir Charles Warren and the ranks below him are, at the same time, apparently incapable of telling the difference between a newspaper report and an actual fact, and dig into the Leather Apron narrative like chumps. This means they inherit the same fears of race riots and decide investigation is secondary to keeping the peace. They try and utterly fail to suppress the sensitive details and, even when their feared race war fails to happen, continue to balls up the investigation by managing to miss, or by deliberately destroying, key evidence.

But lets' address a simple question staring us in the face – what was the Jewish connection? Well, of the many pieces of testimony we've seen so far, we have only two reliable witnesses; Joseph Lawende, and Elizabeth Darrell. Only Darrell claims the suspect had a "foreign appearance," yet heard the man speak English. No mention of him appearing Jewish and no foreign accent. Lawende made no comment in this regard, only suggesting he looked like a sailor. And let's not forget that this Leather Apron business began way back before Mary Ann Nichols' murder, with the death of Emma Smith and the murder of Martha Tabram. Murders connected in the press to both the Ripper and this shifty character. *The Star* newspaper had pounced upon it during the early days of September 1888 to empty newsagent's shelves as profitably as possible, and by the time they were forced to frame poor Pizer during the Annie Chapman inquest, the Police were sold on this Leather Apron narrative as it provided a nice easy answer to the murders – some mad foreigner did it, a Jew, a cobbler or butcher gone mad with a Jewish slaughtering knife. No Englishman could have done this, after all. By the time Catharine Eddowes was being dissected by the Ripper the police were out looking for a ghost, the mysterious Jew, Leather Apron.

The inquest closed on 11th October 1888 with a finding of unlawful death by persons known. The jury donated their fees to Annie Phillips, Catharine's daughter. Catharine Eddowes was buried in the City of London Cemetery on 8th October 1888, with crowds lining the streets to watch.

Letters From Hell

"Dear Boss"

News of the double-event spread quickly through the district. By dawn it was common knowledge that two murders, attributed to the Whitechapel Murderer, had been committed the previous night. The public outcry was tremendous, and the police were to spend the following days and weeks conducting door-to-door inquiries. One consequence of these was that Joseph Lawende and his friends would be located and give their crucial statements, allowing for one of the best witness descriptions in existence for the killer. But within 24 hours, the unfolding story of the Whitechapel murders would take on a new complexion.

On 27th September 1888, the Central News Agency received a letter. Addressed to "The Boss," it was written in red ink and in pristine, almost beautiful, handwriting. It was soon in the hands of the police, and would eventually be reproduced across billboards, leaflets and in the daily newspapers. Written across two sides of paper, the now-notorious letter would kickstart a century of words and phrases associated with the Ripper case. It read;

189

JACK THE RIPPER

Dear Boss,

I keep on hearing the police have caught me but
they wont fix me just yet. I have laughed when they
look so clever and talk about being on the <u>right</u>
track. That joke about Leather Apron gave me real
fits. I am down on whores and I shant quit ripping
them till I do get buckled. Grand work the last job
was. I gave the lady no time to squeal. How can
they catch me now. I love my work and want to
start again. You will soon hear of me with my funny
little games. I saved some of the proper <u>red</u> stuff in
a ginger beer bottle over the last job to write with
but it went thick like glue and I cant use it. Red ink
is fit enough I hope <u>ha. ha.</u> The next job I do I shall
clip the ladys ears off and send to the police officers
just for jolly wouldn't you. Keep this letter back till
I do a bit more work, then give it out straight. My
knife's so nice and sharp I want to get to work right
away if I get a chance. Good Luck. Yours truly

Jack the Ripper

Dont mind me giving the trade name

PS Wasnt good enough to post this before I got all
the red ink off my hands curse it. No luck yet. They
say I'm a doctor now. <u>ha ha</u>

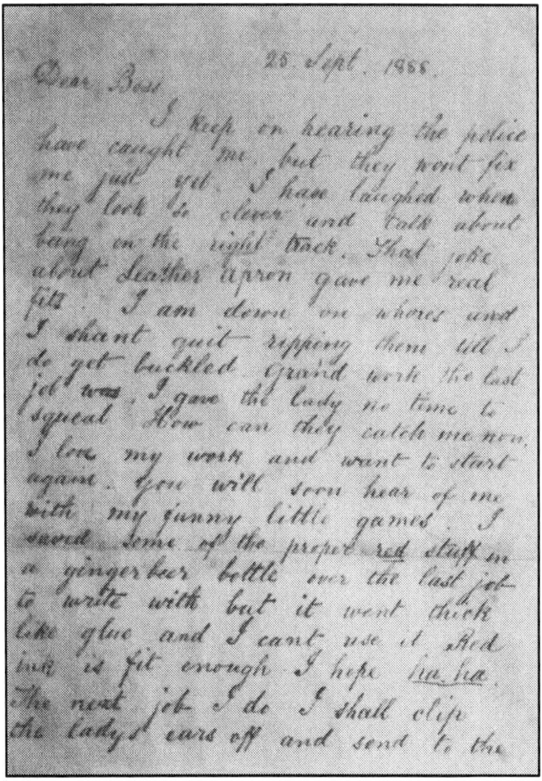

Illustration 10: "Dear Boss" letter, page 1/2, 27th September 1888

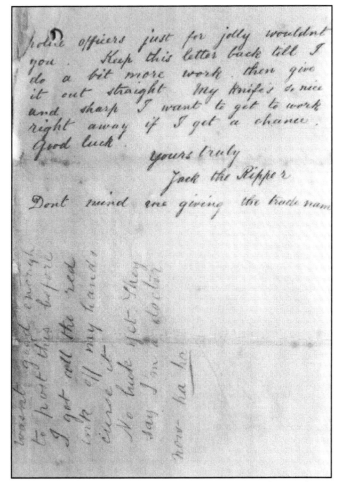

Illustration 11: "Dear Boss" letter, page 2/2, 27th September 1888

It is a gloating, sneering missive, the rantings of some moustache-twirling villain. It is almost comic if you disregard that an actual killer may have written it. Despite being in the hands of the press and Scotland Yard for a few days, it wasn't until the 1st October 1888, the day after the double event, that the evening edition of the *Daily News* printed the letter, pleading for information. This poured fuel into the fire of public and police concern, and only added to the (now global) attention the case was garnering.

It is no small understatement to say the letter caused a stir. It coined the name "Jack the Ripper" and the name has become immortal. Immediately following the letter's printing, newspaper offices, the police, even private individuals were flooded with imitators, copying the writing style and the phraseology. One woman, a 21-year-old from Bradford named Maria Coroner, was even arrested for sending a fake Ripper letter, and the variety and number of them are staggering. Some poor contemporary investigators, such as Patricia Cornwell, seem to have fallen headlong into the myth that the letters are all, or mostly, from the killer. In her book *Portrait of a Killer,* she paints an elaborate and unlikely picture of a killer criss-crossing the country and posting letters in disparate locations, apparently just to confuse the police. I can't blame her for trying to create some order out of the chaos, but the sheer fact of the matter is that nearly all the letters are considered hoaxes. And unfortunately for Ripperology purists, that includes the "Dear Boss" letter.

Whilst the letter caused an enduring and tangible link to the case, making famous the words, the "trade name," the phrases and the very sight of that unmistakeable handwriting, the romance of the case mustn't get in the way of the facts. For those of you still infuriated that I have joined the ranks of those who shoot down the idea of the Ripper killing Stride (because you like the idea of the double event, and you won't let the facts get in the way of a good story), I suggest you buckle up, buttercup.

The Dear Boss letter has a few problems that raise severe red flags. For starters, the letter was sent to the Central News Agency (CNA). Two things here; the CNA acted like Reuters or the Associated Press does today, a sort of high-level news agency that filters down to the smaller agencies like the BBC or Sky News. Notice how often on these networks, they'll quote one of these agencies, or some other foreign ones, as the sources of breaking news? The same was true back then. So, imagine if the so-called Wearside Jack letters claiming to be from the Yorkshire Ripper back in the 1970s had been sent to Reuters in London rather than a local paper or the local police. It would have been rather odd, a jarringly out-of-step action for a killer clearly operating within a particular area and impacting upon a particular community to do. And whilst we are familiar with such agencies now, with our 24-hour rolling news and the rise of the internet, back in 1888 such agencies were just not commonly known, certainly not to the extent that someone would purposefully write to one with the aim of communicating with, presumably, their local community.

But that's not all – the CNA had a reputation for pretty much inventing stories, embellishing details, fudging facts. A story about the 1895 Battle of Weihaiwei during the First Sino-Japanese War was almost entirely fabricated by the journalists at the CNA, for example. They were the original purveyors of fake news.

So, when taken in context, the letter, and the subsequent ones sent to the CNA, have more than a smell of rats about them. When an obscure, high-level news agency, a known source of questionable or even fabricated "news," suddenly produces these immaculately presented letters full of horrid imagery, gloating and sarcastic lines of quotable monologue, and a handy trade name, apparently from a famous killer, you have to start asking some questions.

Onto the letter itself, and as I said, it is immaculate. Neatly, carefully and quite beautifully written, in the sort of practiced hand you'd see produced from a public schoolboy. Certainly not some dock worker in the East End, and certainly not from a poor Polish Jew working some menial task in Wentworth Street. No, this wasn't the work of the killer – at one point he speaks about keeping blood in a ginger beer bottle to write with, but I'd like to see any evidence that he attempted to collect blood from the scene of Annie Chapman's murder. He also suggests they keep the letter back until he can kill again – how nice of Jack the Ripper to show so much care for their marketing strategy? And sure enough, after the double event, they did publish the letter, the very next day.

I'll admit something here. It seems like an awful, and unlikely, coincidence that the letter is sent on the 27th September, asks for the letter to be kept back until he'd killed again, and then within days he does kill at least once more. But that said, the press had already made a show of connecting the murders of Emma Smith and Martha Tabram and linking them to Leather Apron, so the chances are even if there were no further genuine Ripper murders in the district, they would have leapt on any other remotely similar attack and claimed it as proof of the letter's authenticity. That said, the coincidence remains a chilling reminder than for all the arguing in the world, the truth blowing in the wind and lost to history could be that the letter, after all, is genuine. But I do not believe it is, and I require far harder proof than a coincidence in timing to convince me otherwise.

JACK THE RIPPER

The writing is far too neat and unemotional. "Jack the Ripper" is written in the same scrupulous schoolboy hand as the rest of the letter with none of the flourish and narcissism the text itself indicates of the writer. It is also without errors, and without hesitation, a sure sign of re-drafting – all the hallmarks of a press hoax.

"Saucy Jacky"

On the same day as the Dear Boss letter was printed, a postcard was received and published in the press. Again, the CNA received the card, and again it added to the fire by apparently "predicting" the double event murders of the 30th September.

Purists argue that the postcard simply must be genuine for two reasons; firstly, it clearly shows that the writer knew of the double event murders before anyone else, the letter having arrived on the 1st October, the implication being that the killer must either have had insider knowledge that two murders had occurred, or that he'd sent it the day before that. Second is the suggestion that the writer of this missive clearly wrote the Dear Boss letter, which purists are desperate to believe is genuine. It is compelling to believe the two were written by the killer, I must agree. Here is the text of the postcard;

> I was not codding dear old Boss when I gave you the tip, you'll hear about Saucy Jacky's work tomorrow double event this time number one squealed a bit couldn't finish straight off. Had not got time to get ears off for police thanks for keeping last letter back till I got to work again.

It is basically a short sequel to the Dear Boss letter – it's basically an "I told you so" and a brief acknowledgement that the press held up their end of the bargain. However, there's a timing issue here.

The postmark for this letter is a full 24 hours after the murder of Catharine Eddowes. As we know from the testimony of PC Long, by 3am on the 30th September it was common knowledge that two murders had occurred in the area. With several postal deliveries a day, this could have been written at any time after the crack of dawn almost a full two days beforehand. Not only that but the letter specifically thanks the press for holding back on the Dear Boss letter, meaning whoever wrote this definitely read it in the papers, or knew it was being run in the morning editions of the *Daily News* on the 1st October. Even then it wouldn't be until the evening of the 1st October when the Saucy Jacky postcard would be printed in *The Star.*

The point I'm making is that the letter's attention to detail, even the statement about "holding [the Dear Boss letter] back until I do more work," could have been easily replicated by anyone because all the necessary facts were public knowledge in some shape or form for the best part of two days before the letter was sent. That said, the writing is very similar, the destination of the letter the same as the previous one, and the similarities are close enough to assume that the author wished, for whatever purpose, to be recognised as the same man with the same tag lines, same nickname, same style.

The publicity these letters brought was unprecedented. The letters were reproduced on billboards, leaflets and posters and plastered all over the district. Within days images of the letters were printed in newspapers not just across the country, but worldwide, as the fledgling global communications networks carried news of the crimes across the Atlantic and across the Empire. At home, this only increased pressure on the police – the City Police and the Metropolitan Police, two forces very much in competition and reticent to work together or aid one another's investigations, were now forced to share a multiple murder investigation that so far had given the best detectives in the East End the run-around. And as far as anyone could tell, the letters had to be treat as serious, coming from this elusive killer and providing the first real clues that could lead to the man himself.

Unfortunately for us in the 21st Century, we have the benefit of hindsight. Dr. Robert Anderson and Sir Melville McNaughton both indicated in their respective memoirs that the author of these letters was a readily identifiable journalist, a man who worked for *The Star* newspaper, despite wasting time during the investigation treating them seriously.

Anderson, in his memoirs, *The Lighter Side of my Official Life* (1910), stated that he was tempted to disclose both his prime suspect in the murders, and also the author of the hoax letters, but that doing so would "harm the traditions" of his force, and that "...I will only add here that the 'Jack-the-Ripper' letter which is preserved in the Police Museum at New Scotland Yard is the creation of an enterprising London journalist."

McNaughton wrote in his memoir, *Days of My Years* (1914), "In this ghastly production I have always thought I could discern the stained forefinger of the journalist indeed, a year later, I had shrewd suspicions as to the actual author!"

DANIEL JOHNSON

Even Sir Charles Warren wearily commented in a report to the Home Office on 10th October 1888, "...at present I think the whole thing a hoax but of course we are bound to try and ascertain the writer in any case." It seems the police were duty-bound to investigate letters they were sure were all hoaxes perpetrated by a particular journalist.

But who was this journalist they spoke of?

On 7th July 1890 a letter was received by Henry Massingham, the editor of *The Star* newspaper, sent from a former Liberal politician, John Brunner. It complained of the conduct of one of the newspaper's journalists, a penny-a-line hack named Frederick Best. In the midst of the letter is a very interesting sentence; "Furthermore, Mr. Best's attempt to mislead Central News during the Whitechapel Murders should have led to an earlier termination of his association with the newspaper."

"Attempts to mislead Central News during the Whitechapel murders?"

That is not the end of the matter.

In 1966 the magazine *Crime and Detection* published an article by Nigel Morland, a celebrated crime novelist, who spoke of interviewing a journalist named "Best" in 1931 who had admitted that he and a colleague at *The Star* newspaper had written the letters. Morland wrote,

> Returning homewards with me, Best discussed murders, the Whitechapel Murders in particular. With much amplifying detail he talked of his days as a penny-a-liner on 'The Star' newspaper. As a freelance he had covered the Whitechapel murders from the discovery of Tabram. He claimed that he, and a provincial

199

colleague, were responsible for all the Ripper
letters, to 'keep the business alive.'"

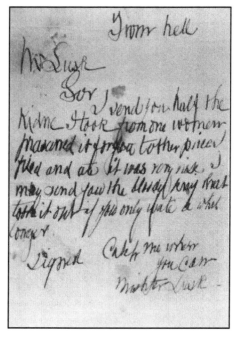

Illustration 12: The "From Hell" letter, 16th October 1888

As for the identity of the unnamed colleague,
there is further evidence here, too. DCI John George
Littlechild, the head of Special Branch during the Ripper
murders, wrote in 1913 to crime writer George Sims. He
claimed that it was "common knowledge" that man he
called Tom Bullen had written the letters, alongside his
superior, Sir Charles Moore. In reality the journalist's name
was Thomas J. Bulling, and he worked alongside Frederick
Best at *The Star*. Between them, these three – Frederick
Best, Thomas J. Bulling and Sir Charles Moore – appear to
have concocted the nickname "Jack the Ripper" and

written the letters themselves to exploit the murders and boost their circulation. It would explain why the letters were sent to the Central News Agency, too – if the letters had been sent to *The Star,* it would have attracted suspicion. If they'd been sent elsewhere, *The Star* loses out on the scoop. But by having the CNA receive them, *The Star* can easily report on them and still boost their sales even if all the other papers have the same story.

There were, of course, many Ripper letters received over the years. Some are given more prominence than others but ultimately, they are generally regarded as all fake, and in the case of these most famous letters, the Dear Boss and Saucy Jacky letters, their authorship can be quite easily ascertained. However, there is one letter and its accompanying package that refuses to easily shrug off the claims and counter claims of authenticity.

"From Hell"

On 16th October 1888, two weeks following the Saucy Jacky postcard, at a time when the district was gripped by the spectre of Jack the Ripper, the red writing and his suspiciously quotable catchphrases plastered all over town and the story dominating the papers, a grim development occurred. As well as the Met and City police forces patrolling the district, there were several "vigilance committees" who provided civilian patrols.

The most well-known was the Whitechapel Vigilance Committee, which based itself in The Crown public house and formed just days following the murder of Annie Chapman. It hired local men to patrol the streets of the district with blunt instruments and whistles, and even stumped up reward money for information when the police and government refused.

Its leader was a local businessman named George Lusk. Acting as the group's public face, he had already been the subject of hoaxes, threats, pranks, and abuse. But on the 16th October 1888 a package arrived for him at his home containing a ghastly surprise. A letter, scrawled in an almost illegible hand, and a small cardboard box. Inside, wrapped in paper, was half a kidney. Lusk apparently believed it to belong to a dog, and dismissed it at first as a cruel joke. He mentioned it at a meeting of the committee the next day and this raised the attentions of several of the group's prominent members, among them Joseph Aarons and Charles Reeve. On the 18th the group met to view the kidney and decided it required taking seriously. They sought medical advice and the kidney ended up in the hands of Dr Thomas Openshaw of the Pathological Museum at London Hospital, who examined the kidney and relayed his findings back to Lusk and the others via an assistant. This is where the details get fuzzy.

The message they got back from the assistant went public via the Press Association, and it was horribly misleading. According to this second-hand tale, Dr. Openshaw had claimed the kidney was from a 45-year-old female who had a drinking problem, and that it had been removed from the body at around the same time as Catharine Eddowes had died. Dr. Openshaw vehemently disputed this in an interview with *The Star* the next day, saying instead that all that could be determined was that it was a human kidney, cut in half, and preserved in wine. Determining gender, age and even the owner's alcoholism cannot possibly be determined from the kidney alone.

By now the kidney was in the hands of City coroner Dr. Gordon Brown, whose report is long lost along with so many City files because of World War II. However, his conclusions are included in the report to the Home Office, dated 6th November 1888, from Chief Inspector Donald Swanson. Now, before I show you what he said, I'll point out that two of my sources for this book are *Jack the Ripper: An Encyclopaedia* by John J. Eddleston (2010), and *The Crimes, Detection and Death of Jack the Ripper* by Martin Fido (1987). Whilst both relate the story thus far in about the same manner, their conclusions differ in part because of their differing interpretations of the following passage quoted from the Swanson report. Fido concludes the kidney to be a hoax, whilst Eddleston implies it is more likely the real deal. Eddleston (p. 174) quotes Swanson thus;

> "The result of the combined medical opinion they have taken upon it, is that it is the kidney of a human adult, not charged with a fluid, as it would have been in the case of a body handed over for purposes of dissection to an hospital, but rather as it would be in a case where it was taken from a body not so destined."

Eddleston confidently suggests this "negates" the suggestion of a sick hoax by a medical student or someone with access to bodies.

Compare with Fido's (p.79) extended quote of Swanson and his conclusion;

> "The result of the combined medical opinion they have taken upon it, is that it is the kidney of a human adult, not charged with a fluid, as it would have been in the case of a body handed over for purposes of dissection to an hospital, but rather as it would be in a case where it was

taken from a body not so destined. *In other words, similar kidneys might and could be obtained from any dead person upon whom a post mortem has been made for any cause, by students or dissecting room porter..."*

Fido ends his discussion of the matter by pleading for us to "please...forget about the kidney!" Swanson's report actually suggests that the lack of a fixative fluid in the kidney means nothing in determining its origin.

The point I make here is the importance of fact-checking, and the minefield that is the path to truth in this case. I make no comment on Eddleston's methods or motives in his writing this version of the Swanson report, as I consider his book exemplary and a crucial and much recommended reference in the case of Jack the Ripper. But I do urge anyone reading up on this case to make sure they check their facts -for God's sake, check the facts I present and question my conclusion, I implore you! The time for childishly sticking your head in the sand of easy answers and fantasy stories about this case are over – ditch the Royal conspiracies and the Masonic rituals nonsense and remember this is a messy and very real case of unsolved murder, not a TV show with a neat and tidy and satisfactory ending. Eddleston's book is an impressive effort in pulling together the facts and busting the myths, but there's always more to dig into, and nobody is going to do a perfect job. Sadly, this means that there's no smoking gun hot enough to silence the mutterings that would persist even if we found it, and Ripperologists are basically chasing a wild goose, and we know it. That said, we'll return to the case of the kidney.

The public opinion that the kidney could be from none other than Catharine Eddowes was not supported by the medical consensus. Dr. Brown had ostensibly drawn much the same conclusion as Dr. Openshaw, and said only that it was the left kidney of an adult human and had been preserved in spirits. He also mentioned that the renal artery of the kidney had been "trimmed," meaning no conclusions could be drawn about whether it was once attached to Catharine's body or anyone else's. In an interview with the *Evening News,* Dr. Sedgwick Saunders further poured scorn on the idea of the kidney being from the body by openly admitting it to be "quite possibly" a student hoax. Crucially he also added that Catharine's body was otherwise healthy – her liver and kidneys showed no signs of disease and she showed no sign of the damaging effects of alcohol abuse. This is important because of the input later on of Major Henry Smith.

Smith, the somewhat self-aggrandising Commissioner of Police for the City and the man with whom the buck stopped in the City Police during the Ripper murders, wrote a famously truth-stretching memoir named *From Constable to Commissioner* in 1910, alongside those of the other key players in the Ripper investigation such as Anderson and Macnaghten. In it he claimed, among other things, to have personally pursued the killer on the night of the double event and barely missed catching him red-handed, finding a sink dirty with bloody water where the killer had washed his hands. There is no evidence of such a find in the annals of the surviving police documents regarding the case. His recall is, shall we say, a little questionable.

Anyway, his contribution to the case of the kidney are a series of details he claims but which can be easily disputed. Smith claimed the kidney had one inch of renal artery attached to it, which matched the two inches left inside Catharine. But of course, as we saw above, the kidney had been trimmed and no artery remained. He claimed that both the Lusk kidney and Catharine's remaining kidney showed signs of "Bright's Disease," an umbrella term for a cluster of related kidney disorders common among the slum-dwelling population at the time. Dr. Brown's autopsy report potentially suggests the symptoms of "Bright's Disease," or the modern ailment most commonly associated with the term, nephritis; a pale bloodless pallor to the kidney and congestion at the base of the pyramids. However, he does not state so, instead commenting that her organs were healthy. Also, these symptoms are only vaguely associated with the condition and no such comment was ever made by the medical professionals who examined the Lusk kidney regarding Bright's Disease or any other ailment. The irony is that even if both Catharine and the kidney had shown signs of Bright's Disease, the condition was so common among the lower classes as to render the observation moot.

In summary, there are three sources of evidence for the kidney being either a hoax, or genuinely from Catharine Eddowes' body; the presence of a renal artery that can be linked to its place of removal; the presence or absence of preservative fluid as would be expected of a body in a medical environment from which a kidney could be obtained; and the presence of absence of Bright's Disease.

In the first case, the kidney had been trimmed and no conclusions could be drawn from the presence or absence of the renal artery. Secondly, Dr. Saunders already stated that it could have been easily acquired by medical students as a hoax and Swanson's report to the Home Office, after reviewing medical opinion on the kidney, stated that the absence of such fluid was a moot point and the kidney could still have come from a medical environment. Put simply, the lack of preservative fluid in the kidney did not pose a problem for medical professionals in considering the kidney a hoax by medical students or mortuary workers. Finally, the only source we have that suggests the Lusk kidney showed signs of Bright's Disease is Major Smith, not a medical professional and not a reliable source. The medical opinion we do have for both the kidney and for the condition of Catharine Eddowes' body make no mention of the disease or any other, and in fact, report on Catharine body as being healthy.

So, the kidney cannot be independently verified as being from Catharine or not. The evidence is either inconclusive or moot.

As for the letter that accompanied the kidney, the text reads as follows;

> from hell.
> Mr Lusk,
> Sor
> I send you half the Kidne I took from one woman prasarved it for you tother piece I fried and ate it was very nise. I may send you the bloody knif that took it out if you only wate a whil longer
> signed
> Catch me when you can Mishter Lusk

It has been argued that the words "sor," "prasarved," "Mishter" and "tother" are evidence of either a genuine or staged Irish dialect, the words written phonetically by someone of substandard literacy. Certainly, the poor state of the handwriting suggests this.

And the letter, as brief as it is, teaches us a few things;

- That the writer claims to have fried and ate the other half of the kidney. Cannibalism is rare among serial killers.
- The letter fails to mention the uterus that was certainly taken by the killer.
- It is addressed and aimed at Lusk himself, rather than the police or the press.
- Finally, the letter only refers to one murder rather than reference the double event.

What can we make of this letter? Well, given that the origin and authenticity of the kidney claimed to be Catharine's cannot be verified at all, we cannot be sure if this letter is genuinely from the killer either. On that basis we need to treat it both ways – consider the implications if it is genuine and those if it is a hoax.

The first thing that leaps out to me is that the writer has not adopted the "Jack the Ripper" moniker, nor any of the phraseology from the other letters. Instead they simply say, "catch me if you can," taunting George Lusk. This is a bold statement of individuality – the writer is not falling in line with the spectre painted in the media, he is communicating as himself. The hoaxers write to the press, painting a lurid picture of some sarcastic, knife-stroking baddie with a taste for one-liners and a catchy nickname, each copying from another, but this person is presenting a matter-of-fact statement, a piece of indisputable evidence, and a taunt. It is a rejection of these hoaxers by appealing directly to this local community leader with a straightforward message, with a bonus lump of evidence – the latest victim's kidney – thrown in as proof. The writer does not piggy back off the other hoaxers, he does not copy them or emulate their long-winded pontifications. It is just a kidney wrapped in butcher's paper and a brief note lending context.

As for the content, as I explained the letter mentions the murder of "one woman" and makes no reference to the double event (unlike the author of the Saucy Jacky postcard, who boasts about it). He also omits the removal of the uterus, and claims to have fried and eaten the other half of the kidney. Now, this is where the psychology comes in. Questions – why not mention the uterus? Would a killer like Jack eat his victims? Why carry out this ghastly act of sending the kidney to anyone, let alone Lusk? Answers? The letter was sent to a particular individual, rather than some vague, faceless entity like the Central News Agency or the Metropolitan or City Police Forces. He wanted one man to see it, one man to react, one man to believe this was real and one man to be affected by it. That is true whether the kidney and letter are hoaxes or not. But if we consider the writer to be the killer, there is an argument that supports his actions as being consistent with his psychological profile.

As we will discuss in more detail later, the killer operates on the basis of control over his victims, complete and total control and treats them as objects in his personal sexual fantasies. He rapidly disables and kills the women, and depersonalises them via the disfigurement and the act of turning their face away from him. In doing this, he totally removes their agency and their identity, before acting to literally dismantle their bodies, destroy their humanity and their womanhood. They become bits and pieces for him to play with. The removal of the victims' organs is a way of taking away, and retaining control, over the victim given his inability to keep the bodies for himself. Killing in public and leaving the bodies in public, posed for shock value, is a way of using the bodies as tools to exert control and influence (or an illusion of) over society by striking fear and suspicion amongst others. In the same way, the removal and retention of the victims' organs can be seen as a way of either completing the process of total control over his victims – by, for example, eating them as the letter-writer claims – or by using them in other ways to further the drama.

First, let's consider the claim of anthropophagy. Cannibalistic murderers are often loners who seek to totally control their victims, and this can mean drinking their blood or eating their flesh. Consuming their victim allows the victim to be part of the killer at all times. It is not a stretch to imagine this killer, whose modus operandi involves the obliteration of another's identity and their use as extensions of their own psychopathology, evolving to the consumption of the organs he removes rather than keep them simply as trophies or masturbatory aids. On that last point, the writer's omission of the uterus he removed is almost certainly because it is being used as a sexual aid, and therefore part of the private sphere of his sexual psychopathy.

Serial killer Jeffrey Dahmer was fascinated by how creatures were put together, their organs and their anatomy, interested only in transforming his victim into some kind of sex slave, a fulfilment of fantasies in which the identity of the victim is irrelevant. The difference between Dahmer and the Ripper is that the Ripper's motivation clearly extended to impacting adversely upon wider society, whilst Dahmer was only interested in maintaining a private world where he could carry out his sexual fantasies. The distress caused by his actions was part of what motivated the Ripper – as we see with the posing of his mutilated victims. Dahmer was asocial whilst

DANIEL JOHNSON

Jack the Ripper was antisocial, with rage and resentment part of the emotional content of his fantasies, and narcissistic traits in his elsewhere inadequate personality. His need for control extended outwards to society, and whilst the hoaxers were whipping up terror in the newspapers, the Ripper may well have decided to use the remaining kidney as a tool to exert further control. Thus, he did not relinquish control over the kidney when he left it in the hands of Lusk, knowing what would happen with it, because it was being used as a tool, a means to an end. It played its part in furthering his fantasies and fulfilling his psychopathic needs.

So, in summary, both the claim of cannibalism and the deployment of the kidney as a tool to cause an impact upon his target are both consistent with the Ripper's psychological profile. His omission of the uterus is also consistent with his desire to control private and public spheres of influence. However, this does not answer the question of why the writer chose George Lusk as his target and not the police or newspapers.

To begin with, there was already a hoaxer keeping the papers and the police happy. The folks over at *The Star* newspaper were happily jotting their Dear Bosses and keeping the city terrified and horrified on his behalf, but clearly, he wasn't too happy with being on the side-lines. It would have felt like the very impact he was dealing on the community was slipping from his control. He rejected the moniker "Jack the Ripper" and wrote his own missive conspicuous in its clear divergence from previous published correspondence. He also included what he considered incontrovertible evidence of his guilt, in the form of the kidney. And rather than aim this at the press or the police, fearful of effectively handing evidence to the cops directly or handing the press a free pass to spin

211

their own story and pollute the killer's own intentions for the communication, he sent it to George Lusk. He was the local public face of the community's vigilance committee, a man who had his face on the posters and his name on the lips of locals rather than a police force considered incompetent (a famous image of the police playing blind man's bluff summed up the public mood).

The Ripper was a local man, who lived and worked in the area. His comfort zone extended as far as Buck's Row and Mitre Square, meaning he lived his life within that area where Lusk would have been a prominent and important figure in the Ripper investigation. Not only that, but exerting control over one individual is much more desirable than trying to influence a self-serving press or a police force that has demonstrated both incompetence and corruption. Therefore, it made sense to buck the trend of the hoaxers and target instead a man local to the killer. It was, in my opinion, an expertly calculated move by the writer of the letter if it was the killer. He could monitor the effects of his missive from right under Lusk's nose, and for a killer who revelled in the impact his actions were having, he will have made every effort to do just that.

All that said, I should also point out that the writer's omission of the second murder of the night lends credibility to the letter being genuine, as we have already seen, Elizabeth Stride's murder was probably the work of a jealous boyfriend and certainly not the Ripper. This guilty knowledge, that the killer would know but not some moron who'd read the Saucy Jacky postcard, is a potential giveaway.

However, we must consider another possibility – that the killer, or at least the writer of the letter, was a member of the Whitechapel Vigilance Committee. This would explain why the killer was so familiar with police and vigilante patrols around Whitechapel to avoid being caught so many times, and it also explains why the letter was sent to George Lusk. This possibility will be touched upon later.

Let's sum up; the letter writer's claim to have eaten the other half of the kidney and their omission of the uterus being removed are both consistent with this killer evolving in his psychopathology. In keeping with the killer's profile, he would have graduated to taking and consuming the organs of his victims as a way of retaining control over them. Also, he would have kept a separation in his life between the private sexual-motivated aspects of his crimes and the public impact aspects. Furthermore, the writer's rejection of the nickname and phraseology in the hoax letters in favour of providing the kidney as proof, and their lack of a reference to the double event, further suggest this letter to be truly from the killer. He also chose a more relatable target, someone closer to home and an individual who would be a more attractive target for causing an impact he could monitor, rather than contacting the police or press whose reactions would have been uncontrolled and unpredictable. Given this evidence, and this argument, the letter appears very likely to be genuine and therefore the kidney quite possibly from the body of Catharine Eddowes.

However, things are not that simple.

In the days leading up to the letter being delivered, George Lusk had reportedly sought police protection from a bearded man he feared was following him (although I can find no verification of this story). At around the same time, Lusk's son reported an incident recounted here in the *News of the World* on 7th October 1888;

213

"On Thursday [4 October], at 4:15, a man apparently from 30 to 40 years of age, 5ft. 9in. in height, florid complexion, with bushy brown beard, whiskers and moustache, went to the private residence of Mr. Lusk in Alderney-street, Mile-end, and asked for him. He happened to be at a tavern kept by his son, and thither the man went, and after asking all sorts of questions relative to the beats taken by members of the Committee, attempted to induce Mr. Lusk to enter a private room with him.

The stranger's appearance however was so repulsive and forbidding that Mr. Lusk declined, but consented to hold a quiet conversation with him in the bar-parlour. The two were talking, when the stranger drew a pencil from his pocket and purposely dropped it over the side of the table saying, "Pick that up." Just as Mr. Lusk turned to do so he noticed the stranger make a swift though silent movement of his right hand towards the side pocket, and seeing that he was detected assumed a nonchalant air, and asked to be directed to the nearest coffee and dining-rooms. Mr. Lusk directed him to a house in the Mile End-road, and the stranger quietly left the house, followed by Mr. Lusk who went to the coffee-house indicated, and found that the man had not been there, but had given his pursuer the slip by disappearing up a court." (*News of the World*, 7 October 1888)

This was followed by a very interesting encounter by a lady by the name of Emily Marsh shortly before the letter and package arrived;

A statement which apparently gives a clue to
the sender of the strange package received by
Mr. Lusk was made last night by Miss Emily
Marsh, whose father carries on business in the
leather trade at 218, Jubilee-street, Mile-end-
road. In Mr. Marsh's absence Miss Marsh was
in the front shop, shortly after one o'clock on
Monday last, when a stranger, dressed in
clerical costume, entered, and, referring to the
reward bill in the window, asked for the address
of Mr. Lusk, described therein as the president
of the Vigilance Committee.

Miss Marsh at once referred the man to Mr. J.
Aarons, the treasurer of the committee, who
resides at the corner of Jubilee-street and Mile-
end-road, a distance of about thirty yards. The
man, however, said he did not wish to go there,
and Miss Marsh thereupon produced a
newspaper in which Mr. Lusk's address was
given as Alderney-road, Globe-road, no
number being mentioned. She requested the
stranger to read the address, but he declined,
saying, "Read it out," and proceeded to write
something in his pocket-book, keeping his head
down meanwhile. He subsequently left the
shop, after thanking the young lady for the
information, but not before Miss Marsh,
alarmed by the man's appearance, had sent the
shop-boy, John Cormack, to see that all was
right. This lad, as well as Miss Marsh, give a
full description of the man, while Mr. Marsh,
who happened to come along at the time, also
encountered him on the pavement outside.

JACK THE RIPPER

The stranger is described as a man of some forty-five years of age, fully six feet in height, and slimly built. He wore a soft felt black hat, drawn over his forehead, a stand-up collar, and a very long black single-breasted overcoat, with a Prussian or clerical collar partly turned up. His face was of a sallow type, and he had a dark beard and moustache. The man spoke with what was taken to be an Irish accent. No importance was attached to the incident until Miss Marsh read of the receipt by Mr. Lusk of a strange parcel, and then it occurred to her that the stranger might be the person who had despatched it. His inquiry was made at one o'clock on Monday afternoon, and Mr. Lusk received the package at eight p.m. the next day. The address on the package curiously enough gives no number in Alderney-road, a piece of information which Miss Marsh could not supply. It appears that on leaving the shop the man went right by Mr. Aaron's house, but did not call. Mr. Lusk has been informed of the circumstances, and states that no person answering the description has called on him, nor does he know any one at all like the man in question. (*Daily Telegraph, 20th October 1888*)

The 4th October incident was reported to the press on the 6th, whilst the Emily Marsh incident was reported on the 20th. The prior example is of a bearded man acting oddly, and such encounters were probably ten a penny and at that heightened time of fear and paranoia, played up for their sinister connotations. Also, if it were the same man, he already knew Lusk's address before he apparently asked Emily Marsh's help. So, we can probably

216

disregard the 4th October incident altogether.

As for the Emily Marsh incident, either the incident is make-believe, and the Irish aspect gleaned from the evident twang in the letter, unrelated and therefore just a coincidence, or else the hoaxer/killer acted without realising, or caring, that their accent would make him stand out. After all, they were still talking about Leather Apron, the Jew, and weren't looking for an Irishman, at least not yet. If the Emily Marsh incident really happened, then we're left considering the possible interpretations;

1. The killer was a moron, or was supremely confident of his ability to act without being caught, and either didn't realise or care that he was giving away his Irish background in both the letter and his memorable appearance at Emily Marsh's workplace asking for Lusk's address.
2. The killer pretended to be Irish in his accent and in the letter to throw witnesses off. This to me suggests that the killer was certainly not Jewish or Polish but a native Englishman whose knee-jerk fall-back position was to pretend to be Irish. Given his penchant for posing crime scenes and his contempt for others, a flair for the dramatic and a preplanned strategy of approach would certainly fit.
3. The hoaxer was an Irish man who made a ham-fisted yet determined effort to scare Lusk by pretending to be the killer. By doing this he would draw attention to an undisguised representation of himself in writing and in person whilst claiming as convincingly as he could, that he was the Whitechapel Murderer. What would this accomplish? It is an absurd idea. What's more is

that Lusk apparently had no idea who the man was when given Marsh's description, meaning if this hoaxer had a grudge against Lusk, the meaning of this act was totally lost on him.

4. Equally stupid is the idea that the hoaxer did this whilst pretending to be someone else, an Irishman. This way the hoaxer lands himself in serious suspicion of being connected to the murders if the evidence is taken seriously, and if he is identified, apparently accomplishes nothing but putting the willies up George Lusk, and hides his identity meaning, again, that the motivation for this act would be a total mystery to Lusk.

5. The penultimate possibility is that the incidents are totally unrelated and that it is merely a coincidence. It appears the Emily Marsh incident did indeed happen, and wasn't invented by the press, though; multiple witnesses are cited providing the same account and the same description in multiple newspapers over two days.

6. The final possibility is that the Emily Marsh encounter and the subsequent package were the work of the Whitechapel Vigilance Committee themselves. This has been suggested by other authors, but I came to consider this explanation myself. Without reference to the other theories in this regard, my personal suggestion is that the Whitechapel Vigilance Committee, keen to whip up public furore over the fact that no reward was being offered by the police or the Home Office, wished to raise their own profile by having their most prominent public figure receive convincing correspondence from the killer along with a disgusting token of apparent authenticity.

I implore the reader to dig into the details of all the information given in this book, as always, to draw your own conclusions. But I am ready to present my own for your consideration here with regards to this letter and the kidney.

I cannot fathom a reasonable payoff for a hoaxer to take the risk they'd need to take to carry out this action. Writing a letter to sell papers? Sure. Writing to the police? Yeah, why not. And maybe Patricia Cornwell was on to something, and maybe Walter Sickert wrote many Ripper letters as some form of performance art, or out of an obsession for the case, I'd even buy that. But to make such a clear effort to pretend to be the killer just to put the willies up a single public figure who isn't even a police officer? And to make such a dumb move as the Emily Marsh encounter as well, leaving a police force in need of a suspect with both your handwriting and physical description (plus, potentially, the fact you're Irish)? I just can't see a reasonable payoff for a hoaxer. The same argument follows on for the idea of the whole thing being a publicity stunt by the Whitechapel Vigilance Committee – the argument is not helped by the fact that the Committee appears to have basically dissolved within weeks; the November 10th edition of *The Star* claims the Committee has "ceased to work." If anything, the letter and kidney had a dramatic effect on the Committee and contributed to its downfall.

Of course, this would be something the killer would wish for.

I'll be honest and say that I hate the idea of this kidney being the real deal. I hate the idea of this letter being from the killer. I hate it because it is a dead-end piece of evidence that cannot be verified one way or another and one that is overlooked by those who seek to write it off as a hoax when it could be mined for whatever clues it can still provide. However, I must grit my teeth and admit that the evidence and the argument are in favour of the "From Hell" letter and accompanying kidney being genuine correspondence from Jack the Ripper.

For starters, I cannot rule the kidney out as having come from Catharine Eddowes. The renal artery was trimmed by the time Dr. Brown got to see it, but by whom, and to what extent it was trimmed is unknown. The state of the renal artery inside Catharine Eddowes' body is not reported with any reliability. The health or otherwise of both Catharine and the kidney are not really reported on with any detail or reliability; Dr. Saunders claims Catharine's body was healthy, but he never actually saw it. Dr. Brown appears to have described Bright's Disease in Catharine's surviving kidney, but never confirms it. Major Smith reports the disease in both her body and the kidney, but he is unreliable and his claims uncorroborated. The absence of preservative fluid in the kidney means nothing in the context of determining a mortuary hoax, as confirmed by Swanson. So in lieu of a DNA test (the kidney is now long lost), we are left to simply state that we cannot determine its authenticity either way.

As for the letter, it appears to be such a departure from the other Jack the Ripper letters, adding and omitting just the right details, to fit with a profile of the killer that accounts for his known behaviours. Anthropophagy is consistent with his profile. Omitting the sexually-motivated aspects of his crime are consistent, too. Omitting the double event, particularly Elizabeth Stride's murder, is again consistent with this being from the actual killer if he did not kill her as I argue. Targeting a particular individual is also consistent with his desire for control. However, if he also intended to disrupt the Committee and its activities, then it was a job well done.

In reality we cannot know for certain if this letter and the kidney were genuinely from the killer until cast-iron forensic evidence swings it one way or another, but as the years slide by the chances of that are slimming. But for this analysis, I think we should certainly not rule out the very real possibility that it is from the killer and that it helps provide a crucial insight into the killer's psyche.

*   *   *

October drew to a close. There were no murders that month, after the four in as many weeks that preceded it. These letters from hell occupied the press and the public in the meantime, the police apparently hitting dead ends, inquests opening and closing, the Whitechapel Vigilance Committee folding, and the victims buried by growing crowds. The news of the crimes and the grisly moniker of "Jack the Ripper" was now global, with wires reporting on the news in America and beyond.

But with the first few days of November, the peace was to be shattered by the Ripper's grisliest murder yet, at 13 Miller's Court.

Mary Jane Kelly

Illustration 13: Illustration of Mary Jane Kelly, circa November 1888

Not much is known of Mary Jane Kelly, including her real name, variously styled as Mary Janet Kelly, Marie Jane Kelly, Mary Jeanette Kelly, Fair Emma, Ginger, Mary Ann Kelly, etc. Similarly, her past seemed to be up for revision; her affectation of "Jeanette" stemmed from her brief stay in France with a wealthy gentleman. Much of what we know of her background comes from the testimony of her lover, Joseph Barnett, and is largely unverified by documentary evidence. What is presented below is an approximation based on what was reported at the inquest.

Born in Limerick, in Ireland, in 1863, one of up to eight children, her family moved to Wales when she was still young, after her father John Kelly got a job at a steelwork in either Carmarthenshire or Caernarvonshire. At the age of 16 she married a young man named Davies, who was killed in a mining explosion a matter of years later. This loss seemingly prompted her to move to Cardiff where she spent time in an infirmary, sometime around 1881. Although police in Cardiff could not verify this, it is believed she became a prostitute whilst living in the city with her cousin. There is no documentary evidence to corroborate any of this.

In 1884 she moved to London. It is reported that she spent her time working in a high-class brothel in the West End, and it is during this time she spent some weeks in France. After this she referred to herself as Mary Jeanette Kelly and started living with a man by the name of Morganstone in Pennington Street, Stepney.

After this, things get fuzzy. She is reported to have moved repeatedly for some years; she apparently scrubbed floors at Providence Row Night Convent and Refuge on Crispin Street, Spitalfields. Apparently, for years there was a tale told of a maid who absconded and was later killed by Jack the Ripper, and it is believed that this story refers to Mary. She is reported to have lived with a Mrs Buki at St George's Street, and then with a Mrs Carthy at Breezer's Hill, Ratcliff Highway. In 1886 she reportedly moved in with a man in the building trade named Joseph Fleming on Bethnal Green Road. Little evidence corroborates any of this either.

On 8th April 1887, she was living at Cooney's Common Lodging House in Thrawl Street, when she met

Joseph Barnett. He was a fish porter and dock worker who was of Irish stock, and who worked at Billingsgate Fish Market. After only two meetings, they agreed to live together. They moved around the area, always in disreputable neighbourhoods (George Street, Little Paternoster Row, and Brick Lane), before settling at 13 Miller's Court. This single-room flat was one of several in a back-alley behind 26 Dorset Street, a dingy but cheap accommodation, although Mary had managed to run up around £1.50 in arrears by the time she died.

She was known to be a loud and boisterous drunk, and routinely prostituted in the area. One of her nicknames, "Black Mary," stemmed from her notorious temper and habit for violence. In many ways she was a contrast to some of the other victims – young and temperamental, and known for certain to work as a prostitute. Her landlord, John McCarthy, ran the properties in Miller's Court and knew of her activities, and that of several other residents, but turned a blind eye at the very least. She worked the streets the entire time the Ripper scare was taking place, and admitted to friends that the murders scared her. It is an unsettling fact that Mary would have been the only one of the women named as a Ripper victim to have heard the name Jack the Ripper, and may well have known the other victims by sight.

By the start of November 1888, the Ripper letters were now plastered across billboards, posters and flyers, the words reprinted in newspapers and the press and police wondering when, or if, the killer would return after an absence of more than a month. She was still working the streets, but she was also terrified of the Ripper, and told friends that it was getting to her. At the very end of October, Mary and Joseph argued, and he left. He offered a several explanations for why, including his displeasure at her working as a prostitute again, and the fact that Mary was allowing a prostitute called Julia to sleep at 13 Miller's Court. To lend context, Barnett had lost his job at the fish market in July or August, and their relationship had previously been somewhat passionate – the window pane was broken during one recent argument and now allowed the pair to lock and unlock the door from outside. Despite their differences, he continued to visit her daily and provided whatever money he could.

Then came the 8th November 1888.

Last Movements

Joseph Barnett visited 13 Miller's Court at around 7:30pm/7:45pm according to his reckoning to find Mary with company. Currently he was dossing at Buller's Boarding House in Bishopsgate and returned there after 8pm. Mary's companion that night was apparently one Lizzie Albrook, although as with everything in this case, the details are disputed. A woman by the name of Maria Harvey originally claimed it was her until she was further questioned in an interview with *The Times* newspaper. It seems she and Mary, who according to Joseph Barnett had been lovers, spent the evening together drinking until around 7:30pm. Between then and 8pm, Joseph had visited 13 Miller's Court to find Mary with Lizzie Albrook. However, to confuse matters even more, a woman named Elizabeth Foster told the press she'd spend the day with Mary drinking in the Ten Bells pub with no mention of Maria Harvey! For some reason, the case of Mary Jane Kelly is littered with these sorts of foggy and contradictory sources of information, so bear with me as I try and guide us through it. In this case I think we can ignore Elizabeth Foster's claim as it really does not fit at all with corroborated statements regarding Mary's last movements as given by more established witnesses, no less her boyfriend, close friends and neighbours and even her lover.

Nevertheless, the hours between 8pm and 11:45pm are a bit fuzzy. A local tailor named Maurice Lewis, who claimed to know Mary Kelly by sight, said he saw her drinking at the Horn of Plenty pub on the western corner of Dorset Street between 10pm-11pm on the night of the murder with her mysterious lodger "Julia" and a man he called "Dan" and who he claimed was Kelly's fish porter lover. This from the *Illustrated Police News*, 17th November 1888;

> Maurice Lewis, a tailor, living in Dorset-street, stated that he had known the deceased woman for the last five years. Her name was Mary Jane Kelly. She was short, stout, and dark; and stood about five feet three inches. He saw her on the previous (Thursday) night, between ten and eleven, at the Horn of Plenty in Dorset-street. She was drinking with some woman and also with "Dan," a man selling oranges in Billingsgate and Spitalfields markets, with whom she lived up till as recently as a fortnight ago. He knew her as a woman of the town. One of the woman whom he saw with her was known as Julia.

In an interview with *The Star on* 10th November 1888, Barnett confirmed he was aware his brother Daniel visited Mary. That said, Lewis clearly identifies "Dan" as being her lover. Indeed, earlier in the article, we find this comment;

JACK THE RIPPER

The victim was another of the unfortunate class, who occupied a miserably- furnished room in a court off Dorset-street, a narrow thoroughfare out of Commercial-street, not far removed from the police-station. She had lived in the court for some little time, and was known as Mary Jane Kelly, alias "Ginger." She was a Welsh woman, and it is believed was married, but separated from her husband. Recently she had lived with a man who was known in the neighbourhood as Dan, but the couple parted a few days ago.

So, Lewis (who may have been their source for that detail in the first place), certainly appears to have believed the man who she spent the night drinking with was actually Joseph Barnett, but whose name he knew as "Dan." Either he's gotten Joseph's name wrong or he's misidentified Daniel Barnett as his brother.

However, the real reason Lewis' testimony is curious is because he would claim to have seen Mary Kelly twice after her estimated time of death, once at 8am and again at 10am the next morning. As we will see later, he won't be the only one, adding to the mystery.

The next recorded sighting of Mary Jane Kelly was by Mary Ann Cox, who described herself as "a widow and an unfortunate," a resident at 5 Miller's Court and a fellow prostitute. At 11:45pm, after returning home from a night on the game, she claims to have seen a drunken Mary in the company of a man – described as mid-30s, blotchy-faced, with a carrot moustache, shabby dark clothing and a derby hat, carrying a can of beer – entering her flat. She called out with a greeting, and was met with singing from Mary. At 12am she left again, hearing Mary's voice singing an Irish folk song called, "Only a violet plucked from my mother's grave." She was still singing an hour later at 1am when Cox returned to Miller's Court.

At about the same time, Elizabeth Prater, who lived above Mary Kelly, returned to the Court and waited for a man whom she lived with for a while before retiring to her room and going to sleep at 1:30am, claiming to have heard no singing from Mary's room.

At this point, we reach the testimony of a man named George Hutchinson. Ripperologists will know this name, and know this is the part of the book where I sigh and hold my weary face in my palm. At 6pm on 12th November 1888, the very same day the inquest into Mary's death had concluded, he made an unlikely and unusual statement to police about having seen Mary in the company of a well-dressed man. Apparently a friend of Mary's for some time, the out-of-work labourer made the following statement to police;

> About 2 am 9th I was coming by Thrawl Street, Commercial Street, and saw just before I got to Flower and Dean Street I saw the murdered woman Kelly. And she said to me Hutchinson will you lend me sixpence. I said I cant I have spent all my money going down to Romford. She said Good morning I must go and find some money. She went away toward Thrawl Street. A man coming in the opposite direction to Kelly tapped her on the shoulder and said something to her. They both burst out laughing. I heard her say alright to him. And the man said you will be alright for what I have told you. He then placed his right hand around her shoulders. He also had a kind of a small parcel

in his left hand with a kind of strap round it. I stood against the lamp of the Queen's Head Public House and watched him. They both then came past me and the man hid down his head with his hat over his eyes. I stooped down and looked him in the face. He looked at me stern. They both went into Dorset Street I followed them. They both stood at the corner of the Court for about 3 minutes. He said something to her. She said alright my dear come along you will be comfortable He then placed his arm on her shoulder and gave her a kiss. She said she had lost her handkercheif he then pulled his handkercheif a red one out and gave it to her. They both then went up the court together. I then went to the Court to see if I could see them, but could not. I stood there for about three quarters of an hour to see if they came out they did not so I went away.

Description age about 34 or 35. height 5ft6 complexion pale, dark eyes and eye lashes slight moustache, curled up each end, and hair dark, very surley looking dress long dark coat, collar and cuffs trimmed astracan. And a dark jacket under. Light waistcoat dark trousers dark felt hat turned down in the middle. Button boots and gaiters with white buttons. Wore a very thick gold chain white linen collar. Black tie with horse shoe pin. Respectable appearance walked very sharp. Jewish appearance. Can be identified

Hutchinson later gave more details to the press;

DANIEL JOHNSON

The man was about 5ft 6in in height, about 34 or 35 years of age, with dark complexion and a dark moustache, turned up at the ends. He was wearing a long, dark coat, trimmed with astrachan, a white collar, with black necktie, in which was affixed a horseshoe pin. He wore a park of dark "spats" with light buttons, over button boots, and displayed from his waistcoat a massive gold chain. His watch chain had a big seal, with a red stone hanging from it. He had a heavy moustache, curled up, dark eyes, and bushy eyebrows... He looked like a foreigner... The man carried a small parcel in his hand about eight inches long, and it had a strap around it.

He had it tightly grasped in his left hand. It looked as though it was covered with dark American cloth.

He carried in his right hand, which he left upon the woman's shoulder, a pair of brown kid gloves. One thing I noticed, and that was that he walked very softly

The subject of this description has been described mockingly as "the perfect villain" by author Bob Hinton, and through the years has attracted derision and fascination in equal measure. Before we pick this apart, however, it is worth noting that Inspector Abberline, the man in charge of detectives on the ground in Whitechapel, considered Hutchinson a credible witness. He assigned officers to accompany him around the area to hunt down the man he saw.

Not only that, but another witness actually corroborates part of his story; the questionable testimony of a woman named Sarah Lewis, stating that at 2:30am

231

(according to the clock on Spitalfields Church), she arrived at Miller's Court to visit a friend who lived at number 2, when she saw a man standing opposite the Court and staring in, as if waiting for someone to leave. Since Hutchinson claims to have seen Mary at the Court at 2am and only stopped watching for them leaving at 2:45am, this man would appear to have been Hutchinson himself. The reason Lewis' testimony was questionable is because it appears identical to that of a Mrs Kennedy who reported much the same encounter, with some differences, but along with Sarah Lewis claimed to have been accosted by a man with a black bag during the previous week and claims to have encountered the man again that night.

So, if we take Sarah Lewis' claim to have seen the man who we can argue within reason to have been Hutchinson seriously, then we can claim with some confidence that Hutchinson did indeed stand watching the Court between 2am and 2:45am, saw a man enter with Mary but not leave. This is the important detail for the timeline so far, a rare piece of evidence we can put some trust in.

What about Hutchinson's suspect, though? A dark-featured, curly-moustached Jewish fellow with a thick gold chain and almost theatrical costume? It's complete rubbish in my opinion. In the police statement and in the press statement he made a point of the suspect's "Jewish" appearance, "foreign" appearance, and that – unsurprisingly – he claimed he could identify the man again. Now, this brings to mind the claims of Michael Kidney who (killer or not), claimed that he could find the Ripper himself with all his special knowledge. Give me a troop of strange constables and I'll find the man, he said. But as I argue, he was an egotistical bastard who possibly murdered his girlfriend. Maybe George Hutchinson was just one of those people, some arrogant blowhard who couldn't keep his nose out of the circus that erupted around Miller's Court. The fact that he provided such a comically specific and detailed description of the man he is clearly claiming looked dodgy, and therefore guilty, and only did so after the official business was concluded, is evidence enough for me.

Nonetheless, his inclusion in Ripper lore is measured both by dismissal, such as mine, and by suspicion. Hutchinson has been named a suspect himself in recent years, but I think he's just an easy target. The annals of the Ripper crimes are littered with witnesses who turn out to be time wasters and liars, as well as those who are mistaken or simply try to help in a misguided way. Hutchinson certainly did stand staring down the Court if Sarah Lewis is to be believed, so he was certainly interested in what was happening in there and could well have seen Mary with a client, and could well have been worried about her safety. But upon her death, he may well have decided to just describe the most comic-book-villain-like Jewish suspect he could dream up rather than shamefully admit that it was dark, and he saw little to nothing of the man she was with. Who knows.

Anyway, back to the timeline.

Back to Ms Cox, who claims she arrived back at about 3:10am and saw and heard nothing further. The singing had finished, and the lights were off in Miller's Court. At 5:45am, after an unsettled night, she claims to have heard someone leave the court.

During this time, Elizabeth Prater would awaken at a time she estimated to be between 3:30am-3:45am, woken by her kitten running across her neck. At this point, she claims to have heard a cry of "Murder!" She apparently guessed the time because the lights of the lodging house were off. At 5:30am she left for a drink at the Ten Bells pub, before returning to bed. Thus, she may have been the person Ms Cox heard leaving the Court at around 5:45am.

At the same time, Sarah Lewis – the corroborator of Hutchinson's story – was spending the night at her friends' house in Miller's Court when she heard a cry of "Murder!" around about 4am. This was apparently during a spell of sleeplessness between 3:30am and 5am.

As previously noted, in *The Star* of 10th November 1888, an interview was printed with a woman named Mrs Kennedy, apparently a neighbour of Mary's who was staying at her parent's house opposite 13 Miller's Court. In the interview she gives a story so similar to that of Sarah Lewis that most commentators assume them to be the same person. I certainly see similarity in the fact that Lewis was staying with a family named "Keyler," and possibly a journalist could mistake it for Kennedy. However – and this point will become crucially important later – in Mrs Kennedy's interview, she states that at 3am on the morning of 9th November she passed three people standing by The Britannia yards from the Court, one of them a young, respectably dressed man with a dark moustache, and two women, one "poorly clad and without headgear." The man and the first woman apparently were drunk, and parted ways on bad terms, the woman storming off in the opposite direction to where he wished her to go. Mrs Kennedy claims that she then went to bed in Miller's Court and would hear a cry of "Murder!" between 3:30am-3:45am, the very same times given by Sarah Lewis.

This is interesting in light of Maurice Lewis' claim to have witnessed Mary drinking with Julia and the man named "Dan" earlier in the night. Could they have spent the night drinking? If so, then this has implications for the timeline. It is possible that she was out with "Dan" and "Julia" at 11pm, returned to the flat at 11:45pm with a client, apparently leaving at some point to pick another one up by 2am, when Hutchinson claims to have seen her. She leaves the flat sometime after 2:45am after he stops watching for her, and returns to the nearby Britannia pub and meets "Dan" and "Julia" again. Within fifteen minutes Mrs Kennedy (which may be Sarah Lewis), sees the trio and therefore witnesses Mary, "Dan" and "Julia" apparently ending their night with a disagreement – two of them, "Dan" and one of the women, heading in one direction and a second woman heading in another. Then, between thirty and forty-five minutes later, the murder occurs in 13 Miller's Court.

If there is any validity to the testimony that provides this timeline, then we potentially have two things here; holes in Joseph Barnett's testimony, and a minute-to-minute timeline of Mary Kelly's final few hours. However, I would be willing to give Maurice Lewis the benefit of the doubt in assuming that "Dan" is the same person as Mary's boyfriend, whom he may have had factual knowledge of but did not know by sight; I once had to correct a statement I gave to police regarding argumentative neighbours because I had named one of the newcomers "George." That turned out to be the name of their pet parrot. So, mistakes can be easily made!

Nevertheless, we have established what could be a far more detailed timeline for Mary Jane Kelly's actions that night, depending upon the witnesses' reliability;

10pm-11pm – seen at The Britannia with "Dan" and "Julia" by Maurice Lewis

11:45pm – seen at 13 Miller's Court by Mrs Cox with a client.

1am – is heard still singing by Mrs Cox.

2am – Hutchinson sees Mary with a client speaking for a few minutes before entering the Court.

2:30am – Sarah Lewis sees a man, believed to be Hutchinson, watching the Court, and a man and a drunken woman speaking nearby.

2:45am – Hutchinson apparently leaves his vigil.

3am – Mrs Kennedy/Sarah Lewis sees man and two women outside the Britannia, possibly Mary, "Dan" and "Julia."

3:30am-3:45am – Elizabeth Prater, Sarah Lewis and Mrs Kennedy hear cry of "Murder!"

If there is any truth in this, then is begs plenty of questions. Was the "Dan" seen by Maurice Lewis actually Daniel Barnett as the comments by Joseph Barnett suggest? If not, and it was actually Joseph Barnett himself, then his alibi is in tatters. Occam's Razor suggests that if we have a statement from one source suggesting it's Daniel, and another describing Joseph but calling him Dan, then we can reasonably argue that the man seen by Maurice Lewis with Mary Kelly that night was indeed Daniel Barnett, but we can't be sure as Daniel Barnett offered no statement as far as we know to confirm this. As for "Julia," it has been suggested that this homeless prostitute was actually Miller's Court resident Julia Van Turney, who testified at the inquest. However, there is no evidence to suggest this; Van Turney lived with a man in the Court and was a laundress, and she also did not report having drunk with Mary on the night of the killings; in fact, she would testify that the drunken row that lead to the window being broken at number 13 was an unusual occurrence. The real "Julia" remains unaccounted for.

Nevertheless, we do have a timeline to work with, and that puts the time a cry of "Murder!" was heard at

DANIEL JOHNSON

3:45am, as corroborated by at least two independent witnesses (this number depends on whether Mrs Kennedy counts given that she may be Sarah Lewis. If not, then that makes three independent witnesses).

This would usually be the part where I jump to the discovery of the body, but on this occasion, I must digress to another truly bizarre part of this story; two separate witnesses who place Mary Jane Kelly out of doors well into the morning of the next day, long after medical opinion says the victim at Miller's Court died.

The first witness is Caroline Maxwell, the wife of Miller's Court landlord John McCarthy. Despite only knowing Mary for four months and speaking to her twice, she claims to have met with her twice within an hour on the morning of the 9th November 1888. The first time was at the corner of Miller's Court at around 8am-8:30am, where she encountered a worse-for-wear Mary being sick. "I have the horrors of drink upon me," she reportedly said, pointing out vomit in the gutter. At around 9:30am, she again saw Mary Jane Kelly at The Britannia pub with a young, well-dressed man. She was, predictably, confronted on her timing at the inquest and particularly the date of these encounters but insists that she recalled the date exactly because she was returning china dishes to a neighbour's house that day.

Now, I'd be willing to follow the other researchers in the field by simply dismissing Caroline Maxwell's testimony as "somehow mistaken," were it not for the fact that her sighting is corroborated. At 8am that morning, the very same time as Caroline Maxwell claimed to have met her, Maurice Lewis – who we've encountered previously – claimed to see Mary Kelly at Miller's Court.

From *Morning Advertiser*, 10th November 1888;

237

JACK THE RIPPER

There is no direct confirmation of this statement, but a tailor named Lewis says he saw Kelly come out about eight o'clock yesterday morning and go back again to the house. Another statement is to the effect that Kelly was seen in a public-house known as "Ringers," at the corner of Dorset-street and Commercial-street at about ten o'clock yesterday morning, and that she there met Barnet and had a glass of beer with him. This statement is not substantiated

He also claimed to have seen Mary Kelly at The Britannia, drinking, at just after 10am, again, at about the same time as Maxwell. From *Illustrated Police News*, 17th November 1888

Soon after ten o'clock in the morning he was playing with others at pitch and toss in M'Carthy's court, when he heard a lad call out "Copper," and he and his companions rushed away and entered a beer-house at the corner of Dorset- street, known as Ringer's. He was positive than on going in he saw Mary Jane Kelly drinking with some other people, but is not certain whether there was a man amongst them. He went home to Dorset-street on leaving the house, and about half an hour afterwards heard that Kelly had been found in her room murdered. It would then be close upon eleven o'clock.

Now, given that Lewis' previous statement about seeing Mary Kelly with Julia and "Dan" can be corroborated and treat as reliable, despite the possibility he has misidentified Joseph Barnett as his brother Daniel, then

Illustration 14:

The Miller's Court victim, 9th November 1888

we have no reason to doubt the validity of these sightings either.

For context, the time of death can be ascertained, through medical evidence, as being between 3am-4am (McClain *et al*, "Estimating Mary Kelly's Time of Death", accessed 08/08/2017, casebook.org).

Two independent witnesses, claiming to see Mary Kelly at the same places and at the same times, long after two or three independent witnesses report hearing the cry of "Murder!", and long after medical evidence suggests she died, and only three-quarters-of-an-hour before her body would be found. Now, we could dismiss the medical evidence as flawed – in the Annie Chapman case, the time of death was probably mistakenly placed hours earlier because of the unusual cooling effect of the disembowelment. However, in this case the scene was caked in blood, and the smell and sight of the remains would have been evidence enough for an experienced police officer and particularly a medical examiner of Thomas Bond's credentials to know the difference between a body dead and mutilated for about 45 minutes and one dead and mutilated for seven or more hours. My point is that I am not inclined to suggest these witnesses saw Mary Kelly and that the medical evidence "must" be wrong, however I am equally not willing to say the medical evidence was correct so these witnesses "must" be wrong, either.

That is the big problem with Ripperology – the inclination to simply dismiss evidence that is inconvenient. We shall dismiss the evidence of Maurice Lewis and Caroline Maxwell because, well, it doesn't exactly fit. We shall sidestep the differences between the Elizabeth Stride murder and the others because, well, it all seems a lot more interesting with two murders in one night. And we shall airbrush from history the Ripper's use of strangulation, the evidence of preplanning in his crimes, and the consistencies and escalations in his behaviour that mark him as an organised killer rather than the raving loon we'd feel more comfortable him being because, well, it suits us.

The conflicting evidence in this final murder case is everywhere. A victim whose history is untraceable. Witness statements that contradict each other. Sightings of the victim that are entirely inconsistent with the medical evidence. Even the story of how the body was found is one of foul-ups and dangling questions. I shall move onto this presently.

At 10:30am on 9th November 1888, John McCarthy sent his assistant Thomas Bowyer to collect the overdue rent from 13 Miller's Court. Getting no answer from the door, which was locked, he peered through the broken window and was the first to see the horrible sight – piles

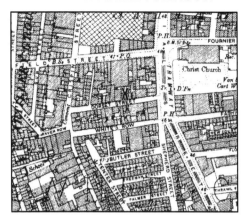

Illustration 15: Dorset Street, circa 1894

of flesh and "a lot of blood." He brought Mr McCarthy, and they went to the police. At around 11am, Bowyer, McCarthy, Inspector Walter Beck and Inspector Walter Dew arrived, with Dr Bagster Phillips arriving around fifteen minutes later. Inspector Abberline turned up around another fifteen minutes after this at 11:30am and ordered the assembled men to await the arrival of bloodhounds which Sir Charles Warren was expected to bring. In an incredible development, Warren had in fact resigned over his failure to catch the Ripper and news had yet to filter down – leaving the men standing around until 1:30pm, when Superintendent Thomas Arnold finally arrived to break the news that no dogs were coming. With that, Arnold ordered McCarthy to break the door down with an axe, about three hours after the body was found. Dr Phillips was first inside to officially pronounce death.

The scene was like a horrible tableau; it was a tiny single-bedroom doss, 12ft by 10ft. Plain walls now spattered with blood, dry for hours. A bed stood in the top-right-hand corner of the room upon which lay the mutilated remains of a female, wearing the torn remains of a chemise. Next to the head of the bed was a nightstand upon which lay strips of flesh. Next to that was a small grate, inside which were the burnt remains of woman's clothes. Mary's own clothes were piled up on a chair at the foot of the bed.

The victim's mutilations were extensive. I shall provide the medical report but here are the essential details as seen by the first responders; her face was utterly unrecognisable, all the features hacked off, leaving a ragged mess, her head turned left towards the door. She lay on her back, her legs open in a stirrup position, her left hand laying upon her abdomen, or rather inside it. Flesh had been carved from her legs leaving white bone showing, her genital region was just gone. The entirety of her abdomen had been stripped and her organs and breasts removed and placed between her feet, under and around her head. Her throat was deeply cut, her head hanging on by bone and skin, and her arms showed deep defensive wounds. It was one hell of an escalation from the previous murders, the consequence of Jack the Ripper having all the time and privacy in the world to act out his deepest desires.

**RIPPER MYTH:
"VICTIM'S ENTRAILS HUNG AROUND THE ROOM"**

In an interview with The Pall Mall Gazette, 4th November 1889, Inspector Henry Moore, who would take over from Abberline in the Whitechapel murders investigation in that year, provided details of the Miller's Court murder that would go down in legend, but which are not true. He is quoted as saying;

"He cut the skeleton so clean of flesh that when I got there

I could hardly tell whether it was a man or woman. He hung the different parts of the body on nails and on the backs of chairs. It must have taken him an hour-and-a-half in all. And when he was ready to go he found the door was jammed.... believing he was locked in with the bleeding skeleton with the bits of flesh that he had hung so fantastically about the room..."

This rumour of the Miller's Court victim having her entrails hung like Christmas decorations around the room has become a grisly trope repeated time and again. It is not true.

As in the previous murders, evidence of ritual can be seen. Again, we see him position the body with the legs open, the left hand laid across the abdomen, and the face turned to face the left. Again, we see deep dissection of the throat and mutilation of the face, as well as a focus on the genitals and abdomen for extensive mutilations and organ removal. The consistencies mark this out as a Ripper crime for sure.

Unlike the previous crimes, this time he appears to only have taken away the heart, although he did remove the other organs at the scene without taking them with him. Similarly, the presence of defensive wounds on her arms suggests she put up a fight, as does the cry of "Murder!" heard by multiple witnesses. We can attribute this to the killer altering his modus operandi by attacking a victim from the front, and in an indoor location. The differences in this murder compared to the others can be explained reasonably, but that does not take away from the increasingly strange and confused nature of the murder.

JACK THE RIPPER

The body – identified as Mary's by Joseph Barnett by her eyes and an ear – was moved to Shoreditch Mortuary at 4pm, whilst the doss was boarded and padlocked, and the Court kept under 24-hour police guard.

Joseph Barnett, Mary's lover, was duly arrested and interrogated during his four hours at the police station. His clothes were searched for bloodstains, but he would later be released without charge. His alibi – that he played whist until bedtime after meeting Mary at 7:45pm the previous night – was accepted.

The inquest into Mary Jane Kelly's murder opened 12th November 1888 at Shoreditch Town Hall, presided over by Dr Roderick MacDonald, coroner.

Inquest
(Source: The Daily Telegraph, 13th November 1888)

The inquest into the death of Mary Jane Kelly began with controversy, as two of the jurors objected to having to sit on a jury that was concerned with a murder which took place not in their districts – Whitechapel and Spitalfields – but in Shoreditch. The Coroner, Dr. MacDonald, firmly put them in their place and told them jurisdiction lies with where the body is kept rather than where it was found.

Following this, the jury saw the body itself at the mortuary, the wounds having been stitched and the body cleaned and dressed. Then onto the guarded and boarded-up doss itself at Miller's Court. Back to the court, testimony began with Mary's lover, Joseph Barnett;

Joseph Barnett: I was a fish-porter, and I work as a labourer and fruit- porter. Until Saturday last I lived at 24, New-street, Bishopsgate, and have since stayed at my sister's, 21, Portpool-lane, Gray's Inn-road. I have lived with the deceased one year and eight months. Her name was Marie Jeanette Kelly with the French spelling as described to me. Kelly was her maiden name. I have seen the body, and I identify it by the ear and eyes, which are all that I can recognise; but I am positive it is the same woman I knew. I lived with her in No. 13 room, at Miller's-court for eight months. I separated from her on Oct. 30.

Coroner: Why did you leave her?

Barnett: Because she had a woman of bad character there, whom she took in out of compassion, and I objected to it. That was the only reason. I left her on the Tuesday between five and six p.m. I last saw her alive between half-past seven and a quarter to eight on Thursday night last, when I called upon her. I stayed there for a quarter of an hour.

Coroner: Were you on good terms?

Barnett: Yes, on friendly terms; but when we parted I told her I had no work, and had nothing to give her, for which I was very sorry.

Coroner: Did you drink together?

Barnett: No, sir. She was quite sober.

Coroner: Was she, generally speaking, of sober habits?

Barnett: When she was with me I found her of sober habits, but she has been drunk several times in my presence.

Coroner: Was there any one else there on the Thursday evening?

Barnett: Yes, a woman who lives in the court. She left first, and I followed shortly afterwards.

Coroner: Have you had conversation with deceased about her parents:

Barnett: Yes, frequently. She said she was born in Limerick, and went when very young to Wales. She did not say how long she lived there, but that she came to London about four years ago. Her father's name was John Kelly, a "gaffer" or foreman in an iron works in Caernarvonshire, or Carmarthen. She said she had one sister, who was respectable, who travelled from market place to market place. This sister was very fond of her. There were six brothers living in London, and one was in the army. One of them was named Henry. I never saw the brothers to my knowledge. She said she was married when very young in Wales to a collier. I think the name was Davis or Davies. She said she had lived with him until he was killed in an explosion, but I cannot say how many years since that was. Her age was, I believe, 16 when she married. After her husband's death deceased went to Cardiff to a cousin.

Coroner: Did she live there long?

Barnett: Yes, she was in an infirmary there for eight or nine months. She was following a bad life with her cousin, who, as I reckon, and as I often told her, was the cause of her downfall.

Coroner: After she left Cardiff did she come direct to London?

Barnett: Yes. She was in a gay house in the West-end, but in what part she did not say. A gentleman came there to her and asked her if she would like to go to France.

Coroner: Did she go to France?

Barnett: Yes; but she did not remain long. She

said she did not like the part, but whether it was the part or purpose I cannot say. She was not there more than a fortnight, and she returned to England, and went to Ratcliffe-highway. She must have lived there for some time.

Afterwards she lived with a man opposite the Commercial Gas Works, Stepney. The man's name was Morganstone.

Coroner: Have you seen that man?

Barnett: Never. I don't know how long she lived with him.

Coroner: Was Morganstone the last man she lived with?

Barnett: I cannot answer that question, but she described a man named Joseph Fleming, who came to Pennington-street, a bad house, where she stayed. I don't know when this was. She was very fond of him. He was a mason's plasterer, and lodged in the Bethnal-green-road.

Coroner: Was that all you knew of her history when you lived with her?

Barnett: Yes. After she lived with Morganstone or Fleming. I don't know which one was the last - she lived with me.

Coroner: Where did you pick up with her first?

Barnett: In Commercial-street. We then had a drink together, and I made arrangements to see her on the following day - a Saturday. On that day we both of us agreed that we should remain together. I took lodgings in George-street, Commercial-street, where I was known. I lived with her, until I left her, on very friendly terms.

Coroner: Have you heard her speak of being afraid of any one?

Barnett: Yes; several times. I bought newspapers, and I read to her everything about the murders, which she asked me about.

Coroner: Did she express fear of any particular individual?

Barnett: No, sir. Our own quarrels were very soon over.

Coroner: You have given your evidence very well indeed.

(Addressing the Jury): The doctor has sent a note asking whether we shall want his attendance here to-day. I take it that it would be convenient that he should tell us roughly what the cause of death was, so as to enable the body to be buried. It will not be necessary to go into the details of the doctor's evidence; but he suggested that he might come to state roughly the cause of death.

The jury acquiesced in the proposed course.

We learn of Mary's life story pretty much from this exchange in court only. Other sources are far sketchier and as I have commented, documentary evidence is thin on the ground to corroborate any of this. There is no reason to suspect any deception and the thin details leave arguably little room for Barnett to be mistaken about most of it. One thing we do learn is that Mary was gobbling up the press coverage of the murders and that it made her afraid, although apparently not of any particular individual. She feared Jack the Ripper, and would have stopped her street work if she could. Lizzie Albrook, the woman who was with Mary at the time Joseph Barnett visited on the night in question, had this to say to the press later;

"About the last thing she said was, 'Whatever you do don't you do wrong and turn out as I have.' She had often spoken to me in this way and warned me against going on the streets as she had done. She told me, too, that she was heartily sick of the life she was leading and wished she had money enough to go back to Ireland where her people lived. I do not believe she would have gone out as she did if she had not been obliged to do so to keep herself from starvation."

As with so many street walkers, Mary had little choice but to turn tricks to survive, and all the time she was doing so she was eating up the popular press' characterisation of the Ripper, which was a deliberately trumped-up scare tactic to sell papers. Take this snippet from *The Star*, published in the aftermath of the discovery of Annie Chapman's murder;

London lies to-day under the spell of a great terror. A nameless reprobate - half beast, half man - is at large, who is daily gratifying his murderous instincts on the most miserable and defenceless classes of the community. There can be no shadow of a doubt now that our original theory was correct, and that the Whitechapel murderer, who has now four, if not five, victims to his knife, is one man, and that man a murderous maniac. There is another Williams in our midst. Hideous malice, deadly cunning, insatiable thirst for blood - all these are the marks of the mad homicide. The ghoul-like creature who stalks through the streets of London, stalking down his victim like a

Pawnee Indian, is simply drunk with blood, and
he will have more. The question is, what are the
people of London to do? Whitechapel is
garrisoned with police and stocked with plain-
clothes men. Nothing comes of it. The police
have not even a clue. They are in despair at
their utter failure to get so much as a scent of
the criminal. (*The Star,* 8th September 1888)

This laughably pantomime prose may inspire a wry grin at
the familiar sensationalism of the tabloid press we're used
to now, but imagine being Mary Kelly, a young woman,
barely literate (given that she made Joseph read the
stories out to her), living in the heart of the district and
experiencing these horrible murders in real-time. Imagine
having never experienced tabloid news before, and
reading these stories or hearing them read to you – that's
probably worse – without the instinct to take them with a
pinch of salt. It would have been absolutely terrifying.
Walter Dew, who wrote of Mary Kelly in his
autobiography, quotes her as telling Lizzie Albrook that
she plans to leave London after the Lord Mayor's show
and return to Ireland, so terrifying were the Ripper
murders.

That aside, we must also note that in a twist, the
court decides not to disclose the medical evidence,
instead have Dr. Phillips merely step in to confirm the
cause of death. In all the previous cases the evidence was
heard, even if the pathologist needed to be persuaded to
read the awful details (as in the case of Annie Chapman).
This possibly is related to the fact that this inquest was
also remarkably short, calling only a dozen witnesses
giving short testimony, the whole affair concluding within
24 hours. As you can imagine, all these factors feed into

conspiracy theories ranging from the reasonable to the irrational. To be perfectly honest, the confusing and mysterious nature of this murder have me seeing why. As I write this, I am very aware of alarm bells ringing and red flags flying in my mind regarding this case. There definitely seems to be something very odd going on, and I will at least try later to make sense of it.

Back to the inquest and the next witnesses were Thomas Bowyer and John McCarthy, who recounted the circumstances of their discovery of Mary's body. McCarthy confirms Mary had lived there with Barnett for 10 months and was 29 shillings behind on the rent. Other than that, their testimony is unremarkable.

Perhaps the most crucial testimony came from the next few witnesses. Mary Ann Cox was first;

Mary Ann Cox: I live at No. 5 Room, Miller's-court. It is the last house on the left-hand side of the court. I am a widow, and get my living on the streets. I have known the deceased for eight or nine months as the occupant of No. 13 Room. She was called Mary Jane. I last saw her alive on Thursday night, at a quarter to twelve, very much intoxicated.
Coroner: Where was this ?
Cox: In Dorset-street. She went up the court, a few steps in front of me.
Coroner: Was anybody with her ?
Cox: A short, stout man, shabbily dressed. He had on a longish coat, very shabby, and carried a pot of ale in his hand.
Coroner: What was the colour of the coat?
Cox: A dark coat.
Coroner: What hat had he?
Cox: A round hard billycock.

Coroner: Long or short hair?

Cox: I did not notice. He had a blotchy face, and full carrotty moustache.

Coroner: The chin was shaven?

Cox: Yes. A lamp faced the door.

Coroner: Did you see them go into her room?

Cox: Yes; I said "Good night, Mary," and she turned round and banged the door.

Coroner: Had he anything in his hands but the can?

Cox: No.

Coroner: Did she say anything?

Cox: She said "Good night, I am going to have a song." As I went in she sang "A violet I plucked from my mother's grave when a boy." I remained a quarter of an hour in my room and went out. Deceased was still singing at one o'clock when I returned. I remained in the room for a minute to warm my hands as it was raining, and went out again. She was singing still, and I returned to my room at three o'clock. The light was then out and there was no noise.

Coroner: Did you go to sleep?

Cox: No; I was upset. I did not undress at all. I did not sleep at all. I must have heard what went on in the court. I heard no noise or cry of "Murder," but men went out to work in the market.

Coroner: How many men live in the court who work in Spitalfields Market?

Cox: One. At a quarter- past six I heard a man go down the court. That was too late for the market.

Coroner: From what house did he go?

Cox: I don't know.

Coroner: Did you hear the door bang after

him?

Cox: No.

Coroner: Then he must have walked up the court and back again?

Cox: Yes.

Coroner: It might have been a policeman?

Cox: It might have been.

Coroner: What would you take the stout man's age to be?

Cox: Six-and-thirty.

Coroner: Did you notice the colour of his trousers?

Cox: All his clothes were dark.

Coroner: Did his boots sound as if the heels were heavy?

Cox: There was no sound as he went up the court.

Coroner: Then you think that his boots were down at heels?

Cox: He made no noise.

Coroner: What clothes had Mary Jane on?

Cox: She had no hat; a red pelerine and a shabby skirt.

Coroner: You say she was drunk?

Cox: I did not notice she was drunk until she said good night. The man closed the door. There was a light in the window, but I saw nothing, as the blinds were down. I should know the man again, if I saw him. I feel certain if there had been the cry of "Murder" in the place I should have heard it; there was not the least noise. I have often seen the woman the worse for drink.

Cox heard no cry of "Murder!" unlike the other witnesses, although she claims she would have heard one if it occurred. Otherwise her testimony is important for timeline purposes when considered alongside those of Elizabeth Prater and Sarah Lewis, whom we shall consider next.

The man Cox witnessed with Kelly was sighted at 11:45pm, whilst if George Hutchinson's statement can be at all believed (and we have Sarah Lewis to thank for us even considering it), Mary was picking up a new client at 2am. So, we can probably rank Cox's description of a man seen with Mary as low priority.

Next to give evidence was Elizabeth Prater;

Elizabeth Prater: My husband, William Prater, was a boot machinist, and he has deserted me. I live at 20 Room, in Miller's-court, above the shed. Deceased occupied a room below. I left the room on the Thursday at five p.m., and returned to it at about one a.m. on Friday morning. I stood at the corner until about twenty minutes past one. No one spoke to me. McCarthy's shop was open, and I called in, and then went to my room. I should have seen a glimmer of light in going up the stairs if there had been a light in deceased's room, but I noticed none. The partition was so thin I could have heard Kelly walk about in the room. I went to bed at half-past one and barricaded the door with two tables. I fell asleep directly and slept soundly. A kitten disturbed me about half-past three o'clock or a quarter to four. As I was turning round I heard a suppressed cry of "Oh - murder!" in a faint voice. It seemed to proceed from the court.

Coroner: Do you often hear cries of "Murder?"

254

Prater: It is nothing unusual in the street. I did not take particular notice.

Coroner: Did you hear it a second time?

Prater: No.

Coroner: Did you hear beds or tables being pulled about?

Prater: None whatever. I went asleep, and was awake again at five a.m. I passed down the stairs, and saw some men harnessing horses. At a quarter to six I was in the Ten Bells.

Coroner: Could the witness, Mary Ann Cox, have come down the entry between one and half-past one o'clock without your knowledge?

Prater: Yes, she could have done so.

Coroner: Did you see any strangers at the Ten Bells?

Prater: No. I went back to bed and slept until eleven.

Coroner: You heard no singing downstairs?

Prater: None whatever. I should have heard the singing distinctly. It was quite quiet at half-past one o'clock.

Prater heard no singing, but did hear a cry of "Murder!" at between 3:30am-3:45am. One aspect of her testimony that I find troubling is that she apparently got into the habit of barricading her doors at night, presumably against the Ripper.

In terms of timeline, Prater saw nobody in the Court at the times she was out, between 1am and 1:30am. This fits with the other witnesses, although at 1am Cox heard Mary still singing, whilst Prater, who is in a much better position to have heard her, did not.

Next comes the testimony of Caroline Maxwell. This is where the story gets strange, as she swears under oath that she saw Mary Jane Kelly twice on the 9th November after the time she certainly met her death. This fact is not lost on the Coroner, who warns her that her testimony differs and that she is under oath, which she responds by stating she is still willing to testify;

Caroline Maxwell: My husband is a lodging-house deputy. I knew the deceased for about four months. I believe she was an unfortunate. On two occasions I spoke to her.

Coroner: You must be very careful about your evidence, because it is different to other people's. You say you saw her standing at the corner of the entry to the court?

Maxwell: Yes, on Friday morning, from eight to half-past eight. I fix the time by my husband's finishing work. When I came out of the lodging-house she was opposite.

Coroner: Did you speak to her?

Maxwell: Yes; it was an unusual thing to see her up. She was a young woman who never associated with any one. I spoke across the street, "What, Mary, brings you up so early ?" She said, "Oh, Carrie, I do feel so bad."

Coroner: And yet you say you had only spoken to her twice previously; you knew her name and she knew yours?

Maxwell: Oh, yes; by being about in the lodging-house.

Coroner: What did she say?

Maxwell: She said, "I've had a glass of beer, and I've brought it up again"; and it was in the road. I imagined she had been in the Britannia beer-shop at the corner of the street. I left her, saying that I could pity her feelings. I went to

Bishopsgate-street to get my husband's breakfast. Returning I saw her outside the Britannia public-house, talking to a man.

Coroner: This would be about what time?

Maxwell: Between eight and nine o'clock. I was absent about half-an-hour. It was about a quarter to nine.

Coroner: What description can you give of this man?

Maxwell: I could not give you any, as they were at some distance.

Inspector Abberline: The distance is about sixteen yards.

Maxwell: I am sure it was the deceased. I am willing to swear it.

Coroner: You are sworn now. Was he a tall man?

Maxwell: No; he was a little taller than me and stout.

Inspector Abberline: On consideration I should say the distance was twenty-five yards.

Coroner: What clothes had the man?

Maxwell: Dark clothes; he seemed to have a plaid coat on. I could not say what sort of hat he had.

Coroner: What sort of dress had the deceased?

Maxwell: A dark skirt, a velvet body, a maroon shawl, and no hat.

Coroner: Have you ever seen her the worse for drink

Maxwell: I have seen her in drink, but she was not a notorious character. I should have noticed if the man had had a tall silk hat, but we are accustomed to see men of all sorts with women. I should not like to pledge myself to the kind of hat.

We shall also include Sarah Lewis' testimony here, too;

Sarah Lewis: I live at 24, Great Pearl-street, and am a laundress. I know Mrs. Keyler, in Miller's-court, and went to her house at 2, Miller's-court, at 2.30a.m. on Friday. It is the first house. I noticed the time by the Spitalfields' Church clock. When I went into the court, opposite the lodging-house I saw a man with a wideawake. There was no one talking to him. He was a stout-looking man, and not very tall. The hat was black. I did not take any notice of his clothes. The man was looking up the court; he seemed to be waiting or looking for some one. Further on there was a man and woman - the later being in drink. There was nobody in the court. I dozed in a chair at Mrs. Keyler's, and woke at about half-past three. I heard the clock strike.
Coroner: What woke you up?
Lewis: I could not sleep. I sat awake until nearly four, when I heard a female's voice shouting "Murder" loudly. It seemed like the voice of a young woman. It sounded at our door. There was only one scream.
Coroner: Were you afraid ? Did you wake anybody up?
Lewis: No, I took no notice, as I only heard the one scream.
Coroner: You stayed at Keyler's house until what time?
Lewis: Half-past five p.m. on Friday. The police would not let us out of the court.

258

Coroner: Have you seen any suspicious persons in the district?

Lewis: On Wednesday night I was going along the Bethnal-green-road, with a woman, about eight o'clock, when a gentleman passed us. He followed us and spoke to us, and wanted us to follow him into an entry. He had a shiny leather bag with him.

Coroner: Did he want both of you?

Lewis: No; only one. I refused. He went away and came back again, saying he would treat us. He put down his bag and picked it up again, saying, "What are you frightened about ? Do you think I've got anything in the bag ?" We then ran away, as we were frightened.

Coroner: Was he a tall man?

Lewis: He was short, pale-faced, with a black moustache, rather small. His age was about forty.

Coroner: Was it a large bag?

Lewis: No, about 6in to 9in long. His hat was a high round hat. He had a brownish overcoat, with a black short coat underneath. His trousers were a dark pepper-and- salt.

Coroner: After he left you what did you do?

Lewis: We ran away.

Coroner: Have you seen him since?

Lewis: On Friday morning, about half-past two a.m., when I was going to Miller's-court, I met the same man with a woman in Commercial-street, near Mr. Ringer's public-house (the Britannia). He had no overcoat on.

Coroner: Had he the black bag?

Lewis: Yes.

Coroner: Were the man and woman quarrelling?

Lewis: No; they were talking. As I passed he looked at me. I don't know whether he recognised me. There was no policeman about.

This testimony is extraordinary because Caroline Maxwell insists on speaking despite the warnings that she is contradicting the evidence given so far. She absolutely insists the woman she had a face-to-face conversation with was Mary, and that this was the same morning as the body was found. Although she only spoke to Mary twice before she certainly knew her by sight, it seems. It would be disingenuous to suggest she was lying or mistaken offhand, but at the same time we are left in a quandary. Was this sighting genuine? Has Maxwell gotten her timing right? Well, the fact that her testimony is corroborated by Maurice Lewis is one hell of a smoking gun – placing Mary at the same places, and at the same times, as Caroline Maxwell's testimony!

So, was Mary Kelly alive and well and having a pint at The Britannia at 10:00am on the 9th November 1888, having been seen there by two independent witnesses, after being seen leaving Miller's Court by the same witnesses at 8am? If so, then who the hell was lying dead in 13 Miller's Court while all this was happening? One could suppose that the only person unaccounted for in all this is the mysterious "Julia," the homeless prostitute Mary took in shortly before Joseph Barnett left her in October. But even if we suggest that "Julia" was the woman killed by the Ripper at or around 3:45am at 13 Miller's Court, why did Joseph Barnett identify his lover as the woman in the mortuary?

A clue could be found in Caroline Maxwell's testimony. She reports that Mary looked ill, and had vomited in the gutter nearby and blamed the drink, but she also suggesting that it was unusual to see her up at that time. What if she had returned to her flat and found the horribly mutilated remains of "Julia" on her bed, and in shock, locked the door as she left, vomited in the gutter and then found herself presented with Caroline Maxwell. Blaming drink, she leaves and finds someone – possibly Joseph Barnett – at The Britannia, where she is seen by both Caroline Maxwell again and Maurice Lewis. Horrified by what she has seen, she drinks hard to settle herself and they agree to claim the body she found is hers.

Why?

For starters, given what we've heard of Mary's movements that night, she likely spent the last few hours of the night with the Ripper. We know she spent between 10pm and 11pm with "Julia" and "Dan," and that she took a drunken punter home at 11:45pm, and at least one more before the night was over. Mrs Kennedy saw a woman, though to be Mary, with a woman, probably "Julia," and a third man at 3am. This was certainly the killer. The following morning, upon finding the horribly mutilated remains of, presumably, "Julia" in her own bed, she would have panicked, realising the Ripper knew her by name, by sight and knew where she lived. Believing the police to be incompetent from the news reports she'd been devouring, and terrified at her plight, she would have been inclined to flee.

Also, as we know from the interview with Lizzie Albrook, Mary was sick of her life as it was and wished to return to Ireland anyway. She still had family in Ireland, so she could potentially flee London and have a place to stay. Also, we know she was terrified of the Ripper crimes but was forced onto the streets due to poverty, and she apparently owed McCarthy money that was due to be collected the following morning (which lead to the finding of the body). She had every reason and the stated intention to leave London, however, there are questions still to be asked. How could she afford to leave, if she was in rent arrears and prostituting out of sheer desperation? Is it a coincidence that she intended to leave just as the murder occurred? And exactly why she would have vanished, apparently willingly, after the murder, is hard to explain. That said, there are some very controversial possibilities that could explain this, and I will explore them in more detail later.

This leaves the evidence of Joseph Barnett. He testified to the court – according to some news reports, stammering and repeating questions back to himself, which may be evidence of a disorder called "echolalia" - that the dead woman was his partner. He was also arrested and held for four hours by police, and was interrogated about his partner's murder, but not about making her vanish. His actions to hide his girlfriend occurred unexpectedly after 10am, within an hour of the body being found. And don't forget that the police already believed the body to have been sitting there for several hours prior to this due to medical evidence – there'd be little purpose in pushing him about his actions at around the time of the discovery of the body (although given their record regarding time of death, as in the Annie Chapman case, we can be doubtful their questions were time appropriate).

After the murder, Joseph Barnett vanishes from public records for nearly twenty years, until he receives a new porter's license at Billingsgate in 1906. After that records sporadically place him in various addresses, mostly in Shadwell a few miles from Whitechapel, apparently with a common-law wife named Louisa. He died on the 29th November 1926 of pulmonary edema, outliving his wife by a matter of weeks.

According to census records, Joseph and this Louisa character list their marriage in the 1911 census as having commenced 23 years prior. This would be sometime between April 1887 and April 1888, and would place the marriage's earliest commencement at the same time Joseph began his relationship with Mary Kelly. The deeper connotations of this finding will be discussed later in the book.

We are still in the dark about what was happening in Joseph's life between 1888 – 1906. We have no answers to the giant plot holes in the witness statements and the official version of events relating to the Miller's Court murder. The evidence we have collected here suggests that Mary Jane Kelly was in the company of her fellow sex worker lodger "Julia" and probably, in the latter part of the night, the Ripper himself.

This is one scenario to consider if indeed Mary wasn't the Miller's Court victim. At around 2am they parted ways – where Mary went is debatable – but "Julia" and the Ripper went back to Miller's Court where he murdered her. She would have been killed around 3:30-3:45am and the killer may have spent an hour or more mutilating the body. Mary Ann Cox's claim to have heard someone leave the Court at around 5:45am could tally with the killer leaving the flat. It may be that he stayed for two hours, intending to kill Mary herself when she returned to eliminate his wayward witness. When he saw movement in the Court – Elizabeth Prater leaving, for example- he decided to cut his losses and flee.

At some time just before 8am another resident, Catherine Pickett, knocked on the door to number 13 to borrow a shawl from Mary because of the rain. There was no answer. Then, minutes later, Mary herself was seen leaving the flat and then returning by Maurice Lewis. At that moment she vomited in the gutter having seen the remains in 13 Miller's Court, and was confronted by Caroline Maxwell. Dismissing her illness as drink-related, she departed immediately to find someone, the man she would later be seen with by both Maxwell and Lewis at The Britannia.

As for Mary's absence from Miller's Court between the period around 3am, when she was seen by Mrs Kennedy, and 8am, when she was seen at her flat by Lewis, other than an all-night bender, there is another, albeit unlikely, possibility.

Just to add to this increasingly bizarre case, it is also suggested that Mary Kelly had a child of 6 or 7 living with her occasionally – and this comes from Joseph Barnett's statement to the press (*The Star*, 10th November 1888)

> She used occasionally to go to the Elephant and Castle district to visit a friend who was in the same position of life as herself. Kelly had a little boy, aged about six or seven years, living with her.

This suggestion that Kelly had a son was further reinforced by a story in the Press Association by a woman named Margaret who claimed Kelly was contemplating suicide for want of money, and that she lived with her young son. There is confusion over who exactly Margaret is describing, and it is probably someone else entirely, but Joseph Barnett's comments are very interesting. If that is the case, then possibly during the missing hours she was with her son at a secondary location and that may also explain why she was so keen to flee London after realising the Ripper could recognise her. As with so much in this case, however, there is little evidence that Mary Kelly did have a child, but that said, there's little in the way of evidence to the contrary. This case truly is a bizarre mixed-bag of supposition and contradiction.

To recap; the timeline provided by witnesses makes for a strong case that Mary Kelly was out and about hours after the Miller's Court victim was murdered. The potential presence of a child at a secondary location could explain Mary's night-long absence from Miller's Court, and her early-morning return. The fact that she likely drank with the Ripper that night contributed to her fear that he would target her following the Miller's Court murder, but she did already have plenty of motivation to flee the life she was living, owing to poverty and her life on the streets.

Extraordinary.

That said, we must also play devil's advocate. What if the estimated time of death is all wrong? If these witnesses saw Mary Kelly right up until 10am on the morning of her death, is it possible that she met her killer after 10am, possibly at The Britannia, only to be taken back to her doss and murdered then? After all, Dr. Phillips, who conducted the autopsy on Mary Kelly and who was present at the scene to declare death, used merely the suggestion of a cry of "Murder!" at about 3:30am as his guide in estimating death, as well as body temperature. That said, he used the same method in estimating the time of death for Annie Chapman and was out by several hours. It is entirely possible that these witnesses are indeed wrong, that they got their days wrong, misidentified Kelly, or simply that they tried to be helpful and did what some folk do and make something up (yes, that does happen). I very much doubt that last option, whilst misremembering times and dates and faces is far more likely, and is in any witness statement. But as for the medical evidence, as I have already suggested, there is little room for doubt.

Earlier, I cited an article by McClain *et al* (accessed 2017) in which they determine the victim's time of death by examining the autopsy report by Dr. Bond. In the article they provide a rough guide to the setting-in and dissipation of rigor mortis, arguing that it takes around 12 hours to peak before receding. In Dr. Bond's report (reproduced later), he suggests rigor was setting in during the autopsy, at 2pm on the day of the murder, and that it likely peaked at 3pm. Winding the clock back 12 hours takes us to 3am, around the time the cry of "Murder!" was heard, and corroborating the witnesses who heard the cry. Thus, the victim at Miller's Court most likely did die at around the time estimated by the coroner and indicated by the witnesses. The question about whether the victim was killed later becomes academic, and the only question is whether two independent witnesses can both be wrong about seeing a particular individual in the same locations, at the same times, on the same day. If so, then we can chalk this up to poor memory and bury Mary Jane Kelly, but if not, then we must seriously consider the facts of the case.

For my part, I shall henceforth refer to the woman killed in Miller's Court as simply "the Miller's Court victim," whether it be Mary Jane Kelly or not, and if I am honest, I doubt that she was. I did not expect to reach such a conclusion. I'd heard for years of errant witnesses placing Mary Kelly alive and well hours after her alleged death, but I never put any stock into the idea until the evidence left that conclusion unavoidable. But there we have it – make of it what you will. I just hope, as we all do, that somewhere there are more unseen documents and pieces of evidence that will clarify all this. Until then, let's move onto the medical evidence from Dr Thomas Bond and Dr George Bagster Phillips.

Dr. Phillips was present at the scene and gave brief evidence at the inquest;

Mr. George Bagster Phillips: I was called by the police on Friday morning at eleven o'clock, and on proceeding to Miller's-court, which I entered at 11.15, I found a room, the door of which led out of the passage at the side of 26, Dorset-street, photographs of which I produce. It had two windows in the court. Two panes in the lesser window were broken, and as the door was locked I looked through the lower of the broken panes and satisfied myself that the mutilated corpse lying on the bed was not in need of any immediate attention from me, and I also came to the conclusion that there was nobody else upon the bed, or within view, to whom I could render any professional assistance. Having ascertained that probably it was advisable that no entrance should be made into the room at that time, I remained until about 1.30p.m., when the door was broken open by McCarthy, under the direction of Superintendent Arnold. On the door being opened it knocked against a table which was close to the left-hand side of the bedstead, and the bedstead was close against the wooden partition. The mutilated remains of a woman were lying two- thirds over, towards the edge of the bedstead, nearest the door. Deceased had only an under- linen garment upon her, and by subsequent examination I am sure the body had been removed, after the injury which caused death, from that side of the bedstead which was nearest to the wooden partition previously mentioned. The large quantity of blood under the bedstead, the saturated condition of the palliasse, pillow, and sheet at the top corner of the bedstead nearest to the partition leads me to the conclusion that the severance of the right carotid artery, which was the immediate cause of death, was inflicted while the deceased was lying at the right side of the bedstead and her head and neck in the top right-hand corner.

Dr. Phillips suggests the killer cut her right carotid artery to kill her, and that the body had been moved from where it had been when the killing occurred. Certainly, when she was found, the victim's body was lying on her back and her head was lying on the left side, her face pointing to the door. Her legs were laid open quite deliberately, and her left arm was lying across her abdomen. This tallies with the tell-tale pose the killer adopted with Annie Chapman. In her case, her legs were also parted in a suggestive way, the face turned to the right, and the left hand has been placed across the abdomen. In the Catharine Eddowes case, the killer had not placed the left arm across the abdomen, but her face was turned to the left. Also, the legs were not drawn up – however, as discussed, it is possible that the killer puncturing the bowel during the assault cut his attack short, and posing the body would likely have been his final actions at the scene. The Miller's Court scene displayed all the characteristics, though.

Next, we will consider the evidence of Dr Thomas

DANIEL JOHNSON

Bond, police surgeon. This post-mortem report was lost until 1987 when it was returned to police anonymously;

Position of body

The body was lying naked in the middle of the bed, the shoulders flat, but the axis of the body inclined to the left side of the bed. The head was turned on the left cheek. The left arm was close to the body with the forearm flexed at a right angle & lying across the abdomen. the right arm was slightly abducted from the body & rested on the mattress, the elbow bent & the forearm supine with the fingers clenched. The legs were wide apart, the left thigh at right angles to the trunk & the right forming an obtuse angle with the pubes.

The whole of the surface of the abdomen & thighs was removed & the abdominal Cavity emptied of its viscera. The breasts were cut off, the arms mutilated by several jagged wounds & the face hacked beyond recognition of the features. The tissues of the neck were severed all round down to the bone.

The viscera were found in various parts viz: the uterus & Kidneys with one breast under the head, the other breast by the Rt foot, the Liver between the feet, the intestines by the right side & the s pleen by the left side of the body. The flaps removed from the abdomen and thighs were on a table.

The bed clothing at the right corner was saturated with blood, & on the floor beneath was a pool of blood covering about 2 feet square. The wall by the right side of the bed & in a line with the neck was marked by blood

269

which had struck it in a number of spearate splashes.

Postmortem examination

The face was gashed in all directions the nose cheeks, eyebrows and ears being partly removed. The lips were blanched & cut by several incisions running obliquely down to the chin. There were also numerous cuts extending irregularly across all the features.
The neck was cut through the skin & other tissues right down to the vertebrae the 5th & 6th being deeply notched. The skin cuts in the front of the neck showed distinct ecchymosis. The air passage was cut at the lower part of the larynx through the cricoid cartilage.
Both breasts were removed by more or less circular incisions, the muscles down to the ribs being attached to the breasts. The intercostals between the 4th, 5th & 6th ribs were cut through & the contents of the thorax visible through the openings.
The skin & tissues of the abdomen from the costal arch to the pubes were removed in three large flaps. The right thigh was denuded in front to the bone, the flap of skin, including the external organs of generation & part of the right buttock. The left thigh was stripped of skin, fascia & muscles as far as the knee.
The left calf showed a long gash through skin & tissues to the deep muscles & reaching from the knee to 5 ins above the ankle.
Both arms & forearms had extensive & jagged wounds.
The right thumb showed a small superficial

incision about 1 in long, with extravasation of blood in the skin & there were several abrasions on the back of the hand moreover showing the same condition.

On opening the thorax it was found that the right lung was minimally adherent by old firm adhesions. The lower part of the lung was broken & torn away.

The left lung was intact: it was adherent at the apex & there were a few adhesions over the side. In the substaces of the lung were several nodules of consolidation.

The Pericardium was open below & the Heart absent.

In the abdominal cavity was some partially digested food of fish & potatoes & similar food was found in the remains of the stomach attached to the intestines.

It is hard to know where to begin with this evidence. Clearly the Ripper has obliterated the victim's identity as an individual but also as a woman, removing her uterus, vulva and breasts while eviscerating the body wholesale. But we must not let the daunting mess of his frenzied cuts confuse us. Let's break it down.

For starters, there is a crucial clue amid the evidence that is often overlooked; *The skin cuts in the front of the neck showed distinct ecchymosis.* This is basically bruising which, when found on the neck, is evidence of strangulation. So as with Mary Ann Nichols and Annie Chapman, here we have evidence of strangulation. After this, as Dr. Phillips suggests, she was killed with a couple of deep and swift cuts to the throat, more specifically the right carotid artery. Then, the killer moved the body into the centre of the bed to commence his further mutilations. It is likely he began with the depersonalisation of the victim – he attempted, as he did with Annie Chapman, to decapitate his victim, as shown by the "deep notches" in the 5th and 6th cervical vertebrae. He failed at this despite his time advantage, and instead attacked the victim's face. He quite literally slashed the face in all directions, removing or damaging all features. Once the face was an unrecognisable ragged mess, he turned it to the left and away from himself, and began the abdominal mutilations.

If we assume he began with a similar method as he'd applied previously, he would have begun by cutting the victim's genital and abdominal area open with long, deep, jagged slashes. From there, we can assume he simply carried on to his heart's content, removing the flesh from the thighs and genitals wholesale. He probably removed the breasts later as this behaviour was new, and he had exhausted his signature behaviours by now. The fact that strips of flesh were simply dumped on the bedside table, but the internal organs were carefully placed about the body, suggests that to begin with he dumped the contents of his victim's abdominal cavity wherever he could (the presence of considerable pools of blood at the scene would lend weight to this conclusion), moving and posing them later.

He removed the victim's intestines, spleen, liver, kidneys, uterus and stomach. The breasts, as mentioned above, were also removed. Now this is where it gets really, really weird.

This is an excerpt from the article in *The Star* newspaper on 8th September 1888 which broke the news of the murder of Annie Chapman, with customary and fictional sensationalism. The article describes the scene as being far more horrific than it actually was, and here I quote the most interesting section (emphasis in the article is mine);

> ...She was lying on her back with her legs outstretched. Her throat was cut from ear to ear. Her clothes were pushed up above her waist and her legs bare. The abdomen was exposed, the woman having been ripped up from groin to breast-bone as before. **Not only this, but the viscera had been pulled out and scattered in all directions, the heart and liver being placed behind her head, and the remainder along her side**. No more horrible sight ever met a human eye, for she was covered with blood, and lying in a pool of it, which hours afterwards had not soaked into the ground.

And again, from Dr. Thomas Bond's report of the body at the scene;

> The viscera were found in various parts viz: the uterus & Kidneys with one breast under the head, the other breast by the Rt foot, the Liver between the feet, the intestines by the right side & the s pleen by the left side of the body. The flaps removed from the abdomen and thighs were on a table.
> The bed clothing at the right corner was saturated with blood, & on the floor beneath was a pool of blood covering about 2 feet square

I'm tempted to suggest that the killer was deliberately trying to copy the news reports. Of course, I'd need to explain away the gap in time and the fact that between this newspaper article and the Miller's Court murder, there was the double event, I hear you cry! Yes, and I do have an explanation.

One of the mysteries of the Catharine Eddowes murder is why exactly the Ripper went to so much trouble to remove a kidney from her body, that is, if indeed it was the Ripper who removed that particular organ. Anyone with even basic anatomical knowledge knows just how hard the kidney is to reach from the front, particularly if your point of entry is the genitalia. The killer cut her body from the vulva upwards to the breastbone and tore out her intestines in a haphazard manner, then apparently dug about to remove the kidney. I am sceptical that the Ripper did remove the kidney in such a methodical manner, but given two pieces of evidence – first, that I have reluctantly concluded the "From Hell" letter and accompanying kidney are more likely than not to be from the killer, and second the argument I'm presenting presently – I am willing to argue in favour of the possibility for the sake of openness.

In the Catharine Eddowes case, the body was not posed in any meaningful way aside from her face being turned away following mutilation (which, as I have argued, is part of the process of depersonalisation rather than an example of posing). What the killer did accomplish was the removal of considerable lengths of intestine, the removal of the uterus and the removal of a kidney, before puncturing the bowel caused the killer to abort his mission and flee. If I am right and posing the body is the final act in his script, then he was aborted before he could even complete his mutilations on Catharine Eddowes. This means he quite possibly planned to commit even more extensive mutilations at the scene. And stage one, it seems, was the removal of multiple organs, possibly to re-enact that *Star* article as he would later at Miller's Court, only his clumsiness interrupted his plans.

In short, the killer seems to have planned to empty out his victim and scatter the organs in the way this news story describes way back with the Catharine Eddowes murder.

Of course, the scene at Miller's Court is not an exact replica. Behind the victim's head were not the heart and liver, but tellingly, the kidneys and uterus. The two organs the killer had taken from Catharine Eddowes. It is a knowing wink-and-nod by the killer to his earlier work. He is planning his crimes, fantasising about his scenes, trying to manipulate what the responders will see, getting off on the horror they will witness. He is proud of his work, showing off and boasting of his kills. He is posing the bodies in two main ways; personally relevant ways, as with the depersonalisation actions, and in spectacular ways, by posing the victims in a sexually degrading way and by scattering the organs to mimic lurid press reports. This tells us he is at least semi-literate, which reinforces the idea of him writing the "From Hell" letter. It tells us he reads the press and reacts to it, which may explain why he targeted George Lusk and why he was willing to move his murders indoors to avoid the increasing police presence and jittery public, not to mention Vigilance Committees.

The victim's hand showed evidence of injury, too, and we know the victim cried out "Murder!" as the attack commenced. Therefore, she put up a fight. This is likely because the killer was forced to attack her from the front rather than from behind due to the change in circumstances from his previous victims. Nevertheless, he was able to subdue her, strangle her, and cut her throat just as rapidly as with other victims. But it is at least a small victory that she was able to fight back momentarily.

The viciousness of the victims' mutilations often clouds the judgement of commentators, who in a panic declare the killer must have gone totally mad to commit these acts, or that more than one person "must" have been responsible, but the truth is somewhat banal. The killer simply had private space and all the time he wanted to indulge himself. A similar argument can be made for the killers of Jamie Bulger in 1996. Reading the litany of horrendous acts carried out by those two boys upon their young victim is enough to make your stomach churn, and it is easy to assume that they went into that situation with their attack somehow preplanned. But reading the acts in context, I realised that this was a stream-of-consciousness sequence of events. Ideas would pop up and the boys would try it. By the end, you have a horrible accumulation of violent acts, some quite bizarre and all cruel. This does not excuse their actions by any measure, but provides context for them. And just the same is true with Jack the Ripper's final canonical victim – alone with his victim, he simply indulged himself over the course of possibly two hours. In his previous murders, he'd been alone with his victim for a matter of minutes, not enough to live out every fantasy. The indoor location of Miller's Court was a welcome opportunity for him.

We shall return now to the inquest testimony. The rest of the testimony was given by Maria Harvey and Julia Van Turney, and provide nothing of substance. Inspector Beck makes a brief appearance, but the only noteworthy appearance left is by Inspector Abberline, who notes there were women's clothes burning in the grate, presumably so the killer could see what he was doing. After his testimony, the Coroner told the jury no further proceedings were necessary as this was not a prosecution and the court merely had to decide on the cause of death. Duly, the jury ruled murder against some person or persons unknown.

The Miller's Court victim, whether it was Mary Jane Kelly or not, was buried in a communal grave at Walthamstow Roman Catholic Cemetery. Despite the global publicity the case gathered, no family were traced, and none attended the burial. I cannot resist the temptation to suggest that they did not attend because Mary Jane Kelly was alive and well and living in hiding with said family in Ireland. However, the explanation for her fate which I favour is far stranger as you shall see.

In an interesting development in 2017, plans to exhume the remains of Mary Jane Kelly, to carry out a DNA test to settle the claims of Dr. Wyne Weston-Davis who wished to prove Mary as his long-lost great-great-grandmother, failed. It was decided it would be impossible to identify her remains after so much time, and that it would involve digging through communal graves requiring the consent of multiple next-of-kin who would likely be impossible to trace. I can only imagine the worldwide reaction if researchers ever managed to locate documentation relating to Mary Kelly's family, trace her latter-day relations, then test the DNA of the Miller's Court victim in the grave and proved the victim to not in fact be Mary Jane Kelly. It would blow the world of Ripperology off its feet.

Conclusions

This case has been one of the most confusing, complex, bizarre and thought-provoking I've ever come across. I assumed it would be a short-and-sweet chapter to write, with such a rapid inquest, hearsay information on Mary's background, and a handful of witnesses. Instead, I have with great reluctance found myself considering a theory I had poured scorn on for years; that the Miller's Court victim was not Mary Jane Kelly, and that she likely found the body and fled in terror.

Mary Jane Kelly is a woman we know virtually nothing about. No documentary evidence exists to corroborate the story of her life provided by Joseph Barnett. He is not to be trusted either, given that he is potentially a killer or a liar concealing his wife's survival. The presence or absence of a child in Mary Kelly's life cannot be verified. Her movements potentially put her having a night on the lash with Jack the Ripper shortly before his next victim is murdered in her own home. And most critically, the murder at Miller's Court is the fullest and most telling expression of the serial killer's depraved psychopathy.

In one final twist to this case, on the 10th November 1888 a pardon was offered in the case of accomplices of the killer, specifically in the Miller's Court case. Prior to this, the notion of handing out pardons was to be limited to those who had no hand in the crime, as explained in this piece in the *Morning Advertiser* dated 15th October 1888;

> The following communication has been received by Mr. Lusk, of 1, Alderney-road, Mile-end, from the Home Office, Whitehall, in answer to his recent letter asking that a free pardon might be proclaimed to an accomplice or accomplices of the murder:-"October 12, 1888.-Sir,-I am desired by the Secretary of State to thank you for the suggestions in your letter of the 7th inst. on the subject of the recent

Whitechapel murders, and to say in reply that, from the first, the Secretary of State has had under consideration the question of granting a pardon to accomplices. It is obvious that not only must such a grant be limited to persons who have not been concerned in contriving, or in actually committing the murders, but the expediency and propriety of making the offer must largely depend on the nature of the information received from day to day, which is being carefully watched, with a view to determining that question. With regard to the offer of a reward, Mr. Matthews has, under the existing circumstances, nothing to add to his former letter.-I am, Sir, your obedient servant, GODFREY LUSHINGTON."

Following the Miller's Court murder came this official statement (quoted from *The Munster News*, an Irish newspaper 10th November 1888);

"MURDER - PARDON"

"WHEREAS on November 8th or 9th in Miller Court street, Spitalfields, Mary Jane Kelly was murdered by some person or persons unknown, the Secretary of State will advise the granting of Her Majesty's gracious pardon to any accomplice not being the person who contrived or actually committed the murder, who shall give such evidence as shall lead to the discovery and conviction of the person or persons who committed the murder."

"Signed) CHARLES WARREN"

The details of why this pardon was offered were elaborated upon by Home Secretary Henry Matthews in a statement to the Commons (*The Times*, 24th November 1888);

> ...In the case of Kelly there were certain circumstances which were wanting in the earlier cases, and which made it more probable that there were other persons who, at any rate after the crime, had assisted the murderer.

It can be assumed that the "circumstanced which were wanting" could be that the murder took place at an extended period indoors, meaning the killer may have required a lookout, despite no witnesses offering anything in the way of evidence to this conclusion. Or, possibly, due to the extremely bloody crime scene, the Ripper would certainly have needed to escape with bloody clothes, and it could be argued that escaping in a carriage would make sense in this regard.

Either way, no such pardon was ever granted to anyone and no rewards ever paid out. But it does suggest that potentially, the police had more evidence regarding the Miller's Court case than they ever let on.

The "Apocryphal" Victims

All in all, up to 11 murders are linked to the Ripper outrage. Sometimes, these fluctuating numbers are down to careful, reasoned argument. Often, it is inflated by wishful thinking on the part of those crime buffs who are less interested in treating the case seriously as they are maintaining the story – and this often allows the accommodation of as many alleged victims as the writer can shoehorn into the narrative. I have termed these murders "Apocryphal" to contrast the use of the phrase "Canonical" in discussing the five murders most often linked to the Ripper.

Here I will briefly discuss the four murders most often linked to the case.

Emma Elizabeth Smith

On 3rd April 1888, 45-year-old Emma Elizabeth Smith was attacked by a gang of three men, one of them estimated to be only around 18-years-old, in a savage assault that included the assailants object-raping her. The force of the attack tore her vagina and perineum and left her dazed, bruised and bleeding at the door of her lodging house, where the deputy of the lodge found her and took her to hospital.

She fell into a coma and died from her injuries a few days later. This attack, despite being entirely unlike the others, is optimistically linked to the Ripper murders by some presumably because of the assault upon her genitals. It is widely considered the word of a notorious street gang known as the Old Nichols Gang. Nobody was ever arrested for the murder.

Martha Tabram

On 7th August 1888, at 4:45am, the body of a woman was found in a pool of blood lying in the doorway of the George's Yard building, Wentworth Street by one of the residents, John Sanders Reeves. She had been stabbed repeatedly and left to die. Reeves called for a police officer and quickly the police surgeon was on scene to pronounce death.

The woman proved to be that of Martha Tabram, a 39-year-old prostitute who lived just around the corner at 19 George Street. She had been separated from her husband Henry Tabram for 13 years and was in an on-off relationship with one William Turner, although her heavy drinking had put paid to that coupling within the previous few weeks too. Both seemed unaware she was a sex worker. Now her only true friend was a woman named Mary Ann Connelly, who went by the nickname "Pearly Poll."

Both women had been out drinking the previous night and had last seen each other at around 11:45pm after picking up a pair of soldiers at The Two Brewers pub, according to Poll, a Corporal and a Private. Poll took her soldier, the Corporal, into an alleyway called Angel Alley, whilst Martha took the Private into George's Yard, where her body would later be found.

Dr. Timothy Killeen conducted the post-mortem on her body once it was found. There was huge dissimilarity between this attack and the rest, however. Unlike the other Whitechapel murders, Martha had been repeatedly stabbed with a penknife in a frenzy, whilst the other victims had been subject to slashing wounds inflicted in stages. A wound in the chest was singled out as being caused by a bayonet, although Trevor Marriott argues that the wound caused by a regular knife, as caused the other wounds, would be split by the softer skin to resemble that of a dagger (Marriott, 2005, p.13-14). The body also showed signs of sexual intercourse having taken place during the attack, again unlike the other attacks. However, this was only assumed as the victim's clothes were cast open as with the other victims.

The attack was focused on Martha's vital organs but also targeted her beasts, throat and genitals, although nowhere near to the extent to suggest a deviant hand such as the Ripper. It was an "overkill" attack but not one motivated by a highly developed sexual fantasy as with the Ripper's murders. The question was asked later as to whether this murder could be the work of the Ripper, and although the press immediately linked it, experts and police officers were divided on the issue.

Dr. Robert Anderson and Inspector Frederick Abberline both believed her to be a Ripper victim, but Sir Melville Macnaghten firmly refuted the notion. In his notorious Memorandum, which we will discuss later, Macnaghten stated there were "five victims [and] five victims only" and that these were the so-called Canonical Five as we know them (Mary Ann Nichols, Annie

Chapman, Elizabeth Stride, Catharine Eddowes, Mary Jane Kelly), and attacks Pearly Poll for "failing or refusing" to identify the soldier Martha was with. This is a reference to Pearly Poll being taken to identify the soldiers she and Martha picked up that night by visiting Wellington Barracks, but failing to provide accurate information or confidently identify the individuals she was presented with.

Most commentators are weary of placing too much stock in the idea that Martha Tabram was a Ripper victim. In many ways, her victimhood is tempting to consider; murders were relatively rare even in the brutal East End, and Martha's murder came at a time where there was a sudden spree. She was a prostitute, and she was in the same age range as the other victims, excluding the Miller's Court victim. The fact she was knifed to death in such a brutal way also warrants consideration, given how serial killers evolve over time. But, consider this; we're meant to believe a serial killer goes from such a messy, frenzied stabbing attack to the clinical assassination and evisceration of his victims within the space of little under five weeks? Even taking the tentative wounds in the Polly Nichols murder as evidence of the killer's nerves and inexperience rather than the situation limiting his freedom to act out his fantasies, it is still a radically different method of attack. The only saving grace for those who suggest Martha was a Ripper victim is a throwaway remark in *Illustrated News* suggesting she was throttled, although no medical evidence or testimony backs this up.

I am curious about this murder, and given it is by far the most widely connected "Apocryphal" Murder to the Ripper case I will refer to it occasionally. However, the jury is still out on this one. It certainly would fit the pattern of a serial killer escalating in brutality but without additional evidence it is hard to tell if it is the work of the Ripper or not.

Alice McKenzie

The case of "Clay Pipe" Alice McKenzie is the only one of these few apocryphal murders that I am curious about as a potential Ripper victim. The method of attack and the scene itself bear a superficial resemblance to the murders of Polly Nichols and Catharine Eddowes, although in this case the mutilations are extremely tentative. Given that the Ripper's previous crime was the horrid mutilations at Miller's Court eight months previously, this is one hell of a come-down.

On 17th July 1889, PC Joseph Allen and PC Walter Andrews were covering the beat around Castle Alley, a street running just off Commercial Street and Whitechapel High Street, right in the heart of the area the Ripper committed his earlier murders. At 12:20am and 12:30am they saw nothing but upon returning at 12:55am found the body of 44-year-old Alice McKenzie lying in a pool of blood beneath a street lamp. She'd been stabbed in the neck, and her killer had tried to slash her throat – indeed, her cause of death was the severance of the left carotid artery as with the other victims, although in this case none of the wounds were anywhere near as deep. Her clothes had been pulled up to her chin and she'd been slashed and stabbed in the abdomen and genitals. Bruising on her chest suggested she'd been pushed to the ground and held there as her attacker commenced his attack. Superficial wounds around her pubis were found to be from the killer's fingernails as he clawed her undergarments away, and a seven-inch slash between her left breast and navel recall the long slashes made by the Ripper.

Another interesting piece of evidence was the presence of farthings found at the scene, as they were at the Annie Chapman scene. If this was the Ripper, this could be another aspect of his signature. Then again, it could simply be dropped coins.

Dr Phillips, Dr Bond, and Dr. Robert Anderson all disagree about whether her murder was carried out by the Ripper. Dr. Phillps said this;

> After careful and long deliberation, I cannot satisfy myself, on purely Anatomical and professional grounds that the perpetrator of all the "Wh Ch. murders" is our man. I am on the contrary impelled to a contrary conclusion in this noting the mode of procedure and the character of the mutilations and judging of motive in connection with the latter

Dr Thomas Bond's comments are quite to the contrary and to be frank, somewhat bizarre;

> I see in this murder evidence of similar design to the former Whitechapel murders, viz. sudden onslaught on the prostrate woman, the throat skillfully and resolutely cut with subsequent mutilation, each mutilation indicating sexual thoughts and a desire to mutilate the abdomen and sexual organs. I am of opinion that the murder was performed by the same person who committed the former series of Whitechapel murder.

"[T]hroat skillfully and resolutely cut?" Alice McKenzie had been stabbed twice, the wounds dragged across by the killer, and a slash added across the neck. Compare to the Ripper murders where the killer could silence and kill his victims with two slashes that cut all the way through all structures of the throat to the bone itself. And although I agree that on an extremely superficial level the Alice McKenzie mutilations are of a sexual nature, they are nowhere near the level of the Ripper's desire to obliterate the human being in front of him – to depersonalise, disassemble and pose her for shock value. The question dangling in front of us is why there was such a decline in the killer's skill and degree of destruction compared to not just the Miller's Court murder, but the general trend of his previous murders becoming increasingly grisly.

Met Police Commissioner James Munro unerringly stated the murder to be that of Jack the Ripper. Anderson disagreed.

All in all, there are broad similarities (a prostitute victim in her 40s, cuts to the throat, abdomen and genitals) but specific differences that make it unlikely to be a Ripper murder (no evidence of asphyxia, cuts are extremely shallow and disorganised, no posing of the body, attack in a well-lit area rather than dark corner as with Annie and Elizabeth). By the time this murder took place, the popular press would have gushed over every aspect of the crimes, so a copycat would know broadly what to do to mimic the Ripper's crimes. The tentative nature of the wounds suggests just that. However, if ever it came to light that the actual Ripper likely suffered some degenerative illness during his last days, and this limited his capacity to kill as effectively, I would not be at all surprised if the Alice McKenzie murder was reconsidered a Ripper crime.

Frances Coles

Frances Coles was only 23-years-old when she was killed on 13th February 1891. Her throat was cut by an attacker who fled following the immediate arrival of a police officer who would have captured the culprit had he ignored his training to stay with the body.

She was found by PC Ernest Thompson in a dark spot in Swallow Gardens far to the south of Whitechapel High Street; she'd been thrown to the ground and her throat cut across three times, with no further molestation or mutilation taking place. A man named James Thomas Sadler was arrested and charged with her murder but freed when the best witness to the case, a man named William "Jumbo" Friday was discredited. Later, it emerged that despite having spent time in Frances' company in the days leading up to her murder, he had an alibi – even a credible explanation for wounds and bloodstains on his person! He had been in a series of fights that night and thus, his actions were accounted for satisfactorily.

Afterwards, the police were still convinced of Sadler's guilt, although at the time of the murder, the idea of Frances Coles' murder being a Ripper crime was taken very seriously, with Sir Robert Anderson, Chief Inspector Swanson and Melville Macnaghten all attending the scene. Swanson would be the only one to believe this was a Ripper crime, and although Thomas Sadler was arrested, charged and acquitted, her murderer was never identified.

PART TWO: Truth, Lies, and Conspiracy

Kosminski: The Police's Suspect

Numerous sources point to the widespread, though not universally accepted, belief within the Metropolitan Police that the Ripper was a lunatic Polish Jew who'd ended his days in an asylum – a belief held by the top brass and one which eventually became the Yard's official position on the matter. However, the true story is a mess, a confusing and controversial mix of fact, speculation and contradiction.

Much of the work on this "Polish Jew suspect" narrative has been done by the esteemed Martin Fido, a giant in Ripperology circles and a man whose contributions are the result of hard work, steadfast research and above all, pragmatism. His book on the subject, a labour of love and a seminal text on the Ripper crimes is the 1987 tome, *The Crimes, Detection and Death of Jack the Ripper.* In this, (and the 1999 compilation *The Mammoth Book of Jack the Ripper* by Jakubowski and Braund [eds]) Fido outlines his own theory based on the scant evidence available, concluding that a case of mistaken identity may have led to the wrong man – a poor Polish Jew named Aaron Kosminski – getting the blame for crimes he did not commit. My theory differs from Fido's in many ways, but either way his findings are irreplaceable in the field and I doff my hat to him.

I debated whether to lead with the "conspiracy" line in this book, and whether to make a big deal of the Kosminski line either, but in the end, I realised that they are integral parts of history. I must give all credit to Mr. Fido as he appears to be the first, and only, serious historian to investigate these strands of evidence and consequently my inclusion of this information in this book relies heavily upon his work. I have cited him on every occasion I draw upon his work and I recommend readers check out his writings for themselves.

With that context, I think we should begin with a brief overview of this theory.

The story of the mysterious Jewish suspect began with rumours in the 1890s, and judging by the comments made by Asst. Commissioner Sir Robert Anderson in his memoirs (as we shall see), his focus on this "solution" during the investigation was more than likely the reason. After door-to-door inquiries and discreet investigations into lodging houses following the death of Annie Chapman and continuing until early-October, Sir Robert returned to London and took charge of the Ripper investigation. He claims that following consultation with the top brass at the CID, the result of these searches was that the killer was certainly a low-class Jew whose occupation allowed him to come and go without notice and allowed him to clean up following his murders. With this conclusion in mind, and bearing in mind the sustained pressure from various quarters – not least Sir Charles Warren – he pressed ahead looking for his Jewish suspect. According to Sir Robert, at some time following the murder of the Miller's Court victim (which he considered the final Ripper crime), a suspect was identified. Whilst in an asylum, this low-class Jewish man was positively identified by "the only man to ever get a good look at the killer," an apparently Jewish witness who then refused to swear that he was the killer because he was also Jewish. Sir Robert leaves it at that.

The pot is sweetened by the discovery of the McNaughton Memoranda. Public reporting of its contents began in 1959, and the full publication of the documents came about in 1975. Written by the then-Chief Constable, Melville Macnaghten, three copies are known to have existed, two of which still exist and a third is lost. Essentially, they are drafts of a confidential report, written squarely to exonerate a suspect – a man named Thomas Cutbush – who was named by *The Sun* newspaper in 1894. Call me a cynic, but it is no small coincidence that Cutbush was the son of a police officer. These memoranda are crucial because they offer two things – the first recorded time the name "Kosminski" is named in relation to the Ripper crimes, and second, a clue to how widespread the "Polish Jewish lunatic" narrative is within the police. Macnaghten goes to great lengths to attack each and every aspect of what has subsequently been determined to be the narrative in question. Perhaps the most telling aspect of these documents is that in the third, and lost copy, the name "Kosminski" is spelled differently. Various recollections have been reported, one of which is "Kaminsky." Keep that in mind for later, folks, as well as the memoranda's' take on this Kosminski character – reporting him across the various versions as a homicidal Jewish cobbler with a hatred for women, and as the man believed to be "Leather Apron." He reports in these memos that the man Kosminski was detained in an asylum "around March 1889" and is still there as of the writing of the memos. A note of caution must be sounded when discussing Macnaghten's contribution to the case, however – he was not involved in the investigation, and arrived on the scene only after the case was cold. His knowledge is, as he admits, second-hand, and his recollections of even the facts he should know is demonstrably faulty.

The story does not stop there. Martin Fido was the first to link Anderson's Jewish suspect with Macnaghten's Kosminski, and this spurred him on. During his work on his seminal book, he was party to a final and crucial, if confusing, piece of evidence; the so-called "Swanson Marginalia." Handwritten in pencil in the margins and endpapers of Chief Inspector Donald Swanson's personal copy of Sir Robert Anderson's memoirs, *The Lighter Side of My Official Life,* are Swanson's own corrections, comments, annotations and memories. These include his comments on Anderson's Jewish suspect. There is no longer any reasonable doubt as to their authenticity. The comments he makes endorses Anderson's claim that the Jewish witness refused to testify against a fellow Jew (a claim hotly disputed by his contemporaries, who accuse him of rash and offensive comments and conduct), and they explain that the suspect was identified at "The Seaside Home", a convalescent home for injured police officers in Brighton, whereupon he was taken to his brother's care, and was watched round-the-clock by City CID. Eventually Swanson claims he was carted away with his hands bound to "Stepney Workhouse," and finally to Colney Hatch Lunatic Asylum where he died shortly afterwards. Indeed, Swanson can be quoted by the *Pall Mall Gazette* on 7th May 1895 as saying he believed the Ripper crimes to be the work of a man "now dead." Crucially, at the very end of his notes, Swanson appears initially to be the second independent source to use the name, stating, "Kosminski was the suspect."

The problems arise when trying to determine the exact sequence of events, and why the identification is described as having been organised "with difficulty." Also problematic is the fact that "Stepney Workhouse" never existed, and that the term probably refers to multiple 19th Century workhouses, including Mile End Old Town Workhouse. The Swanson Marginalia are infuriatingly incomplete, confusing and tantalising in equal measure. Notes scribbled in margins that could have cleared everything up actually muddy the waters – his mention of the involvement of the City Police in this identification process are infuriating when you realise the entire City Police archives were destroyed in the firebombing of London during the Second World War. As a result, the Marginalia, as with all this evidence, is up for interpretation.

Don't worry, you will have the chance to review these pieces of evidence in their entirety yourself, with relevant context. But this overview gives you an idea of the key pieces of evidence that appear to point to a widespread conclusion among the highest-ranking police of the time; either the killer was, or was believed to be, a Polish Jewish maniac named Kosminski, who was a homicidal, misogynistic cobbler known as Leather Apron. A man who was locked in an asylum and died soon afterwards.

The truth, however, is far less clear-cut than that.

"A Definitely Ascertained Fact": Anderson's Suspect

Dr (later Sir) Robert Anderson was a key figure in the

Ripper investigation as Assistant Commissioner of the CID and a distinguished figure in his own right. A barrister, a former secret service man involved in the fight against Fenian terrorists, and a noted writer and theologian, he was jack of all trades and a master of most of them. His autobiography, *The Lighter Side of My Official Life*, is available to read on the casebook.org website having passed into the public domain many years ago, and is a fascinating insight into his recollections of a long life well lived. Fido (1987) provides an excellent biographical account of Anderson, and I recommend it heartily. However, it is Anderson's role in the Ripper murders, particularly in the emerging truth in the years following the crimes, that are the focus of this chapter.

Sir Robert retired from the Metropolitan Police in 1901 after spending the last 13 years of his career as Assistant Commissioner, and would be appointed the prestigious titles of Companion of the Order of Bath (CB) and Knight Commander of the Order of Bath (KCB). Nine years after his retirement, he published the memoir at around the same time as another key figure; Melville Macnaghten published *Days of My Years* in 1914. In both memoirs, the writers attempt to lay to rest the case of Jack the Ripper.

Anderson claimed to know the Ripper's identity as a "definitely ascertained fact" on several occasions, two of them will be examined here; the first was in his book *Criminals and Crime* (1907), and the second in his memoirs. Not only did he claim that the killer's identity was known, but that the offender had been locked away in an asylum many years prior and the case was so neatly wrapped up it barely merited attention any more. In his writing, he speaks of the Whitechapel Murders with a snide tone that seem to me to be a man having to drag it up and talk about it because the readers expect it. There is no mystery in Anderson's eyes – the case was closed, and the killer dealt with.

Here is the except from *Criminals and Crime:*

"At that time the sensation-mongers of the newspaper press fostered the belief that life in London was no longer safe and that no women ought to venture abroad in the streets after nightfall. And one enterprising journalist went so far as to impersonate the cause of all this terror as Jack the Ripper, a name by which he will probably go down in history. But no amount of silly hysterics could alter he fact that these crimes were a cause of danger only to a particular section of a small and definite class of women, in a limited district of the East End, and that the inhabitants of the metropolis generally were just as secure during the weeks the fiend was on the prowl as they were before the mania seized him or after he had been safely caged in an asylum."

In these few lines he gives away several important things; first, that a journalist was believed responsible for the Jack the Ripper letters, and second that the killer had been "safely caged in an asylum." No details, no explanation, nothing. He just states it as fact. Now, as we have seen, the Dear Boss letter and probably most of the follow-up letters, including the Saucy Jacky postcard, were more than likely the work of *The Star* journalist Frederick Best and his colleagues, and it is clear from the hilariously over the top prose provided by said newspaper on the case that the papers were indeed blowing the thing up like murder was going out of fashion. But to state in passing that the killer was locked in an asylum?

Anderson famously went into further detail about this mysterious suspect in his memoirs. In Ripperology there is a continuing argument over the identity of two figures; Anderson's suspect and the witness who identified him, both Jewish according to Anderson. The suspect is, of course, the more contentious of the two figures to attribute an identity, but not so the witness. There are only three possible Jewish witnesses each of them during the double event; Israel Schwartz, Joseph Hyam Levy and Joseph Lawende. I suspect those eager to point to Schwartz are just trying to do one of two things; head-off accusations that Elizabeth Stride wasn't a Ripper victim (as I have argued, she wasn't), or to plug a conspiracy theory involving multiple assailants. They ignore that Joseph Lawende's description of the man he saw at Mitre Square was considered of utmost importance and withheld from the inquest into Catharine Eddowes' death, or that he was at least twice called to identify potential Ripper suspects by police. However, Joseph Hyam Levy is equally likely to have been the witness Anderson mentions, as his personal connections to suspects and to the wider context of what happened during the investigation cannot be underestimated.

Let us examine the passage in *The Lighter Side of My Official Life* that brought these figures to the world:

> During my absence abroad, the Police had made a house-to-house search for him, investigating the case of every man in the district whose circumstances were such that he could go and come an get rid of his blood-stains in secret. And the conclusion we came to was that he and his people were certain low-

class Polish Jews; for it is a remarkable fact that people of that class in the East End will not give up one of their number to justice.

And the result proved that our diagnosis was right on every count. For I may say at once that "undiscovered murders" are rare in London and that the Jack-the-Ripper murders are not within that category [...] I will only add here that the Jack-the-Ripper letter which is preserved in the Police Museum at New Scotland Yard is the creation of an enterprising London journalist.

Having regard to the interest attached to this case, I am almost tempted to disclose the identity of the murderer and the pressman who wrote the letter above referred to...I will merely add that the only person who ever saw the murderer unhesitatingly identified the suspect the instant he was presented with him, but he refused to give evidence against him.

In stating that he was Polish Jew I am merely stating a definitely ascertained fact.

In a serialised version of his memoirs in *Blackwood's Magazine*, Anderson says this;

I will only add that when the individual whom we suspected was caged in an asylum, the only person who ever had a good view of the murderer at once identified him, but when he learned that the suspect was a fellow-Jew he declined to swear to him.

So, let is break down the claims made by Anderson. First, he claims that prior to his arrival back from extended leave on 6th October 1888, whereupon he took his place at the helm of the Ripper investigation, door-to-door searches had taken place to find anyone who could have come or gone with blood on them. For starters, as you may recall, Inspector Collard gave the following evidence at the inquest into the death of Catharine Eddowes;

> ...Mr. M'Williams, chief of the Detective Department, on arriving shortly afterwards sent men to search in all directions in Spitalfields, both in streets and lodging-houses. Several men were stopped and searched in the streets, without any good result. I have had a house-to-house inquiry made in the vicinity of Mitre-square as to any noises or whether persons were seen in the place; but I have not been able to find any beyond the witnesses who saw a man and woman talking together.

This was in the early hours of 30th September 1888 following the double-event, and it lead to the identification of "the witnesses who saw a man and woman talking together." Of course, at this inquest we heard from Joseph Lawende and Joseph Hyam Levy, both Jewish men who were leaving a Jewish club when they spotted a man with a woman Lawende later identified as Catharine Eddowes. But there were of course extensive house-to-house enquiries during the Ripper outrage, starting after the Annie Chapman murder and continuing in fits and starts until after the Miller's Court murder, the police distributing flyers and searching lodging houses, etc., and an important observation must be noted about

them; Fido (p. 173-4) quotes Swanson on the range of all
of the searches from the Annie Chapman murder until
after the double event; they extended across the area of
Whitechapel that included the majority of the Jewish
population centred on Wentworth Street. I believe these
searches, directed by Swanson as head of the
investigation until Anderson's return in October, are the
key to understanding the importance of their Jewish
suspect theory.

Now, as I mentioned, we know that Joseph
Lawende's description was treat with the utmost
seriousness, and was withheld from the inquest testimony
for that reason (despite it being reported in the press, of
course). But we also know he was called by police to
identify possible Ripper suspects at least twice. I promised
to explain, and now I will. In 1891 23-year-old Frances
Coles was found with her throat cut, and a violent
seaman, Thomas Sadler, was charged with her murder,
although later acquitted. At the time, the top brass took
the idea of this being a new Ripper murder very seriously.
A witness, certainly either Joseph Lawende or Joseph
Hyam Levy, was asked to identify Sadler as the man he
saw in Mitre Square. Here is the report from *The Daily
Telegraph*, 18th February 1891;

> Probably the only trustworthy description of
> the assassin was given by a gentleman who, on
> the night of the Mitre-Square murder, noticed
> in Duke Street, Aldgate, a couple standing
> under the lamp at the corner of the passage
> leading to Mitre-Square. The woman was
> identified as the victim of that night, September
> 30, the other having been killed half an hour
> previously in Berner-Street. The man was

described as aged from thirty to thirty-five, height 5ft 7in, with brown hair and big moustache; dressed respectively. Wore pea jacket, muffler, and a cloth cap with a peak of the same material. The witness has confronted Sadler but has failed to identify him

A fact many commentators point out with good reason is that an eyewitness who could potentially convict a man of murder in the 19th Century would be putting the man to his death. It is more than likely that a witness would be unwilling to hammer the last nail in a man's coffin, and therefore the witness' unwillingness to identify the alleged Jewish suspect Anderson describes, or Thomas Sadler whether he recognised him or not, shouldn't be unexpected. It has subsequently been proven that Sadler could not have been the Ripper, his movements are accounted for quite reliably, but nevertheless it is possible when the report says the witness "failed" to identify Sadler he was in fact refusing point-blank. But that was only the first occasion he was called in.

In 1895 a man named William Grant Grainger was arrested for the slashing of a prostitute named Alice Graham. She had been brutalised in her genitals and abdomen by a knife after apparently trying to rob Grainger during a sexual encounter. The news of a man feared to the Ripper being caught at least hit newspaper stands across the world and on 23rd March 1895 William Grainger was convicted of malicious wounding and sentenced to 10 years penal servitude. In an article dated 7th May 1895, the *Pall Mall Gazette* reported;

There is one person whom the police believe to have actually seen the Whitechapel Murderer

with a woman a few minutes before that
woman's dissected body was found in the
street. That person is stated to have identified
Grainger as the man he then saw...

Given the clues in the previous case, this is evidently
Lawende. And in this case, he is stated to have "identified
Grainger as the man he saw." Bear in mind that this is
1895, and back in 1888, only a few days since the
Catharine Eddowes murder, Lawende said on the stand
that he was unlikely to recognise the man he saw again.
As for the role this could play in this theory, in the very
same article Swanson is quoted as saying he believed the
Ripper to already be dead.

Nevertheless, here we appear to have tentatively
identified our Jewish witness: Joseph Lawende – although
as I said earlier, Joseph Hyam Levy plays a key role which
means we cannot rule him out as the witness either.

As for the suspect, Anderson provides few clues. A
low-class Polish Jew, whose occupation allowed him to
come and go unnoticed and clean up his bloodstains in
secret. One who was locked in an asylum after the
murders. More information is given in the so-called
Macnaghten Memoranda.

The Macnaghten Memoranda

The earliest known mention of a man named
"Kosminski" as a suspect in the Jack the Ripper case is in
the Macnaghten Memoranda, at least three versions of
which exist, and which first came to public attention in
1959. Two versions are still in existence – the "Lady
Aberconway" version and the "Scotland Yard" version, so
named because the former, a handwritten transcription

from original documents, was made public whilst in the possession of 2nd Baroness Christabel Mary Aberconway, Macnaghten's daughter, and made public in 1959 by Daniel Farson. The latter was among Scotland Yard files and was discovered by Donald Rumbelow in 1975. A third has been described but never located. Finding it would be invaluable since it reportedly spells the name of the suspect "Kosminski" differently, and this could be vital in solving the mystery.

Written by Chief Constable Melville Macnaghten after the 13th February 1894 in response to the naming of Thomas Cutbush (nephew of a superintendent) as a Ripper suspect by *The Sun* newspaper, the documents go to great lengths to exonerate Cutbush, the argument taking up almost four out of seven pages in the Lady Aberconway version, and more in the Scotland Yard version. This is no surprise – I suspect the creation of this document was almost certainly politically-motivated. However, of more importance, is the latter halves of the documents describing three suspects Macnaghten considers "more likely than Cutbush to have been the Ripper." His favoured candidate is barrister Montague Druitt, who was found dead in the Thames some time after the Miller's Court murder. However, of far more interest are the two others; Russian criminal Michael Ostrog, and low-class Polish Jew "Kosminski."

What is fascinating about the documents is not the expansive deconstruction of the case against Cutbush, nor the error-laden recital of the crimes, but the bias of the argument. Take for example the apparent randomness of the selection of Ostrog. Despite the Russian crook being labelled by Macnaghten "a homicidal maniac," a quick check of his criminal past shows him to be a thief and a con artist, but that's about it. Oddly enough, being a known habitual criminal who was indeed "on the loose" in Whitechapel during 1888 – apparently his only qualifying feature as a remotely plausible Ripper suspect – he therefore stands a better chance of being the Ripper than Macnaghten's clearly demarcated prime suspect, Montague Druitt. Even back in 1894, Macnaghten could have had his pick of far more plausible suspects than either of these two to set up and knock down in the Memoranda, a fact he even admits when he suggests a great many "homicidal lunatics" were considered at one time or another. This brings me of course to "Kosminski," here labelled as having "strong homicidal tendencies," yet just as quickly dismissed in favour of Druitt. The difference between Ostrog and Kosminski is however, that Macnaghten apparently goes to great lengths to dismiss Kosminski's candidacy in particular.

Let's take a look at what the documents have to say about the Ripper, and the suspects, and I will explain as we go the telling details that I believe, help us to unpick the Kosminski case (quoted portions are concurrent and are taken from the Lady Aberconway version);

> [...]A much more rational and workable theory, to my way of thinking, is that the rippers brain gave way altogether after his awful glut in Miller's Court, and that he then committed suicide, or as a less likely alternative, was found to be so helplessly insane by his relatives that they, suspecting the worst, had him confined in some Lunatic Asylum.

Why leap to the conclusion, as if it is the most likely one, that the killer committed suicide versus the very specific suggestion that the killer was confined by his family to a lunatic asylum? Why bring the suggestion of an asylum up at all? Clearly, he is referring to a specific narrative his intended audience is aware of. This is a point I will revisit.

> No-one ever saw the Whitechapel murderer (unless it was possibly the City PC who was a beat near Mitre Square) and no proof could in any way be brought against anyone, although a great many homicidal maniacs were at one time, or another, suspected.

Hold on – nobody ever saw the killer? No proof could ever be brought against anyone? He appears to have forgotten about several witnesses who are widely considered to have definitely seen the killer shortly before the murders with the victims – for example, Joseph Lawende, who we've discussed, and Elizabeth Darrell who saw Annie Chapman with the killer at the entrance to 29 Hanbury Street. In fact, this comment about the "City PC near Mitre Square" seems to imply this very sighting.

So important was Lawende's evidence that the description he gave was withheld from the inquiry. This information is a matter of public record, and yet here we have an official document written by a chief constable stating that not only is it very unlikely that the killer was committed to an asylum, (but far more likely that he killed himself), that nobody ever saw the killer, and that no proof existed at all that could be brought against any suspect. It is here that he suggests, offhand, that many "homicidal maniacs" were variously considered and dismissed as suspects. Absolute statements and offhand vagary seem to mix in the Memoranda to both make the case for Macnaghten's prime suspect, and bury "Kosminski." A little too hard in my opinion. Also, the suggestion that "a City PC" was a witness at Mitre Square is curious. A workable hypothesis is that he is mixing his Double Event details up, as a Metropolitan, not City, officer, PC William Smith, did witness Elizabeth Stride with a man shortly before her murder, and in the Scotland Yard version of the memoranda, Macnaghten suggests that Stride's killer was disturbed "by some Jews who drove up to a Club." Eddows was seen with a man by Jewish witness Lawende and his friends as they left a club near Mitre Square. Not only that, but Israel Schwartz certainly witnessed an attack upon Stride, and despite her questionable candidacy as a Ripper victim now, back then it wasn't in question as far as senior policemen were concerned – Macnaghten reviews the crimes in the Scotland Yard version, and includes Stride without question. This mysterious City cop does turn up in other places, and I believe this story holds a great deal of importance in understanding the flow of information within the ranks of the police. Later, this will become clear as I make my case.

There is another explanation though – he was being deliberately vague, referring to the Double Event but tactically evading two Jewish witnesses in favour of a policeman. Perhaps a policeman's testimony would be considered unquestionable, and that if a policeman ever got a good look at a suspect, he would certainly testify to it. The suspicion that a Jewish witness refused to testify, therefore, is subtly whitewashed alongside the very existence of the Jewish witnesses.

Next, Macnaghten begins his take-down of the other suspects in the case;

I enumerate the case against 3 men whom the Police held very reasonable suspicion.

Personally, after much careful and deliberate consideration, I am inclined to exonerate the last two, but I have always held strong opinions regarding no. 1, and the more I think the matter over, the stronger do these opinions become. The truth however, will never be known, and did indeed, at one time, lie at the bottom of the Thames, if my conjections be correct.

Before even outlining the three cases, he sets out his conclusions, having already planted the seeds suggesting an asylum inmate is far less unlikely to be the killer than someone who killed themselves, and that nobody witnessed the killer at all besides "maybe" a policeman. The purpose of this appears to be a polemic, directing the reader to accept his conclusions regarding the case, but also, surreptitiously discrediting the candidacy of "Kosminski." He didn't just exonerate Cutbush, or attempt to, but he purposefully expounded his theory about Druitt and apparently introduced Kosminski purely to discredit him. Nowhere does Ostrog's credentials get set up and shot down like Kosminski's.

He begins by outlining his own preferred suspect, Montague Druitt;

No. 1 Mr M. J. Druitt, a doctor of about 41 years of age and of fairly good family, who disappeared at the time of the Miller's Court murder, and whose body was found floating in the Thames 31st December, i.e., 7 weeks after said murder. The body was said to have been in the water for a month or more – on it was found a season ticket between Blackheath and London. From private information I have little doubt but that his own family suspected this

308

man of being the Whitechapel murderer – it
was said he was sexually insane.

His previously stated belief that the Ripper killed himself
and that no other suspect appeared to fit the bill is further
reinforced not by this description but by other statements
he has made since retirement about the case. What of
Druitt as the Ripper? Well...there's not much. The barrister
and cricketer apparently drowned himself in the Thames
in December 1888 after expressing fears about losing his
mind. He was believed to be a homosexual and at the
time, that was enough to be considered "sexually insane."
If you're still curious, I'd always suggest you check out any
suspect you choose but I'd personally recommend you put
Druitt at a lower priority than many others, put it that
way.

What I am suggesting here is an attempt by
Macnaghten to whitewash the idea of Jewish witnesses
and Jewish suspects, tacked on for political reasons at the
end of a polemic written to exonerate one accused man –
the relation of a fellow cop no less. I suggest that maybe
the effortful demolition of the idea of anyone ever seeing
the killer, of there being Jewish witnesses at Mitre Square,
of the killer being committed to an asylum, and the
deliberate naming of Kosminski among a pool of far more
plausible suspects – which Macnaghten himself mentions
– are all intended to address a specific body of thought
among the intended audience of the memorandum and
discredit it. There does certainly appear to be evidence for
this belief.

If Anderson's memoirs are to be believed, there
was a narrative among post-Ripper officers that a low-
class Jew in an asylum had already been identified as the
Ripper and the case was secretly closed. Macnaghten's

Memoranda expressly attacks each and every aspect of that narrative, particularly the scathing Lady Aberconway version. Instead, Kosminski is named amidst a carefully constructed assault on the very premise of his supposed guilt. Possibly Macnaghten wrote the memo in part to attack the narrative, but there is a far more mundane and plausible explanation – he genuinely did believe Druitt to be the killer, at the expense of any and all other theories and evidence. In the field of Ripperology, he wouldn't be the first or last to fixate on a suspect and suffer blinding confirmation bias. There certainly is evidence to support this claim. Following his retirement in 1913, Macnaghten claimed to the *Daily Mail* (2nd June 1913) that the killer was a

> maniac, but I have a very clear idea who he was and how he committed suicide, but that, with other secrets, will never be revealed by me. I have destroyed all my documents and there is now no record of the secret information that came into my possession at one time or another.

Presumably, this secret information is the Druitt family's correspondence to Macnaghten, if it indeed existed, suggesting Montague Druitt as the killer. This would not be too surprising – every time a serial killer is on the loose, the general public queue up to accuse their husbands, fathers and brothers as the culprit in droves.

But the point here is, that even as far as 1913, three years after Anderson published his own memoirs, Macnaghten apparently still believes Druitt as the killer. He reiterates this belief in his memoirs *Days of My Years*.

So, if Macnaghten genuinely believed Druitt as the

killer, why is he so keenly discrediting the line of argument that could lead specifically to Kosminski? I suspect it is because he couldn't single-mindedly argue the case for Druitt as he would have wished without discrediting the more commonly-held beliefs of fellow officers regarding the case first, and probably assumed his rank would buttress his opinion. Ostrog was simply thrown in the mix to further make Kosminski look like another unimportant suspect among a wider pool.

Next, Macnaghten details the case of Kosminski himself;

> No.2, Kosminski, a Polish Jew, who lived in the very heart of the district where the murders took place. He had become insane due to many years indulging in solitary vices. He had a great hatred of women, and strong homicidal tendencies. He was (and I believe still is) detained in a lunatic asylum about March 1889. This man, in appearance, strongly resembled the man seen by the City PC near Mitre Square.

The Scotland Yard version differs slightly from the above-quoted Lady Aberconway edition only slightly, suggesting Kosminski hated women, "especially of the prostitute class," and again saying there were "many circs connected with this man that made him a strong suspect." Some of the polemic is also watered down, including the notion of the killer being committed, which is given even credence with the notion of suicide. Otherwise the details relating to Kosminski, including his admission to an asylum in March 1889, are unaltered. However, the aforementioned third, and lost version of the memo differs substantially. Begg *et al* (1991, p. 289-90) quotes Phillip Loftus in his recollections of that lost version of the memoranda, suggesting that Kosminski was referred to only as "A Polish Jewish cobbler named Leather Apron." This detail is omitted in the other versions, and provides a crucial clue; the police clearly believed Kosminski to be Leather Apron.

So, the story given here is quite clear; Druitt is set up as the killer, and Kosminski is the poster-boy for the "Jewish lunatic" narrative, whilst Ostrog is thrown in to make the document look like a broad sweep of suspects when it is in fact nothing of the sort. And the Kosminski line is not some random choice – it is the establishment line that he is fighting to discredit, and as we shall see from the Swanson Marginalia, Kosminski is indeed the suspect. He fights to attack the idea of any witnesses seeing the killer (the foundation of the Jewish suspect narrative is a witness identification, probably by Joseph Lawende), fights the idea of the killer being locked in an asylum (when Anderson stated it, various sources including Chief Inspector Frederick Abberline refer to it, and as we shall see, Aaron Kosminski certainly was detained in an asylum), and fights the idea of any evidence pointing to anyone else but Druitt (claiming that he obtained, and destroyed, the only and singularly damning evidence of his guilt).

Like I said, Melville Macnaghten wasn't the first and won't be the last to become fixated on "their suspect" and blindly refute any evidence to the contrary. But the fight in him to attack the Kosminski narrative is very, very telling. To my mind it is the best evidence yet of the pervasive narrative's hold on the police at the time – one man's efforts to refute it.

DANIEL JOHNSON
"Kosminski": The Swanson Marginalia

It wouldn't be until nearly a century after the Ripper murders ceased that new evidence of the name "Kosminski" would come to light, and when it did it would pay out for newspapers wanting to fill the August silly season with filler news on the "startling new evidence" proving Jack the Ripper's identity for decades to come. Yes, even as recently as 2014 have I seen headlines in certain questionable publications citing the Swanson Marginalia as the "new" ground-breaking proof that the Ripper was a mad Jew. And yes, that despicable hate bait still sells.

In 1987, the grandson of Chief Inspector Donald Swanson, James Swanson, released to *The Daily Telegraph* newspaper his grandfather's annotated copy of Anderson's *The Lighter Side of My Official Life*. In the margins and back pages of the book, Swanson, a man who ran the Ripper investigation on the ground from day one until Anderson's return in early October 1888 – and is considered likely the most knowledgeable man on the subject – had written clarifications and notes on some of Anderson's comments. The notes were in drips and drabs all the way through the book but for the purposes of this analysis I have quoted the passages relating to the Ripper crimes.

At the point where Anderson claims his Jewish witness unhesitatingly identified the suspect, but wouldn't testify, Swanson jotted this;

> because the suspect was <u>also a Jew</u> and also because his evidence would convict the suspect, and witness would be the means of murderer being hanged which he did no wish to

be left on his mind D.S.S.

The emphasis there is Swanson's own. As I suggested, the witness did not wish to be an executioner. And recall, the original draft of this passage which included the detail that the witness wouldn't swear against "a fellow-Jew" was only printed once in a serialisation. Swanson's comments are essentially a corroboration of this sentiment. In a separate note Swanson claims;

> And after this identification which suspect
> knew, no other murder of this kind took place
> in London

Given that several murders occurred after Miller's Court that were variously considered Ripper murders, such as Alice McKenzie and Frances Coles, it is worth examining what Swanson personally considered a Ripper murder or not.

Among the private papers released to the public upon the publication of the marginalia was a list of murders Swanson linked to the Whitechapel killer. The list extended to the murder of Alice McKenzie on 17th July 1889, but has Frances Coles' murder in 1891 pencilled in at the bottom. Swanson personally handled the case of Frances Coles and interviewed Thomas Sadler and his wife himself, so he is certainly able to know the case well enough and be capable of deciding if the case was linked to the Ripper murders. As I said, Sadler can be alibied for the murders and certainly was not the killer, but that apparently did not stop the police considering him a suspect in not just the Frances Coles murder (for which he was quite thoroughly cleared) but for the Ripper crimes as well.

DANIEL JOHNSON

To recap – Swanson appears to consider the Frances Coles murder the last in the Ripper series. Himself, Dr Anderson and Melville Macnaghten all attended the scene of Frances Coles' murder the morning after the body was found and took the suggestion of a new Ripper killing incredibly seriously. Despite Swanson's conviction that this was a Ripper murder, both Anderson and Macnaghten would later claim the Miller's Court murder to be the last, and this will be an interesting point to remember for later. For now, we must move on to the final notes made by Swanson in his "marginalia."

On the back page of the memoirs, Swanson handwrote a final long passage, and this is the one that provides the most confusion and controversy. It reads;

> After the suspect had been identified at the Seaside Home where he had been sent by us with difficulty in order to subject him to identification and he knew he was identified. On suspect's return to his brother's house in Whitechapel, he was watched by police (City CID) day and night. In a very short time the suspect with his hands tied behind his back he was sent to Stepney Workhouse and then to Colney Hatch and died shortly afterwards – Kosminski was the suspect.

And there we have it – Kosminski was the suspect. The name again, in a reference directly to Anderson's suspect. Identified at "The Seaside Home" (a colloquial name for the Police Convalescent Home in Brighton, which opened in 1890, its main purpose was as a rest and recuperation facility for police officers) watched by City CID, and finally marched off to a workhouse and an asylum where he died. Just as Anderson said, and just as Macnaghten had tried so hard to discredit.

The story seems cast-iron now; Anderson picks up the thread of the house-to-house searches that had been going on since early September upon his return a month later, determines that the Leather Apron line they'd been pursuing – and heartily trying to cover up – was the right one, and that a suspect they knew as Kosminski was the guy. Sometime after the Frances Coles murder they come across the man, organise an identification at this "Seaside Home," but strike out when Lawende refuses to identify him. Nevertheless, Kosminski ends his days in Colney Hatch Asylum.

The end.

But...not quite.

Let us take a moment to look at the man accused of being the Ripper – Aaron Kosminski.

Aaron Kosminski

Aaron Kosminski was a 26-years-old hairdresser who lived in Whitechapel, although it was reported he had "attempted no work in years" when he was admitted to Mile End Old Town Workhouse due to his deteriorating mental illness on 4th February 1891. His malady was reportedly the consequence of "self-abuse," or masturbation. His problems appear fairly harmless and in many ways, he appeared to be garden-variety schizophrenic; he apparently believed "instincts" guided his behaviours, and these told him (in the form of auditory hallucinations) never to trust others, never wash, and to only eat food from the gutters. His only recorded incidents of violence were threatening his sister with a knife shortly before his admission, and throwing a chair at a member of staff at Colney Hatch. Hardly Jack the Ripper. This poor man would spend the rest of his life in asylums. He was later transferred to Colney Hatch on 7th February 1891, and later to Leavesden Asylum for Imbeciles 19th April 1894, dying in aged 53 in March 1919, an emaciated shell of a man. His only family was a brother named as Woolf Kosminski in asylum records, although as he shall see there were other Kosminskis in the area who may or may not be relations.

Quite how Swanson and Anderson came to confuse this man with their homicidally violent, woman-hating serial killer is incredible. Yet it seems to have happened, and I think I know why. The key breakthrough for me came with a simple misprint that might just explain exactly what is going on here. Upon admission to Mile End Old Town Workhouse in February 1891, Aaron Kosminski's next-of-kin's address is given as 3 Sion Square, and the police misread this as Lion Square, a mistake the writer Martin Fido himself made. Keep this in mind for later.

Not only is Aaron Kosminski patently not a vicious serial killer, but the suggestion of a Jewish killer enraged the community and the press.

Anderson's Critics

Anderson's comments in his serialised memoirs had filtered into the press in small doses, but upon the serialisation of his memoirs in 1910, just prior to their publication in book form, his theory went down like a lead balloon. Jewish newspapers went ballistic at the unfounded allegation that the killer was a Jew, yet he stuck to his guns.

JACK THE RIPPER

Here, the columnist "Mentor," for the *Jewish Chronicle* (4th March 1910), aka Leopold Jacob Greenberg, takes aim at the content of the serialised memoirs of the distinguished copper which first alerted the public to the "Lunatic Jew" theory;

AN ASPERSION UPON JEWS.
POLICE "THEORY" AGAIN.
By Mentor.

Sir Robert Anderson, the late head of the Criminal Investigation Department at Scotland Yard, has been contributing to *Blackwood's* a series of articles on Crime and Criminals. In the course of his last contribution, Sir Robert tells his readers that the fearful crimes committed in the East End some years ago, and known as "Jack the Ripper" crimes, were the work of a Jew. Of course, whoever was responsible for the series of foul murders was not mentally responsible, and this Sir Robert admits. But I fail to see - at least, from his article in *Blackwood's* - upon what evidence worthy of the name he ventures to cast the odium for this infamy upon one of our people. It will be recollected that the criminal, whoever he was, baffled the keenest search not alone on the part of the police, but on the part of an infuriated and panic-stricken populace. Notwithstanding the utmost vigilance, the man, repeating again and again his demoniacal work, again and again escaped. Scotland Yard was nonplussed, and then, according to Sir Robert Anderson, the police "formed a theory" - usually the first essential to some blundering

318

injustice. In this case, the police came to the conclusion that "Jack the Ripper" was a "low-class" Jew, and they so decided, Sir Robert says, because they believe "it is a remarkable fact that people of that class in the East End will not give up one of their number to Gentile justice". Was anything more nonsensical in the way of a theory ever conceived even in the brain of a policeman? Here was a whole neighbourhood, largely composed of Jews, in constant terror lest their womenfolk, whom Jewish men hold in particular regard - even "low-class" Jew do that - should be slain by some murderer who was stalking the district undiscovered. So terrified were many of the people - non-Jews as well as Jews - that they hastily moved away. And yet Sir Robert would have us believe that there were Jews who knew the person who was committing the abominable crimes and yet carefully shielded him from the police. A more wicked assertion to put into print, without the shadow of evidence, I have seldom seen. The man whom Scotland Yard "suspected," subsequently, says Sir Robert, "was caged in an asylum." He was never brought to trial - nothing except his lunacy was proved against him. This lunatic presumably was a Jew, and because he was "suspected," as a result of the police "theory" I have mentioned, Sir Robert ventures to tell the story he does, as if he were stating facts, forgetting that such a case as that of Adolph Beck was ever heard of.

But now listen to the "proof" that Sir Robert Anderson gives of his theories. When the

319

lunatic, who presumably was a Jew and who was suspected by Scotland Yard, was seen by a Jew - "the only person who ever had a good view of the murderer" - Sir Robert tells us he at once identified him, "but when he learned that the suspect was a fellow-Jew he declined to swear to him." This is Scotland Yard's idea of "proof" positive of their "theory"! What more natural than the man's hesitancy to identify another as Jack the Ripper so soon as he knew he was a Jew? What more natural than for that fact at once to cause doubts in his mind? The crimes identified with "Jack the Ripper" were of a nature that it would be difficult for any Jew - "low-class" or any class - to imagine the work of a Jew. Their callous brutality was foreign to Jewish nature, which, when it turns criminal, goes into quite a different channel. I confess that however sure I might have been of the identity of a person, when I was told he had been committing "Jack the Ripper" crimes, and was a Jew, I should hesitate about the certainty of my identification, especially as anyone - outside Scotland Yard - knows how prone to mistake the cleverest-headed and most careful of people are when venturing to identify anyone else. It is a matter of regret and surprise that so able a man as Sir Robert Anderson should, upon the wholly erroneous and ridiculous "theory" that Jews would shield a raving murderer because he was a Jew, rather than yield him up to "Gentile justice," build up the series of statements that he has. There is no real proof that the lunatic who was "caged" was a Jew - there is absolutely no proof that he was responsible for the "Jack the Ripper" crimes,

and hence it appears to me wholly gratuitous on
the part of Sir Robert to fasten the wretched
creature - whoever he was - upon our people

A scathing assault on Anderson's theory, to which he duly
replied *(The Jewish Chronicle*, 11ᵗʰ March 1910);

The "Jack the Ripper" Theory:
Reply by Sir Robert Anderson.

TO THE EDITOR OF THE "JEWISH
CHRONICLE."
SIR, - With reference to "Mentor's" comments
on my statements about the "Whitechapel
murders" of 1888 in this month's *Blackwood*,
will you allow me to express the severe distress
I feel that my words should be construed as "an
aspersion upon Jews." For much that I have
written in my various books gives proof of my
sympathy with, and interest in, "the people of
the Covenant"; and I am happy in reckoning
members of the Jewish community in London
among my personal friends.

I recognise that in this matter I said either too
much or too little. But the fact is that as my
words were merely a repetition of what I
published several years ago without exciting
comment, they flowed from my pen without
any consideration.

We have in London a stratum of the population
uninfluenced by religious or even social
restraints. And in this stratum Jews are to be

found as well as Gentiles. And if I were to
describe the condition of the maniac who
committed these murders, and the course of
loathsome immorality which reduced him to
that condition, it would be manifest that in his
case every question of nationality and creed is
lost in a ghastly study of human nature sunk to
the lowest depth of degradation.

Yours obediently,
ROBERT ANDERSON

To his discredit, he trots out the old, "some of my best
friends are Jews" line to wave off his anti-Semitic
comments. Dear Lord. Nevertheless, he tries to sweet and
innocently suggest that the killer's depravity transgresses
any boundaries of nationality or creed – a nice little way of
batting the Jewish issue aside yet again. This letter is a
stubborn non-apology ("I'm sorry you got offended") and
a syrupy attempt at appeasement. But a reaction such as
this can be expected from the Jewish press, surely?
Yes...but what of his colleagues in the Met and
counterparts in the City?

Inspector Edmund Reid disagreed with Anderson's
suggestions of a Jewish witness too, and along the way
made some interesting comments that could fill in a few
gaps in our theory. Writing in the *Morning Advertiser* 23rd
April 1910:

Now we have Sir Robert Anderson saying that
Jack the Ripper was a Jew, that I challenge him
to prove, and what is more it was never
suggested at the time of the murders. I

challenge anyone to prove that there was a tittle
of evidence against man, woman or child in
connection with the murders, as no man was
ever seen in the company of the women who
were found dead

No witnesses, no evidence of a Jewish suspect, no
suggestion the killer was ever supposed to be Jewish. To
put Reid's comments into context, he was one of the men
on the ground working his fingers to the bone under the
guidance of Abberline during the Ripper crimes. He, like
Swanson, is a valuable source of information. That said,
he does make some basic errors; men were seen in the
company several of the women; Annie Chapman was seen
with a man minutes before her death, a man was seen
with Catharine Eddowes next to Mitre Square, a man was
seen attacking Elizabeth Stride (who police considered a
Ripper victim at the time), and the carrotty moustached
man was seen with a woman believed to be Mary Kelly in
Miller's Court. Possibly what he meant was that none of
these folks were ever identified as a viable suspect, and
therefore no outstanding sightings of unidentified men
with these women exist to suggest the killer's gender. This
is just hair-splitting though – we can be sure the killer was
male for two reasons, one of them being the sightings at
Hanbury Street and Mitre Square, but also nearly a
century-and-a-half of our society's experience with serial
murder since 1888.

The real meat and potatoes of Reid's comments
are in the suggestion that there was no evidence that the
Ripper was Jewish, and no suggestion even at the time
that he might be. So where does that leave Anderson's
insistence that the "diagnosis" of the "definitely
ascertained fact" of a low-class Jewish suspect was

formulated and followed through after the house-to-house searches and his own meetings with the top brass? Well, given that Swanson backs up Anderson's claims in the marginalia, and both folks outrank Reid and Abberline (Anderson being Asst. Commissioner of the Met CID, Swanson being Chief Inspector, Abberline being an Inspector first-class and Reid an Inspector), we can assume that those two were the ones covertly arranging the investigation towards their preferred conclusion, without feeling the need to filter this information down to the lower ranks. Anderson's consultation with others following his return, and following the house-to-house searches, was merely a meeting with Swanson, whereby Swanson informed Anderson of the concentration of their searches in the predominantly Jewish parts of the area and the suspicion that Leather Apron was their man – with or without the influence of the press.

Further damning attack comes from the somewhat colourful, and arguably unreliable, pen of City Chief Superintendent Major Henry Smith in his autobiography *From Constable to Commissioner;*

> Sir Robert talks of the "Lighter Side" of his Official Life." There is nothing "light" here ; a heavier indictment could not be framed against a class whose conduct contrasts most favourably with that of the Gentile population of the Metropolis.

> [...]

> How Sir Charles Warren wiped out - I believe with his own hand, but will not speak positively - the writing on the wall, how he

came to my office accompanied by Superintendent Arnold about seven o'clock the same morning to get information as to the murder of Catharine Eddowes, I have already stated on p. 153. The facts are indisputable, yet Sir Robert Anderson studiously avoids all allusion to them. Is it because "it would ill become him to violate the unwritten rule of the service," or is he unwilling to put on record the unpardonable blunder of his superior officer ? I leave my readers to decide.

Sir Robert says "the Ripper could go and come and get rid of his blood-stains in secret." The criminal, no doubt, was valeted by his co-religionists -warned not to run too great risks, to come home as soon as he could after business, and always to give notice when he meant to cut up another lady ! On three occasions - the only three of which I can give reliable details - there was no need to provide the murderer with hot water and Sunlight soap. In Berners Street he did not mutilate the woman, and probably had very few blood-stains about him ; in Mitre Square he used the woman's apron ; and in Dorset Street he carefully washed his hands at the sink.

The writing on the wall may have been written - and, I think, probably *was* written - to throw the police off the scent, to divert suspicion from the Gentiles and throw it upon the Jews. It may have been written by the murderer, or it may not. To obliterate the words that might have given us a most valuable clue, more especially after I had sent a man to stand over them till

325

they were photographed, was not only
indiscreet, but unwarrantable.

Sir Robert Anderson spent, so he tells us, the
day of his return from abroad and half the
following night "in reinvestigating the whole
case." A more fruitless investigation, looking to
all he tells us, it would be difficult to imagine.

The "lighter side," we learn, is "to be
continued." Meantime, if Sir Robert can spare a
few minutes, there are two books, I think, well
worthy of his perusal - "Bleak House" and the
Bible. In the former book Mademoiselle
Hortense, to divert suspicion from herself,
writes "Lady Deadlock, Murderess" - with what
result Inspector Bucket tells us. In the latter,
Daniel interprets the writing on the wall which
brought things to a crisis at Belshazzar's Feast.
Sir Robert is fortunate to live in times like the
present. Mr. Blackwood's readers seem pleased
with his tales, but I fear the King of the
Chaldeans would have made short work of him

Again, his department are accused of blundering, and of
needlessly attacking an entire segment of the population.
Smith also suggests that the Goulston Street graffiti –
which may or may not have been by the killer, he says –
was probably made to implicate Jews by some malicious
Gentile. That last paragraph is, I admit, a little too Boris
Johnson for my appreciation but I get the jist of it.
Anderson is being told to read the writing on the wall and
grow the hell up. In fact, Major Smith's suggestion that
the re-investigation of the case was "fruitless" is more
than likely a reference to the total lack of clues they had

and still had at the time of writing. However, as I have shown, by the time Anderson returned, Swanson had already focused his investigation onto the Jewish population, and possibly even a suspect, as we shall see. So what Anderson did was listen to his colleague's apparently sound line of enquiry that they decided to keep hush-hush from the lower ranks. How to explain the "unpardonable blunder" of Sir Charles Warren scrubbing off the graffiti at Goulston Street? Simple; he was part of this little clique, too, committed to keeping the "fact" of a Jewish suspect secret. This was the most absurd of conspiracies – a tiny little clutch of men believing they needed to keep a tight lid on need-to-know information when all they did was follow a line of thought driven less by evidence and more by prejudice. But the truly sad thing is that it had little to do with Anderson, newly promoted, fresh to a red-hot investigation, or a top-ranking official under so much pressure he was forced to resign before the last victim was even cold...it was all about a certain Chief Inspector Donald Swanson.

Swanson's Suspect

One more thing to note about Reid's contributions that offer a vital clue to this whole mystery. In a letter to a newspaper written during a fiery exchange with an anonymous writer named "Unofficial," Reid disputes the assertion that a student who drowned in the Thames (ostensibly Druitt) was the killer, and recollects (in *The Morning Advertiser* 30th March 1903) that

> [a murder was] committed in Mitre Square in the City, but whatever Police Constable Thompson was doing there out of Metropolitan

district one is at a loss to know. Perhaps
"Unofficial" can explain since he knows so
much about it.

"Unofficial" cites a book by Major Arthur Griffiths named *Mysteries of Police and Crime* (1898) as the source of his information that a police officer was the witness at Mitre Square. I've checked this book out, and it is free to access now the copyright has expired, and it does indeed recount the details of the Ripper crimes in its preface, particularly those claims made in the then-secret Macnaghten Memoranda, positing three suspects – a Polish Jew, a mad doctor, and a suicidal student. It does indeed repeat the notion of the police officer witnessing the killer at Mitre Square. Tellingly, "Unofficial" also refers to the police officer as having been since murdered, as PC Ernest Thompson was in 1900 – the man who found the body of Frances Coles in 1891. Reid picks this up and runs with it, recounting the circumstances of PC Thompson's discovery and of him hearing "receding footsteps" at the scene, but dismisses any knowledge of PC Thompson having anything to do with Mitre Square. Further evidence that there was a long-standing confusion between these specific details is found in an interview with former police officer Robert Sagar in 1905, who said that he recalled a police officer heard "receding footsteps" from Mitre Square as the body of a Ripper victim was found. Clearly, at some level there was a mix-up between the details of two murders; Catharine Eddowes and Frances Coles, with PC Ernest Thompson being mixed up with the Jewish witnesses at Mitre Square. But the earliest reference to this confusion is the Macnaghten Memoranda, a document written on-the-fly by Melville Macnaghten and meant for confidential reading.

As I have already noted, Macnaghten joined the Met after the Ripper crimes had ended. His memoranda were written with second-hand information. However, these claims – particularly about the confusion of PC Ernest Thompson, and the Polish Jew suspect which Macnaghten names as Kosminski – had to come from somewhere. Of the three main figures in this narrative, Anderson, Swanson and Macnaghten himself, only Swanson believed that Frances Coles was a Ripper victim. Reid's comments express surprise that Thompson had anything to do with the events at Mitre Square, and he seemed unaware the man wasn't even a cop at the time! He recounts Thompson's involvement with the Frances Coles murder, showing he does know what he is talking about. So, this bring us back to the book by Major Griffiths, which re-treads the words of Macnaghten, and back to the source of Macnaghten's comments on the Ripper crimes. I think it is clear that his source believed that the Ripper murdered Frances Coles, and therefore, that Macnaghten's source was Swanson, who unthinkingly transposed the PC Ernest Thompson near-encounter at Swallow Gardens with the events at Mitre Square when filling Macnaghten in on the details. This inevitably means that the details about the suspect "Kosminski" also came from him.

We can trace the two times "Kosminski" is named as the Jewish suspect to one man; Donald Swanson. The Macnaghten Memoranda and the Swanson Marginalia aren't independent sources of information about the suspect "Kosminski" - they are sourced from the same man. The same man who we can show zeroed in on a Jewish suspect in the earliest days of the investigation, who persuaded Sir Robert Anderson of his "discovery" of the suspect's background – possibly even his assumed identity – and finally who was the source of the name "Kosminski" in two different places many years later.

If Donald Swanson seemed to barrel through the Ripper investigation with a clear idea that his suspect "Kosminski" was the man, and managed to convince Anderson of this to the extent that he would singularly defend the notion until his dying day, even against the Jewish press themselves, then maybe it is time we took a closer look at what Swanson had to say about him, a closer look at the real Aaron Kosminski, and a closer look at the research of Martin Fido. But let's start at the beginning; the "Leather Apron" scare of Autumn 1888.

"Leather Apron"

Historically the first mention of the character named "Leather Apron" was in *The Star* newspaper on 5th September 1888 following the Mary Ann Nichols murder. And as we shall see, they milked that cow until it sang the national anthem. But an earlier reference does exist in a small local newspaper that interviews a friend of Mary's named "German Moggy," who in the context of the article is certainly Emily Holland, the last person to see Mary alive at 2:30am on 31st August 1888. In the brief piece, printed on the 1st September 1888 in the *Sheffield and Rotherham Independent*, the figure of "Leather Apron" is introduced;

> The women in a position similar to that of the deceased allege that there is a man who goes by the name of the "Leather Apron" who has more than once attacked unfortunate and defenceless women. His dodge is, it is asserted, is to get them into some house on the pretence of

330

offering them money. He takes whatever little
they have and "half kills" them in addition.

That he "half-kills them" possibly indicated strangulation.
Either way this detail from such a small newspaper, but
such an important source, indicates that the figure of
Leather Apron was at the heart of the inquiry into Mary
Ann Nichols' murder right from the off. If Emily Holland
reported this to the newspaper she certainly passed it
onto the police.

However, we have evidence that prior to the
murder of Polly Nichols, when the press was still pouring
over the "Bank Holiday Murders" of Emma Smith and
Martha Tabram, the police already had Leather Apron on
their radar. In an article in the *Echo* dated 20th September
1888, this is reported;

> The Whitechapel murders are as inexplicable as
> ever, and at present the utmost energy on the
> part of the police has failed to secure sufficient
> evidence to justify an arrest in a quarter where
> suspicion lurked shortly after the commission
> of the fatal outrage at George-yard-buildings.
> Inspector Reid, Detective-sergeant Enright,
> Sergeant Goadby, and other officers then
> worked upon a slight clue given them by
> "Pearly Poll." It was not thought much of at the
> time; but from what was gleaned from her,
> coupled with statements given by Elizabeth
> Allen and Eliza Cooper, of 35, Dorset-street,
> Spitalfields, certain of the authorities have had
> cause to suspect a man actually living not far
> from Buck's-row. At present, however, there is
> only suspicion against him

This suggests that "Pearly Poll"- that is, Mary Ann Connolly, the companion of Martha Tabram on the night of her death – implicated a man "living not far from Buck's Row," a detail specific to police references to Leather Apron. This detail, plus the fact that several streetwalkers implicate the man at different times, tallies with our overall picture of Leather Apron as we shall see. Not only that, but here we have acquaintances of three Whitechapel murders – "Pearly Poll"/Martha Tabram, Emily Holland/Mary Ann Nichols, and Elizabeth Allen and Eliza Cooper/Annie Chapman – all reporting on, or informing police about, Leather Apron. This is by 20th September, three weeks since the Mary Ann Nichols murder, but crucially, also a little less than three weeks since *The Star* newspaper decided to run its infamous Leather Apron story.

On 5th September 1888, *The Star* ran this as its headline story;

"LEATHER APRON."
THE ONLY NAME LINKED WITH THE
WHITECHAPEL MURDERS.
A NOISELESS MIDNIGHT TERROR.

The Strange Character who Prowls About Whitechapel After Midnight - Universal Fear Among the Women - Slippered Feet and a Sharp Leather-knife.

The mystery attending the horrible murders in Whitechapel shows no sign of lessening. The detectives at work on the case, who were quick to confess themselves baffled, only continue to make the same confession, and there is every prospect that the last ghastly tragedy will go unpunished like its predecessors. Whitechapel is loud in its indignation over the inefficiency of the detectives, and is asking several questions to which there does not seem to be any satisfactory answer. Among other things the people wish to know why the police do not arrest "Leather Apron."

"Leather Apron" by himself is quite an unpleasant character. If, as many of the people suspect, he is the real author of the three murders which, in everybody's judgement, were done by the same person, he is a more ghoulish and devilish brute than can be found in all the pages of shocking fiction. He has ranged Whitechapel for a long time. He exercises over the unfortunates who ply their trade after twelve o'clock at night, a sway that is

BASED ON UNIVERSAL TERROR.

He has kicked, injured, bruised, and terrified a hundred of them who are ready to testify to the outrages. He has made a certain threat, his favorite threat, to any number of them, and each of the three dead bodies represents that threat carried out. He carries a razor-like knife, and two weeks ago drew it on a woman called "Widow Annie" as she was crossing the square near London Hospital, threatening at the same time, with his ugly grin and his malignant eyes, to "rip her up." He is a character so much like the invention of a story writer that the accounts of him given by all the street-walkers of the

Whitechapel district seem like romances. The remarkable thing is, however, that they all agree in every particular.

Ever since the last murder the name "Leather Apron" has been falling repeatedly on the ears of the reporters. On the afternoon of the day following the murder a group of women in Eagle-place, near the mortuary, were busily discussing something to the detriment of their household duties. The subject was "Leather Apron," and the report had spread that

"LEATHER APRON" HAD BEEN ARRESTED

for the murder. Ever since then women have been shaking their heads and saying that "Leather Apron" did it. The strangest thing about the whole case is that in view of public opinion in Whitechapel, the man has not been arrested on suspicion, and his whereabouts on the night of the murder inquired into.

About 50 of the unfortunates in the Whitechapel district gave a description of "Leather Apron" to a *Star* reporter between midnight and three o'clock this morning. The descriptions all agreed, and most of them added to it a personal experience with the man during the last two years in which they were more or less injured. From all accounts he is five feet four or five inches in height and wears a dark, close-fitting cap. He is thickset, and has an unusually thick neck. His hair is black, and closely clipped, his age being about 38 or 40.

DANIEL JOHNSON

He has a small, black moustache. The distinguishing feature of his costume is a leather apron, which he always wears, and from which

HE GETS HIS NICKNAME.

His expression is sinister, and seems to be full of terror for the women who describe it. His eyes are small and glittering. His lips are usually parted in a grin which is not only not reassuring, but excessively repellant. He is a slipper maker by trade, but does not work. His business is blackmailing women late at night. A number of men in Whitechapel follow this interesting profession. He has never cut anybody so far as known, but always carries a leather knife, presumably as sharp as leather knives are wont to be. This knife a number of the women have seen. His name nobody knows, but all are united in the belief that he is a Jew or of Jewish parentage, his face being of a marked Hebrew type. But the most singular characteristic of the man, and one which tends to identify him closely with last Friday night's work, is the universal statement that in moving about

HE NEVER MAKES ANY NOISE.

What he wears on his feet the women do not know, but they all agree that he moves noiselessly. His uncanny peculiarity to them is that they never see him or know of his presence until he is close by them. When two of the Philpott-street women directed the *Star* reporter to Commercial-street, opposite the Princess Alice Tavern, as the most likely place to find him, she added that it would be necessary to look into all the shadows, as if he was there he would surely be out of sight. This locality, it may be remarked, is but a few steps from the model dwellinghouse in George's-Yard, where the murdered woman of four weeks ago was found.

The noiselessness of 'Leather Apron's' movements recalls the statement of Mrs. Colwell, of Brady-street. She said that about the time the murder was said to have been committed she heard a woman running up the street shrieking "Murder; Police." "She was running away from somebody," said Mrs. Colwell, "who, from the way she screamed, was hurting her as she ran. And it struck me as very strange that I did

NOT HEAR THE SOUND OF ANY FOOTSTEPS

whatever except hers. This took place where the bloodstains were found, and where the woman evidently received her death cuts. Taken together with the absolutely noiseless way in which she was carried up Brady-street; so noiselessly that three people wide awake and only a few feet distant heard no sound, this looks as though "Leather-Apron" was worth interviewing, to say the least.

"Leather-Apron" never by any chance attacks a man. He runs away on the slightest appearance of rescue. One woman whom he assailed some time ago boldly prosecuted him for it, and he was sent up for seven days. He has no settled place of residence, but has slept oftenest in a fourpenny lodging-house of the lowest kind in a disreputable lane leading from Brick-lane. The people at this lodging-house denied that he had been there, and appeared disposed to shield him

This shameful display of journalistic masturbation terrified the people of the East End. They weren't used to the kind of joyfully over-the-top tabloid journalism we are today – in those days, papers like *The Star* were called "New Journalism," a populist venture designed to sell copy to the newly-literate slum-dwelling classes. They had no reason to doubt what they read, and if it seemed to grab the attention and play to one's prejudices (and anti-Semitic prejudices were rife), then it was drank in deeper. So this article single-handedly kicked-off the "Leather Apron" scare that continued more or less until the publication of the Dear Boss letter on 4th October 1888 after the double event popularised the name "Jack the Ripper." Even on that night, passers-by yelled "Leather Apron" at Elizabeth Stride's date for the night in jest.

The reaction to this was public outrage. *The Star* followed this article up with more, and their sales rocketed week on week, a fact of which they proudly boasted. The very next day, the paper printed a follow-up. Unlike their usual pigswill, this article actually provides some interesting details;

"LEATHER-APRON."
More About His Career - His Latest

JACK THE RIPPER
Movements - In the Borough.

The sense of fear which the murder of the
unfortunate woman Nicholls has thrown over
the neighborhood, and especially over her
companions, shows no sign of decreasing. A
number of the street wanderers are in nightly
terror of "Leather-Apron."

One of our reporters visited one of the single
women's lodging-houses last night. It is in
Thrawl-street, one of the darkest and most
terrible-looking spots in Whitechapel. The
house keeps open till one o'clock in the
morning, and reopens again at five. In the
house nightly are 66 women, who get their bed
for 4d. The proprietor of the place, who is also
owner of several other houses of a similar
character in the neighborhood, told some
gruesome stories of the man who has now
come to be regarded as the terror of the East-
end. Night after night, he said, had women
come in in a fainting condition after being
knocked about by "Leather-Apron." He himself
would never be out in the neighborhood after
twelve o'clock at night except with a loaded
revolver. The "terror," he said, would go to a
public-house or coffee-room, and peep in
through the window to see if a particular
woman was there. He would then vanish, lying
in wait for his victim at some convenient
corner, hidden from the view of everybody.

The police are making efforts to arrest him, but
he constantly changes his quarters. Some of the
unfortunate women state that he is now in one

of the low slums in the Borough. One of them said she saw him crossing London-bridge as stealthily as usual, with head bent, his skimpy coat turned up about his ears, and looking as if he were in a desperate hurry.

The hunt for "Leather Apron" began in earnest last evening. Constables 43 and 173, J Division, into whose hands "Leather-Apron" fell on Sunday afternoon, were detailed to accompany Detective Ewright, of the J Division, in a search through all the quarters where the crazy Jew was likely to be. They began at half-past ten in Church-street, in Shoreditch, rumor having located the suspected man there. They went through lodging-houses, into "pubs," down side streets, threw their bull's-eyes into every shadow, and searched the quarter thoroughly, but without result.

THE HUNT CONTINUED

later down in the Brick-lane neighborhood, Florendene-lane being "Leather Apron's" preferred lodging place lately. He was not found here, however, and the search, which then took the direction of the London Hospital, resulted in nothing. It is the general belief that the man has left the district.

The clue furnished by the woman who denounced the man on Sunday is a very unfortunate one. Her offer to prove by two women that "Leather Apron" was seen walking with the murdered woman in Baker's-row at two o'clock last Friday morning, is the most direct bit of evidence that yet has appeared. The belief in "Leather Apron's" guilt, whether it be well or ill founded, is general, and the instant he is recognised by any one he is sure to be reported and arrested. His conduct on Sunday was as usual. He never answers a question when it is put to him, and only speaks under strong compulsion. Mike --- , the grocer in George's-yard, dwelt a long time last evening on this peculiarity. He knows "Leather Apron" very well, and has known him for six years. He says that

THE MAN IS UNQUESTIONABLY MAD,

and that anybody who met him face to face would know it. That his eyes are never still, but are always shifting uneasily, and he never looks anybody in the eye. "Leather Apron" used to live in the lodging-house around the corner from the grocery, and was turned out of there some months ago with an order not to return. The lodging-house is a few doors below the "model" doorway in which the Turner woman was found with 39 stabs.

Great activity prevails among the police all through Whitechapel. All are sharply on the look-out for "Leather Apron," though many of them, strangely enough, do not know him by sight, and have only his description to go by.

Meanwhile other clues are not neglected. Inspector Hellson has the case in his charge, and is aided by the full division force, by Detective Abberlene, and others from Scotland-

yard who are familiar with East-end work.
Quite a number of men are necessary, for
several parties are under constant supervision.
"Leather Apron" is not the only possibility, but
he is the only one suspected whom the police
cannot lay their hands on at a moment's notice

Leather Apron is described as constantly moving around,
shifty and with darting eyes, "unquestionably mad" and
reticent to speak. His eagerness to flee police attention
and avoid his preferred dwelling place of Flower-and-
Dean Street, and the suggestion that he has fled the
district, kind of rules him out of the later murders. But
more importantly, it provides some pretty useful
indicators of identifying the man when we see him. The
reticence to speak, the shifting demeanour and the
darting eyes, and the unwillingness to look anyone in the
eyes, plus his stalking paranoid and suddenly violent
behaviour could be indicators of some kind of mental
illness, possibly a form of paranoid schizophrenia – that is,
if "Mike the Grocer" and the nice men of *The Star*
newspaper haven't just made all that up.

So, by the 6th September 1888, the district was in
terror, and on the hunt for Leather Apron – and this
included a substantial investment by the police under
Inspector Joseph Helson and Inspector Abberline,
apparently. However, soon a name emerged in the mess
of it all. On 7th September 1888, the day after the second
Leather Apron article, Inspector Helson filed a report with
the Yard stating thus;

The enquiry has revealed the fact that a man
named Jack Pizer, alias Leather Apron, has, for
some considerable period, been in the habit of

ill-using prostitutes in this, and other parts of
the Metropolis, and careful search has been and
has continued to be made to find this man in
order that his movements may be accounted on
the night in question, although at present there
is no evidence whatever against him.

For the first time we have a name for Leather Apron –
Jack Pizer. That said, in the same report Helson also states
there's "not an atom of evidence" linking anyone to the
murder of Mary Ann Nichols, although in naming Pizer as
Leather Apron, he is at least stoking the fires of a useful
lead. As we saw in the Annie Chapman inquest, however,
it was not quite that simple. But before we get that far, we
need to focus on the 48 hours between the discovery of
Annie Chapman's body at 29 Hanbury Street on the 8th
September 1888, and Pizer's unceremonious appearance
in the dock on the 11th September 1888.

At approximately 6am on the 8th September 1888,
John Davis finds the body of Annie Chapman, dissected
and displayed in a horrendously degrading manner in the
back of 29 Hanbury Street. It is barely a week since the
murder of Mary Ann Nichols and mere days since *The Star*
published its stories about "Leather Apron." Worse still, is
the discovery in the same backyard of a recently-washed
leather apron by Inspector Joseph Chandler. Although
quickly identified as belonging to an innocent resident of
Hanbury Street, it wasn't enough to stop social unrest.

Fido (1987, p. 37-8) cites the *Daily News, The East
London Observer* and *The Jewish Chronicle* as reporting a
spike in racial violence akin to pogroms erupting against
the Jewish population in the district, with doctors
overworked to treat the wounded and crowd hurling
abuse and assaulting the locals. Remember that

Whitechapel was a tight maze of decaying and
claustrophobic alleyways and side-roads, extremely
densely populated and sporting a heavily immigrant and
destitute population already home to socialist agitators,
Irish migrants that made the authorities fearful of Fenian
violence, and a huge migrant Jewish population. By far
the greatest single concentration of poor Jewish
immigrants in the West existed in the abyss of the East
End. Media-fuelled hatred and fear in the midst of an
unprecedented killing spree such as this – again,
remember that the press counted Emma Smith and
Martha Tabram as Ripper victims – were a recipe for
chaos. The authorities were terrified of a district-wide race
riot, the East End descending into violence that would
spill out of control into the adjacent districts, including the
City. Something had to be done.

On 10th September 1888, the aforementioned John
"Jack" Pizer, a boot-finisher living in Mulberry Lane, was
arrested by a police officer he'd known for nearly twenty
years. Sergeant William Thicke lifted the bewildered man
on the charge of being Leather Apron, and within 24
hours he was up on the dock at the Annie Chapman
inquest, to great public attention. As we saw during the
Annie Chapman inquest, his tit-for-tat exchange with the
coroner was remarkably curt. He explains that he was the
subject of false suspicion, and that he was in hiding at his
family home at 22 Mulberry Street. He admits he is known
by the name Leather Apron, and proceeded to provide his
cast-iron alibi for the murder (that he witnessed a fire
miles from the scene near the docks, and was able to back
this up with the help of a policeman's own witnessing of
the event). He was then discharged.

After this, something odd happened.

Mentions of a Jewish aspect to their suspected

murderer were dashed from all official communications. Fido suggests (p.213) that this was when "the cover-up" began. Sure enough it would be after this that the police no longer made any reference to Leather Apron. The Goulston Street Graffiti would be erased, Rabbi Adler would tacitly suggest that "Juwes" did not mean "Jews" contrary to common sense, and no more Jewish suspects would be so unceremoniously rounded up and hurled into the public spotlight. I suggest that Sir Charles Warren's personal order to erase the graffiti pretty much sticks the buck at his desk on this one, meaning the conspiracy to silence the Jewish connection and bury the Leather Apron story probably began and ended with him, the man at the top. He would have involved his subordinates – Sir Robert, and by extension Swanson during his turn as lead investigator on the case – but as we have already seen, those two had their own theory. Swanson, it seems, played along with the cover-up and even with the "identification" of Pizer as Leather Apron, but on his own time and later with the collusion of Sir Robert Anderson, pursued the Jewish suspect line. Since Sir Charles Warren never publicly commented on the Ripper's suspected identity, we can only speculate as to whether he had any hand in perpetuating this line of inquiry or whether Swanson and Anderson carried on regardless.

But this leaves an obvious question; if indeed Pizer had been named by Helson, and arrested by Thicke, as "Leather Apron" prior to the real incidents of violence kicking off, and he even admitted being the figure in court, why did the Jewish suspect line continue? Why, after he was cleared of being the Ripper, did Swanson apparently still inform Macnaghten of a suspect called "Leather Apron" called "Kosminski" at some time prior to the writing of the memoranda?

This is where the Pizer problem begins to unravel.

On 11th October 1888, John Pizer actually sued a woman who called him Leather Apron, and was successful, winning 10 shillings. Not only that, but he would sue the police themselves for wrongful arrest, and successfully sued several newspapers who named him as Leather Apron. He protested his innocence at every turn. Upon a closer look at the evidence, had every reason to. The *Daily News* reported the arrest of Pizer in Plumber's Row, when in fact he was arrested in nearby Mulberry Street. And the earlier-quoted report about Pearly Poll and two others naming a suspect living near Buck's Row, is dated a week after Pizer's appearance at the inquest. I think it is clear what has happened; Pizer, whether his name legitimately emerged as a suspected Leather Apron or not, was identified as such, hurled onto the stand with a script, and made to play-act this stupid yes-sir-no-sir for the figurative cameras. The press would have their Leather Apron, and he would be exonerated as the Whitechapel murderer. This allowed them to kill the Leather Apron scare and bury it without the fear of more race rioting. It was a cynical move designed purely to make the police's life easier. Certainly, Pizer's reaction afterwards is one I would class as indignation and rightly deserved – he reported being chased and almost lynched when his name started doing the rounds. Even if he was "a" Leather Apron, it seems he wasn't "the" Leather Apron. All of this is so far included in Fido's research, barring one observation I have made that I think warrants closer examination.

Plumber's Row runs south from Whitechapel Road to Commercial Street. Parallel to it, runs Mulberry Street. So far, it is easy to see how a journalist could make a simple mistake. But it was a comment Fido made about the current location of the street that stunned me. Upon checking a map of the area, I was astounded that he'd missed it. In his book, Fido (p.212) says;

> Mulberry Street was not Plumber's Row, but the road parallel to it (it ran from today's Mulberry Street – then Sion Square – to Commercial Road).

Sion Square was the address given for Aaron Kosminski upon his admission to Mile End, the location misread at Lion Square by Fido upon initial consultation.

But that, reader, is just the tip of the iceberg.

Fido contends that the police continued their search for the real Leather Apron after Pizer's exoneration, as the above quote about the Elizabeth Allen/Eliza Cooper lead suggest. It seems they were after someone who lived on or near Plumber's Row or Mulberry Street (the report confuses the two), and Sion Square runs atop Mulberry Street adjacent to Plumber's Row. They were looking for a violent, paranoid, and apparently mentally unwell Jewish individual who conned and threatened women with knives, as well as attacking them in some violent manner, half-killing them. It clearly wasn't Pizer, and as the following excerpt reveals, even the general public had their own ideas about a particularly violent and eccentric individual who was suspected of being both Leather Apron, and of being the killer.

In the *Echo* on 16th September 1888, nearly a week since the exoneration of Pizer, an article interviewing the Richardsons, who were witnesses at Annie Chapman's inquest, made this remarkable digression;

> Passing afterwards through Spitalfields with

DANIEL JOHNSON

John Richardson, a curious incident occurred. A
rough, demented-looking fellow came from a
group, grinning, and with clenched fist,
muttered some threat to John Richardson. In
answer to the question, "Who is he? What does
he mean?" Richardson replied, "That is a man
they say is mad. A great many of the women
and the people around our house think that he
is the most likely man that they know of to
commit a murder. In fact many of them say that
he is the real "Leather Apron." When asked to
go back to enquire what the man meant,
Richardson said, "You had better not. For he
would be most likely to spring upon you and
knock you down, at once, without a word. I
shall not stop to speak to him for he is very
dangerous; and a great many of the women
think that he is the murderer.

Remarkable. So not only are the police still hunting their
man "near Buck's Row," but here we have an encounter
with "the real Leather Apron." Again, he is presented as
"mad." Politically incorrect as it seems, this encounter
dovetails with the other descriptions of a man showing
physical and behavioural evidence of mental instability. If
one thing is clear, the intelligence-trained, "need-only-
basis" thinking of the top cops came into full swing. They
had already contrived the search area for their door-to-
door enquiries based on their hunt for their suspect, and
they were clearly not interested in Pizer as a legitimate
Leather Apron suspect. Their real suspect, whoever it was,
was being named in whispers in the corridors of the Met
Police's HQ and careful work was done to ensure it didn't
leak to the hungry and ruthless press. Even the cops
ranked below Swanson were out of the loop by all

accounts. They were keeping their Leather Apron suspect hush-hush.

It seems there is reason to believe that they were still after their Leather Apron, and the proximity of Aaron Kosminski to Pizer, and the apparent focus of attention of the police's search for Leather Apron, is compelling evidence that after all this, Swanson's suspect, the mysterious violent Jew Kosminski, aka Leather Apron, is right here under our noses. Certainly, everything appears to be heading this way; Pizer was the scapegoat, Kosminski was the suspect, and nothing could be pinned on him until at some time in the future when he would finally be carted off to Colney Hatch. But one last fact sinks this convenient arrangement and reveals a truth that can only be met in the 21st Century with an almighty facepalm.

Nathan Kaminsky and Aaron Davis Cohen

On 19th October 1888, Chief Inspector Swanson reported back to the Home Office on the extent of the enquiries being conducted into the murders. As previously written, house-to-house enquiries began following the Annie Chapman murder and continued into October, and they covered the area of maximum Jewish settlement. Here we have an idea of the search area;

> 80,000 pamphlets to occupiers were issued and a house to house enquiry made not only involving the result of enquiries from the occupiers but also a search by police and with a few exceptions – but not such as to convey suspicion – covered the area bounded by the City Police boundary on the one hand, Lamb

348

St., Commercial Street, Great Eastern Railway
and Buxton Street, then by Albert St., Dunk St.,
Chicksand St., and Great Garden St. to
Whitechapel Road and then to the City
Boundary.

Begg *et all* (1991) helpfully trace this boundary in their
work *The Jack the Ripper A-Z*. Remarkably, it doesn't
include Plumber's Row, Pizer's address or even Sion
Square where Swanson's suspect Kosminski lives. It does,
however, include another location. Black Lion Yard, a
mere 142 yards from Kosminski's address, and where at
number 15 lived a man named Nathan Kaminsky.

     This is where the research paid off. Initially
intending to find the mysterious Kosminski appear as the
evidence suggested as an inmate at East End infirmaries
and asylums, Fido came across Nathan Kaminsky first.
Admitted to Whitechapel Infirmary on 24th March 1888 for
syphilis, and discharged as "cured" on the 12th May 1888,
the 23-year-old cobbler lived at 15 Black Lion Yard, at the
heart of the district, a short walk from Buck's Row,
Hanbury Street and Miller's Court. After this, he vanishes
from all known records. Desperate to see if the man
reappeared in East End asylums, Fido struck gold and
found both court and asylum records – but not for Nathan
Kaminsky.

     On 7th December 1888, weeks after the Miller's
Court murder, police raided a brothel above a cigar shop
at 254 Whitechapel Road. Several people were arrested;
Mary Jones was accused of keeping the brothel, alongside
Gertrude Smith and Ellen Hickey, but also a man named in
court documents as Aaron Davis Cohen. He was referred
to simply as a "lunatic wondering at large and unable to
take care of himself." Now, I've read numerous accounts

of Cohen's detention and in each case barring Fido's own, this phraseology is taken literally, and the circumstances of his arrest are ignored. Fido helpfully clears this up; this particular use of words is, as Fido (p. 223) says, "Lunacy Act wording," the specific definition provided in the law to have someone brought in under the Act and be detained in an asylum. He was in fact found among the women of the brothel, arrested, and then under the purview of the court, "sectioned." Aaron Davis Cohen was admitted to Whitechapel Workhouse Infirmary as a "lunatic at large" and later transferred to Colney Hatch Lunatic Asylum on 21st December 1888. He would die on 15th October 1889 from exhaustion. Records show Cohen to be violent, mischievous, who danced and tried to attack staff if unrestrained. He refused to eat, tore his clothes and destroyed the fittings of his room, and was clearly in the depths of severe mental illness.

What made Aaron Davis Cohen such an attractive suspect was that he matched both Aaron Kosminski and Nathan Kaminsky in every way – he was a low-class Jew, 23-years-old, who lived in Whitechapel. As Kaminsky vanished, Cohen appeared, and together, they seemed to wrap the mystery up. The suspect "Kosminski" must really be "Kaminsky," the police having gotten the names easily mixed-up, having started their hunt for Jack the Ripper suspecting Nathan Kaminsky of being the "real" Leather Apron. Indeed, his address, Black Lion Yard, was certainly a short walk from Buck's Row and a matter of yards from Plumber's Row. He must have vanished from there in September 1888 when the Leather Apron scare began, and moved around the area ever since.

Cohen's behaviour in the asylum certainly accords with that of the reports of Leather Apron, too. It certainly rings a bell when recalling the reports about Leather

Apron – the twitchy, threatening, paranoid brute who had bouts of homicidal violence and constantly moved or was thrown out of lodging houses for drinking and violence. Interestingly, alongside those arrested in the brothel raid, the court records note of his arrest show that missing from the roster was an individual named only as N. Cohen, who apparently was the complainant to a charge of assault levelled against Ellen Hickey. This person has never been identified but it isn't too great a stretch to imagine that it could have been the "incoherent" Aaron Davis Cohen, who in turn may have been Nathan Kaminsky using the nom de plume "Nathan Cohen," (and later Aaron Davis Cohen), as cover while he hid from the police's hunt for Leather Apron. The fact that the women of the brothel and Cohen appeared in separate occasions in court could explain in part why he was never identified as such.

This all seemed, and still seems, a plausible and convenient narrative for explaining what happened to Nathan Kaminsky, where the name Kosminski may have come from, and where the confusing details of the Swanson marginalia came from. The argument is that the name Kaminsky was confused with Kosminski, and when Swanson recalls events that could only ever have happened after 1890 (when the Seaside Home in Brighton opened), he's recalling the Met's dealings with Kaminsky/Cohen but telescoping it forwards to the 1890s to account for the City's observation of the real Aaron Kosminski – assuming they're all the same person. But these conclusions have problems.

I believe Martin Fido is right in one respect; 23-year-old Jewish cobbler Nathan Kaminsky of 15 Black Lion Yard was probably the prime suspect as Leather Apron. Soon after the Leather Apron press scare began in

351

September 1888, he fled, and he may well have gone by the name Nathan Cohen or Aaron Davis Cohen, and hidden out at the Poor Jew's Shelter and the brothel at 254 Whitechapel Road. Now, where I differ with Fido is on the importance of Aaron Davis Cohen, and whether he was indeed Nathan Kaminsky. For a start, there is reason to believe that Cohen may have been a recent migrant to the country, or that possibly that he had family in Whitechapel. Upon his arrest, his address was listed as 86 Leman Street. Not only is this right across the road from Leman Street Police Station, effectively Ripper HQ, but the address is Whittington Protestant Boy's Club. However, next door at 84 Leman Street is the Poor Jews Temporary Shelter. Ideal, it seems, except for a small fact about the place that sheds considerable doubt on the theory; the shelter only housed recent migrants to the UK and only for two weeks. If he'd indeed been living there, he'd only been in the country since mid-November at the earliest, after the murders ceased. There are alternatives that could explain this, though; the man, who spoke only German, may have simply been assumed to be a recent migrant and the authorities just used the shelter as a placeholder; his real purpose at the shelter could have been weeks and weeks of round-the-clock observation by police at the station opposite, explaining Swanson's claims of such surveillance of their suspect (except that he specifies it was City Police who did the observing of the suspect, and that it occurred after he'd been identified at the Seaside Home which wouldn't be built for another two years); or alternatively, that his presence there was because he had family in the area. Indeed, the night-watchman of the Protestant Boy's Club that is recorded as Aaron Davis Cohen's address is named Henry Cohen, and could be a relative. That said, there's nothing to link them beyond the similar name.

Another problem comes from the demographic similarity of Cohen and Kaminsky, and the lack of evidence supporting them being one and the same. Quite simply, not a scrap of evidence of any kind indicates in any way that Aaron Davis Cohen is anyone but Aaron Davis Cohen. And not a scrap of evidence exists as to the whereabouts of Nathan Kaminsky after May 1888. Absolutely nothing exists to support Fido's supposition that these are the same men – a fact he admits in his summary of the theory in *The Mammoth Book of Jack the Ripper* (Jakubowski and Braund [eds] 2008, p. 173-195). He rests his case on the idea that the two are so similar, and also similar to Aaron Kosminski. However, I take a bigger-picture view on this.

For example, their presence at Colney Hatch Lunatic Asylum is not a particularly strong common denominator, as it was the biggest and most widely used asylum in the area. When looking at populations of the mentally ill in Victorian London, Colney Hatch is going to crop up an awful lot. It was home to two-and-a-half-thousand inmates at its height and the name seeped into popular culture as a by-word for mental illness. Given that Fido was looking for asylum inmates, this alone is not much of a surprise.

Also, the ages of these individuals aren't a surprise either. Schizophrenia tends to present in a serious way in the sufferer's early twenties. Aaron Davis Cohen and Aaron Kosminski were both 23 in 1888, and were admitted only three years apart to Colney Hatch, and both showed signs of psychosis. Two Jewish men (from a Jewish population in Whitechapel of up to 50,000) of about the same age, both showing signs of psychotic illness, ending up in the region's largest asylum within three years of each other, seems less of a startling coincidence now, and it seems even less of a coincidence if Cohen is not Kaminsky after all.

Fido's timings are also wrong. For Cohen to be Kaminsky, and for the Police to know this and be in a position to ever confuse the facts, they should have known of his existence. Fido's claim that Nathan Kaminsky/Aaron Davis Cohen was Jack the Ripper relies in there having been a positive witness identification of the man before his death in 1889 – but there's a problem; Anderson seems to believe the killer was still free in 1889. In his autobiography, *The Lighter Side of My Official Life*, after crediting the Ripper with "just" five murders, ending with Miller's Court, he says this of the murder of Alice McKenzie;

> I am here assuming that the murder of Alice M'Kenzie on the 17th July, 1889, was by another hand. I was absent from London when it occurred, but the Chief Commissioner investigated the case on the spot and decided that it was an ordinary murder and not the work of a sexual maniac. And the Poplar case of December 1888 was a death from natural causes, and but for the "Jack the Ripper" scare, no one would have thought of suggesting a homicide.

He assumes the McKenzie murder was not the Ripper, suggesting that he believed even as late as 1910 that the Ripper was still free by July 1889, when Aaron Davis Cohen, Fido's suspect, was dying in Colney Hatch and had been since December 7th the previous year. As for the "Poplar case," that too occurred in December 1888,

354

after Cohen had been arrested, put in front of a court and later sent to the asylum. It was the death of Rose Mylett, and is not seriously considered a Ripper case by any but those desperate to up Jack's body count for their own amusement. Thus, if Cohen's case was known to the top brass, under these circumstances it is highly unlikely such confusion would take place.

I believe it is immaterial if Kaminsky and Cohen were the same man, and I do not believe that either man had any meaningful involvement with the Ripper investigation ever again. I believe there is another interpretation of events which I will outline as we progress.

Conspiracies and Confusion

What conclusions, and what questions, have emerged so far from this discussion?

In September 1888, as the name of Leather Apron came to the attention of police investigating the murder of Mary Ann Nichols. Nathan Kaminsky – the real Leather Apron – flees his lodgings at 15 Black Lion Yard, and either leaves the area entirely or flits from doss to doss to escape the police dragnet. The Leather Apron scare really hits on 6th September with the front-page article in *The Star* and the Police's priority to find their suspect needs to become a covert operation while they engage in damage-control and try to prevent an outbreak of racial violence in the teeming abyss of the East End.

At this point, there are two small-scale conspiracies going on; the first was Swanson's obsession with his Jewish suspect (Nathan Kaminsky, aka Leather Apron), and his intention to drag the East End for him (a conspiracy that would later include Anderson at the very least, and possibly even Sir Charles Warren), using the name Kaminsky only in conversation and keeping the hunt off the books – hence the total lack of documentary evidence for any hunt for a Jewish suspect despite Anderson's later insistence of one. The second conspiracy was directed by Sir Charles Warren and involved community leaders such as Rabbi Adler and lower-ranked officers discharged to do his bidding and keep their mouths shut; this was to silence the very line of enquiry the police were pursuing, and erase all mention of a Jewish suspect, even whitewashing Jewish witnesses from recollections of the case (hence the possibly deliberate addition of the City PC witness at Mitre Square, who never existed). This extended as far as framing John Pizer just to quell the public's and press' thirst for some kind of resolution to the Leather Apron scare, and even destroying the Goulston Street graffiti to prevent racial violence in the soon-to-be-busy Wentworth Street and Commercial Street nearby. If the City PC story was a deliberate concoction to scrub Lawende and co. from history, then Swanson was certainly a co-conspirator to Warren.

By the Miller's Court murder, the threat of racial violence and the Jewish line in the investigation appears to have calmed down. However, references in witness George Hutchinson's statement to seeing a "Jewish looking" man in Miller's Court would be tactfully edited out for wider publication. As we have seen, this conspiracy was like something out of the Pink Panther – Joseph Lawende's description leaked to the press, as did the text of the Goulston Street graffiti, so their moronic attempts to cover this up seemed a waste of effort. The real end for the threat of racial violence came with the publication of the Dear Boss letter on 1st October 1888, in which the writer names himself Jack the Ripper and also pokes fun at the Leather Apron theory (in my own mind I have not ruled out the idea that this letter was composed in this manner at the direction of the police as part of the cover-up, but exploring that theory is a little beyond the scope of this book). Nevertheless, the murders ceased, but the police continued their hunt. Once the threat of racial violence was gone, it became apparent that the authorities had come to believe that a lunatic Jew was the killer. The cover-up was a waste of time, but those involved believed they had successfully identified the Ripper and that he was off the streets forever, a victory in the end.

However, quite how they came to the conclusions they did about this killer, that he was some vulnerable asylum inmate rather than the evidently violent Nathan Kaminsky (and under what circumstances they came to put Aaron in front of a witness for identification) has been a bone of contention. Having looked the evidence over, I think I know what happened.

I believe that in February 1891, Met CID came across the name of Kosminski in the admissions logs at Mile End Infirmary, whom they identified as being connected to a "Lion" Square, making the same error as Fido did, and immediately confused him with their hush-hush Leather Apron suspect whom they had spent so much time trying to capture. Quite possibly, they'd been using the name "Kosminski" in error in describing Nathan Kaminsky for years, since they appear to have been reticent to write down much about their more covert motives and operations. One of their observations about their freshly "rediscovered" suspect would be that they realise they'd missed him from the original door-to-door

357

inquiries by a matter of yards – Nathan Kaminsky's dwelling at Black Lion Yard is fifty yards inside the search area, but Aaron Kosminski's address at Sion Square is fifty yards out. They would have realised their mistake, but I believe they made the reverse assumption; that their identification of Black Lion Yard was wrong years before, and that their Kaminsky/Kosminski was from Sion Square all along. Thinking their long-missing Leather Apron had reappeared as an asylum inmate, they rapidly arrange an identification.

You may be wondering why I date the identification to February 1891. Allow me to explain. Anderson and Swanson differ on when this took place. Anderson, in his original drafts serialised in *Blackwood's Magazine*, states the identification took place whilst the suspect was already in an asylum. Swanson, in his marginalia, states it took place before, with the suspect being taken back to his brother's house for observation by the City Police, before being sent to "Stepney Workhouse" (Stepney being a name that appears to be used to describe a sweeping portion of the East End back in those days) and on to Colney Hatch. This contradiction suggests one of them is wrong – and it is likely Swanson, the only man of the top brass to consider Frances Coles to be a Ripper victim. One thing they all agree on is that there were no more murders after the suspect was identified and this is the latest murder any of them believe to have been committed by the Ripper. Aaron Kosminski was already in an asylum when Frances was killed, which would account for Anderson's recollection, because he believed the Miller's Court murder to be the last Ripper crime, but also Swanson's recollections. Given that Swanson's statements basically tally with the facts about Aaron Kosminski, who did indeed spend some time at his brother's house between his release from Mile End on 15th July 1890 and his re-admission on 7th February 1891 (facts he would have become aware of later and assumed to comply with a timeline favourable to his beliefs), and given that Swanson believed Frances Coles to have been a Ripper victim whilst Anderson did not, we can understand why he is so keen in 1910 to recall the identification occurring in a time frame which allows Kosminski to have killed Frances Coles – since in reality he had been transferred to Colney Hatch already when the murder occurred. This tells me that Anderson was probably correct in his timings and Swanson's recollections are wishful thinking.

However, the final piece of evidence dating the identification to February 1891 is that we know for a fact that the Mitre Square witness certainly did participate in at least one witness identification in February 1891. *The Daily Telegraph*, 18th February 1891 reports;

> Probably the only trustworthy description of the assassin was given by a gentleman who, on the night of the Mitre-Square murder, noticed in Duke Street, Aldgate, a couple standing under the lamp at the corner of the passage leading to Mitre-Square. The woman was identified as the victim of that night, September 30, the other having been killed half an hour previously in Berner-Street. The man was described as aged from thirty to thirty-five, height 5ft 7in, with brown hair and big moustache; dressed respectively. Wore pea jacket, muffler, and a cloth cap with a peak of the same material. The witness has confronted Sadler but has failed to identify him

JACK THE RIPPER

Thomas Sadler was arrested for the Frances Coles murder on the 15th February 1891, and the article dates from the 18th – thus, the identification parade likely involved both Kosminski and Sadler with the witness tasked with identifying either of them as the Ripper. As Sadler wasn't identified by the witness but Kosminski was – but also, that Kosminski was already in an asylum when the Coles murder occurred – Swanson is trying to have his cake and eat it too in his recollections.

Another thing to consider when speaking of Swanson's recollections as far as the marginalia are concerned, is that he is speaking of City of London Police surveillance, and City Police witnesses – I conclude that in all likelihood, these Met officers are recalling details provided to them of a City Police operation, not one of their own. Therefore, confusion of the details and misremembered details are quite likely. However, it cannot be understated that these men, Anderson and Swanson, are recalling second-hand information decades after the events. Even an event as important as a positive identification of a suspect can be fogged-up by time and Chinese whispers.

I genuinely believe that what the police describe as their identification of Kosminski was correct, and that they were talking about Aaron Kosminski. However, I believe that they mistakenly thought this was the very same man they'd been hunting. To put it another way, they had an idea about the first half of this man's life, as the violent misogynist Leather Apron, and just assumed this Aaron Kosminski fellow was the same man, now confined to the asylum years later. So, when they put a witness in front of Aaron Kosminski, any admission that they recognised him would have been interpreted as the witness admitting Kosminski was Leather Apron, and by

360

extension Jack the Ripper. The witness then trying to explain that they know the man but not as the suspect they saw would fall on deaf ears – indeed, Anderson and Swanson put the witness' unwillingness to testify down to him being unwilling to send a fellow Jew to the gallows. Racial solidarity, an ignorant stereotype they fell back on when the truth just wouldn't sink in.

As to who the witness was, Fido himself says that Aaron Kosminski's eccentric behaviour, such as eating bread from the gutters, meant he was probably "a visible City and East End figure" (p. 226), meaning the witness, whoever it was, may have recognised the man anyway. With this in mind, we are left to assume the police were simply not willing to believe that Kosminski wasn't the man they thought he was, and instead accused the witness of being deliberately difficult.

This does somewhat raise the question of exactly who the witness was, yet again. Despite both mine and the wider Ripperology community's assumption that Anderson's witness was probably Joseph Lawende, there is a strong possibility that it was in fact his friend Joseph Hyam Levy, who if you recall was also present that night in Mitre Square. If so, then I believe this provides the final clues to exactly what happened.

Joseph Hyam Levy: Curious Connections

The Kosminski Family

Levy's candidacy as an important witness has leverage in media reports at the time. His comments during the incident itself – not wanting to be around when certain "sorts" of people are around, and commenting that Mitre

Court "ought to be watched," lend some weight to this. But there is also a very interesting press report that refers to Joseph Hyam Levy in unflattering terms around the time of the inquest. In the *Evening News*, 9th October 1888, he is referred to in this way;

> Mr. Joseph Levy is absolutely obstinate and refuses to give us the slightest information. He leaves one to infer that he knows something, but that he is afraid to be called on the inquest. Hence he assumes a knowing air

This certainly suggests he knew more than he was letting on and that he feared for his personal safety (thought denied this at the inquest). A very interesting figure, his importance only grows when you look deeper into his character. For example, there is an argument, however slight, that Joseph Hyam Levy may have known Aaron Kosminski.

Scott Nelson (2008) makes the case for this. Pointing out that one of Aaron Kosminski's sisters changed her name to Cohen by the time of the 1901 census, and that a Jacob Cohen witnessed Aaron's admission to Colney Hatch Asylum in 1891, there may have been a family agreement to abandon the Kosminski name by the turn of the century. Indeed, living relatives of Aaron Kosminski in the present day refer to his incarceration as a "scandal." This gets juicier when you consider that a Jacob Koski (possibly a mis-spelling of Kosminski) lived next door to Joseph Hyam Levy at 2 Hutchinson Street in 1891, and that Levy apparently abandoned his prosperous butchery business in 1891 or 1892 and vanished from the census altogether. Jacob Koski and family also vanish from 1901 onwards – after the time the identification of Aaron Kosminski in Colney Hatch would have occurred. The links only deepen, though; in 1877, Joseph Hyam Levy sponsored the naturalisation of a man named Martin Kosminski to the UK. His family appears to have migrated to the UK too – Polish census records reveal a Mosiek and Szmul Kosminski, who appear to be the brothers listed in the UK census as Martin and Samuel Kosminski, and a third brother Jacob – who may indeed be Jacob Koski. Records for Poland in the 19th Century are patchy and incomplete so there is no record of an Aaron in the family, however, so far, no definitive paper trail on Aaron Kosminski has been identified. Also, there is only a weak paper trail on Aaron's brother Woolf, who again, could be part of the same Kosminski clan.

This theory is quite simple; Joseph Hyam Levy knew the Kosminski family, and therefore probably knew Aaron by sight. If he, and not Joseph Lawende, was in fact the Jewish witness called to identify the suspected Ripper at the Seaside Home in February 1891 as I hypothesise, he may well have told police he knows exactly who the man is, and identified him as Aaron Kosminski. But then, when pressed, refused point-blank the notion that he was the Mitre Square suspect, because he wasn't. Swanson and Anderson, by now convinced of their suspect's identity and guilt, put this uncooperative behaviour down to Jewish solidarity and contented themselves with the fact that their man was locked away in an asylum never to trouble London again.

But this still leaves inconsistencies.

Swanson said the killer was not only incarcerated in an asylum, but had died shortly afterwards. He also elaborated that City Police had watched the man on Met territory round-the-clock before he was carted off. How to

363

explain these details? For starters, I will make one thing clear – I believe Swanson is getting his cases mixed up, in a similar fashion to how Fido believed he was mixing up Aaron Davis Cohen and Aaron Kosminski. However, the link between these cases is not the suspects, not quite to the same extent, but the witness. See, Joseph Hyam Levy had the dubious honour of being a Ripper witness with a personal connection to at least two Jewish asylum patients in the 1880s and 1890s, each of whom are potential candidates for Anderson's and Swanson's suspect, but also according to some commentators, the Ripper himself. I believe that the answers we seek to understand the esoteric comments and recollections of the officers in charge can be found in the story of Jacob Levy.

Cousin Jacob

I believe that Joseph Hyam Levy's cousin, Jacob Levy, could provide a lot of answers to our unresolved questions.

Joseph Hyam Levy's uncle, also called Joseph Levy, had a son named Jacob. Jacob Levy was a man who became a butcher like his father, lived mere yards from Joseph Hyam Levy near Butcher's Row in Aldgate, and had a history of both criminal activity (theft of meat from a rival butcher), and mental illness. Indeed, on 15th August 1890 he was admitted to Stone Asylum in Surrey for "mania," dying on 29th July 1891 from complications to an infection of syphilis, potentially picked up from local prostitutes. Jacob Levy's wife said of his illness,

> [H]e also feels that if he is not restrained he
> will do some violence to someone; he

364

complains about hearing strange noises; cries
for no reason; feels compelled to do acts that
his conscience cannot stand; and has a
conscience of a feeling of exaltation.

She also suggested he walked aimlessly for hours.

This is all well and good, but where is the real
reason to place any suspicion on this guy, I hear you ask?
For one thing, Jacob Levy lived and worked within the
boundaries of the City Police, and only just. As previously
noted, it seems Swanson in his recollections is working
from second-hand information provided by the City Police
with regards his suspect, and it is more than likely that
details have been confused in transit. So what
involvement did Jacob Levy have with the City Police? The
answer comes from the recollections of a City Policeman,
no less than the force's liaison with the Metropolitan
Police over the Ripper investigation, Detective Inspector
Robert Sagar.

In 1905 he gave a series of interviews about his
long career with the force to mark his retirement. The
details differ depending on the source, as it was printed in
papers around the world, but the facts can be drawn out
to a reliable standard. Whilst the interview covers many
key aspects of Sagar's life, the final part focuses on the
Ripper crimes. Tellingly, he speaks of being present at
nightly meetings with the Met at Leman Street Police
Station regarding the Ripper murders, and this would
have put him in daily and direct contact with Swanson
first, then Swanson and Anderson together. This provides
context for what follows in the interview, considering
what we have already discussed regarding their
collaboration in pushing the Jewish suspect theory.

A cast-iron clue as to the two-way-influence of

JACK THE RIPPER

Swanson and Sagar upon one another is Sagar's
regurgitation of the erroneous "City PC at Mitre Square"
story – a sure-fire dog-whistle of Swanson's influence.
From the *Seattle Daily Times*, 4th February 1905;

> "We believe," he said, "that he came nearest to
> being captured after the Mitre Square murder in
> which the woman Kelly was the victim. She
> had been detained in Bishopsgate police station
> until 1 a. m. At 1:45 a. m. she was dead. A
> police officer met a well dressed man of Jewish
> appearance coming out of the court. Continuing
> on his patrol he came across the woman's body.
> He blew his whistle, and sent the other officers
> who rushed up in pursuit, the only thing to
> guide them being the sound of retreating
> footsteps. The sounds were followed to King's
> Block in the model dwellings in Stoney Lane,
> but the search got no further.

As with the other occasions this story has emerged, the
line about "retreating footsteps" marks this as a fudged
recollection of the Frances Coles murder, but the Jewish
suspect he refers to is more than likely the one Joseph
Lawende and Joseph Hyam Levy allegedly saw, according
to Anderson! Nonetheless, we move on. In speaking of the
suspects, Sagar explains that "suspicion fell upon a man
who, without doubt, was the murderer." From the
Morning Leader, 9th January 1905;

> We had good reason to suspect a certain man
> who worked in 'Butcher's-row,' Aldgate," he
> said, "and we watched him carefully. There was
> no doubt that this man was insane, and after a
> time his friends thought it advisable to have

366

him removed to a private asylum. After he was
removed there were no more Ripper atrocities.

Butcher's Row was the colloquial name for a short section
of Aldgate High Street, yards from the boundary between
the City Police and Met Police jurisdictional boundaries. In
geographical terms, the site is a short walk from a few
very crucial sites; yards from Mitre Square where
Catharine Eddowes was murdered, a street away from
Castle Alley where apocryphal Ripper victim Alice
McKenzie was killed, and a short walk to Dorset Street
where Miller's Court saw murder. It was, as the name
suggests, a row of butcher's shops and slaughterhouses,
and we know from census records that Jacob Levy lived
with his family just around the corner at Middlesex Street.
Sagar suggests the suspect worked on Butcher's Row and
it is quite likely that is true given Levy's proximity.

As a butcher or a slaughterman, Jacob would have
the knowhow and the stomach for the Ripper murders.
Cutting animals' throats and gutting them would have
been his stock-in-trade, and if anything is to be read into
his wife's comments that he is driven to commit "acts his
conscience cannot stand," and that his ultimately fatal
syphilis infection probably came from prostitutes, a
simple argument can be made to his supposed guilt.
Certainly, it was Jewish butchers and slaughtermen that
were being touted as potential Ripper suspects almost
from the get-go. It would certainly explain why the killer
of Mary Ann Nichols seemed to stray far from the other
murder sites, given a horse slaughterer's yard was
immediately next to the scene, suggesting he knew it
from experience. I cannot doubt that Levy is a convincing
suspect, and if he was the Ripper, it would also account for
Joseph Hyam Levy's obstinate demeanour and his uneasy

behaviour at Mitre Square.

From these few details, one can see how the "clearly insane" Jacob Levy, the Jewish butcher, may have fallen under suspicion. And what's more, he was a relation and neighbour of one of the Mitre Square witnesses! However, a comment by Sagar reported in the *City Press*, 7th January 1905, brings up a troubling variation to his retirement story;

> Identification being impossible, he could not be charged. He was, however, placed in a lunatic asylum, and the series of atrocities came to an end.

Identification being impossible. So, despite being a relation of one of the key witnesses, he was apparently not formally identified. That said, we're working from one newspaper report, and the reports of the very same story across different newspapers do not concur, so who knows what Sagar actually said – one of the sources basically quotes Sagar as saying the killer fled to Australia whilst another opens by refuting reports the killer fled the country at all!

My theory, then, is this; Swanson – writing in 1910 or after – confused the Kosminski case with his incomplete, second-hand recollections of the Jacob Levy case, as he'd gleaned back in 1891 from his City counterpart Detective Inspector Robert Sagar, who it seemed also believed the lunatic Jew theory. Jacob Levy, whether he was being watched by the police or not, would die in July 1891. As I argue, the Kosminski identification at the Seaside Home occurred between 15th-18th February 1891, within days of the events of the Frances Coles murder, which appears to explain Swanson's recollection that the killer died "soon after" his incarceration in an asylum. It also explains nicely why Swanson, in 1910 or later, recalls a Jewish suspect being watched round-the-clock by City police, as he knew only that of Sagar's suspect and attributed it to Kosminski. That the Met found Kosminski whilst following the slim details provided of the City suspect is unsurprising – the timings involved are astonishing;

12th July 1890 – Aaron Kosminski admitted to Mile End
15th July 1890 – Aaron Kosminski leaves Mile End
15th August 1890 – Jacob Levy admitted to Stone Asylum
7th February 1891 – Aaron Kosminski was admitted to Colney Hatch
13th February 1891 – Frances Coles was murdered.
15th February 1891 – Thomas Sadler arrested for Frances Coles murder
13th - 18th February 1891 – Met Police arrange Sadler identification
29th July 1891 – Jacob Levy dies

There is nothing to really indicate that Sagar is speaking of Jacob Levy, but there is one more source to consider. Researcher Steward Hicks, an accountant who investigated his own theory on the murders, is cited as recalling a story told by none other than Sir Robert Anderson's wife, Lady Anderson, suggesting that Jack the Ripper was incarcerated in an asylum near Stone. It seems likely she was referring to the City of London Asylum, in Stone, Kent. This would appear to mean Jacob Levy when you consider Sagar's testimony, and thus, this provides a somewhat satisfactory conclusion to the riddle – that the facts in this case are fluid, and are thrown around depending on the theory you prefer. Ripperology is much the same today.

Truth, Lies and Conspiracy

Let me now summarise this section and outline my final theory.

What started out as a murder investigation soon became an exercise in political posturing, damage-limitation, community relations work and racial politics. As we saw, there were likely two conspiracies in play, each related to the other – a conspiracy that started with Chief Inspector Donald Swanson, and would later involve Sir Robert Anderson and Detective Inspector Robert Sagar to focus the investigation of the Ripper murders onto the Jewish community to pin down their prime suspect since day one, the violent thug "Leather Apron," and a conspiracy from the very top, spearheaded by Sir Charles Warren, the Commissioner of the Metropolitan Police, to silence any mention of a Jewish suspect. This meant everything from framing John Pizer as Leather Apron to destroying the Goulston Street graffiti, to even editing politically sensitive material from witness statements (as in George Hutchinson's statement). These motivations ran counter to each other and made the investigation a cloak-and-dagger affair, with the intelligence-trained Anderson keeping the hunt for their suspect off the books and "need-to-know," and therefore, left the details open to confusion.

This lead to an almighty error on the part of the police; their mistaken belief that in 1891, they finally found their prime suspect, the figure known as Leather Apron, detained in an asylum. This was partly thanks to their rivals in the City evidently providing titbits of information about their operations but leaving out the important details.

Since the murders began, Swanson, and later Anderson, had nightly meetings with their City counterpart, Detective Inspector Robert Sagar, who since probably mid-1890 has been watching his own suspect – a Jewish butcher named Jacob Levy, the cousin of Joseph Hyam Levy – and who sharing scant information on this operation with the Met. The Met, still hunting their prime suspect Leather Apron, assumed that the City's suspect is the same man, and later added what they know of the City's observation of their suspect to what they think they know of the suspect. This confusion leads Swanson to later report two facts incorrectly about his suspect Kosminski; that the City had him under 24-hour surveillance, and that he died "shortly after" admittance to Colney Hatch. Jacob Levy was likely under surveillance during July 1890, only to be admitted in the August, and he in fact died in July 1891 not long after the Kosminski identification would have happened.

Since Kosminski was admitted to Mile End in July 1890, the Met may have trawled asylum and infirmary admissions for the past few months to try and catch up with their rivals in the City. They then found Aaron Kosminski's admission to Mile End in July 1890. It was this admission log that showed Kosminski's brother's address as Sion Square, that could be misread as "Lion" Square, and which lead them to believe he was their Leather Apron suspect. They realise that this address falls a matter of yards outside of their original house-to-house search area during the Ripper hunt, whilst Black Lion Yard lies just inside. Assuming they'd misidentified their suspect all the way back in 1888 and that this Aaron Kosminski, and not Nathan Kaminsky, is their real Leather Apron – and therefore attributing all they'd heard of their suspect and his violent and perverted deeds to this poor innocent man – they proceed with a witness identification. Since the identification of Thomas Sadler took place at the same time as part of the Frances Coles investigation, it is possible that the Mitre Square witness, whether it was Joseph Lawende or Joseph Hyam Levy, was asked to identify at least two potential Ripper suspects in one go.

If the witness was Joseph Hyam Levy, and if he did indeed know the same Kosminski family, then it is more than likely he was able to identify Aaron Kosminski immediately. The police, by now convinced that this was the very same man as their long-sought Leather Apron, simply can't absorb what their witness is telling them – yes, he recognised Aaron Kosminski, but no, he's not the man he saw at Mitre Square. The police obstinately put this down to a Jew being unwilling to testify against a fellow Jew, and send Kosminski back to Colney Hatch. The proximity in time to the Frances Coles murder, which Swanson believed to be a Ripper crime, also explains why he recalls the witness identification as occurring prior to the suspect's detention in the asylum, whilst Anderson correctly recalls the suspect being incarcerated already. Thus, the witness identification by Lawende or Levy of Aaron Kosminski must have occurred at the Seaside Home in Brighton, in between 13th-18th February 1891.

Scotland Yard would eventually claim that Jack the Ripper was a lunatic Jew who had been detained in an asylum, whilst Anderson's memoirs cause a stir as it becomes apparent that this fixation on a Jewish Ripper did not extent further down the ranks than Swanson, and was not shared by his counterparts in the City, with the apparent exception of Robert Sagar.

In conclusion, Aaron Kosminski was the police's

suspect, but only because they were too keen to be correct about their Leather Apron theory – and scrambled the details horribly. Largely the mistakes made by the police to reach this conclusion were down to their secretive and off-the-books search for a Jewish suspect, one that had to remain active by word of mouth only with little or no paper trail because at the very same time, Sir Charles Warren was directing a conspiracy of silence and mounting a cover-up over the suggestion of a Jewish suspect for political reasons. Only years later, in 1910, did Sir Robert Anderson feel the need to break the silence and admit their conclusions about the Jewish suspect.

I think all Ripperologists hope more documentary evidence comes to light someday, and I hope one day we will know the whole truth about the police's suspect, "Kosminski."

PART THREE: Profiling Jack the Ripper

JACK THE RIPPER

"Blowing In The Wind..."

Whilst the police of 1888 believed they had a solid theory – and maybe even solution – as to the identity of Jack the Ripper, this does not equal a resolution. I like to think sometimes that the truth of the identity of the Ripper is one of those truths that exist yet are unreachable to our memory, blowing in the wind and forever a part of the world that we just can't see. Theories and suppositions and beliefs are all well and good but there is one objective truth regarding the Ripper's identity, the number of murders he committed, his motives and his eventual fate. Somewhere in this world the real Ripper's bones lie unrecognised in a cemetery, or his ashes still litter where they were scattered in minute particles. Getting a theory to fit, loving the hell out of it and believing it to be the truth even when the theory is being dismantled by your peers or even lauded and praised is no substitute to knowing this truth.

To get anywhere near this truth requires throwing away the pre-existing theories and looking at the cold, hard evidence. Therefore, I have had to grit my teeth and accept some tough notions in the writing of this book. Elizabeth Stride was killed by someone else, and not Jack the Ripper. Mary Jane Kelly looks likely to have survived

Miller's Court and her mysterious companion "Julia" is likely immortalised as a mutilated corpse on a blood-soaked bed for all eternity. I even hated the idea of Sir Robert Anderson and Donald Swanson ever getting their mitts anywhere near Aaron Kosminski, hoping that they'd learnt about him second-hand, but it seems more likely given the evidence that he was subjected to a (probably bewildering) identity parade by police who thought him a pervert and murderer. Sometimes one must accept truths that are not palatable and in writing this book I've had to accept many. I hope, reader, you approach my theories and suggestions, whether they be original to me or reconstitutions of suggested by others over the years, with an open and inquisitorial mind. Between us we can uncover the truth.

The same is true of understanding the killer himself. Many theories abound about "why" the killer murdered four or five, or more, victims in the East End. Most, sadly, are Hollywood inspired; the killer was picking off a circle of friends one by one like some slasher movie villain to cover up a secret that involves the Royal family; the killer was a mad midwife; he was a mad surgeon; he was carrying out a religious or Masonic ritual. You name it. The truth is, each of these theories have the same thing in common; the search for a meaningful pattern, some goal in mind the killer "must" have had. Human beings in general search for meaning and when they cannot find it, substitute it for their own ideas – usually projections of their own inner beliefs, such as those who insist the killer was "cleaning the streets" of sex workers as part of a moral mission, which is a purely fictional motivation for serial killers. We have been spoon-fed a diet of detective dramas and slickly-packaged news that focuses on crime and murder for so long that we are used to viewing crime in such a way, particularly murder. The killer simply had to have had a motive, otherwise...why did he do it?

Serial killers are a huge part of our popular culture, but sadly they are often misrepresented in the media. The off-the-shelf motives ascribed to serial killers are trotted out often – including the old canard of a killer murdering a series of victims just to cover a single murder, as in Agatha Christie's The ABC Murders, for example. This just does not happen in real life. Men like Jack the Ripper – and yes, as if the witness statements weren't enough, the Ripper's crimes are unequivocally that of a man – are driven by more complex, unseen and idiosyncratic motivations that often revolve around their deep-seated perceptions, beliefs, sexual and violent urges, fantasies and cycles of addiction and arousal. But the idea of a killer randomly, or semi-randomly, targeting and murdering women and subjecting them to debauched and humiliating mutilations to satisfy his psychopathic sexual fantasies just does not tally with our Hollywood education. Worse, it does something far more tough to swallow; it reminds us of our own base urges, our secret sexual and violent fantasies, our capacity for cruelty and perverse satisfaction. The Ripper reminds people we are all animals, predators, and that anyone could be the Ripper. If the Ripper was murdering the witnesses to a Royal secret, then he's some paid lackey. If he's a pervert hunting and killing women for sexual kicks, he could be anyone. And that's the scary part.

In this chapter, I will outline three pre-existing theories and psychological profiles put across about the killer by various sources – Dr. Thomas Bond in 1888, Sir Robert Anderson in 1910, and the Federal Bureau of Investigation (FBI) in 1988 – before analysing the crimes myself, pointing out the killer's "cardinal behaviours," the evidence of escalation and threads of evolution and signature in the murders, in order to develop a psychological profile of the killer based on the evidence.

Thomas Bond and Sir Robert Anderson: Contemporary Profiles of the Killer

Thomas Bond is considered by many to be the first offender profiler. He was certainly qualified – he swapped his life in the Prussian military for a distinguishing career in medicine and became the Police Surgeon to Westminster's A Division twenty years prior to the Ripper murders. He attended to the Miller's Court murder, and his autopsy report on the victim – lost for years – was finally located in 1987 among papers returned anonymously to Scotland Yard. He would also write reports for Alice McKenzie and Rose Mylett, as well as being directly involved in the so-called Torso Murders that occurred concurrent to the Ripper crimes. In fact, he was in the right place and the right time to have developed a keen eye for unusual crime scenes and a unique insight into the methods and motives of murderers, particularly in the sense of their psychological motivation and their characteristics. This is reflected in his report on the Ripper murders, delivered to Sir Robert Anderson on 10th November 1888, the day after the Miller's Court murder. In it, he makes some interesting observations about the five cases but also provides the very first example of an offender profile relating to Jack the Ripper;

I beg to report that I have read the notes of the
4 Whitechapel Murders viz:
1. Buck's Row.

2. Hanbury Street.

3. Berner's Street.

4. Mitre Square.

I have also made a Post Mortem Examination of the mutilated remains of a woman found yesterday in a small room in Dorset Street -

1. All five murders were no doubt committed by the same hand. In the first four the throats appear to have been cut from left to right. In the last case owing to the extensive mutilation it is impossible to say in what direction the fatal cut was made, but arterial blood was found on the wall in splashes close to where the woman's head must have been lying.

2. All the circumstances surrounding the murders lead me to form the opinion that the women must have been lying down when murdered and in every case the throat was first cut.

3. In the four murders of which I have seen the notes only, I cannot form a very definite opinion as to the time that had elapsed between the murder and the discovering of the body. In one case, that of Berner's Street, the discovery appears to have been made immediately after the deed - In Buck's Row, Hanbury Street, and Mitre Square three or four hours only could have elapsed. In the Dorset Street case the body was lying on the bed at the time of my visit, 2 o'clock, quite naked and mutilated as in the annexed report -

Rigor Mortis had set in, but increased during the progress of the examination. From this it is difficult to say with any degree of certainty the exact time that had elapsed since death as the period varies from 6 to 12 hours before rigidity sets in. The body was comparatively cold at 2 o'clock and the remains of a recently taken meal were found in the stomach and scattered about over the intestines. It is, therefore, pretty certain that the woman must have been dead about 12 hours and the partly digested food would indicate: that death took place about 3 or 4 hours after the food was taken, so one or two o'clock in the morning would be the probable time of the murder.

4. In all the cases there appears to be no evidence of struggling and the attacks were probably so sudden and made in such a position that the women could neither resist nor cry out. In the Dorset Street case the corner of the sheet to the right of the woman's head was much cut and saturated with blood, indicating that the face may have been covered with the sheet at the time of the attack.

5. In the four first cases the murderer must have attacked from the right side of the victim. In the Dorset Street case, he must have attacked from in front or from the left, as there would be no room for him between the wall and the part of the bed on which the woman was lying. Again, the blood had flowed down on the right side of the woman and spurted on to the wall.

6. The murderer would not necessarily be splashed or deluged with blood, but his hands' and arms must have been covered and parts of his clothing must certainly have been smeared with blood.

7. The mutilations in each case excepting the Berner's Street one were all of the same character and shewed clearly that in all the murders, the object was mutilation.

8. In each case the mutilation was inflicted by a person who had no scientific nor anatomical knowledge. In my opinion be does not even possess the technical knowledge of a butcher or horse slaughterer or any person accustomed to cut up dead animals.

9. The instrument must have been a strong knife at least six inches long, very sharp, pointed at the top and about an inch in width. It may have been a clasp knife, a butcher's knife or a surgeon's knife. I think it was no doubt a straight knife.

10. The murderer must have been a man of physical strength and of great coolness and daring. There is no evidence that he had an accomplice. He must in my opinion be a man subject to periodical attacks of Homicidal and erotic mania. The character of the mutilations indicate that the man may be in a condition sexually, that may be called satyriasis. It is of course possible that the Homicidal impulse may have developed from a revengeful or brooding condition of the mind, or that Religious Mania may have been the original disease, but I do not think either hypothesis is likely. The murderer in external appearance is quite likely to be a quiet inoffensive looking man probably middleaged and neatly and respectably dressed. I think he must be in the habit of wearing a cloak or overcoat or he could hardly have escaped notice in the streets if the blood on his hands or clothes were visible.

11. Assuming the murderer to be such a person as I have just described he would probably be solitary and eccentric in his habits, also he is

most likely to be a man without regular
occupation, but with some small income or
pension. He is possibly living among
respectable persons who have some knowledge
of his character and habits and who may have
grounds for suspicion that he is not quite right
in his mind at times. Such persons would
probably be unwilling to communicate
suspicions to the Police for fear of trouble or
notoriety, whereas if there were a prospect of
reward it might overcome their scruples.
I am, Dear Sir,
Yours faithfully,
Thos. Bond.

In summary, Bond says the following of the killer, his
methods and motives;

- That he killed all five victims
- That he murdered the victims whilst they lay on
  the ground
- That the victims were given no time to struggle,
  and in fact the Miller's Court victim may have had
  her face covered during the assault
- That the killer likely had little blood on him
  because of the attacks
- The object of the murder was the mutilation
- The killer possessed absolutely no anatomical
  knowledge, not even that of a slaughterman
- That a sharp, pointed, six-inch strong bladed knife
  was used in each case, such as a butcher's knife.
- The killer was cool, physically powerful, outwardly
  ineffectual, and driven by some deep-seated
  sexual mania.

- The killer had no accomplices
- The killer would be middle-aged, unemployed, solitary and eccentric, raising concern and suspicion among those closest to him.

These are astute comments for the time they were written. The comments about the killer suffering bouts of homicidal and erotic mania are astonishingly prescient – in fact, credit must be given to Bond but also to Dr. Gordon Brown on his presence of mind to examine Catharine Eddowes' body, including her abdomen and thighs, for evidence of ejaculate as would be expected of a sexually-motivated serial killer. These men were certainly encountering a type of killer they'd likely never seen before, but they did so with a fresh and keen perspective that proved they were no fools to what was going on. As such, they were able to lend their opinion as to the type of man they expected to find committing these murders – not some knuckle-dragging bloodstained lunatic raving about whores and randomly attacking folk in the street, but someone quiet and solitary, a nobody who blends in, suffering a private psychosis that lead him to indulge his twisted desires when the mood took him, efficiently and cleanly murdering his victims with the goal of mutilating them.

However, Sir Robert Anderson – who suspected a lunatic Jew was the killer – commented in his memoirs that;

> "One did not need to be a Sherlock Holmes to discover that the criminal was a sexual maniac of a virulent type; that he was living in the immediate vicinity of the scenes of the murders; and that, if he was not living

385

absolutely alone, his people knew of his guilt,
and refused to give him up to justice."

In his world the killer was someone venturing not far from home to kill in his insane state, and his obvious guilt was being concealed by "his people" evidently because the Jewish heart of the district, where he deduced the killer must be living, turned up nothing of substance during the extensive house-to-house searches. Nevertheless, he did recognise the sexual element of the crimes, despite an absence of sexual contact between killer and victim in all cases. I find it amazing that even today, 2st Century commentators struggle to accept this obvious fact; that the Ripper was sexually motivated, when even someone as blinkered as Anderson saw the obvious way back in 1888.

All in all, the police and medical professionals of 1888 seemed aware of the nature of the killer. A loner, a sexually-motivated killer who acted on his impulses with some degree of cunning and cool calculation but who also was acting on base urges that meant his swift executions were followed up by horrendous mutilations that appeared to be the very motive for the crimes. A man living in the very centre of the district within easy reach of the crimes. A middle-aged unemployed man of eccentric habits, who was otherwise the sort of person who blended in.

It would be another century before the experts would have their say. To mark the centenary of the murders, the Federal Bureau of Investigation (FBI) in the United States, who had coined the term "serial killer" in the 1960s and pioneered psychological profiling of offenders, released a psychological profile of Jack the Ripper. On 6th July 1988 the profile was released from the

National Centre for the Analysis of Violent Crime (NCAVC) having been compiled by renowned profiler John Douglas. Let's take a look.

FBI Profile 1988

The FBI's profile of the Ripper is available to view online at **vault.fbi.gov/JacktheRipper.** It is a fascinating read, a real insight into how the FBI would approach a latter-day criminal profile. I implore you read it to learn exactly how they come to their conclusions. It is divided into sections and I will use those as a guide to provide you with the best insight into the material I can. Sadly, I cannot quote the material directly, but I will give an overview of the contents and a discussion of their meaning as we proceed.

First, victimology. The Ripper's victims were all either prostitutes or were poor, vulnerable and resorted to sex work during their lives. Serial killers often target such women because of their vulnerability. This is true then and today; serial killers such as Peter Sutcliffe, Stephen Wright, Alun Kyte and Stephen Griffiths hoovered up sex workers because of their easy access and worse, the fact that they could be made to vanish with little fanfare. The sexual element can be seen here by comparing these crimes with those of, for example, Michael Lupo, Stephen Port or Colin Ireland, gay men who murdered gay men and got away with it for a longer time again because of the victims' high risk and the lack of social concern that follows them. Dennis Nilsen similarly targeted those who fell through the cracks of society, killing as many as 16 victims without anyone apparently noticing.

How the killer carried out his crimes proved key to how the FBI constructed their profile. As has become apparent in the earlier examination of the cases, the killer was almost passive in his actions – silencing his victims rapidly with a blitz attack, strangling them and mutilating them after death. There was no torture, little blood and no sexual molestation of the victims. He took trophies including organs, which to the FBI suggested at least some anatomical knowledge. This is a behavioural pattern the FBI would be familiar with as they deal with serial killers of all varieties, yet encounter sexually-motivated killers most regularly. It is for this reason that their profile can be trusted – the very agency that coined the phrase "serial killer" and pioneered criminal profiling work with such offenders as their stock-in-trade. Analysis of the crime scenes is vital to understanding how the criminal behaves and how they think.

The FBI profile continues with a breakdown of the key characteristics of the crime and the crime scenes;

- All but one victim killed outdoors.
- All the murders occurred within a quarter of a mile of each other,
- The murders all occurred in the early hours of Friday, Saturday or Sunday.
- There may have been other attacks not connected by authorities to the Ripper

The profile then moves on to make a clear distinction between *modus operandi* and *signature/ritual.* This is vitally important so that the layman can understand the crimes in a criminological context. I will explain here but the profile says much the same thing.

Modus operandi literally means "method of operation" and refers to those actions that are necessary for the commission of a crime. The "MO" is a practical concern and is therefore malleable, the killer learning and adapting as he goes. Therefore, killers can and do change their *modus operandi* to suit their needs, or to accommodate their learning and development. In the case of the Ripper, he did indeed have an MO that changed as he went, the starkest change to that MO coming when he murdered the Miller's Court victim indoors having killed the rest outdoors. To those who immediately point and declare that to be "proof" the Ripper did not murder her because "killers don't change their MO," I point to the murder of Patricia "Tina" Atkinson on 23rd April 1977 by Peter Sutcliffe. After murdering three victims and attacking several more in outdoor locations, Sutcliffe murdered Tina inside her flat. Serial murderers do change their MO.

Signature or Ritual is those actions unnecessary to the commission of the crime, but which reflects the offender's psychopathology. Usually, these actions are, in the context of serial murder, reflective of the killer's motivating fantasies or perversions, and can also reflect images, scripts or actions the killer is compelled to carry out to obtain their psycho-sexual satisfaction. In the case of the Ripper, his ritual is the post-mortem mutilation of his victims. Strangling his victims and swiftly cutting their throats are necessary actions to commit the murder, but the abdominal and genital mutilations are not, and reflect motivations on the killer's part that go beyond that which is practical or utilitarian. Because of the psychological and sexual roots of this signature/ritual, it rarely changes. This is the motivation for the crime, and whilst the method of carrying out the crime may change, this does not.

As for the letters allegedly sent by the killer, the FBI, like myself, place no value on them, although my opinion on the "From Hell" letter is a begrudging acceptance that it is more likely than not to be a genuine communique from the killer. This is controversial as it is very rare for serial killers to send communiques to anyone – the Zodiac killer was an exception, but that is likely related to the fact he claimed numerous attacks as his own that demonstrably were not. He was an egomaniac whose letters included demands for the citizens of San Francisco to wear Zodiac badges for him to admire as he went about his day-to-day existence – an exercise in control rather than an honest communication. He set puzzles and made threats, boasted and mocked, but never gave anything away. Serial killers who write to the media or the police either go big or go home. The Ripper letters were just long-winded rants written to sell newspapers (except, possibly, the "From Hell" letter), and that is the opinion of the FBI.

Next, the profile explains the assumed characteristics of the killer. To be clear, the FBI are not guessing or applying some esoteric laboratory logic to their estimations; they develop their information on the characteristics of murderers through their investigative successes. When they make an assertion, they have an explanation for it based on real-world investigatory experience. Hence, they can offer a breakdown of the killer's likely characteristics because they have dealt with similar killers before and have developed their information from there.

I will summarise their description of the offender profile;

- The Ripper is a lust killer, one whose psychopathology is focused on the victims' genitals and sexual organs due to his own sexual deviancy.

- A white male, owing to the demographics of the area and the predominance of male sexually-motivated serial killers.
- 28-36 years old.
- Appears to be ordinary-looking and approachable to his victims.
- Raised by a domineering, alcoholic mother, father absent, and had inconsistent care and inadequate adult role models. This would result in poor socialization and acts of cruelty and violence which add fuel to the fire which would link in with a sexual component later in life that results in fantasies of domination and mutilation of women.
- Works Monday to Friday in a profession where he can act out his desires (like as a slaughterman, for example)
- His feelings of inadequacy are compounded by some abnormality, such as scarring or a speech impediment, that feeds his paranoia.
- Probably carries weapons on him because of this paranoia
- His lack of social skills means his only relationships are probably with prostitutes, and he likely became infected with sexually-transmitted diseases as a result, further fuelling his hatred for women. Therefore, he probably wasn't married.
- A shy loner who lives and drinks in the vicinity of the murders.
- Would have been interviewed by police during house-to-house searches but likely overlooked.

The degree to which this agrees with Thomas Bond's profile is striking. Both assume the killer to be someone quiet, ordinary-looking, defiantly sexually-motivated, and living in the area of the murders. The meeting of two minds – one the thoroughbred serial murder investigator, John Douglas of the FBI, the other a 19th Century doctor going off his gut, shows to me that these are examples of Occam's Razor in action, cutting to the heart of the killer's method and motives.

When discussing the killer's pre-crime and post-crime behaviours, the FBI profile strays a little into storytelling. They paint a picture of the killer drinking in the local pubs for Dutch courage, before setting out to stalk and kill his victims. And whilst he is not expected to have targeted individuals specifically, he "fished" for victims in all the right places. In a similar way, Gary Ridgeway, the killer of 49 sex workers in Seattle between the 1980s-2000s, is believed to have similarly "fished" dry the strolls of the city as he went. There certainly is evidence that the Ripper drank in the local bars – the victims were often in pubs on their final nights, and Mary Jane Kelly, whether she was the victim or not, certainly drank with the Ripper on the night of the 8th November 1888 if the testimony of Mrs Kennedy is to be believed.

So, the FBI draw up a picture of a shy loner with deep-seated issues of repressed anger, sexual dysfunction and who in some way suffered a physical defect that provides a barrier between himself and others, only exacerbating his isolation, paranoia and bitterness. He has developed fantasies of control, dominance and destruction that became fused with sexuality and directed by his frustrations with the opposite sex into a violent fantasy world which he is living out with each murder. The crimes are to some extent premeditated, with the killer being armed and deliberately taking some Dutch courage and stalking particular hunting grounds, but the victims are simply chosen for their symbolic value – as "whores" – and for their easy access. He subjects his victims to a controlled yet rapid blitz attack before commencing his signature mutilations. He leaves, cleans up, and then attempts to draw out the high from the crime by revisiting the scene and/or visiting the graves of his victims. He was a white male in his late-20s or early-30s from a broken home, and probably works as a butcher or mortuary attendant weekdays, and his home and/or work is likely near Buck's Row.

Profiling is not an exact science – it is a tool, only as good as the person using it and only useful if it is used in the correct manner. The FBI are the pioneers of offender profiling and they are still the experts in the field of serial murder. Although I will present my own profile based on my own education in this subject, I bow to the authority of the FBI and in the end, it is their profile that will help to shape how I reach my conclusions. That said, I believe I have identified several key points of interest that will shed new light onto the killer's behaviour.

My Analysis of the Crimes

Here I will outline and analyse the series of events, behaviours and criminological elements common to each of the four murders I attribute to Jack the Ripper.

Trolling: A Geographical Profile

The murders all occurred in the early hours of the morning on Fridays, Saturdays and Sundays; Mary Ann Nichols was

JACK THE RIPPER

murdered around 3:40am on Friday, 31st August, Annie Chapman at around 2:30am on Saturday 8th September, Catharine Eddowes at around 1:35am on Sunday 30th September, and the Miller's Court victim at around 3:30am on Friday, 9th September. The striking similarities suggest that the killer for some reason was out and about at these times, and not during the week. To my mind, and the FBI seems to agree, this suggests he works weekdays and is accustomed to being up and about at the crack of dawn. On his days off and at weekends he doesn't break this routine and instead heads out into the district, where he probably patronises the prostitutes of Whitechapel. The fact that even during the height of the Ripper scare he was able to procure the services, and the apparent trust, of prostitutes to either go with him to dark corners or into their homes, and put them at easy enough so they put themselves in a vulnerable position to allow his attack, suggests he was superficially harmless and trustworthy, and almost certainly a regular user.

Serial killers who target prostitutes are always regular users of prostitutes. Joel Rifkin, the New York killer of 17 women, lost his virginity to a prostitute on his 18th birthday and never stopped using them since. Gary Ridgeway, Arthur Shawcross, Alun Kyte, and Peter Sutcliffe were all regular users of sex workers, and Suffolk murderer Stephen Wright lived in the heart of the red-light district – sex workers interviewed at the time expressed their shock at having serviced the man days prior to his arrest for multiple murder. This pattern is indicative of the psychopathology of the killer but most importantly, the vulnerability of the women. They are extremely high-risk victims and they are in constant danger from men who could exploit this, all the time aware that the odds of their victimization by a violent "john" is high, but is unlikely to be taken seriously by the police. Killers depend upon this, whilst outreach workers and campaigners continue to fight it and help women get off the streets and improve the lives, prospects and representation of those who are still there. Until our society addresses these issues, killers will continue to target sex workers.

Thus, the killer's time off was more than likely spent with the street-walkers of Whitechapel, where he was both friendly and invisible, arousing no suspicion and capable of committing his murders without ever being identified. He operated over a small area, within a particular time of day, and was enough of a forgettable regular that he was able to continue to operate even during the height of the murders. As for each particular murder, his "pick-up" of the victims cannot be easily determined, however, we can gain some insight into the geographical profile of this killer by examining the clues he did, unwittingly, leave.

Mary Ann Nichols was last seen at the corner of Osborn Street and Whitechapel Road, a full hour before she was found dead, heading towards Buck's Row. She claimed she was off to make her doss money before the night was out. The next time she's seen, it is by Charles Cross, lying dead in Buck's Row. It can be deduced that she met her killer somewhere near where she was killed, but exactly where is a mystery. This could be important, as it could tie the Ripper to a nearby location – a house, business, pub, etc. - but instead all we have is the clue that her body was found outside the locked stable gates of Brown's Stable Yard. I believe this overlooked detail provides evidence of an aspect of the Ripper's trolling and behaviour that is often underestimated; he pre-selects his crime scenes, and that in the case of Polly Nichols, he made an error and panicked.

Put simply, the Ripper is not simply grabbing women in the street, dragging them into a dark corner and slashing them to shreds like some common portrayals would lead us to believe. Compare the later scenes with this first one to start; the Hanbury Street scene was an enclosed yard, accessible via a discrete doorway onto and off the street. Slipping in and out would be quite effortless. The scene itself is enclosed, private, especially at such early hours. The killer's method of silencing his victims meant that in the darkness of the early hours, without a struggle or a noise, he could work secure in the knowledge that he wouldn't be disturbed and could escape or hide if necessary.

Illustration 16, below, is a contemporary illustration of the Mitre Square crime scene, and shows Catharine's body in the bottom right-hand corner of the Square next to the Mitre Street entrance, with Church passage at the top right and St James' Passage in the top-left.

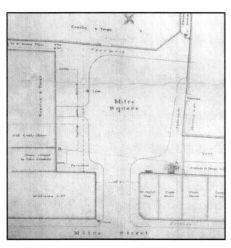

Illustration 16: Map of Mitre Square

Similarly, Mitre Square was not just an enclosed area, but the buildings surrounding the square were nearly all abandoned. He also chose to kill his victim in the one corner without a streetlamp. With three passages into the court, and the murder taking place in the darkest corner, the killer could easily flee in the confidence that his victim would probably go undiscovered just long enough for him to get away. And Miller's Court was a locked room off the street, but quite different from the other doss-houses in the area as each doss was separate, with no communal rooms, allowing him to enter and exit in the early hours unseen. In each case, the Ripper is either working from prior knowledge (as with the entrance to 29 Hanbury Street, which according to the residents was often used by people for disreputable purposes), or he was possibly improvising the best use of a location (possibly the case at Mitre Square, where he took Catharine Eddowes to the darkest corner of the square, next to the entrance to Mitre Street and opposite Church Passage, allowing him a dark working environment, a clear vantage point for anyone approaching, and a quick getaway).

Why then, was Mary Ann murdered in the street, where the Ripper ran a very real risk of being not just seen, but arrested red-handed? The key is in the exact location of the murder; the locked gates of Brown's Stable Yard. Like the other murder scenes, the Ripper intended for the crime to take place somewhere secluded and enclosed, where he could carry out the mutilations in relative security of not being discovered. He meets Mary Ann somewhere between Osborn Street and Buck's Row along Whitechapel Street, takes her to Brown's Stable Yard, expecting it to be accessible, but finds it is not. Not only does the Ripper appear to have been patrolling the area between Osborn Street and Buck's Row for a victim, but he appears familiar with the area enough to have pre-selected a location for murder. His familiarity with the area extends to the businesses there, in particular the stables. Also on that row was a slaughterhouse, which – given the FBI's profile of the killer's likely occupation – seems to raise a red flag. In this context, plus the "local knowledge" of the back yard of Hanbury Street as a good place to take a woman, we appear to be looking at a killer who is premeditating his crimes to an extent (as if walking around with a knife wasn't premeditation enough).

However, I cannot overlook the possibility that he is being taken to these locations by the women themselves. After all, Annie Chapman would probably know about 29 Hanbury Street, and Catharine Eddowes probably knows about Mitre Square as a good location to have sex, given its proximity to St Botolph's Church in Aldgate, which was also near to where she was arrested earlier in the night, and was a location notorious for prostitution during the end of the Victorian era. However, what suggests the Ripper himself was guiding the encounters and where they end up is the evidence of both the locked gates of Brown's Stable Yard, but also his increased confidence in the subsequent crime scenes. The wounds inflicted on Mary Ann Nichols were far tamer than those on the later victims, and the body was covered up by the killer as he fled, rather than the wounds being left on display. He was spooked, and acted tentatively before fleeing. He would kill again only a week later, despite the gap between his second and third victims otherwise being three weeks, and the gap between his third and fourth murders being almost six weeks. This second murder would display all the usual characteristics of a Ripper crime – the body ripped open, posed and left on display – in a more secure setting. The third murder would occur a considerable distance from the first two, and show even greater violence, and the fourth and final one would occur within an indoor environment where he felt far more comfortable. In that case, his mutilations were obscenely extensive, and the whole scene posed for shock value. This growing confidence comes not just from the change in environment, but in his capacity to feel safe in the choice of location – for someone like the Ripper, this increased sense of confidence stems from a sense of control. Therefore, even if the women have input as to the locations they go to, he is to a significant degree controlling where these murders occur, and his preference for an enclosed environment is evident in each of the murders – Brown's Stable Yard, the enclosed back yard of 29 Hanbury Street, the enclosed space of Mitre Square, and 13 Miller's Court.

With this in mind, it is evident that he spends some time during his everyday life scouting locations where he could kill. Serial killers become obsessed with their crimes, their minds always on the hunt, always selecting potential victims, scouting potential locations to kill or dispose of bodies, and the Ripper is no exception. This also explains how he was able to evade police patrols and slip away from crime scenes so effectively; he made it a priority to know these things ahead of time. This sort of research is part of the killer's process of actualising their fantasies, continually fusing their fantasy life with their real life and greasing the wheels of the process of crossing the line and committing their murders. Therefore, when a scenario comes around that slots nicely into these extended fantasy scenarios – such as encountering a victim and being able to use a pre-selected location to kill them – acting on the opportunity can be irresistible to the killer.

What then, of the sites he did select? What importance can be assigned to the pattern we see in his murder sites? Let us note a few things about these scenes;

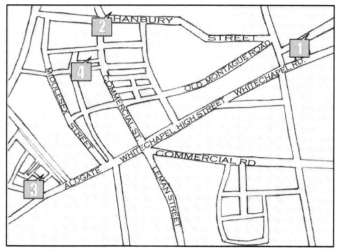

Illustration 17: Map of the murder scenes

All the murders occurred near to major roads; murders one and three took place just off Whitechapel Road and the concurrent Aldgate High Street, whilst murders two and four took place off Commercial Street. All occurred north of Whitechapel Road, and in general they cluster near the Wicked Quarter Mile (two of the four murders occurring within yards of Flower-and-Dean Street). The importance of the pattern of murders cannot be overlooked. The first three occur almost equidistant to one another, sweeping across the district from Buck's Row to Hanbury Street, and to Mitre Square. But for his final murder he kills close to a previous location – Miller's Court is a stone's throw from Hanbury Street. To understand why, we must explore the concepts of geographical profiling.

The geographical activity of serial killers can be explained with the following concepts;

- Journey-to-Crime – the notion that offenders will commit crimes close to their *base,* with crimes occurring less frequently further away.
- Routine Activity Theory – that offenders and victims will likely intersect during their everyday lives. The offender's selection of scenes of crime or victims will be largely bound by their activities between work, home and recreation. Criminals are unlikely to strike out in totally unknown and alien environments far from their base. The areas they strike are within areas they are familiar with in some way – their *comfort zone.*
- Rational Choice Theory – this concept is related to the first, and suggests that the offender decides on which opportunities to take advantage of based on their familiarity with the location, how safely far from the individual's base the site is, and the difficulty of reaching it. Offenders tend not to work harder than they need to when taking opportunities, but at the same time they do not wish to draw attention to or compromise their base. Like the concept of the comfort zone, the offender surmises a *buffer zone* around their base within which they will not commit crimes. Also, they tend to avoid previous crime locations, as they have been potentially made "hot" by the presence of law enforcement following the earlier event.
- Crime Pattern Theory – putting all of this into

context is the idea of *mental maps,* the internal representations and perceptions people carry of their environments. Distances between locations, the perceived dangerousness of areas, or the perceived opportunities for crime, plus the practical knowledge of the ins- and outs- of an environment, all form part of the mental maps criminals use.

How crimes are distributed in relation to the offender's base(s) can be categorised in several different ways. David Canter, in his seminal work on profiling murderers, *Criminal Shadows* (1995), posits the "circle hypothesis," in which he claims offenders tend to live within an area bound by a circle drawn with the furthest crimes at the very edge. Such a criminal is known as a marauder. Another type of serial offender is the "commuter," who travels from a home base to a secondary location to hunt victims and opportunities for crime. Finally, research points to a style of offending that produces what is known as a "windshield wiper pattern," whereby crimes occur with a directionality from the offender's base.

Taking all this into consideration, how does it help us understand the Ripper's geographical profile? Well, let us go back briefly to the first suspect we named, Charles Allen Lechmere, the man who gave his name as Charles Cross and who found the body of the first victim.

His home at 22 Doveton Street is close to the first crime scene as the FBI suggest the killer's may have been, and his workplace on the other side of the district in Broad Street means he would have needed to cross the heart of the district where the crimes occurred every morning. Since he left work around 3:20am on a normal working day, he would have been out and about at about the times the crimes took place. Not only that, but the two quickest routes to work take him either via Old Montague Street (via the scenes of both the Mary Ann Nichols and Martha Tabram murders), or via Hanbury Street and Dorset Street (and therefore, near the Mary Ann Nichols, Annie Chapman and Miller's Court murders). Adding his mother's home at 1 Cable Street into the mix further raises red flags, as this route to work would take him close to the Elizabeth Stride and Catharine Eddowes murders.

However, let's not get carried away. Whilst the objectively quickest routes to his workplace put him near the crimes, they also take him from relatively respectable areas, where he lived, directly into the most dangerous streets in the slums such as Dorset Street. It is more likely he avoided these alleyways and followed the main roads – the supposition that he took the routes that conveniently place him near the crimes is the theorists' own. Also, when you consider that Robert Paul's route was similarly close to the crime scenes in both location and timings, it starts to look all a little less compelling. That said, it is a good illustration of what the theories concerning geographical profiling mean; if Lechmere was the Ripper, it would make a lot of sense for him to be choosing locations he is familiar with, locations far from his home and work and clustered in the centre of his route. His journey-to-crime behaviour is derived from his journey to his workplace, which tallies with the predictions of Routine Activity Theory. He is also selecting off-road locations because he is a regular along the route and prefers not to be recognised by anyone, which makes sense in terms of rational choice theory, especially since he is remaining along his route despite his need for privacy. Finally, his perception of the district being larger than it actually is can be understood when you consider his selection of Mitre Square as a scene of murder, a location he may be familiar with from his journeys to work from his mother's home, yet still somewhere he feels is far enough from the "heat" the first crimes generated in the district.

These concepts informed a paper-and-pen approach to geographical offender profiling until the intervention of Dr. Kim Rossmo who, in 1995, wrote a paper entitled "Geographic Profiling: Target Patterns of Serial Murders." This paper provided the groundwork for a piece of software patented by Rossmo called Rigel, which uses a special algorithm to calculate the likelihood of offenders' base of operations within a target area. Rossmo's Formula takes all the concepts explained above and puts them into a mathematical format that allows for the creation of probability maps showing areas of increasing likelihood where an offender may live. These maps are known as *jeopardy surfaces.*

It works like this; the software divides a map containing information points, in this case scenes of murder, into a grid of fine squares, and runs the algorithm for each of the squares on the map. It calculates the distance from each square to each crime scene, and it uses figures for the buffer zone input based on the programmer's own trial-and-error efforts (drawn from their experience and accumulated data on offenders' environmental activity in past cases) to provide the square with a value. Once complete the squares are shaded depending on their value, and this results in a map shaded hues of red, orange and yellow, with the darker shades indicating the areas of increased likelihood – areas close to the crimes but outside their buffer zones. These darkest spots indicate the most likely areas of personal connection to the offender; home, work, or recreation.

DANIEL JOHNSON

Over the years, I have seen many attempts made at jeopardy surfaces for the Ripper crimes. For some reason, even those researchers who use just the canonical five murders as their information points still produce wildly different maps...which often happen to support their conclusions. In my case I will use the most trusted source in my opinion – Dr Rossmo's own profile, outlined in his 1999 book *Geographic Profiling*. Rossmo (p. 239-241) argues that the residencies of the victims are "suspiciously close together" - the victims lived within yards of each other at various times, at Thrawl Street, Flower-and-Dean Street and Dorset Street, at the doss houses there, as well as plying their trade in those areas, too. Rossmo suggests the close residencies take up only about 1.5% of the whole hunting ground (p. 239-240) Whilst this closeness of the victims is often considered evidence the victims knew each other – which may be true – it is irrelevant. What is relevant is that the killer knew the victims to some passing degree, allowing him to gain their trust before murdering them even amid the Ripper scare. According to Rossmo, the geographic profile "peaks" at Flower-and-Dean Street, the location considered the most dangerous in the whole district. Does this mean the Ripper lived there? Possibly. However, credence must now be given to something that Major Henry Smith, top dog at the City Police, said in his unreliable memoirs in relation to the Catharine Eddowes murder;

> In Dorset Street, with extraordinary audacity,
> he washed them at a sink up a close, not more
> than six yards from the street. I arrived there in
> time to see the blood-stained water.

This claim has been widely panned by critics as being part

of Smith's fanciful imagination, and is no longer taken seriously. He claimed to have found this evidence as far north as Dorset Street, a bloody sink near where the final victim, possibly Mary Kelly, was found dead next. Whether you consider the Goulston Street apron (or the graffiti for that matter) to be left by the killer, one cannot ignore that both Dorset Street and Flower-and-Dean Street lie just north from this spot.

But there is one more thing to consider when speaking of the geography of the area. One thing I have argued is that the killer drank at The Britannia public house on the corner of Dorset Street, as he was undoubtedly seen with Mary Kelly and possibly "Julia" shortly before the Miller's Court murder by Mrs Kennedy. All the victims were drinkers, and were known to drink at pubs including the Ten Bells, which was down the road from The Britannia, and sat opposite Spitalfields Market. Indeed, Mary Kelly was rather territorial in her pitch outside the Ten Bells, whilst Annie Chapman was rumoured to have been seen there on the morning of her murder. So, their watering holes were close by as well as their residencies. Thus, we have a clue to the killer's pattern of activity; he lives and/or works near to or within this small area, 1.5% of the whole hunting ground, drinks at The Britannia and probably therefore also The Ten Bells, and was probably a regular customer to the victims themselves. His residence is probably close to or within Dorset Street or Flower-and-Dean Street, given Dr. Rossmo's geographic profile. This contrasts with the FBI's geographical profile, but does so based upon sound scientific and investigative reasoning.

Another thing to consider is the FBI's suggestion that he drinks to steady his nerves before his attacks, which brings me onto the assaults themselves. He is witnessed by both Elizabeth Darrell and Joseph Lawende speaking calmly to his victims, no sign of agitation or aggression, outside where they would eventually be murdered. We can assume that he meets his victims as a customer and takes them somewhere he has pre-selected – a location that probably doubles as a popular spot for prostitution anyway, which he would be familiar with as a regular customer – and then persuades them using his disarming demeanour to turn their backs on him and place themselves in danger of the blitz attack to come.

Blitz Attack – Strangulation and Assault

Surprisingly, Jack the Ripper appears to require his victims to be totally passive and compliant for him to be able to act. He seems to employ violence only briefly and uses it in a purely utilitarian way; the act of seizing control of the victim. A rapid and violent attack to render the victim insensible or dead is known as a blitz attack, and is the hallmark of a disorganised offender as far as the FBI are concerned. However, this broad conceptualization of certain behaviours equating to certain types of offenders neglects the nuances of behaviour. In the case of the Ripper, his actions are powerful, utilitarian and fast, and show skill – compared to Peter Sutcliffe's method of blitz attack, whereupon he simply whacked his victims with a hammer until they fell down, it is clear the Ripper was bringing to his scenes pre-existing skills which were reflected in his initial attack. Let us examine his method in more detail.

The Ripper appears to commence his attacks with a sudden and violent seizure of power. Within moments, he has silenced and incapacitated his victim, and has murdered them swiftly and with considerable violence. This violence appears totally unexpectedly, as the victims in each case appears to have turned her back on the killer, or at least been disarmed enough to allow him close contact without resistance, prior to the killer beginning his rapid assault.

In the cases of Mary Ann Nichols, Annie Chapman, and the Miller's Court victim, the evidence of the pathologists who carried out the autopsies concur that the killer strangled his victims prior to cutting their throats, and he did it with such speed and strength that none of the victims, except for the Miller's Court victim, had any defensive wounds on them, and none but the last victim was heard to cry out. Strangulation is by far the most common method of murder among serial killers, and this is no coincidence; strangulation is a personal attack, a demonstration of the killer's dominance over the victim, and also a tactile method of connecting with the victim as they die. The phrase most often used about stranglers is that they feel as though they "hold the power of life and death in their hands," and it is this sense of power and control that intoxicates them.

Here is the inquest testimony of Dr. Llewellyn relating to the strangulation of Mary Ann Nichols, which also suggests she may have been subjected to greater violence;

> Five of the teeth are missing, and there is a slight laceration of the tongue. On the right side of the face there is a bruise running along the lower part of the jaw. It might have been caused by a blow with the fist or pressure by the thumb. On the left side of the face there was a circular bruise, which also might have

been done by the pressure of the fingers

Her killer may have hit her in the face during the assault as well as strangled her. Next, consider the testimony from the Annie Chapman inquest by Dr. Phillips;

> The face was swollen and turned on the right side, and the tongue protruded between the front teeth, but not beyond the lips; it was much swollen

Later, when questioned about this, the doctor had this to say;

> [...]From these appearances I am of opinion that the breathing was interfered with previous to death, and that death arose from syncope, or failure of the heart's action, in consequence of the loss of blood caused by the severance of the throat.
>
> [...]
>
> **Coroner:** The thickening of the tongue would be one of the signs of suffocation?
>
> **Phillips:** Yes. My impression is that she was partially strangled.

Finally, there is a comment from Dr Thomas Bond's autopsy report, not elaborated upon by Dr. Bond in the inquest, that strongly indicated strangulation in the case of the Miller's Court victim;

> The skin cuts in the front of the neck showed distinct ecchymosis.

Ecchymosis is bruising indicative of strangulation when

found around the throat. Given the evidence of strangulation in the previous cases, this seems the best interpretation of the evidence.

In each of these cases, there is the evidence itself, and the expert opinion to go along with it, indicating that the killer employed strangulation to incapacitate his victims. Psychologically, the role of strangulation in his crimes cannot be underestimated as evidence of his need to dominate and control his victims. However, the use of strangulation may have had a secondary benefit to the killer; it is likely that strangulation significantly lowered the victims' blood pressure, allowing the killer to cut through the throat without risking a fountain of blood spraying everywhere. Certainly, there was evidence of blood spatter and spurting, particularly visible at the Miller's Court scene and also at the scene of the Annie Chapman murder, but in each case the majority of blood had pooled around the victims' throats or soaked into her undergarments, rather than flowed like a stream away from the body as seen with the extensive amounts of blood at the scene of Elizabeth Stride's murder.

This brings me onto the next step of the killer's attack; the trademark throat-cutting, which in each case severed all the structures of the neck down to the bone. These wounds are among the best-known aspects of the Ripper crimes. However, rather than simply slice his victims' throats where they stood, the killer appears to have cut their throats whilst they lay on the ground. Dr. Thomas Bond's report to Sir Robert Anderson, reproduced above, bears this idea out, whilst the blood pooling and spatter evidence from the Annie Chapman and Miller's Court scenes indicate this. He also appears to employ a particular method of avoiding getting blood on himself; staying at the victim's right side whilst cutting the left carotid artery.

Here is the testimony of Dr. Llewellyn again, reporting on the wounds to Mary Ann Nichols;

> On the left side of the neck, about an inch below the jaw, there was an incision about four inches long and running from a point immediately below the ear. An inch below on the same side, and commencing about an inch in front of it, was a circular incision terminating at a point about three inches below the right jaw. This incision completely severs all the tissues down to the vertebrae. The large vessels of the neck on both sides were severed. The incision is about eight inches long. These cuts must have been caused with a long-bladed knife, moderately sharp, and used with great violence

He cut his victim's throat in two swipes, standing to the right of his prone victim and cutting from the extreme left to avoid blood splatter. This method is silent, clean and quick, and demonstrates about the only pre-existing skill the Ripper brings to his scenes; serial killers rarely develop whole new skills to apply to their murders, but rather adapt existing skills and tools to their purpose. This is in evidence with modern serial killers such as Peter Sutcliffe, who, rather than go out and buy a set of shiny chef's knives to kill with, simply sharpened his own set of screwdrivers. Jack the Ripper's only deft skill appears to be the swift method of killing, and that comes from somewhere else in his life, possibly his profession. In fact, this two-swipes method is seen in the other cases, too. Here is the evidence from the Annie Chapman case;

The throat had been severed. The incisions of
the skin indicated that they had been made
from the left side of the neck on a line with the
angle of the jaw, carried entirely round and
again in front of the neck, and ending at a point
about midway between the jaw and the sternum
or breast bone on the right hand.

"Incisions" plural, and apparently focused on the
left-hand-side of the throat, causing death by
exsanguination via the severance of the left carotid artery.
Compare with the autopsy report of Dr. Brown on
Catharine Eddowes;

The throat was cut across to the extent of about
six or seven inches. A superficial cut
commenced about an inch and a half below the
lobe below, and about two and a half inches
behind the left ear, and extended across the
throat to about three inches below the lobe of
the right ear.

The big muscle across the throat was divided
through on the left side. The large vessels on
the left side of the neck were severed. The
larynx was severed below the vocal chord. All
the deep structures were severed to the bone,
the knife marking intervertebral cartilages. The
sheath of the vessels on the right side was just
opened.

The carotid artery had a fine hole opening, the
internal jugular vein was opened about an inch
and a half -- not divided. The blood vessels

contained clot. All these injuries were
performed by a sharp instrument like a knife,
and pointed.

The cause of death was haemorrhage from the
left common carotid artery. The death was
immediate and the mutilations were inflicted
after death.

These wounds are fast and effective, cutting
through all the major tissues and severing or wounding
the key blood vessels, the wound extending down to the
bone. This is apparently done in one, or two, swift
motions, with death occurring instantaneously. Finally,
compare with the damage done to the final victim at
Miller's Court, which again sees all tissues cut to the bone;

The neck was cut through the skin & other
tissues right down to the vertebrae the 5th &
6th being deeply notched. The skin cuts in the
front of the neck showed distinct ecchymosis.
The air passage was cut at the lower part of the
larynx through the cricoid cartilage.

So, in three of the four cases the killer is quickly
and adeptly seizing control of his victims, throttling them
insensible, and in all four cases making extremely deep, if
rapid, cuts through the victims' throats as they lie on the
ground, killing them.

Psychologically, this initial phase is important
because it shows the killer displaying control, skill, and a
utilitarian efficiency that isn't present in his later actions,
which are reflective of a heady mix of emotion, sexual
fantasy and some improvisation. If we were looking at a

killer who did not commit the later mutilations, and instead simply strangled and killed his victims in this manner, then nobody would ever suspect that some raving lunatic committed these crimes. His is rapidly and expertly executing these women, so fast and so effectively that they utter no sound and offer no defence. The only exception to this rule is the Miller's Court victim, who did show evidence of defensive wounds and was heard to cry "Murder!", although the key difference with that murder is the changed circumstances the killer found himself in; an enclosed space with a victim in bed, rather than a standing victim he could easily incapacitate. This alone is interesting as the victim in that case suffered the most extensive injuries, and it could be partly due to her fighting back and enraging the killer, something we will look at a little later. For now, let's focus on another function the throat-cutting plays in the killer's methodology; depersonalization.

Depersonalization

After incapacitating and killing his victims by strangling and exsanguinating them, the Ripper begins a process of depersonalizing his victims. In the autopsy reports of both the Annie Chapman and Miller's Court cases, there is evidence of attempts by the killer to remove the victims' head. Also, in the cases of Catharine Eddowes and the Miller's Court victim, the faces of the victims were extensively mutilated. Finally, in each case, the victims' faces were turned away from the side where the killer likely stood or sat. These are all evidence of attempts at depersonalization, a behaviour whereby the offender will in some way obscure or remove the victims' own identity, usually so that the victim ceases to represent themselves and instead can be substituted by a fantasy victim. Projecting a "source" victim into the current victim allows the killer to act out fantasies and repressed emotions relating to that source victim. American serial killer Ted Bundy murdered co-eds with long, brunette hair who bore a striking resemblance to his former girlfriend Stephanie Brookes. Levi Bellfield attacked and killed young blonde women who resembled his girlfriend. In a similar vein, Ed Kemper killed girls like the ones his domineering mother used to tell him he would never be able to date – before he finally murdered her, and turned himself in to police. Strikingly, in the cases of Kemper and Bundy, both decapitated their victims, whilst Bellfield attacked his victims from behind, attracted only by their blonde hair. We can draw from this that the Ripper's actions to depersonalize his victims were in part so that he could act out fantasies relating to a source victim somewhere in his life, one who was a source of some emotional and sexual frustration to him, and he attempted several means to accomplish this.

In the cases of Mary Ann Nichols and Annie Chapman, the victims' faces were unharmed, but they had been turned away from where the killer had been crouched. No physical mutilations took place on these victims' faces, but this is unsurprising, as the bodily mutilations were tentative in the Mary Ann Nichols case and escalated quickly in the Annie Chapman case. The killer was getting into his stride with these early murders.

As with the first murders, Catharine Eddowes' head had been turned, this time to the left, reflecting that the killer had worked from her right side due to the geography of the place; from there, he could look right at the entrance to Mitre Street and flee down Church

Passage and onto Duke Street to escape if necessary, or run onto Mitre Street and away if he heard someone approaching from the more distant St James or Church Passages. One other difference with this case besides the directionality of the victim's face is the presence of facial mutilations for the first time. As we move onto the case of Catharine Eddowes we also move on in the killer's evolution.

Catharine Eddowes had been subject to a series of stabs and cuts and slashes, particularly to the eyes, nose, and across her face. Commentators have tried to insert all sorts of interpretations into the story of the facial mutilations on Catharine Eddowes, including the killer planting his initials, Masonic symbols, or indecipherable nonsense that is the product of an insane mind. In fact, the interpretation of these injuries is quite plain; the v-shapes on the cheeks and eyes are due to the killer attempting to slide the knife flush against her face and hack off her features all in one go. He would have quickly realised this was a stupid idea and instead resorted to stabbing and slashing at her features.

It has been suggested that the killer did this because he knew the victims, but this is a fallacy; yes, it is true that some killers who know their victims may cover the victim's face out of guilt, but this is not usually the first act of mutilation they do before a frenzy of enraged sexual butchery, followed by degrading posing of the body. Facial covering is an act of remorse, contrition, shame. What the Ripper is doing here is something quite different – erasing the victims' identities. Guiltily covering a murder victim's face is a way of acknowledging their identity after killing them, whereas this is about starting out by erasing it. Without a face, the victim can become either something other than a human, or they can become another person entirely. In each case, the killer's first act after murdering the victim would have been these depersonalizing actions; this is evident in the fact that he was probably interrupted in his murder of Catharine Eddowes by his accidental severance of her bowel during his ferocious mutilations, which cut short the scale of the mutilations he may have been planning and caused him to flee there and then, and her face had already been mutilated with no evidence of faeces in her facial wounds that would indicate otherwise.

Despite the ferocity of Eddows' abdominal injuries, the facial injuries are comparatively tentative. He pokes and prods at the eyes, trying to hack the face off in one fell swoop but failing because he doesn't put enough gusto into it. This was his first effort at facial mutilation, and he was not confident in his method. It exposes several flaws in his character; the Ripper struggles to cope with change and challenge in his environment, such as; dealing with new elements even if he introduces them purposefully; dealing with filth, as he fled after bursting Catharine's bowel; and he has an almost childlike reaction to the prospect of a victim "seeing" him kill and mutilate her, stabbing the eyes very gently and cutting the cheek, before pushing her face away. This I believe is simply down to the killer's shame over the sexual element of his crimes, but also an element of regressive behaviour.

Here, I will stray a little into Freudian psychodynamics to better explain mine and the FBI's profile. You have probably heard of the ideas of Sigmund Freud who, although his ideas are dated, fathered many revolutionary theories which can help us understand how our childhood influences our development. Since his lifetime, Freud's ideas have been developed and adapted for the times. The reason the FBI specifically say the

Ripper probably had a domineering mother is because of psychodynamic principles; specifically, that our capabilities in forming relationships have their origin in how we are exposed to, and form, relationships in our early years. Broadly speaking, in Freud's theories of "traditional" heterosexual development there is a dynamic relationship between mother, father and child which helps the child crystallise their gender-identity via their identification with the parent of the same sex. Our future ability to pursue romantic and sexual relationships, as well as our ability to trust and our locus of self-worth, are all developed during our early childhood years, around the ages of 3-6 (the "phallic" stage of psychosexual development). It is during this stage that paraphilias can become cemented, as abnormal stimuli can be associated with sexual pleasure (although the full expression of this will be essentially dormant until the dawning of sexual maturity).

The reason why the profile of the Ripper suggests he had an absent father, a domineering mother and is incapable of ordinary relationships is because these are the errant elements in this crucial developmental stage which would lead to withdrawal, solitary sexual pursuits, paraphilias and a failure to properly internalise the appropriate "pattern" of sexual relationships through his dynamic observation and interaction with his parents' relationship. Remember, these are not "pie in the sky" theories someone dreamt up in a psychology lab somewhere; these principles exist today in developmental psychology because they are reliable and evidence-based observations.

Interestingly, if we push the psychodynamic envelope, we can associate his organised and change-resistant behaviour with his aversion to Catharine

Eddowes' faeces, and his desire, as we shall see, to dismantle and manipulate his victims to the classic "anal retentive" personality. If you're wondering why aversion to faeces should be considered special here, when everyone would presumably have such an aversion, I point to two things; one, not everyone is as averse to filth and bodily functions, and two, this is a man who apparently has no qualms about dissecting women and playing about with their internal organs, but is scared off by the sight and smell of a bit of shit. This is another sign of trouble during early development as per Freudian psychodynamics; anal retentive personalities are so called because during the "anal" stage of psychosexual development (18 months – 3 years), the child learns that control over his bowel movements is their first act of true agency in the world around them, and it can be used to tip the balance of power between themselves and the parent by refusing to release the faeces when required. Anal retentive personalities are those who unsuccessfully learn to relinquish the desire for total control in their lives and can end up fastidious, organised, stressful and intolerant in later life. The killer's aversion to faeces yet his methodical dissection of his victims I think reflects this. To understand why faeces should still play a part in his perception when such stages of development occur in very early childhood, I direct you to two elements of psychodynamic theory; one is the unconscious, which is the repository of all that is inaccessible to the conscious mind, yet which has the biggest influences (and contains, among other things, repressed memories), and second, the concept of the "child" in Transactional Analysis (a modern offshoot of psychodynamics), which posits that our personalities can be understood as nesting dolls, and interact with others through these three layers; adult, child and parent. Thus, an unconscious aversion to faeces triggers his actions during the Catharine Eddowes assault, but it is a regressive and childlike reaction to his solitary and undeveloped sexual activities – shunning the attention of the female he is acting upon in what is essentially for him a sexual interaction, rather than engaging with her – which explains his pushing away of the victim's face when his initial efforts at depersonalisation did not work. His later efforts, however, served a slightly different purpose; removing the identity of the victim to substitute it with that of his source victim.

In summary, the contrast between his tentative actions, usually "firsts" such as these first facial mutilations, and his balls-to-the-wall actions such as the horrendous degree of evisceration he carried out on Catharine Eddowes and later the Miller's Court victim, points to a man who does not easily adapt to change. The nature and motivation for these facial mutilations, and how they were carried out, appears to show the killer's deeper psychological state, whereby he is already acting as if the victim reflects his "source victim," and acts in an appropriately regressive manner, showing that there is a root issue with his psychosexual development that is probably causing pathological frustration throughout his life.

After his first steps in Mitre Square, the killer would go onto enact the full gambit of his deepest fantasies at Miller's Court six weeks later. The Miller's Court victim's face was simply gone, and her throat as far cut through as he could manage. The mutilations done to the Miller's Court victim were savage but that was only because, I suspect, he had the time and unlike his other victims he had light with which to see her;

The face was gashed in all directions the nose cheeks, eyebrows and ears being partly removed. The lips were blanched & cut by several incisions running obliquely down to the chin. There were also numerous cuts extending irregularly across all the features.

The killer literally just slashed her face to pieces. Trying to decipher a face from the crime scene photograph of the Miller's Court victim is impossible. However, this murder provides another piece of evidence that completes the picture of what, how and why the killer carried out these initial depersonalization actions; in the cases of Annie Chapman and the final victim, autopsy reports show that attempts had been made to decapitate them.

Dr Phillips at the inquest on Annie Chapman's murder reported this;

There were two distinct clean cuts on the body of the vertebrae on the left side of the spine. They were parallel to each other, and separated by about half an inch. The muscular structures between the side processes of bone of the vertebrae had an appearance as if an attempt had been made to separate the bones of the neck

Similarly, Dr Bond reported this on the Miller's Court victim;

The neck was cut through the skin & other tissues right down to the vertebrae the 5th & 6th being deeply notched

The killer did not simply cut down to the bone but made an effort to break through. In both cases, the killer lacks the skill to separate the victims' bones, but makes the effort to try – and remember, he had all the time in the world with his final victim, and still couldn't do it. I think we can quietly shelve the idea of a butcher being the killer in this case. Nevertheless, it reflects his intentions, and his failures. Removing the victims' head is an efficient way of removing their identity, although quite what he was going to do with the head once he removed it is anyone's guess. This, it seems, was his original aim, but when he failed to take Annie Chapman's head off, he gave up and instead mutilated Catharine Eddowes' face. With the time and opportunity to try again he attempted to decapitate the Miller's Court victim. He again failed, and instead took his frustrations out on her face, before turning the ragged mess away from him so that it faced the window. Interestingly, Dr Bond would comment that he thought the killer may have used the bed sheet to cover his victim's face during the initial attack, yet another form of depersonalization!

All in all, these initial phases of attack took mere moments out of the killer's time. Picking up his victim and guiding her to a suitable, and probably pre-selected location, before suddenly seizing and strangling her, and finally subjecting the victim to a series of efforts at depersonalization, sets the groundwork for his main objective; the abdominal and genital mutilations. Remember, these are the killer's primary motivation, and the most psychologically important in understanding his motivation.

Mutilations

In each case, the Ripper subjected his victims to extensive abdominal and genital mutilations. This is one reason the Elizabeth Stride murder is not considered a Ripper crime; despite the timeline indicating that her killer should have had ample time to have subjected her to mutilations, he did not, although this is only one of several disparities that rule her out as a victim of the Ripper, not least the fact that her throat had been cut without strangulation, accomplishing the goal of killing her and nothing else. In the other four cases, as Dr Thomas Bond points out, the object of the murders appears to have been the mutilations. Certainly, the killer's rapid silencing and execution of his victims is a highly functional behaviour compared to the unnecessary mutilations. This, as I explained previously, is the difference between *modus operandi* and *signature.* The Ripper's signature, and the key to understanding his motivations, are these mutilations.

Each of the murders teaches us something new about the killer, and I will explore the mutilations in each case before drawing together some broad observations and conclusions.

Mary Ann Nichols: Confidence & Control

In the Mary Ann Nichols case, the Ripper's actions seem far more tentative than in the latter cases. True, this was his earliest known murder, and therefore his method could still have been developing, but I believe that there is a reason for his nervousness; his exposure in the open environment of Buck's Row compared to his intended seclusion in Brown's Stable Yard. Thus, instead of eviscerating his victim as he would in his later crimes, he contented himself to a series of slashes, only one of which was deep enough to penetrate the abdominal cavity. Not only was this his first known act of mutilation, but he also does not appear to have interacted with Mary Ann sexually. Both of these things can be explained by considering the psychosexual motivations of the killer and the crucial role the locked stable door played in his on-the-fly thinking.

It was a major problem for the Ripper to find the doors to the stable yard locked. Thwarted by this obstacle, he doesn't simply abort his mission and dismiss Mary Ann, or even go through with the sex act – he still kills her. The wounds are far more tentative in Mary Ann's case than with the others, as indicated in the autopsy reports, and his final action appears to be to cover the wounds as he leaves, apparently not confident that his tableau will be found sufficiently long after his escape. Instead, he is covering up, quite literally. This stands in stark contrast to the other crimes, where the bodies were hacked open and left with their entrails hanging out on display, posed for maximum shock value. What we see here is the real Ripper – a coward, ashamed of his actions, fearful of being caught, the bravado of the later crimes nowhere to be seen. The fact that he dares not try to dismiss Mary Ann shows he doesn't want to incite ridicule from her – she needed the money and she was drunk. A punter turning her down after picking her up would have gotten her angry, and even a single, passing flippant comment on her part as she left would have been an affront to the damaged, inflated ego of the Ripper, and he knew it. Remember, these crimes are remarkably passive – he invites trust from his victims right up until the point he murders them, an act he carries out from behind, and with swiftness and efficiency. Then he has his victims entirely passive, dead, as he wants them, as is the purpose of the murders. Confronted with the option of dismissing Mary Ann, he does not. I don't buy the idea that as a serial killer, his urge to kill was too strong to ignore. Even in this challenging scenario the crime is still clean and efficient, not some sort of psychosexual feeding-frenzy brought on by desperation. No, instead he goes through with the crime but under the great stress of the open-air scene and the real risk of capture. That said, neither does he have sex with Mary Ann. Instead he kills her, looking over his shoulder the entire time, carrying out far less extensive mutilations than he'd have liked, taking no trophies and finally having to flee, ashamed and covering up his work.

Why does he not have sex with her, though?

There are psychosexual reasons; sex in the conventional sense just doesn't cut it for Jack. His crimes are sexual but lack clearly sexual components. He interacts with the victims' genitals by slashing at them. The Miller's Court victim had her whole vulva removed as part of one of the long flaps of skin cut from her torso, and her uterus was cut out and stuffed under her head. Both Chapman and Eddows had their uteri cut out entirely with various external cuts to the vulva of Eddows evidence of an attempt to similarly mutilate it as he would the last victim. No mutilations at all were apparent around Mary Ann' genitals, the focus of the mutilations being the abdomen during the short and stressed time he had. According to autopsy reports, none of the victims appeared to have been raped prior to death, and in each case, the killer appeared to have upped his ante by increasing abdominal mutilations rather than carry out any overtly sexual manipulation of the body. Why then,

the Ripper did not simply have sex with Mary Ann is clear
– his whole purpose in obtaining a prostitute that night
was to act out his perverse sexual fantasies, his idea of
sex, and that did not involve a live, willing partner for
conventional sex but rather an inert cadaver he could
open and interact with in a grossly abnormal way. Faced
with either rejecting her and being subjected to the very
sort of abuse that had fed his insecurity and hatred in the
first place, or actually having sex with her, the Ripper
decided to risk killing her anyway and doing what he could
before someone came. It was a risky, largely impulsive
decision that almost cost him. Mary Ann Nichols' murder
would have been seen by the Ripper as a shameful failure.
The simple task of making sure a gate was unlocked
thwarted his efforts to obtain satisfaction. So, he fled into
the night as Cross, Paul and Neil came across the body
minutes later, with nothing to show for it.

However, this "nothing" was still horrible, and
provides us with a window into his psychopathology.
From the inquest;

> There were no injuries about the body till just
> about the lower part of the abdomen. Two or
> three inches from the left side was a wound
> running in a jagged manner. It was a very deep
> wound, and the tissues were cut through. There
> were several incisions running across the
> abdomen. On the right side there were also
> three or four similar cuts running downwards.
> All these had been caused by a knife, which
> had been used violently and been used
> downwards. The wounds were from left to
> right, and might have been done by a left-
> handed person. All the injuries had been done

426

by the same instrument.

Dr. Llewellyn suggests the killer may be left-handed because the horizontal injuries to her abdomen are left-to-right. However, this is explained if the killer is sitting at her right side as he slashes her. This makes the left-hand-side deep gash an awkward one to make, but that is apparently what Jack did. We can speculate that possibly that those horizontal slashes are his attempts to quickly cut the abdominal flesh away, having made the deeper cut. Then he makes deeper downward slashes closer to himself, but fails to penetrate the abdomen. In stark contrast to the other cases, these wounds are clumsy, shallow, and are just token slashes enacted just to make the murder worthwhile given his exposed location. Regardless, these injuries tell us a lot. For starters, it is the first evidence of the killer murdering his victim in order to obtain total passivity from her and total control over her, so that he could act out his ultimate desires with her as an unwilling and passive participant. He is not sadistic, at least not in the traditional sense.

Picquerism and Necrosadism

Sadists gain sexual satisfaction from the suffering of their live victims, and often physically, sexually and psychologically torture them before killing them. On the other hand, Jack the Ripper is a "necrosadist." These particular types of sexual deviants derive sexual stimulation from the mutilation of a dead body, and include among their ranks killers such as Andrei Chikatilo, Jeffrey Dahmer, Peter Sutcliffe, Anthony Hardy, although in most of these cases the killers are also necrophiles who sexually abuse corpses. As far as we can tell, and with the assistance of Dr. Gordon Brown, we have evidence for this, he did not perform sexual acts on the bodies. The lack of sexual activity and necrophilia can be attributed to a second sexual deviancy present in his profile; picquerism. A rare phenomenon, picquerism is the sexual satisfaction gained from the stabbing or mutilation of flesh. The subtle difference between the two is that necrosadism is about the pleasure gained in the performance of violent acts upon the dead, whilst picquerism is the pleasure of the act itself. With both of these deviancies in his profile, Jack the Ripper would have carried out these acts to gain a double-whammy of satisfaction, by rendering his victim dead, providing a satisfying scenario for sexual activity, before carrying out the directly sexual actions of stabbing and cutting upon the victim. In the case of Mary Ann Nichols, he was unable to provide a satisfactory scenario in which he could work in privacy, which would have been psychologically very important to him given the sexual nature of his activities, and therefore he took the time he had before having to flee the approach of Charles Cross simply slashing at the abdomen. Only a week later would be murder his second victim, with a considerably greater degree of mutilation.

Annie Chapman: Anatomical Awareness and Theatrics

Moving on to Annie Chapman, we can see a marked evolution in his behaviour and in his signature. The seclusion provided by the back yard of 29 Hanbury Street gave him the confidence to act out his deepest fantasies. The scene bore all the hallmarks of the later cases; the victim was disembowelled and put on display, and an organ was missing from the body; her uterus. Focusing for now on the mutilations, let us again refer to the inquest testimony;

> The abdomen had been entirely laid open. The intestines, severed from their mesenteric attachments, had been lifted out of the body and placed on the shoulder of the corpse; whilst from the pelvis, the uterus and its appendages, with the upper portion of the vagina and the posterior two-thirds of the bladder had been entirely removed. No trace of these parts could be found and the incisions were cleanly cut, avoiding the rectum,and dividing the vagina low enough to avoid injury to the cervix uteri.

A little biology lesson here to provide some context. The mesentery are tissues that connect the small intestines to the abdominal wall, and Jack would have had to cut through these to remove the intestines. The uterus lies just behind the bladder and in front of the bowel, and what the killer has done has cut away most of the bladder and at least half of the vagina without injuring the nearby rectum, which seems quite an achievement until you recall the mess he made of the Catharine Eddowes scene – meaning the credit Dr. Phillips gave to him as being "clearly an expert [in anatomy]" is really just his dumb luck. Nevertheless, a cursory glance at female anatomical diagrams, and after viewing several hysterectomies, shows that the organ isn't exactly easy to access, but that someone could grub about and find the organ without undue hardship if they cut the body open groin to sternum first as the killer did. The question is, how did he know it was there and was he searching for it specifically?

JACK THE RIPPER

In picqueristic offenders, often they have found a "safe" outlet for their drives, where their sexual desire for mutilation can be expressed legally, such as taxidermy as a hobby or butchery as a profession. The key aspects of the killer's behaviour, quick killing via throat-cutting, and the evisceration of the abdominal cavity, suggest he is enacting sexual fantasies grounded in the kind of gore you'd expect in a slaughterhouse. In abattoirs, cattle are stunned, their throats cut, and their abdomens sliced open, their internal organs removed, and it is possible that the Ripper has been exposed to this environment during key developmental periods in his life; from childhood to adolescence. Paraphilias develop when young people are exposed to stimuli that become objects of sexual fixation or fetish during key periods of psychological development, a pattern seen in all serial killers who exhibit a paraphilia. This early exposure may also explain how a man such as the Ripper, who may have no obvious way of having anatomical awareness, could have been proficient enough to know which organs are which and even have a general idea of how he could try to remove them – he would obsess on such things throughout his life and he could also have learned rudimentary anatomy from watching, or being involved with, the slaughter and butchery of animals. As for human anatomical knowledge, there does seem to be evidence of some degree of education in his background.

To expand this argument, let us consider the evidence of the killer's likelihood of being to some degree educated. His murders occurring on weekends suggests he worked during the week. The fact that he was posing as a customer and, as we have discussed, he most likely *was* a regular customer of the local girls, he had the money to pay for their services. The "From Hell" letter is a dead giveaway as it is an example of legible writing which includes the correct identification of the organ that accompanied it; the kidney. If it is genuine, and I argue it may well be, then it means the killer has at least basic anatomical knowledge and that he can also read and write. Further evidence of this is seen at Miller's Court; recall that the scene was arranged in a manner very similar to how a newspaper report had somewhat enthusiastically described the Annie Chapman scene – organs scattered all about her and beneath her head. Underneath the head of the final victim were her uterus and kidneys – this very strongly indicates he was communicating to the authorities that he was the same man who killed the previous victims by leaving the very organs he'd previously removed beneath her head to be found when the body was moved. This also indicates that he knows which organs are which, as he would have been stumped as to what bits were which if he had tried to claim credit for the earlier organ removals in such a way without knowing what they were to start with. Therefore, this very strongly suggests he was indeed responsible for removing them in the first place, but also that he was keeping up with the media reports of the murders and even copying them. So, he was a working man, with some money, able to read and write and he knew which organs were which, and he indicated in his posing of the final victim's remains that he did indeed remove the earlier organs. This also indicates he read *The Star* newspaper, which reported the over-the-top version of the Annie Chapman murder in the first place.

As for his anatomical knowledge, there are two options; one, he had some training or education in anatomy, and may have worked in a mortuary – as the FBI suggest – or in a field with a similar knowledge base such as a fish porter, slaughterman or butcher, where animal anatomy can be similar enough to human to have guided his actions; two, his knowledge is self-taught, and he came to know what he knew in much the same way as Jeffrey Dahmer; his pathological fascination with anatomy became a solitary pursuit, and he learned what he needed to about female anatomy during his earlier years to be able to put his fantasies into practice later. I suspect the truth is a little of both. The FBI note that offenders such as these probably take jobs where they can express their pathological desire to mutilate in a safe environment, and given that the Ripper's "sex" during his necrosadistic crimes are the mutilations themselves, the paraphilia known as "picquerism," then he is likely to both be fascinated with the innards of the objects of his attractions, but also end up in a profession where he can act out his desires. Psychologically, this is known as sublimation, whereby a desire is acted out somewhere else, and the individual may not consciously realise they are doing it. Given the plethora of slaughterhouses and butchers, the local fish market, and businesses such as cat's meat shops, it seems that the Ripper probably was involved in a business like that, where gore, blood, mutilation and disembowelment would have been his daily grind. If he did have exposure to such conditions as a youngster which fed his paraphilias, it is likely it was a family business, too.

The killer's method of murder and mutilation also reflects the methods used by slaughterers in their preparation of animals. Atkins' (2012, p.84) work *Animal Cities: Beastly Urban Histories* quotes Edward Ballard's 1877 comments about the slaughter process of an ox, and offers an intriguing insight into the similarities between the Ripper's actions at the scene and the process occurring behind closed doors across the district;

> As the animal lies on its side, the slaughterman
> then drives a knife deeply into the carcass
> above the sternum so as to cut thoroughly into
> the large vessels behind that part, and the blood
> gushes out freely...the carcass, when
> sufficiently bled, is then turned over upon its
> back...an incision through the skin is then made
> along the whole length of the carcass, the skin
> is turned out sufficiently, and the abdomen
> opened and partially disembowelled.

The passage then describes how the intestines and other organs are removed, skimmed of fat and prepared for various purposes. Also, contemporary sheep slaughter takes a similar path, with the animal having its throat slashed right to the bone before the carcass is skinned and disembowelled. The Ripper's method is extremely similar; cutting the throat right to the bone and then cutting the abdomen open with long, penetrating wounds, before cutting out and removing the intestines and other organs, with a rudimentary knowledge of what they are and where they are. In contrast to a slaughterhouse or butcher's, where the animal's body may be suspended or pulled taught during the cutting process, Jack was working in a dark environment with victims who were laying prone on the floor, dead weight, which could account for the wounds being jagged. The similarities are very interesting, and warrant serious consideration.

So, from these first two cases we can determine that the only real skill the killer brings to his scenes is the execution of his victims, whilst he seems to display a basic knowledge of anatomy and evisceration in his subsequent mutilations. This suggests to me that he is possibly employed in a field related to, or like that of, animal slaughter rather than butchery, as his attempts to behead both Annie Chapman and the final victim failed.

His final act on this poor victim's body was to pose it in a degrading manner. Not content with killing and butchering her, he lifts her legs to a stirrups position and drapes her severed entrails over her body. This manipulation of the scene is part of his fantasy, and shows his desire to control what is seen when the body is found. His fantasy therefore is not merely about the time he spends with the victim, but also the effects of the murder on others, and the wider and longer consequences. This is a man plotting the murder from pick-up right through to the media coverage. However, this planning is not so meticulous that the root cause of his offending – his deviant sexuality and unhealthy emotional coping mechanisms – cannot override his need for control and lead to acts of outright and graceless butchery.

With his skillset and anatomical knowledge discussed, let us point to the focus of his activities. He was not simply emptying his victims of their organs, he was focusing on their genital regions. Nowhere is this more evident that in the murder of Catharine Eddowes, a crime that also displays evidence of the killer's rage and emotional drive during the attacks, and helps us to identify what type of sexual murderer he was.

Catharine Eddowes: Misogyny and Rage

There is only one argument that has me doubt that Elizabeth Stride was killed by someone other than the

Ripper, and that is the rage-fuelled mutilation of Catharine Eddowes. Her murder was certainly an expression of rage – she was stabbed and slashed and eviscerated with a gleeful brutality that shows the Ripper either at his most confident in a state of outrage. It is a very convincing argument to say that the killer, incensed at his failure to mutilate Elizabeth Stride, proceeded to obliterate Catharine Eddowes in a rage. The problem with this is, as I have explained, that the killer appeared so calm when seen by Lawende and co. moments before killing Catharine, and probably most importantly, there's just no evidence of this ever happening in any other serial murder case. But we've had that discussion already, so let's digress no further.

The murder of Catharine Eddowes showed the very same mutilations as in the other cases, only carried out with a greater degree of brutality and emotion. Let us run down the injuries again;

- He cut her body open from the breastbone to the genitals, and opened her abdominal walls to expose her organs.
- Her liver had been stabbed repeatedly, and sections of her stomach and intestinal tissues were torn away, still attached to the displaced flesh.
- Her genitals had been subject to multiple, deep slashes and stab wounds.
- Her intestines had been removed from her abdomen and dumped on her right shoulder
- Two feet of her colon had been cut away and placed beside her body.
- A portion of her intestines had been shoved into the wound in her throat

- The pancreas had been stabbed
- Her left kidney had been removed
- Her uterus had been cut through and the upper portions, and its attachments, removed
- Dr Gordon Brown testified that in his opinion the wounds took at least five minutes to inflict.

The thing that most interests me is the evidence of stabbing and slashing of the organs and particularly the genitals, and that is what gives this away as a sexually-motivated, rage-fuelled assault, but also interesting is the lack of evidence of strangulation. Dr Bond stated that there was a quantity of clotted blood to the left-hand-side of the body and on the victim's shoulder, and no apparent superficial bruising, which goes against the suggestion that she was strangled as with the other victims, but he and Dr Brown suggest the throat-cutting occurred so quickly it would have killed the victim instantly. It is possible that the wounds to the body were so horrendous that either the doctors couldn't recognise the signs of strangulation, such as petechia haemorrhaging in the eyes or ecchymosis of the skin around the throat, or did not report whatever evidence they did come across due to the primacy of the exsanguination as the cause of death. Also, it is possible that the killer experimented with altering his MO here, and dispensed with strangling his victim, relying just on throat-cutting to murder her. Of course, it is equally likely that he acted on the spur and inflicted the wounds he did out of pure rage. This is another attractive idea, bringing back the idea of some foaming-mouthed madman with a knife, but it is also one demolished by the facts.

As previously stated, the killer appeared perfectly

calm immediately prior to the murder. Also, his choice of location is remarkable given he is supposed to have fled murder scene one and miraculously arranged an ideal second murder within half an hour! After all, Mitre Square in general is another enclosed location, this time with ideal vantage points and multiple ways of either escaping (via the passages and via Mitre Street) or hiding (nearly all the buildings were empty), but it is specifically ideal because he was able to coax his victim calmly and collectedly into the darkest corner before murdering her without either of them making a sound. Clearly another of his pre-selected locations, and not the on-the-fly work of a het-up and blindly enraged killer. That said, this man is a master of control, and his fantasy life is a masterpiece of compartmentalisation – his rage is a deep-seated psychological issue that he keeps wrapped up in layers of fantasy and control that he can slot around his life like trademarked plastic building bricks. So, the calm and collected man Lawende saw was more than capable of keeping the mask in place until he got Catharine where he wanted her, whereupon he let loose his fury, but only within the context of a scenario he had engineered. Once it was time to abort, he dropped those internal bulkhead doors and contained whatever rage he had left, and fled. Wherever and whenever he suffered the stressor that enraged him, he was always going to be equipped to contain it until he was able to release it by killing Catharine.

However, this does not automatically mean he *must* have killed Elizabeth Stride to have gotten this angry! Killers like this usually act when triggered by all manner of stressors in their lives, and the Ripper is no different. In fact, all this does is reinforce what we could already deduce about the killer's motive – his depersonalization of his victims points to a man displacing his rage from the source victim in his life onto a murder victim. This leads me to an important method of understanding sexual murderers – to look at their crimes in the context of rape. In both cases, deviant sexuality is expressed as a function of a need for control, and usually sexually motivated murderers begin life as rapists. Luckily, a useful platform for understanding the types and motivations of rapists exists.

Groth's Typology

In Nicholas Groth's typology of rapists, he lists several types of offender, usually falling into two categories based on the rapists' pathology – Power and Anger. The issue for the rapist is not enough of the first, and too much of the second, and the types listed are, Power Reassurance, Power Assertive, Anger Retaliatory, and Anger Excitation.

- Power Reassurance rapists are the most common type and can be called "gentleman rapists." Delroy Grant, the so-called "Night Stalker," and Britain's most prolific convicted sex offender was a textbook example of this type of offender. He would talk to, and even be polite to victims, prior to raping them. He offered apologies, and even assisted his elderly victims around their homes during the assaults if they needed to use the lavatory, drawing on his own experience as a carer. He was not violent or sadistic, yet his actions traumatised his vulnerable victims, and lead to some dying soon after.

- Power Assertive rapists are a type of situational rapist who will force themselves on women who are in a vulnerable position to reinforce a macho self-image. A similar psychological motivation underlies prison rape, where rape becomes a method of domination and power, and us used to prop up or protect an individual's personal or social status as a powerful man.

- Anger Excitation rapists are sadists who will torture their victims, prolong attacks and act out elaborate fantasies. These are the sort who progress to murder and often sadistic serial killers will have started out as Anger Excitation rapists. They need to see their victim reacting to, and suffering during, their assault.

- Anger Retaliatory rapists are the ones we're interested in. Their profile, offered by Groth, reads like a retelling of the Ripper's profile so far; triggered by a stressor in their lives, they will head out and find a victim, subject them to a blitz attack, in which they aim to subject the victim to violence and humiliation, before quickly fleeing the scene. Sound familiar?

It is useful to think of the Ripper in terms of his rape profile to understand the basic motivations underlying his behaviour. He is an evolved anger-retaliatory sexual offender, whose deviant sexuality is underpinned by necrosadism and picquerism. His evolution is marked by the development not only of his method but of the playfulness of it, and his growing confidence. The Annie Chapman murder was gruesome, but it was comparatively clinical, the removal of organs

and displaying of the body somewhat simplistic. The
Catharine Eddowes scene was a display of the killer's
rage, and his confidence in being able to release it in this
manner – once he had his victim dead at his feet in a
location he felt he was able to operate in with relative
safety, he unleashed the full range of his pent-up anger.
The key variation in his psychological make-up from that
of an anger-retaliatory rapist is his capacity for self-
control, as he can be shown and has been shown in my
analysis so far to be an overcontrolled personality who
demands that he is in control of everything around him,
including the setting and the victims themselves, or else
he either fails to act (as in the Mary Ann Nichols case) or
he loses his mind altogether (as in the Miller's Court case,
as we shall see next).

Finally, to really put his actions into context, we
must not ignore the fact that he is consistently targeting
women who are either full-time prostitutes, or who may
occasionally prostitute themselves. Whilst I have serious
doubts about some of the victims being street-walkers,
and I have argued so in this book, it is an unavoidable fact
that women in the East End occasionally had to do it to
survive. Mary Jane Kelly hated her life on the streets, and
Mary Ann Nichols probably drank as much to cope with
her lifestyle as she prostituted herself to pay for her drink.
As I have suggested, though, serial killers choose
prostitutes because they are easy targets; for example,
Peter Sutcliffe began picking up prostitutes to kill but later
took to just attacking any woman he saw on the streets
because the effort of picking women up suddenly became
an unnecessary complication, a time-waster. With all
serial killers who target prostitutes, the killer may tell
himself, and would tell investigators, that he has some
moral opposition to sex work, or that he is cleaning the

streets. Indeed, he may have a real problem with women who sell sex if he is sexually dysfunctional himself (the FBI profile suggests the killer may struggle with ordinary human relationships, suffer some disfigurement or speech impediment, and be fastidious and shy, not exactly boyfriend material), but all that would have done would provide him with a superficial justification for his crimes. In reality, he was little more than a violent, inadequate misogynist.

There is an element of his activities that shine a light on this deep-seated hatred of women; that he would target the sex organs for mutilation but put them in a degrading pose, particularly focused on the genitals, at the same time. He is ripping at their femininity whilst turning it into a sordid and sexually arousing display, destroying and humiliating his victims but only after obliterating their individual identity. He may be unleashing his rage against a source victim upon the women he kills, but at the same time he is creating a tableau that explicitly attacks the very notion of womanhood, a general attack that he arranges for the wider public to find. It is that his efforts to punish one individual in his life reflects a core belief inside of him – that women who do not conform to his demands are deserving of both the destruction of their womanhood and of public, degrading humiliation. On that note, I'd like to refer to the FBI's profile, in which they suggest the killer suffered abuse at an early age. The cycle of abuse, as it is called, is the pattern by which abused children can often become abusers themselves. This cycle exists because abused individuals will attempt to reassert the control they lost, or compensate the hurt they experienced, in the context of that harm. In other words, regaining control in the same way it was taken from them. With that in mind, we could argue that the killer's core belief, stated above, is about his own emasculation and humiliation in childhood. This is nothing special in criminology – this is precisely the pattern we see with most serious violent and/or sexual offenders, including and especially serial killers.

In summary, the Catharine Eddowes scene displays evidence of a killer who acts out deep-seated rage and misogyny within a scenario he feels confident and in control over. His confidence to unleash this emotional torrent to destroy and degrade his victim is very much rooted in his need to control his victim, himself and his environment, something he excels at. The root of his rage and hatred of women likely stems from childhood experiences of humiliation and disempowerment, as well as emasculation, elements that continue into his adult life and act as the primary triggers for his rage-spiral. This lifelong cycle of triggering and brooding, plus his early exposure to deviant sexual stimuli (which must include the cutting of flesh, such as you may see in a slaughterhouse), lead to deviant sexual development and the paraphilias of necrosadism and picquerism. But the final piece of the puzzle comes in Miller's Court.

Miller's Court: Jack the Narcissist

The scene at Miller's Court is now infamous, and the crime scene photo taken on the morning of 9th November 1888 now one of the most widely reproduced photographs in history. In contrast to the previous murders, the victim at Miller's Court was butchered beyond recognition, her body flayed, and the carcass emptied of all its contents in an awful scene of debauchery that is almost unparalleled.

Various myths exist about this murder; that the victims' missing heart was burnt in the grate (in actual fact, women's clothes were found burning), that her entrails were strung about the room like Christmas decorations (a media invention easily disproved by a quick glance at the crime scene photos), or that initials were written in blood on the walls beside her (in reality, the spray from severed arteries and cast-off from the knife as the killer slashed at his victim caused arcs of blood to mark the walls). Of course, in this book I have argued that a strong argument exists for the victim at Miller's Court being someone other than Mary Jane Kelly, but this has been debated for years and knowing the truth one way or another may now be impossible. I cannot be certain, which is why I have referred to her as "the Miller's Court victim" as a placeholder title given that doubt does exist. However, the identity of the victim and the myths of that scene are irrelevant to the current discussion, that of the clues her killer gave in his actions at the scene of the psychological motivations underlying his murder spree.

Immediately, let us make a simple observation about the difference between this murder and the others – that it took place indoors. This is the ultimate step forwards in the killer's theme of seeking secluded spots in which to act. He felt confident at Hanbury Street and he felt even more so at Mitre Square, as evidenced by his increasingly violent acts upon his victims. Here, alone with his victim in a locked room, he was supremely confident, and he also had all the time he wanted to act out his deepest fantasies. But given that context, which he would have found very attractive, things did not go his way.

Unlike the other victims, this final girl did fight back. A cry of "Murder!" was heard by at least two witnesses, and the victim's body showed evidence of defensive wounds. Dr Thomas Bond's report describes;

> Both arms & forearms had extensive & jagged
> wounds.
> The right thumb showed a small superficial
> incision about 1 in long, with extravasation of
> blood in the skin & there were several
> abrasions on the back of the hand moreover
> showing the same condition.

And in his report to Sir Robert Anderson, Bond described how the killer may have covered the victim's face with a sheet at the time of the throat-cutting;

> In the Dorset Street case the corner of the sheet
> to the right of the woman's head was much cut
> and saturated with blood, indicating that the
> face may have been covered with the sheet at
> the time of the attack.

Arguably, there are three possible reasons for this; first, it would prevent blood from spraying onto the killer given that he was attacking from the front, in contrast from behind, in this case; second, it was another example of depersonalisation; third, it could have been an attempt at asphyxiating the victim given that strangulation would have been harder for the killer to carry out given the victim was lying down when the attack took place. However, it seems it didn't work on any count as the body was moved away from where the blood-soaked sheet lay, and the victim's face was still deeply mutilated.

Before we analyse this scene for its clues, let's run down the injuries he inflicted upon her again;

- The victim's throat was severed right down to the bone, which itself was damaged by an attempt at decapitation
- The victim's face had been deeply slashed at multiple angles, destroying all features and rendering it unrecognisable.
- The whole of the abdomen and thighs had been cut away in three flaps which included all connective muscles and tissues, and the external genital organs
- All the internal organs (stomach, liver, intestines, spleen, uterus, kidneys, etc.) removed from the abdominal cavity and scattered about the body
- The breasts removed all the way down to the muscles connecting them to the ribcage
- Arms and legs suffered several deep, jagged wounds and both thighs had been stripped down to the bone which was exposed.
- The heart removed and was missing from the scene, and the stomach and right lung severed

The whole scene was drenched in the victim's blood, suggesting that unlike the other victims, whose blood loss was minimal because strangulation reduced their blood pressure, this victim struggled and was killed with the throat-cutting outright. Once he had his victim under control, he commenced mutilations for which there is no superlative strong enough to qualify. Whilst there is a strong case for believing he was acting out his fantasies to their fullest, and that is an argument I will make, there is another aspect to consider.

Recall that in the Mary Ann Nichols case, when the killer was out of control of his environment, he appeared to lose his confidence and his wounds upon her body were consequently far more tentative and seemed to be more like token gestures, compared to his later work? Well in this case, at Miller's Court, it was the victim he almost lost control over. By fighting back, she threatened his fantasy of control. Instead of running away with his tail between his legs, the Ripper instead lived up to his name and gutted his victim. This ties back to the point made in the previous case, in which I argued that underlying the killer's psychopathology is a core belief that women must conform to his demands or else they deserve destruction and humiliation. His reaction to being confronted with such a trigger in the context of an attempted murder appears to have enraged him even further (given that his actions are triggered by outrage in the first place). Thus, the victim was not just stabbed or disembowelled, but flayed and eviscerated wholesale, her body scraped to the bone and left unrecognisable. It was as if he was saying, "how *dare* she fight back against me! How *dare* she resist my control!" In his warped mind, this victim was deserving of the harshest treatment. But this brings us all the way back to his initial motivation, full-circle; that his rage at disempowerment by significant female figures is enacted in these retaliatory murders in which he regains control through sexual domination and degradation. The victim's actions only poured more fuel on the fire that was going to consume her anyway, and thus his actions are really no different to those enacted on other victims – she just got more of it. Nevertheless, it does show us a key insight into his personality; his feelings of losing control over his victims are not the same as his feelings of losing control over his environment. In the latter case he feels disempowered and flees. In the former case, he is enraged and acts with supreme violence. This to my eye is evidence of narcissistic rage.

The concept of narcissistic injury and rage stem from Freudian psychoanalysis, and describes the ways which narcissistic personalities can break down and fly into rages that can become violent. In short, narcissistic injury occurs when the individual's self-worth is challenged or their self-concept, an often-fragile construct which may mask deep insecurities, is threatened and his true self exposed. In the case of the Ripper, his actual self, a banal and ineffectual figure probably henpecked and certainly inadequate, is hidden by his inflated ego-construct of the powerful and vengeful killer who rips up and humiliates whores. Losing control of the victim risked the ego-construct being exposed as a lie, and his otherwise inadequate self revealed to his victim. This caused him to fly into a violent narcissistic rage in which he proceeded to slice his victim's face to shreds, and empty her body of its contents in a frenzy, evident in the arcs of blood splattering the walls of the room. It is believed he may have spent at least a couple of hours alone with her, with witnesses hearing the cry of "Murder!" around 3:30am, and someone being heard leaving the Court at around 5:45am. Within this time, he was able to satisfy the rage by extending his fantasy-fulfilment as far as possible. Crucially, we know that he left the scene once he was satisfied because there's no evidence of any disturbance to the scene during the time of the attack, and also, he took the time to pose the scene exactly as he wanted it.

The difference between this incident and the Mary Ann Nichols incident is that he did not fly into a rage when his control was lost because of the situation, whereas he did when the source of the loss of control was the victim herself. This is important for understanding the locus of his self-worth, the very thing that is compromised in an act of narcissistic injury. He cannot stand conflict when it comes from a woman, but he can chicken out and run away at the drop of a hat when the situation doesn't go his way. Thus, as I argued previously in the discussion about his transference of rage from a source victim onto a murder victim, I believe that the killer's self-worth is likely connected to a strong female presence or substitute in his life – his mother, wife, girlfriend, sister, etc. – and when this source victim becomes a source of narcissistic injury, the inadequate man displaces his rage onto a victim of his selection (prostitutes) in a location of his selection (enclosed locations) as part of a cycle of sexually-motivated fantasy-trolling-murder.

A final aspect of the Miller's Court murder that points to narcissism in the killer's profile is the posing of the body. In the cases of Annie Chapman, to a lesser degree Catharine Eddowes, and particularly the final victim, the bodies were posed by the killer for his own gratification and to bestow the greatest level of degradation upon the victim and shock for the audience. Let us discuss this next.

Posing of the Body

Let us remind ourselves of the descriptions of the scenes of the Annie Chapman, Catharine Eddowes and Miller's Court murders. First, Annie Chapman;

> **Chandler:** […] I saw the body of a woman lying on the ground on her back. Her head was towards the back wall of the house, nearly two feet from the wall, at the bottom of the steps, but six or nine inches away from them. The

face was turned to the right side, and the left arm was resting on the left breast. The right hand was lying down the right side. Deceased's legs were drawn up, and the clothing was above the knees. A portion of the intestines, still connected with the body, were lying above the right shoulder, with some pieces of skin. There were also some pieces of skin on the left shoulder.

Dr. Phillips: I found the body of the deceased lying in the yard on her back, on the left hand of the steps that lead from the passage. The head was about 6in in front of the level of the bottom step, and the feet were towards a shed at the end of the yard. The left arm was across the left breast, and the legs were drawn up, the feet resting on the ground, and the knees turned outwards. The face was swollen and turned on the right side, and the tongue protruded between the front teeth, but not beyond the lips; it was much swollen. The small intestines and other portions were lying on the right side of the body on the ground above the right shoulder, but attached. There was a large quantity of blood, with a part of the stomach above the left shoulder. I searched the yard and found a small piece of coarse muslin, a small-tooth comb, and a pocket-comb, in a paper case, near the railing. They had apparently been arranged there.

In summary;
- Lying on her back
- Left arm across the left breast

- Head turned to the right
- Legs drawn up, feet resting on the ground
- Intestines lying across right shoulder and stuffed into throat wound
- Portion of stomach above left shoulder
- Items from the body placed away from body
- Uterus removed from the body and taken away

Also, worth considering is that there were two rings and a scarf missing from her body, possibly taken by the killer as trophies.

Now the Catharine Eddowes scene;

Watkins: The woman was on her back, with her feet towards the square. Her clothes were thrown up. I saw her throat was cut and the stomach ripped open. She was lying in a pool of blood

Dr. Brown: My attention was directed to the body of the deceased. It was lying in the position described by Watkins, on its back, the head turned to the left shoulder, the arms by the side of the body, as if they had fallen there. Both palms were upwards, the fingers slightly bent. A thimble was lying near. The clothes were thrown up. The bonnet was at the back of the head. There was great disfigurement of the face. The throat was cut across. Below the cut was a neckerchief. The upper part of the dress had been torn open. The body had been mutilated, and was quite warm - no rigor mortis.

Dr Brown's Autopsy Report: "The body was on its back, the head turned to left shoulder. The arms by the side of the body as if they had fallen there. Both palms upwards, the fingers slightly bent. The left leg extended in a line with the body. The abdomen was exposed. Right leg bent at the thigh and knee. The throat cut across.

The intestines were drawn out to a large extent and placed over the right shoulder -- they were smeared over with some feculent matter. A piece of about two feet was quite detached from the body and placed between the body and the left arm, apparently by design.

Again, in summary;
- Lying on her back
- Arms lying "where they fell"
- Head turned the to face the left
- Clothing torn open and thrown up around the body
- Intestines drawn out and placed over the right shoulder.
- A section of colon was cut away and place deliberately beside the left side of the body
- Uterus and kidney removed from the body and taken away

And Miller's Court:

Position of body
The body was lying naked in the middle of the bed, the shoulders flat, but the axis of the body

inclined to the left side of the bed. The head was turned on the left cheek. The left arm was close to the body with the forearm flexed at a right angle & lying across the abdomen. the right arm was slightly abducted from the body & rested on the mattress, the elbow bent & the forearm supine with the fingers clenched. The legs were wide apart, the left thigh at right angles to the trunk & the right forming an obtuse angle with the pubes.

The viscera were found in various parts viz: the uterus & Kidneys with one breast under the head, the other breast by the Rt foot, the Liver between the feet, the intestines by the right side & the s pleen by the left side of the body. The flaps removed from the abdomen and thighs were on a table.

In summary;
- Body was on its back.
- Head turned towards the left.
- Left arm lying across the abdomen
- Legs wide apart
- Heart removed from the body
- Organs scattered around body

What can be learned from these scenes? What consistencies are there? Well, for starters, there's one scene missing; that of Mary Ann Nichols. In that case, the scene was rather different. As we know, the killer was disturbed in his murder of his first victim, having already been spooked by his failure to secure the stable yards as his preferred murder site. In that case the injuries inflicted upon the body were far tamer but also, crucially, the killer had covered them up by replacing her clothes just prior to fleeing. These mitigating circumstances explain why the scene was incomplete, but in those other scenes, what elements are common and what do they mean?

The following elements occur in all the other scenes;

- Body on its back
- Internal organs removed and placed upon or next to the body, particularly intestines which are placed on the right of the body.
- Face turned away from the killer's position
- Organs removed and taken away by the killer

In the Catharine Eddowes and Miller's Court cases, the faces of the victims were mutilated, and in the Annie Chapman and Miller's Court cases, the victims' legs were drawn up and the genital areas exposed in a degrading manner. The lack of facial mutilation in the Mary Ann Nichols and Annie Chapman cases can be attributed to his evolving methods of depersonalisation, whilst the incomplete posing of the bodies in the Mary Ann Nichols and Catharine Eddowes cases can be attributed to interruption; his exposed position and the approach of Charles Cross in the former, and his accidental rupturing of his victims' bowel in the latter.

Taking these mitigating circumstances into account, we can see the consistency in his method and his intentions, but also gain insight into the sequence of events; he is posing his victims last, leaving the scenes with a final flourish when he is finished. But why pose them at all?

First it is important to explain the difference

453

between posing and staging of a crime scene. Staged crime scenes are those where the scene is manipulated in some way to mask what really happened; burning a crime scene down to mask a crime is a form of staging, as is making a murder look like an accident, or the work of an intruder. Posing a crime scene is when the offender manipulates the scene to express something, or send a message, or to fulfil some desire. The Boston Strangler would pose his victims, leaving greetings cards at the scene or thrusting objects into his victim's vagina. Peter Sutcliffe left a recent copy of a national newspaper at an undiscovered scene and even contemplated taking the victim's head away to leave somewhere else to, in his words, "create a mystery." TV and film are full of killers posing their scenes; the killer in *Se7en* organised each crime scene to be representative of one of the seven deadly sins. Hannibal Lector hung a victim like a huge artwork on the bars of his one-man cell. *Dexter's* Doomsday Killer reflected scenes from the Biblical Book of Revelations in his murders. In real life, this rarely happens, but when it does, often it is the killer's effort to exert control over even greater portions of his environment. His murders are an expression of his own desire to feel powerful and justified and fulfilled, but also, they are fulfilling sexual fantasies. Telling the difference is the key, and in the Miller's Court scene, we can see this difference.

Recall my argument that the scene resembled the description of the Annie Chapman murder as provided by *The Star* newspaper (8th September 1888)?

> ...She was lying on her back with her legs outstretched. Her throat was cut from ear to ear. Her clothes were pushed up above her waist

and her legs bare. The abdomen was exposed, the woman having been ripped up from groin to breast-bone as before. **Not only this, but the viscera had been pulled out and scattered in all directions, the heart and liver being placed behind her head, and the remainder along her side**. No more horrible sight ever met a human eye, for she was covered with blood, and lying in a pool of it, which hours afterwards had not soaked into the ground.

And the scene itself;

> The viscera were found in various parts viz: the uterus & Kidneys with one breast under the head, the other breast by the Rt foot, the Liver between the feet, the intestines by the right side & the s pleen by the left side of the body. The flaps removed from the abdomen and thighs were on a table.
> The bed clothing at the right corner was saturated with blood, & on the floor beneath was a pool of blood covering about 2 feet square

Well, that allows us to break the Miller's Court scene into two themes; theatrical and psychosexual. The theatrical theme is the scattering of organs in the manner of this story, one he undoubtedly poured over like pornography as he refuelled his fantasies between attacks. Also, leaving the legs open in the Annie Chapman and Miller's Court cases was degrading to the victim only if she is seen in this manner by others – so again, sexual content but otherwise, a theatrical action. The same goes for leaving the victim's clothes torn or thrown up around the body, so she is on display, without dignity. He wishes the audience – police, onlookers, press – to see his victim in as great a state of undignified degradation as possible, and to show the damage he has done to her as an expression of his dominance and destruction of her. The themes here – egotism and misogyny, expressed as reversals of inadequacy and emasculation, the killer regaining power in the way it was lost. This inadequacy is reflected in his depersonalisation of the victim, which includes turning the victim's face away from where he sits in relation to the victim, an action we saw in the Annie Chapman, Catharine Eddowes and Miller's Court scenes.

But there is another thread within these scenes. Towards the very end of the assault he does something else – places the victim's left hand across the left breast. We saw this in the Annie Chapman and Miller's Court cases, and it does appear to be deliberate, particularly in the final murder, where the hand lay effectively inside the body where the viscera had been. Quite why he does this is unclear, however, this has no overt meaning to an observer other than to possible draw the eye into the abdominal injuries. I am tempted to speculate that this action has meaning only to the killer, and that there may be a particular image in his mind he wishes to replicate at the scenes when he does this. Also, the consistent placement of the intestines across the right of the body in the Annie Chapman, Catharine Eddowes and Miller's Court cases appears to be deliberate, and constitutes an action he feels compelled to carry out in that manner for his own gratification, in much the same way he gains a sexual kick from the acts of cutting and disembowelling his victims in a manner a regular person would struggle to relate to. These bizarre and idiosyncratic actions reflect the psychosexual theme, of his fantasies and the scene he is creating for his own gratification, hidden among those elements he arranges for the wider audience to see. This reflects his need for control over the reactions of the responders and onlookers. He fantasises, plans and executes these crimes in this manner with a dogmatic script that he resorts to when he suffers a narcissistic injury during his life, a deviant coping mechanism that we see in serial killers the world over.

This need for control, and manipulation of his victim and the wider audience, the arrangement of the scene to reflect ghastly newspaper reports or to degrade the victim, again reflect a narcissistic personality plagued with pathological inadequacy and sexual deviancy. Each tableau he creates is his way of creating a lasting source of private satisfaction that the short-lived thrill of his murders can be enjoyed in some way long after it has ended. However, the killer does carry out one final action that does much the same thing; the removal of trophies from the scenes.

Trophy Taking

In the Annie Chapman, Catharine Eddowes and Miller's Court murders, the killer took away the uteri of two victims, the kidney of one and the heart of another. Potentially, one of those organs, the kidney, turned up again as an accompaniment to the "From Hell" letter. In that missive, he indicated he had eaten the other half of the kidney. Whether or not this letter is genuine, we must consider what role the taking of organs and trophies, such as Annie's rings, may have in the killer's profile so far deduced, and what role, if any, anthropophagy (cannibalism) has, too.

JACK THE RIPPER

In the Annie Chapman and Catharine Eddowes murders, as we have seen, the killer was able to carry out his fantasies in a far more complete way than in his first murder. Being able to instil horror, fear and revulsion in his audience provided the Ripper with an extended thrill outside of the acts of murder and mutilation themselves. But more than that, the victim became both an object to be manipulated to this end, and a human being in the killer's possession. Since his anger-retaliatory profile is all about regaining lost power through the means of its removal, he would be motivated to feel in some way in possession of his female victims, depriving them of agency being the first step, the second being the continued post-crime sense of possession. In other words, he would extend his possession of the victims, asserted through his murders, by retaining part of them after the murder, so that he could continue that possession in the same sense that manipulating the scene allows him a continued thrill in knowing how it will impact others (thereby allowing him to feel a sense of control over others' emotions and perceptions).

But what would he do with these organs once he has taken them away with him from the scene? Taking away Annie Chapman's and Catharine Eddowes' uteri, the very organ of sexual reproduction, should require no deeper analysis. He was grubbing about inside their genital regions, and with or without basic anatomical knowledge (which I suspect he had a thin grasp of), he would have probably realised roughly what it was. He did not remove spleens or gall bladders or pancreases (except in the final murder, when he emptied the cadaver), but uteri. Whilst there is a debate to be had about what he did with them (see below), we do have a clue about his motivations for removing the kidney – in the "From Hell"

DANIEL JOHNSON

letter he claims to have fried and eaten half of it. That said, we cannot be certain of the kidney's or the letter's veracity. The heart missing from the last victim is still missing with no idea what happened to it, and as for Annie Chapman's missing rings, they also never resurfaced. What he did with these items and organs between murders is unclear, but we can make some guesses; usually when items are removed from victims by killers, they serve two purposes; as reminders or as masturbatory aids.

The key lies in the difference between *trophies* and *souvenirs*. Trophies are items taken by the killer as literal reminders of their actions. In general, these items act as a tally for the killer, to recall or gloat over his actions. Sometimes, killers will collect jewellery from their victims and present it to their close friends or family as a gift, and it gives them pleasure to see the individual wearing it. Gary Ridgeway, the Green River Killer, used to leave jewellery he collected from his dozens of victims in the wash-room of his workplace for colleagues to find and pass on to their partners. Harold Shipman hoarded items of jewellery from his victims which were found in his house only after his death. These items hold only the egotistical value of reminding the killer of his conquests. Annie Chapman's rings would be ideal for the killer to value as trophies, and I think that is what became of them. It is possible that the killer passed this on to a significant other in his life, maybe even his "source victim," as a way of blurring the lines between victim and source, and enhance his sense of power over her, or compensate for his continued lack of power.

Souvenirs are items that the killer has a closer connection with, often using them as sexual aids. The organs would have been used in this way, and this

459

includes his consumption of the kidney. Although rare, anthropophagy, or cannibalism, occurs in some highly-evolved sex killers, but also occurs early in the development of killers such as Jeffrey Dahmer, whose desire to possess another human extended to the enslavement, dissection and consumption of his victims. As he would later explain, eating the victim is a way of keeping them part of oneself, a form of ultimate possession. Like British killer Dennis Nilsen, Dahmer would claim that his need for companionship was a major motivation in why he killed people, but in his case, it extended to the need to eat them. This consumption becomes a sexual act of union and physical pleasure, and in this way, we can see how Jack the Ripper would have taken the organs as a way of continuing the sexually stimulation he gained from the crimes. He may have eaten them all, and we have nothing to suggest otherwise, but it is worth noting the alternative. Rather than eating the uteri and heart as he did the kidney, it is possible he used them as masturbatory aids. The heart has multiple openings once removed which the killer could have used in this manner, whilst the uterus could be employed in a similar manner. How long these items would last is questionable, but nonetheless it is worth considering. Personally, I think it makes more sense for him to have eaten all of them, but like many of the unknowns of this case, it is a matter of opinion and argument over this point by now, 129 years later, is merely academic.

The killer's obvious desire to totally dominate and control his victim, his environment and the wider community with his murders, and his pathological sexuality in evidence in his actions, all allow for anthropophagy in his profile, as it provides the killer with a further extension of the pleasure of his crime but also the final possession of his victim (who, in turn, represents something greater to the killer). In this way, sending half the kidney to George Lusk alongside the "From Hell" letter is not relinquishing control of the kidney but employing it as a tool to exert control over Lusk himself, the victim again straddling the line between object and subject to the killer, depending upon what he wants the victim to "do" for him. Lying there dead and depersonalised, the victim becomes another person. Once the mutilations are complete, the victim is dismantled and scattered like an object for use in controlling others and the scene itself. Taking away the organs for consumption or for use in the Lusk letter, the victim and her parts become objects, but giving the rings to someone to deliberately blur the lines between that person and the victim, and she becomes a person again – it all boils down to what the killer gets out of it. In this context, we can see that other people are really, truly, always just objects to this person.

And so, we have reached the end of our examination of the stages of the killer's crimes, and what each stage tells us. Now, I will summarise the findings of this chapter and provide a final and complete profile of the killer based upon the FBI's work and my own discussions here, before moving on to the final chapter in this book.

Conclusions

The FBI provided a professional profiler's take on the Ripper, and I think my conclusion should make that the centrepiece, my own musings merely annotating it, no matter how confident I am in my deductions. That said, let's remind ourselves of what they said;

- White male, 28-36 years old
- Likely unmarried
- Lives in Whitechapel area
- Works weekdays
- His work likely reflects a "safe" environment for him to act out his destructive fantasies, such as butcher, slaughterer, morgue attendant, etc.
- Shy and non-social, appears ineffectual
- May have some physical or speech issue that makes communication difficult
- Family life was dominated by his alcoholic mother, and the father was passive or absent
- Unlikely to be capable of forming intimate relationships, and relies on encounters with prostitutes
- Drinks to lower his inhibitions before murdering his victims

In each of these points, I think the FBI are justified. I would add the following from my profile;

- He is literate, and reads the news reports of the crimes obsessively
- Has scant anatomical knowledge, possibly self-taught to some degree
- His personality is marked by narcissistic and psychopathic traits
- He is sexually dysfunctional and highly deviant, his psychosexual makeup marked by the paraphilias of necrosadism and picquerism.

- He is overcontrolled and does not react healthily to change, challenge or loss of control over his environment
- He has a significant female figure in his life who is the primary source of continual feelings of loss of control and sexual inadequacy.

In closing, we must consider the broader case at hand. We must consider the probability that the "From Hell" letter (and *possibly* Emily Marsh's encounter with the strange man asking for George Lusks' address), is a genuine communication from the Ripper. Let's remind ourselves of these pieces of evidence;

First, the "From Hell" letter;

> From hell.
> Mr Lusk,
> Sor
> I send you half the Kidne I took from one
> woman prasarved it for you tother piece I fried
> and ate it was very nise. I may send you the
> bloody knif that took it out if you only wate a
> whil longer
> signed
> Catch me when you can Mishter Lusk

The words "Sor," "prasarved," and "mishter" are all examples of phonetic Irish dialect. A partially literate man may pronounce words in this way. To back this up is the testimony of Emily Marsh who, if you recall, was confronted by a man asking for George Lusk's address shortly before Lusk received the package containing that letter and the accompanying kidney. Here is what she said;

JACK THE RIPPER

The stranger is described as a man of some
forty-five years of age, fully six feet in height,
and slimly built. He wore a soft felt black hat,
drawn over his forehead, a stand-up collar, and
a very long black single-breasted overcoat,
with a Prussian or clerical collar partly turned
up. His face was of a sallow type, and he had a
dark beard and moustache. The man spoke with
what was taken to be an Irish accent.

She described the man as 45-years-old, six feet tall, sallow
and dark with a beard and moustache and an Irish accent.
The key there being his Irish accent – although as I have
argued, there is considerable doubt about the significance
or veracity of this sighting.

We must consider that the man seen by Joseph
Lawende and Joseph Hyam Levy, and Elizabeth Durrell,
was the Ripper and use his description as a guide. With
those in mind, let us add the following;

- Given the Emily Marsh encounter and the
  phonetics of the "From Hell" letter, the killer may
  have an Irish background.
- Tall, about 5' 7"
- Fair complexion
- Moustache
- Medium build
- "Shabby genteel," with the appearance of a sailor
- Has the appearance of a "foreigner," possibly a
  Jew
- Probably lives and/or works near Dorset Street and
  Flower-and-Dean Street
- Drinks in The Britannia pub, as he did with Mary

Kelly and co. on the night of the Miller's Court murder

Finally, we must consider the work of Dr Kim Rossmo, who's geographical profile places the killer on or near to Flower-and-Dean Street, suspiciously close to the Dorset Street locale where Major Henry Smith claimed in his unreliable memoirs to have chased the killer.

With these points in mind, we are left with a tantalising question...have we encountered anyone during our exploration of this case who fits the profile?

I believe we have.

PART FOUR: Hello, Jack

JACK THE RIPPER

Naming Names

Before I begin outlining my case for the suspect I have identified as best-fitting of the evidence and the profile of Jack the Ripper, I feel I should make a few things absolutely clear. First, I am not going to do as others have done and declare to the world that I have solved the case and I know who Jack the Ripper was. I do not, and neither do you. In this chapter I will outline why I believe a particular individual appears to me the most reasonable suspect given the facts of the case and the input of experts such as the FBI. A holistic consideration of the evidence has lead me to one man who warrants singling out, and I intend to explain why. This is not the same as po-facedly declaring "I know the identity of a murderer" as Patricia Cornwell did, or ending my book with the words "Jack the Ripper has been found" as Martin Fido did. I did not expect to single out this individual as my suspect, and I do not offer a perfect theory either; life is messy, this is a non-fiction book, and therefore I advise the reader to be wary of any theory that appears to be so watertight that every variable, every element, has a neat and tidy explanation. Instead I offer a pragmatic potential solution, with holes, flaws, grey areas and gaps, but also, I hope, profound observations, arguments, and things to think on. This man has been dead nearly a century, and much of the evidence of this case is forever lost. So, if you are looking for the sort of ending fitting of an Agatha Christie novel, where it all fits beautifully together, then forget it. Life isn't that simple. This is not a novel, and real life is complicated, particularly 129 years after the fact.

Second, I'd like to suggest to those readers who disagree with any of my conclusions in this book to please, I implore you, write your own material explaining why, using the evidence, dispensing with the myths, and employing reflexivity in your sources and your arguments to avoid your work becoming a polemic. I speak to the Ripperology "purists" and gatekeepers, those folks who are more interested in maintaining the myth and the story of the Ripper than acting like adults and looking at the case based on the evidence. My own interpretations do not sit comfortably with me – I did not want to suggest there was significant doubt in the identity of the Miller's Court victim. I am not terribly happy that Elizabeth Stride is almost certainly not a Ripper victim. I am somewhat peeved by the role of the gutter press in the Ripper letters being hoaxes, and I would love them to be genuinely from the killer as they would then be tangible evidence from the man himself. It irritates me that the police were so incompetent and self-absorbed that they couldn't tell their Jews apart when it came to jotting their self-aggrandising memoirs twenty years after the murders. If you can argue with total and unquestionable certainty that I am wrong in any of these regards, then by all means, I implore you to do so – maybe the gatekeepers of the Ripperology world (folks with elusive documentation, etc., that they will only share with other folk who ask them nicely and promise not to share any further) will stop dreaming of the day their jealously-guarded possessions are found among their papers after death, like their folk heroes Swanson and Anderson and Macnaghten, and might grow up and start sharing so we as a community can do justice the murdered human beings at the heart of this story.

And that is my final point. Ripperology has become a willy-waving boy's club of theories and suspects and finger-pointing that anyone can have a go at. Here I am, having my own stab at it (pardon the pun), but the difference I hope is that this book remembers that the victims were human beings. Writers who throw around words like "whores" and "tarts" to describe these women, as I have seen countless times while researching this book, should be ashamed of themselves. A man murdered these innocent women, who were living among extreme depravation and resorting to the life they did through desperation, for his own perverse satisfaction, leaving them humiliated and desecrated in the process. By writing works that dismiss them as whores and tarts and then trotting out countless men who could have done the deed – particularly when your suspect is someone powerful or famous (or Royal, I type rolling my eyes) – then you are no better than Jack himself, exploiting these women for your own kicks.

So, I repeat my original point – I do not know who Jack the Ripper was. I am about to name the man I believe fits the bill the best because the evidence of the case has lead me there. And this theory has problems. This is not gasping in awe at the face of the Ripper, it is about being able to visit four (or five) graves with a clearer conscience that 129 years later, I've joined the ranks of those who have at least tried to provide justice to the women the Ripper murdered. With that said, let's move on, and see where my examination of the evidence has lead me.

* * *

Biography

Born 25th May 1858 to Irish immigrants John and Catharine Barnett, the young Joseph Barnett would live his whole life in Whitechapel. A family of fish porters, he would eventually follow his father into the business at Billingsgate Fish Market alongside his brothers Denis, Daniel and John. However, he would also succumb to the lethal conditions of their environments. Lung problems would kill John Barnett and Joseph himself in the years to come, and no wonder. He was born and raised at 4 Hairbrain Court, moving to 2 Cartwright Street by 1861. In a report dated 27th July 1875, John Liddle, the Chief Medical Officer for Whitechapel, would single out the area containing these streets for their narrowness, poor condition, overcrowding, high mortality rate, and the "evils" associated with such conditions (quite possibly crime and prostitution).

The young Joseph would spend his formative years in these conditions, less than a mile from the heart of the district labelled "the Abyss" in later years. Then, his father's death from pleurisy in 1864, when Joseph was only six, prompted a period of increased instability. Never escaping the wretched conditions of the East End slums, but never settling, Joseph and family began moving from one slum to another. For now, the head of his family was his mother Catharine, but that changed sometime around 1871, when records indicate she left the family and became a live-in servant to a man named Thomas Allman at 4 Glasshouse Street, whom she may have married in 1885. That left the family scraping for survival in the worst slum in Whitechapel; their latest address, 24 ½ Great Pearl Street, Spitalfields, was in a notoriously degenerate area, cramped, overpopulated and filthy and would, in 1877, be rendered unfit for human habitation by virtue again of Chief Medical Officer John Liddle. It sat just north of Spitalfield's Market and "Itchy Park," the homeless encampment in the disused graveyard opposite Dorset Street. The very same medical reports relating to these conditions also report on the unsanitary activities of licensed and unlicensed slaughterhouses in the region. Living in these conditions, Joseph's brother Daniel Barnett, now the head of the family, worked at Billingsgate Fish Market as his father had done as a fish porter to put Joseph and John through school. By this time, Denis had already married and left, as had their sister Catherine.

At this point, the living conditions and the gradual breakdown of the family had taken their toll on Joseph, who it seems was suffering what was probably a severe developmental disorder. As previously noted, Joseph appeared to be suffering from echolalia and a severe stammer. Echolalia is a behaviour in which the sufferer repeats back things spoken to them. Most tellingly is that this condition is often a symptom of a more widespread problem, and is seen in cases of autistic spectrum disorder, schizophrenia, frontal-lobe injury or diseases linked to cerebral degeneration, as well as pervasive development disorders. Echolalia performs a function in the early development of language in children, but usually tails off after around 30 months of age. To continue past that into adulthood is a warning sign of an underlying neurological problem. One of the consequences of this is it can seriously impact upon the sufferer's social interactions and their interpersonal development, which appears to be the case with Joseph, who despite attending school thanks to his brother's hard work paying his way, ended up as a fish porter and dock worker like his father, getting his porter's license on 1st July 1878, where he would work solidly for ten years. He never moved out of the East End, and remained a labourer the rest of his life.

Between then and 1888, Joseph would continue with a transient life moving around the worst slums of Whitechapel (his addresses including Osborn Street, Heneage Street, and Wellclose Square), regions heaving with the poor and destitute, and riddled with crime and prostitution. His job, one of hard physical labour and in a masculine environment would have been a challenge for the man described later as nervous, stammering and shy, who would drink hard apparently just to be capable of socializing. That said, it meant he was physically strong and earned enough to dress in a far more dapper way than his colleagues, and he was noted at the inquest for his attire.

Possibly his first real relationship with a woman began on Good Friday, 8th April 1887, when he appears to have met Mary Jane Kelly as a customer at her pitch on Commercial Street, outside The Ten Bells pub. He would be forgiven for his immediate fascination with her – she was his height, 5' 7", with waist-long blonde hair and blue eyes, 25 and remarkably attractive. The very next day after meeting her, the infatuated Joseph Barnett resolved to move in with Mary, and they took lodgings at George

Street, Whitechapel. This street ran south from Flower-and-Dean Street, where Mary was currently dossing when they met, and right through the centre of Thrawl Street. They would move from place to place, ending up at 13 Miller's Court, which ran off Dorset Street yards from George Street.

One thing to note is that Dorset Street, where the Court stood, was another horrible place. Only 150 yards long, it housed nearly 2000 people and was so dangerous that police would only enter if absolutely necessary, and never alone. It sat alongside the tangle of streets dubbed the "Wicked Quarter Mile," Flower-and-Dean Street, Thrawl Street and Fashion Street, and was a hub of prostitution and crime, as well as deprived and subhuman living conditions. Joseph and Mary lived there in as best as can be called comfort thanks to Joseph's work at the fish market, where he earned up wards of £3 a week, packing and loading fish, earning extra money and working twice his usual four-hour morning shifts by cleaning and preparing the fish. His work would have brought in enough to keep Mary Kelly off the streets, a life she hated but that she otherwise needed to stave off starvation, and pay their rent. But all that changed in around July or August 1888.

What happened is not known for sure, but at about this time Joseph Barnett lost his job at Billingsgate after ten years. It has been deduced by Bruce Paley, who first suggested Joseph Barnett as a Ripper suspect, that his immediate dismissal can only have resulted from him being caught stealing. Certainly, he suggested that he loved to provide Mary Kelly with "meat and other things" during his inquest testimony, and theft was an offence punishable by instant dismissal. Either way, he was left penniless, scraping around for work to provide for Mary and himself. Both being heavy drinkers, this meant not simply paying the rent and providing meals. In the aftermath of losing his job, Mary Kelly would venture back on the streets, but the pair would begin to fall behind on the rent from the end of September. Joseph would gain odd jobs working as a "labourer" and by working at an orange market nearby, but they were never as financially sound as they had been.

Having been fired around August 1888, Joseph and Mary stopped paying rent in the last week of September, presumably as their money ran out and Mary reluctantly, and much to the outrage of Joseph Barnett, resumed her streetwalking. Mary's drinking and her prostitution were the main sources of discontent, it seems, made worse by Mary's horrible change in character when drunk. She became a different person, and the apparently ineffectual Barnett became a henpecked husband to his common-law wife, only able to match her when he himself was drunk. Their drunken quarrels continued throughout October, culminating in a fight on 30th October 1888, in which the window pane of 13 Miller's Court was smashed. It seemed that Mary had invited prostitutes, first the unidentified "Julia," and then Maria Harvey, whom may have been her lover, to stay at 13 Miller's Court. Here, in an article from the *Penny Illustrated News* (17th November 1888), are Barnett's own words:

> We lived comfortably until Marie allowed a prostitute named Julia to sleep in the same room. I objected; and as Mrs. Harvey afterwards came and stayed there, I left her, and took lodgings elsewhere. I told her that I would come back if she would go and live somewhere else. I used to call there nearly every day, and if

DANIEL JOHNSON
I had any money I used to give her some

He took lodgings at Bulling's Lodging House at 24-25 New Street, across the street from Bishopsgate Police Station, where he remained until after the murder.

Between the 30th October and 8th November, little over a week, Joseph Barnett visited Mary daily with whatever money he could bring her, as well as "presents" as he alluded to earlier. However, on the 8th November 1888, after visiting her and finding her in the flat with neighbour Lizzie Albrook, the situation appears to have changed. He brought no money, and they talked for 15 minutes. He left at 8pm, and wouldn't see her again. Again, in his own words from the same article;

> I last saw her alive at 7.30 on Thursday night
> (last week). I stopped about a quarter of an
> hour, and told her I had no money. Next day I
> heard there had been a murder in Miller's court,
> and on my way there I met my sister's brother
> in law, and he told me it was Marie. I went to
> the court, and there saw the police inspector,
> and told him who I was, and where I had been
> the previous night. They kept me about four
> hours, examined my clothes for bloodstains,
> and finally, finding the account of myself to be
> correct, let me go free. Marie never went on the
> streets when she lived with me. She would
> never have gone wrong again, and I should
> never have left if it had not been for the
> prostitutes stopping in the house. She only let
> them in the house because she was good
> hearted, and did not like to refuse them shelter
> on cold, bitter nights.

Lizzie Albrook's comments about that night are also worth repeating;

> I knew Mary Jane Kelly very well, as we were near neighbours. The last time I saw her was Thursday night, about eight o'clock, when I left her in her room with Joe Barnett, who had been living with her. About the last thing she said was, "Whatever you do don't you do wrong and turn out as I have." She had often spoken to me in this way, and warned me against going on the streets as she had done. She told me, too, she was heartily sick of the life she was leading, and wished she had enough money to go back to Ireland, where her people lived. I don't believe she would have gone out as she did if she had not been obliged to do so in order to keep herself from starvation.

Mary Jane Kelly was losing her dignity, her financial security and her sobriety, not to mention her partner Joseph, all due to the deprivation of her life in Whitechapel. The 9th November 1888 was the day of the Lord Mayor's Show, and Mary Kelly would say this to Lizzie Albrook;

> This will be the last Lord Mayor's Show I shall see, said Marie tearfully. I can't stand it any longer. This Jack the Ripper business is getting on my nerves. I have made up my mind to go home to my mother. It is safer there. (Dew, 1938, pp.86, 143-155)

Those words were reported by Walter Dew, a beat cop who worked the streets of Whitechapel and knew Mary by sight, in his memoirs, *I Caught Crippen* (1938). Mary was clearly approaching rock bottom, and Joseph meanwhile was brooding over her return to the streets, her shacking up with women who were probably her only friends and confidants in the world. As we've seen, he blamed her for the break-up, denied she ever walked the streets while they were together, and all this after having seen what remained of her body in the blood-sprayed room they shared when he was called to identify her.

Following the murder, he was taken into custody by police and kept for four hours, his clothes checked for bloodstains and his alibi examined. He was released, and after testifying at the inquest into Mary's death, would vanish from records until 1906. After that he is seen to be living with his brother Daniel at 18 New Gravel Lane, Shadwell. He would end his days living at 106 Red Lion Street, Shadwell, with a woman named Louisa Barnett who is listed as his wife but for which no supporting documentation exists. He died 26th November 1926, a few weeks after his wife, aged 68 of similar pulmonary disorders that killed his father.

Fitting the Profile

So that was the biography of my suspect, Mary Jane Kelly's boyfriend Joseph Barnett. But what about this man suggests he could be the killer? In what ways does he fit the profile? I will address this in two ways; first, I will outline briefly the arguments used by previous researchers in naming Barnett as a suspect, and second, I will go through each of the 25 points in the profile provided in the previous chapter, and explore how Barnett matches up, one point at a time.

JACK THE RIPPER

To begin with, what are the arguments provided by writers such as Bruce Paley (A New Theory on the Jack the Ripper Murders', *True Crime,* April 1982) and Paul Harrison (*Jack the Ripper: Mystery Solved,* 1991) nailing Barnett as the killer? In a nutshell, the argument is this; Barnett did not want Mary Kelly working the streets, and thus concocted a plan to scare her away from prostitution by murdering a series of women (who, depending on your preference of theory, may or may not have been known to Mary). His gruesome killings were informed by his experience boning and gutting fish, which he picked up during his ten years as a fish porter, and in the end, he could take her streetwalking no more and slaughtered her in a jealous rage. On the surface it isn't a bad theory – and quite a bit survives, in a highly modified form, in my own work – but the idea of a neatly overarching theory and a tidy explanation of every element in a way any old joe could relate to it are, in my opinion, the downfall of the theory.

The real problem with most of the theories about Jack the Ripper is that the writers try to recast the crimes in a way a layman could understand. In other words, they suddenly decide the crimes were the work of a mind like our own and not the work of a sexually-motivated psychopath. A Royal doctor killing witnesses to a secret wedding? Sure – we've all seen enough TV to be able to relate to that. An abortionist covering up his (or her) botched jobs? Yep, we can relate to that too, everyone's made mistakes they'd rather forget. A jealous lover killing his girlfriend's friends and acquaintances to scare her off the streets before jealousy gets the better of him? Again, it's a goal-oriented mindset, and an emotional journey, we can relate to. But the Ripper crimes were not the work of a man with a goal, or a man trying to cover up something, or achieve something. The hole in our knowledge where motive and the killer's identity should be is begging to be filled and our minds are hard-wired to fill it with a pattern, a relatable explanation. So, this nice little theory that Joseph Barnett was some desperate sap trying to save his girlfriend from the streets, or even that he was a controlling and jealous lover with a masterplan, are just too contrived for my liking. I personally believe in the case of Joseph Barnett, this need for a pattern, a motive, a thread of common sense running through inexplicable crimes, derails the theories and renders his candidacy a curiosity rather than a serious subject for examination.

My version of this relies on one thing; he fits the profile. And this isn't some airy-fairy bullshit psychologists in their ivory towers have dreamt up while universities pay their tenures, this is a practical and grounded basis for placing him under suspicion. It follows the same logic as the suspicion levelled at Charles Allen Lechmere – there's a solid basis for knowing that questions need to be answered. In Lechmere's case, it is his timing regarding the Mary Ann Nichols case and the fact that he appears to be near each murder at about the right times – the only difference is that such a practical plot hole would unquestionably have been addressed at the time and that it could all be quite easily explained, and in all likeliness, was explained to the police's satisfaction. In the case of Barnett, it is simply that he is uniquely befitting of a profile that has been drawn up by experts, including details determined from a close examination of the killer's activities and behaviour, and of facts of the case drawn from the wider context. In case this still seems all a little pie-in-the-sky, I should remind you that a psychological profile was arranged by Professor David Canter in the 1980s in response to a serial killer and rapist terrorising

London. When applied to the police's list of suspects, which numbered greater than 1000, the list reduced to one name; that man, John Duffy, would be jailed for life for three murders and multiple rapes. Again, I do not claim to "know" that Barnett is the Ripper. Nobody "knows" who the killer was, even those whose suspicions are, from a God's eye view, literally correct. That knowledge is lost, blowing in the wind. My contribution here is to add my name to the list of those who believe that Joseph Barnett appears to be a very strong contender from a criminological and psychological point of view.

With that in mind, let's begin. I will revisit each point of the profile outlined in the previous chapter, and discuss them in relation to Joseph Barnett.

His Appearance and Background

- *White male, 28-36 years old*
- *Irish background*
- *Dominant mother, absent father*
- *Tall, about 5' 7"*
- *Fair complexion*
- *Moustache*
- *Medium build*
- *"Shabby genteel"*
- *Looks like a foreigner*

A white male Joseph Barnett undoubtedly was. He was Caucasian and aged 30 when the murders occurred. Studies have shown that the serial killers are aged around 28 on average when they first start killing (Aamodt, 2016), and given the race, gender and occupations of the victims, not to mention what was done to them and the fact that multiple witnesses place them in the company of men shortly before their murders, I think it is virtually certain the killer was a white male. His family were Irish immigrants from Cork, and they grew up in the largely Irish migrant areas of Whitechapel – this would include his and Mary's lodgings in the Wicked Quarter Mile.

Joseph's father died when he was just six, whilst his mother apparently ran the family single-handedly until she abandoned them to work as a servant in 1871, when Joseph was just 13. After that, the household was run by Denis and Catharine, his brother and sister. Both would eventually leave as they married. The debilitating effects of his lung problems probably meant that Joseph's father was less and less capable as a parent as the years progressed, meaning that in the six years Joseph knew him, his mother undoubtedly dominated family life, with his sister acting as a substitute who would also abandon him in the following seven years. Such a cycle of domination and abandonment would have made Barnett incapable of sustaining a trusting and intimate relationship, which is what we see in his controlling, jealous, paranoid and undignified efforts with Mary Kelly. Indeed, Bruce Paley in *The Mammoth Book of Jack the Ripper* (p. 262) quotes the renowned FBI profiler Robert Ressler's landmark work *Whoever Fights Monsters* (1992) in describing the developmental influences on serial killers,

> [P]otential murderers become solidified in their loneliness first during the age period of eight to twelve. Such isolation is considered the single most important aspect of their psychological makeup. Many factors go into fashioning this isolation, among the most important is the

absence of a father.

Barnett would have had a weak or absent father figure for the first six years, and from ages 6-13 was one of several siblings scraping by in dire poverty, and during a very unhealthy social environment in the most dangerous and crime-ridden slums in London, with his overworked mother dominating the family until her abandonment. Joseph appears to have been the runt of the litter, never the head of the household and only just above his brother John in the pecking order due to age. No wonder he would become withdrawn and incapable of ordinary relationships.

Whilst Joseph Barnett certainly has the background that fulfils the profile's criteria, what of his physical description? Let us return to the best description we have of the killer; Joseph Lawende. He described a man in his 30s, around 5 feet 7-9 inches tall, fair complexion, moustache, medium build, a "salt-and-pepper" loose jacket, grey cloth peaked cap and a red neckerchief. He commented that the man looked shabby and a bit like a sailor. This is Joseph Barnett's porter's license from 1877 (my emphasis);

> Badge 853. Barnett, Joseph. Address: 4 Osborne Street [sic], Whitechapel. **Age: 20. Height: 5 ft 7 ins. Complexion: fair.** Issue Date: unfilled. Renewal dates: 1/Jly/1878. Comments: Changes of address to St. Thomas Chambers, 1 Heneage Street, Spitalfields and 4 North East Passage, Wellclose Square.

Also, contemporary drawings of him in the press depict him looking dapper and sporting a moustache, as per the descriptions of the Ripper.

He would have been an exact match for Joseph Lawende's suspect. The same cannot be said for Elizabeth Darrell, who saw a man over 40, dark and foreign-looking, although she did not see his face and couldn't even be sure of the clothes he was wearing. Finally, Emily Marsh described a six-foot man with a dark beard and moustache, aged about 45. In her case, I am still uncertain if the man was the writer of the "From Hell" letter, and whether he is or not, the authenticity of the letter as a genuine Ripper missive is up for debate. One way or another, the best detailed and reliable witness is Joseph Lawende, and his description is a dead ringer for Barnett. You can see the doubt that exists here, and even more can be introduced when you consider the fallibility of eyewitness recollection, but nonetheless it is uncanny to read the two descriptions side by side.

One final detail worth zeroing in on was Elizabeth Darrell's description of the man she saw with Annie Chapman as "shabby genteel." *The Star* (12th November 1888) reports Barnett as "looking very respectable for one of his class," which is precisely how I would define "shabby genteel." I note this only because "shabby genteel" is fast becoming another vapid mantra trotted out on Ripper Walks and by lay Ripperologists but given no further analysis or context.

Personality

- *Shy and ineffectual*
- *Physical and/or speech impediment*
- *Overcontrolled and reacts badly to change*
- *A drinker, who drinks to build confidence*

485

As I described in Barnett's biography, he apparently struggled with echolalia and a stammer into adulthood, which were indicative of a developmental disorder, but which would have severely impacted upon his socialisation. In terms of his behaviour, Barnett is clearly a passive figure; 13 Miller's Court was rented in Mary Kelly's name, meaning their break-up meant he needed to leave and find lodgings. Newspaper reports at the time of the inquest report his stammer (*Standard*, 13th November 1888);

> Witness spoke with a stutter, and evidently laboured under great emotion.

Joseph reported his kindness towards Mary Kelly, saying that he visited her daily to give her money and gifts, whilst witnesses at the inquest reported nothing out of the ordinary with their relationship, other than John McCarthy mentioning the fight in which the window pane was broken. Even then it appears to have been due to both of them being drunk, and Barnett's regular drinking appears to have acted as a social lubricant, helping him to speak at the inquest, and helping him stand up to the drunken Mary.

How do we reconcile this image of the stammering, thoughtful man with the image of an obsessive serial killer, executing and disembowelling women? A clue could be found in the testimony of Julia Van Turney.

> **Julia Van Turney:** I knew the deceased for some time as Kelly, and I knew Joe Barnett, who lived with her. He would not allow her to

go on the streets. Deceased often got drunk.
She said she was fond of another man, also
named Joe. I never saw this man. I believe he
was a costermonger.

A costermonger is someone selling from a cart or a stall,
and often refers to a fruit and vegetable salesman. Of
course, Joseph Barnett was working as an orange seller at
the time, having been sacked as a porter. I suggest that
Mary Kelly had told Julia Van Turney that she liked Joe, but
also disliked Joe, because Joseph Barnett had two sides to
him – a controlling and manipulative, maybe violent side,
and a kinder, ineffectual side that gave her gifts and doted
on her. Van Turney misunderstood what she was saying,
assuming she had a second lover. The controlling side was
the one that demanded she stay off the streets and came
out after a drink, matching Mary's drunken attitude and
fighting with her. The other side was a syrupy
sentimentalist who tried to woo her back over after their
fights and keep her sweet. I'm not talking about "split
personalities" or any such convenient plot device here –
I'm talking about the complex and multifaceted nature of
personality, of layers of the self and the personas people
adopt. Barnett's control was exerted in an unhealthily
polarised manner, through this doting dependency and
gift-giving, or through a demanding, controlling iron fist.
When Kelly tried to convey this to Julia Van Turney, it
came across as if she was referring to two different men.

On the surface, Barnett appears a shy, stammering
hopeless romantic, but the finer details of his and Mary's
relationship belies the truth; a manipulative and
demanding control freak. To illustrate his intolerance to
change, consider that the murders coincide with major
stressors in his life;

- July/August 1888, Joseph is dismissed from his ten-year employment, forcing him into poverty, scrounging for odd jobs, and putting Mary Kelly back onto the streets – Martha Tabram is murdered in George's Yard on 7th August 1888, Mary Ann Nichols is murdered at Buck's Row on 31st August 1888, but unsatisfied by his botched crime, he murdered Annie Chapman a week later at Hanbury Street 8th September.

- On 26th September 1888, the last payment of rent is made before the couple apparently fall into arrears that aren't cleared up by the time of Mary's death – Catharine Eddowes is murdered on 30th September 1888 around the corner from an orange market Barnett may well be familiar with given his employment at the time.

- 30th October 1888 – after arguing over Mary's return to prostitution and her allowing first Julia, and then Maria Harvey to stay at her flat, Joseph leaves. 8th November 1888 – after trying to woo her back empty handed, she ditches him - 9th November 1888, the final victim is murdered inside 13 Miller's Court itself.

His resorting to drink is another sign of his lack of confidence and his inability to deal with stress. He appeared at the inquest "furiously drunk" and was reportedly in drink with Mary regularly according to witnesses including John McCarthy. When *The Star* interviewed him on 10th November 1888 he was in a pub drinking, calmly discussing the murder of his lover over a pint. But this is not something to dwell on as especially suspicious; there's no crime in liking a drink and under the circumstances, whether he's the killer or not his reasons for getting plastered in the days following the murder at Miller's Court are understandable. Even the killer couldn't have walked away from the ruined woman on the bed without it affecting him somehow. But my point is that such behaviour is a distraction from stressors. And whilst financial worries clearly played their part in Mary's regrettable actions and her downward spiral into depression, Barnett appeared more concerned with Mary and how she lived her life. He was outraged not at her rent arrears, as I discussed earlier, but at her association with prostitutes and of her sharing their room with such people. He was worried about his tenuous grasp on power over Mary. This was an obsession for Barnett, and the real source of his stress. So, he drank, and brooded, and simmered, impotent to act and unwilling to take it out on Mary. And as his rage bubbled over inside, he sought a substitute for his rage against Mary, his rage against his own lack of control over her, and he removed that substitute's identity by covering, turning or slashing her face, and lived out a fantasy of possession and control and most of all, cathartic violence by the slashing, stabbing and ripping of the victim.

Relationships

- *Unmarried*
- *Incapable of relationships except with prostitutes*
- *Is sexually dysfunctional*
- *Significant female presence in his life who is a source of stress and emasculation*

As we have seen, Joseph Barnett almost certainly met Mary Jane Kelly as a customer of her services outside her pitch at the Ten Bells pub. He is reported to have hated prostitution, and took exception to Mary Kelly's walking the streets during their relationship, but it seems that's how they met, which indicates that he was using prostitutes up until that point. This contradiction – a moralistic attitude towards prostitution, yet continuing patronising of their services, is one seen in the behaviours of serial killers the world over. A hatred for, yet dependence upon prostitutes is a volatile mix, and this may indicate why he took such a controlling attitude towards Mary. Their relationship was not a healthy one; they were by all accounts sex and drinking buddies, Mary being dependent upon his finances, and Joseph's obsession with her underlying the smouldering tension between them, which came to a head when Mary's drunken personality came out and ignited arguments and fights. There's no indication of any serious relationships preceding this, and evidence only exists for two women in his life – one was Mary, and the other is a woman named Louisa Barnett.

Barnett certainly did not marry Mary Jane Kelly despite some press reports referring to them as man and wife. Following the death at Miller's Court, Barnett vanished from records until 1906 when he is reinstated with his porter's license. However, in the 1911 census, Joseph Barnett makes a reappearance but with a twist, as he is apparently living at 60 Red Lion Square, Whitechapel, with Louisa Barnett listed as his wife. No documentation exists to provide a clue as to who she is, and nothing support the idea that they married but Joseph Barnett's census entry specifically is remarkable - It lists Joseph and Louisa as having "completed" 23 years of marriage, placing the "marriage" between April 1887 and April 1888. Since Joseph met Mary Jane Kelly on 8th April 1887, this raises intriguing possibilities; first, that Joseph wanted to scrub Mary Kelly – and his connection to the murders – from his life altogether and collaborated with his new lover to rewrite his background; second, that he was leading a double-life, secretly shacked up with Mary Kelly whilst maintaining a wife elsewhere; and third, that "Louisa Barnett" is actually Mary Kelly herself, having survived Miller's Court as I suggest, and brought completely under the thumb of Barnett under the pretext of his "protecting" her from the Ripper and keeping her off the streets and they both so desperately hated.

That final suggestion is attractive to say the least. Researchers are continuing to try and pin down any documentation at all that proves the identity of this Louisa Barnett and her relationship with Joseph Barnett, but so far there's nothing concrete. I'm disinclined to believe that he was leading a double-life of some kind, like the plot of some stupid soap opera. I'm more inclined to believe that he met someone new who agreed with him to fudge some dates and erase the Miller's Court business from his past.

However, I'm most intrigued by the coincidence of the earliest possible date for Joseph and Louisa's marriage; April 1887. The very same month and year he met Mary. Given that I have argued that there is substantial evidence to believe Mary Jane Kelly did not die in Miller's Court – medical evidence fixing the time of death at 3:30am, but two independent witnesses placing Mary alive twice long after – I am willing to offer the argument that Louisa Barnett was indeed Mary Jane Kelly, living anonymously after the death at Miller's Court. Believing Jack the Ripper knew who she was and where she lived, and knowing she was a prime target for the killer being a sex worker, she fled as she promised with Barnett. To put this into context, remember that the Ripper was killing victims closer and closer to Miller's Court, attacking women known to the pair even if just in passing, and in the meantime Barnett was reading Mary the lurid, scaremongering press reports of the murders. Part of his psychopathology was his desire to control her, and taking a broken and rock-bottom Mary Kelly completely under his control would have been a satisfying scenario for him, obsessed as he was with her.

After all, we only have Barnett's word that the body at Miller's Court was indeed Mary Jane Kelly – her destroyed face and blood-soaked body was otherwise rendered unidentifiable – he apparently recognised her by an eye and an ear. There's every possibility that he was the man Kelly met at The Britannia that morning, as seen by both Maurice Lewis and Caroline Maxwell, and that after explaining to Barnett what he already knew about Miller's Court, he convinced her to go into hiding while he played the distraught boyfriend and "identified" her as the victim.

This somewhat controversial suggestion might explain the trail-off in murders post-Miller's Court. With his "source victim" now his captive, he may not have felt the desire to unleash his frustrations upon semi-random victims. Mary may have been ground down by life already up until 9th November 1888, but after finding the decimated body in her flat that morning it could have traumatised her into agreeing to put herself entirely in the "protection" of Joseph Barnett.

There are problems with my suggestion. First is a press report from an American newspaper, *The Wheeling Register,* 19th November 1888;

> Last week I saw the man, Joe Barnett, who had
> lived with the woman Kelly up to a short time
> before she was butchered. He then begged for
> money to bury his poor dear, and wanted it
> understood that he 'ad a 'art (i.e. had a heart) as
> well as men with black coats on. He was
> furiously drunk at the inquest and is living with
> a certain notorious Whitechapel character who
> testified at the inquest and became enamoured
> of the drunken brute because, as she said, of the
> romantic interest attaching to him, which
> illustrates life in London's slums. Kelly's
> remains will be buried on Monday.

The only women to testify at the inquest were Maria
Harvey, Caroline Maxwell, Julia Van Turney, Elizabeth
Prater, Mary Ann Cox and Sarah Lewis. It seems that the
"heartbroken" Barnett was begging for money and
shacking up with Mary's neighbours. This does not
diminish my theory of Barnett as a likely Ripper – after all,
Mary's neighbours were mostly prostitutes themselves,
and the profile does suggest that the Ripper would likely
only be able to form relationships with prostitutes – but it
does put a kink in the idea that Mary, calling herself
Louisa, was waiting somewhere with dark glasses and a
scarf for her controlling boyfriend to return from the
inquest to protect her. Also, a workhouse record,
considered to be quite possibly of the genuine Louisa
Barnett, exists dated from 1911 which lists her age as 55 –
making her 32, not 25, in 1888.

All in all, one thing we do know is that Joseph
Barnett did end up living with someone towards the end
of his life, although probably as common-law man and

wife. The details are fuzzy, and given the context of the above article, it may have been another prostitute he ended up living with. The idea that it was Mary Kelly herself is, admittedly, quite far-fetched, but it was worth suggesting until further evidence comes to light.

Joseph Barnett and Mary Kelly's relationship appears to have been otherwise a somewhat usury one. They quarrelled, they made up, they lived together, and he jealously denied ever having seen her drunk and denied she'd ever resorted to prostitution. Those last two things were, of course, demonstrably false and probably his effort to preserve his pride. However, Joseph and Mary's sex life is quite simply unknown, other than his meeting her as a customer. Three things are certain, and that is that Joseph met Mary whilst picking up prostitutes, that Joseph never fathered children as far as we can tell – he and Louisa died childless in the 1920s – and that Mary was turning tricks in hers and Joseph's own bed the night of the murder, hours after their last meeting. Whilst we cannot know about Joseph's sexual predilections, and we have no witnesses who speak of Mary's opinion of his sexual prowess, we can deduce that he was not particularly experienced sexually or in "proper" relationships even by the age of 30. Also, if he did have any deviant sexual desires, without a proper outlet he is likely to sublimate them in some way, such as in the work he does handling dead fish and maybe participating in their preparation. If his late-blooming in seeking a relationship, his work at the fish market in part a way of playing out his picqueristic urges, and his visits to drunken prostitutes a way of letting off steam that ordinary sexual relationships would not fulfil (as many a prostitute will explain, customers will subject them to some strange and disturbing acts they are almost certainly not doing with their regular partners), then this certainly points to some degree of sexual dysfunction.

Whether or not he was deviant or simply impotent in his regular sexual relationship with Mary Kelly is irrelevant to the nature of their relationship when viewed in the context of its usury nature. Mary Kelly lived well with Barnett while he pulled down £3 per week from the docks, working possibly 4-8 hours per day. They lived together with this arrangement for around a year and three months until he was dismissed from the market and had to job around. By September they couldn't afford the rent, and by the end of October she dumped him and returned to the streets. As their relationship deteriorated, he became increasingly frustrated with her behaviour, whilst she steadily sank into drink and her obnoxious alter ago came to the fore.

John McCarthy made this telling comment about her drunken personality;

> **Coroner:** What rent was paid for this room ?
> **McCarthy:** It was supposed to be 4s 6d a week. Deceased was in arrears 29s. I was to be paid the rent weekly. Arrears are got as best you can. I frequently saw the deceased the worse for drink. When sober she was an exceptionally quiet woman, but when in drink she had more to say.

"More to say" is a sly phrase indeed. This, from Elizabeth Phoenix, who spoke to the newspapers about Mary following her death (*Morning Advertiser*, 12th November 1888);

> She is described as being very quarrelsome and

abusive when intoxicated, but "one of the most decent and nicest girls" when sober.

Barnett himself was quoted in *The Star* of 10th November 1888 as saying this;

> In a public-house close by Buller's the reporter succeded later on in finding Barnett, who is an Irishman by parentage and a Londoner by birth. He had lived with her for a year and a half, he said, and should not have left her except for her violent habits.

Incidentally, at the inquest he said he'd left because of the presence of Maria Harvey and Julia, revealing an interesting contradiction in his story. But more to the point we see here that he considered her violent, not just abusive, when drunk.

This change in personality is not unique to Mary Kelly, and as her depression worsened and her situation became increasingly bleak, she would have been in this state more often than not. It is telling that despite weeks of rent arrears, between 30th October and 8th November, when Joseph had steady employment as an orange seller at Spitalfields Market and visited Mary with money daily, she never contributed to the rent. Instead, she was described as being incoherent with drink on the night of the murder. Joseph, a man unaccustomed to close interpersonal relationships, clearly was henpecked – it was Mary's flat, not his, and his money was spent on her, money she drank away. As I said, this was one side of his controlling manner, the other being his demands that she not work the streets, which seemed to be his priority rather than maintaining the more important aspects of her life (for example, he could have paid McCarthy the overdue rent himself, therefore removing the main source of Mary's drinking and prostituting). Instead he enabled her drinking and her irresponsible lifestyle, and continued her dependence upon him. That came with a price, though. It meant that she more and more lapsed into her drunken, quarrelsome state and she disobeyed Barnett's demands by her prostitution. In this way he is setting up the very conflict driving the killer's motivation – growing rage at a dominant female figure in his life.

Now, there does seem to be a contradiction here; Barnett's "controlling" manner with Mary, and Mary figuring as a "dominant" woman to him. Let me clarify; Barnett's control is an expression of his own inadequacy; he desperately seeks her validation and her love through his "softer" side, the gifts and money and support, but this is all really enabling and propping her up, making her dependent upon him materially. This leads to Mary using him for her own wants and needs, spending his money on drink, quarrelling and resorting to prostitution to continue that lifestyle in defiance of him, because she knows his emotional dependency on her is stronger than her material dependency on him, which could just end and which she could acquire from another source. Thus, his need for emotional validation drives his controlling behaviour over her, but Mary's usury motivations in staying with Barnett enable him in this regard, which leads to her exploiting her emotional and psychological hold over Barnett to defy him. His control is really providing Mary with support that she can abuse. This leads to the drunken conflicts that we see reported, and it is Barnett's emotional dependency which causes the greatest problems – after all, once it became clear he couldn't continue providing for Mary's material dependency, she ditched him and resolved to flee London.

Faced with this realisation that the object of his sexual obsession and emotional dependency was slipping from his control, he would seek to redress this with the cycle of depression, fantasy, trolling and murder that serial killers go through. In his case, this is a rapid process driven by impotent rage, and leads to the very anger-retaliatory attacks and murders described in the profile of the serial killer in question. The level of psychological damage Mary Kelly would have suffered after finding the body at 13 Miller's Court, having been reportedly suicidal and desperate by the start of November anyway, would have been tremendous. If she did acquiesce to Barnett's suggestion to "die" at Miller's Court and stay by his side under an assumed name, he would have satisfied his desire for emotional control and his relapse into such anger-retaliatory cycles would have diminished.

This killer clearly is a fantasist, a planner, a strategist and from the evidence we have seen someone with tremendous emotional control. Given the debate over his skills and his anatomical knowledge, in what way does Barnett fit according to his educational background?

Education

- *Literate, reads press reports of murders*
- *Has scant anatomical knowledge*

What we do know about Joseph Barnett is that he was educated to some degree. His older brother Daniel worked as a porter to support his and his brother John's education whilst they hopped from slum to slum as

498

youngsters. This may have included some very, very basic schoolboy anatomy. All the Ripper needed to know was whereabouts in the body the organs were, and roughly their appearance. As for their functions, he seemed only interested in the uterus as a sexual organ, which could be deduced from its location, rather than knowing exactly what it did – plus, his deviant interest in anatomy extended only to a fascination with the inner workings of the female body and how he could take it apart, rather than an anatomically-minded study of the organs' functions. The murders, particularly the last one, seem to be reflections of the killer's desire to control the victim, right down to dismantling and even consuming them. So, thinking medically about his anatomical knowledge is errant. A child plays with plastic blocks not because he is pursuing a career as an architect, but because he likes putting things together and taking them apart. Same with the Ripper. The scant knowledge we see him display is probably all he has, and all he has any real interest in or desire for, and this is knowledge Joseph Barnett could have easily learned in school or in his own time. The Ripper did appear to know that you can eat kidneys, however, which tells us his background was good enough to provide meat in his diet, and that he was aware of the organs he could consume. Once all four Barnett brothers began work at Billingsgate they would be pulling in enough to feed themselves comfortably.

Further evidence of his education, and his psychopathy, can be seen in the fact that he read the newspaper reports about the Ripper murders to Mary Jane Kelly, apparently at her request. Illiterate, Mary asked him to read them aloud, which only made her more nervous about her lifestyle. From the inquest;

Coroner: Have you heard her speak of being afraid of any one?

Barnett: Yes; several times. I bought newspapers, and I read to her everything about the murders, which she asked me about.

Coroner: Did she express fear of any particular individual?

Barnett: No, sir. Our own quarrels were very soon over.

Note how when asked if Mary feared anyone, Barnett quickly bats away any suggestion she feared *him.* But the crucial fact here is that Barnett was reading the reports in the papers, and using the stories to terrify his lover, satisfying her morbid curiosity rather than trying to ease it – evidence he used fear to control her. If he was reading the stories to Mary, he was taking it all in, too – including the overblown description of the Annie Chapman crime scene provided by that paper which would be replicated at Miller's Court itself.

Employment

- *Works weekdays*
- *"Safe" outlet for destructive urges*

Barnett had regular employment up until mid-1888, and after that worked on and off at Spitalfields Market. Therefore, he would be accustomed to the routine of working weekdays.

At the time of the murders, Joseph had worked as a fish porter at Billingsgate Fish Market for ten years. There seems to be debate over whether his job included the gutting and preparation of fish, but the weight of opinion seems to be that he would have been, and not only that, his family's long-standing role at Billingsgate Fish Market means he would have been exposed to these skills from an early age.

The method of slashing the victims' throats right through and then hacking open their abdomens, before pulling out their entrails, appears superficially like the preparation of fish or the process employed by a slaughterman. The crimes grew increasingly grotesque as the killer grew in confidence, so it is entirely possible that he was transferring experience from his work to his crimes. Picqueristic offenders are not simply dipping into their sexual deviance with their murders, they are living their sexual deviance, so it is bound to be expressed in some form during his daily life and not just acted upon on those rare occasions where he kills. That said, it must be pointed out that this is not a hard-and-fast rule.

Peter Sutcliffe, probably the most relatable contemporary analogue to Jack the Ripper, was a picqueristic offender who worked as a lorry driver, and never worked as a butcher or a surgeon or a fish porter. His working environment was devoid of appropriate stimuli, unlike for example, Charles Allan Lechmere, who worked carting meat around to Whitechapel's butchers. With that in mind, we can forgive researchers who argue the dotted i's and crossed t's of the role of a fish porter, suggesting there's no evidence he would have gutted fish. After all, his working environment was a damn sight more stimulating for his picqueristic and necrosadistic tendencies than Peter Sutcliffe's was, given that he would undoubtedly have been working alongside fishmongers and piles upon piles of gutted fish, the entrails and blood everywhere. And after all that, it is still quite probable that a man born and raised in the family business of portering at Billingsgate did have experience in boning and gutting fish from an early age, was used to the blood and gore of it, and was handy with a knife.

Geographic Profile

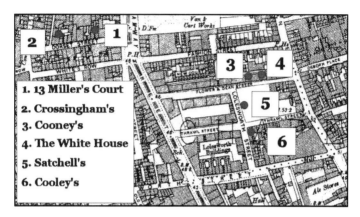

1. 13 Miller's Court
2. Crossingham's
3. Cooney's
4. The White House
5. Satchell's
6. Cooley's

Illustration 17 Barnett's and the victims' addresses

- *Lives in Whitechapel*
- *Lives/ works near Dorset Street and/or Flower-and-Dean Street*
- *Drinks in The Britannia public house*

Joseph Barnett lived in Whitechapel his whole life. As a child and an adolescent, he moved around the worst slums in the district and ended his days living in nearby Shadwell. During the Ripper murders, he lived in the very heart of the district near to where the victims lived, and the murders took place.

Now, this is where the geography of the area becomes important. Take a look at the above map, showing both the locations where Barnett lived with Mary, but also the doss houses used by the victims of the

Ripper;

Barnett met Mary Kelly when she lodged at Thrawl Street, and they soon took up lodgings at George Street, before moving on to Brick Lane, Little Paternoster Street and finally 13 Miller's Court.

Mary Ann Nichols dossed at 18 Thrawl Street (Cooley's) from the 2nd August 1888 to the 24th August 1888. From 24th August 1888 until her death on the 31st, she dossed at 56 Flower-and-Dean Street (The White House). Her local pub, where she was seen on the night of the murder, was the Frying Pan on the corner of Thrawl Street and Brick Lane.

Annie Chapman lived at 35 Dorset Street (Crossingham's), doors away from Miller's Court, from May or June 1888. Catharine Eddowes lived at 55 Flower-and-Dean Street (Cooney's) on and off from 1881 right the way until her death. However, she is also reported to have used a "shed" for homeless women next-door to 26 Dorset Street (Miller's Court itself), up until the night of her murder;

> Telegraph 3rd October 1888 – [of the two double event victims] The former had endured every variety of privation, humiliation, and pollution, moral and physical; the latter had times without number been in so abject a state of destitution as to be compelled to share the nightly refuge - a shed in Dorset-street - of a score or so of houseless waifs, penniless prostitutes like herself, without a friend, a name, or even a nickname. This once most unhappy wretch has been identified, but not by any real or fanciful designation, by some of her no less miserable associates, and by two City

constables, who had arrested her on Saturday evening for drunkenness, a few hours before her assassination. She was still in custody at Bishopsgate-street Police-station at one a.m. on Sunday, at which hour she was released, and sauntered away along Houndsditch towards the place of her death, which must have occurred barely twenty minutes after her release from custody.

And again, following the Miller's Court murder;

Telegraph 10th November 1888 - Dorset-street is made up principally of common lodging-houses, which provide not less than 600 registered beds. In one of these establishments Annie Chapman, the Hanbury-street victim lived. Curiously enough, the warehouse at No. 26, now closed by large doors, was until a few weeks ago the nightly resort of poor homeless creatures, who went there for shelter. One of these women was Catherine Eddowes, the woman who was murdered in Mitre-square.

It is also worth noting that Martha Tabram and her companion that night, Mary Ann Connelly, also lived within this small area. Martha Tabram dossed at Satchell's Lodging House at 19 George Street just before her death, having originally lived at 4 Star Place, which ran off Commercial Street, on the other side of the district. Mary Ann Connelly was resident at Crossingham's at 35 Dorset Street prior to that night, and would have been a neighbour of Joseph Barnett and Mary Jane Kelly at the time of the Tabram murder. It has been suggested by some researchers, particularly Dr Frederick Walker on the

Casebook.org website (Walker, [accessed 14/9/17]), that the killer appeared to target victims with the name or alias "Mary Ann." Indeed, Catharine Eddowes even went by the name "Mary Ann Kelly" prior to her death. However, I think this is either far-fetched or impossible to prove, as Mary Ann was a popular name for the day. However, I do believe it makes the presence of Mary Ann Connolly in the story of the Tabram murder a curiosity that can only reasonably be explained by this theory – that the killer was indeed living within the vicinity of his victims, targeted victims named Mary Ann (a name Mary Kelly apparently used occasionally), and killed Martha Tabram thinking it was her friend Mary Ann Connolly. Regardless, I still believe the Tabram murder to be the most likely of the apocryphal victims to have been murdered by the Ripper.

So, Joseph Barnett would have lived within yards of Mary Ann Nichols, Annie Chapman, Martha Tabram, and next door to Catharine Eddowes at around the times of their murders. Also, his and Mary Kelly's notorious drinking would have taken them to the Frying Pan, where Mary Ann Nichols drank on the night of her death, and The Britannia, where Annie Chapman drank, at the times they were patronising those establishments. The questions over whether the victims knew each other or not is academic – the real question is whether the killer, with whom the victims appeared to feel perfectly safe, was familiar with the victims. It appears that Joseph Barnett is uniquely at the heart of the Ripper case, but also in close contact with the victims, and appears to have been frequenting prostitutes when he met Mary Jane Kelly. His stuttering, shy manner would have easily disarmed the women he approached, and if indeed he did suffer a condition such as autistic spectrum disorder or some other neurological issue, it could easily be that he presented a broadly harmless appearance regardless of what he was thinking or feeling.

Rather than try to rationalise this by saying, "he murdered Mary's friends to scare her off the streets," I will quote Hannibal Lector; "we covet what we see every day" (Harris, 1989, p.339). He chose women he was familiar with and who were comfortable around him, and this allowed him to disarm them in his approach, rather than grab any old streetwalker he saw and risk failing in his attempt. Ultimately, his removal of their identity through his efforts at depersonalisation means who they really were didn't matter to him – and if he'd managed to remove their identity to such an extent that nobody could identify them, choosing Mary's friends would have been a waste of time if his intention was to scare her!

Joseph Barnett's connection to these locations cannot be ignored, and his selection of crime scenes equally so. Catharine Eddowes was killed near an orange market where Barnett most likely was familiar with. Annie Chapman was killed yards from where he and Mary lived, whilst the final victim, whether it was Mary or not, was killed in his own home up until a week prior. The only sticking point – and this is true of all suspects – is Buck's Row. It is so far from any of the other crime scenes, and bears no reasonable excuse for hosting the Ripper at that time. Even if one reasons that the killer selected Mitre Square for the Masonic connection to the name, or because it was across police jurisdictional boundaries, or because an orange market was nearby, one cannot come up with any rational explanation for the murder in Buck's Row. It hosts no obvious spot for sexual activity such as Hanbury Street, and the killer must have been in the area to have met Mary Ann Nichols, who was touting for business for an hour prior to her murder between Osborn Street and Buck's Row. At the time, Barnett and Mary lived in Miller's Court, nowhere near Buck's Row. The only connection apparent is that Mary Ann drank in the Frying Pan pub on the night of her death, and the same pub was just down the street from Barnett and Mary's doss when they met. Possibly, her killer met her there and arranged to meet her later, hoping the doors to Brown's Stable Yard were unlocked when they got there.

Contrasting Dr Rossmo's profile with that of the FBI, the former suggests that the killer's home base was likely in or near Flower-and-Dean Street, whilst the FBI surmise that the killer must live near to the first crime. If Martha Tabram's murder was actually the first murder, as some suggest and which I cannot rule out, then both profiles nicely dovetail, and Joseph Barnett certainly was based near Flower-and-Dean Street – first dossing at George Street, which intersects it, and then at Miller's Court across the road – both spots just yards from the scene of Martha Tabram's murder.

Thus, the geographical spread of doss houses and murder scenes in relation to Joseph Barnett's own movements during 1888 are extremely suspect.

The "Locked Door" Mystery

There's one last thing to consider in relation to the identification of Joseph Barnett as the killer and in relation to the Mary Kelly murder in particular; the so-called "mystery" of the locked door of 13 Miller's Court. The story is this; when police found the body, the door to 13 Miller's Court was locked. The key had gone missing some time ago. However, Inspector Abberline had this to say;

> An impression has gone abroad that the
> murderer took away the key of the room.
> Barnett informs me that it has been missing
> some time, and since it has been lost they have
> put their hand through the broken window, and
> moved back the catch. It is quite easy. There
> was a man's clay pipe in the room, and Barnett
> informed me that he smoked it.

The broken window was close enough to the latch to allow Mary or Joseph to reach in and release the catch manually. Not only that, but it appears the lock was a spring lock that automatically locked when the door closed. Regardless, let us make one thing clear – locking and unlocking the door was something the killer would have witnessed the victim doing. Maybe he had the key, and maybe he nicked it from the victim as he left, but it doesn't really matter too much – the point is that there really is no mystery regarding the locked door; that said, one question is still hotly debated. Let us remind ourselves of the evidence of the case, and answer this question; Who was the last person to have been seen exiting 13 Miller's Court?

Let us review the evidence. The very last Miller's Court witnesses before the body's discovery were Caroline Maxwell and Maurice Lewis. Let's review what they said;

> **Caroline Maxwell:** My husband is a lodging-
> house deputy. I knew the deceased for about
> four months. I believe she was an unfortunate.
> On two occasions I spoke to her.
> **Coroner:** You must be very careful about your

evidence, because it is different to other people's. You say you saw her standing at the corner of the entry to the court?

Maxwell: Yes, on Friday morning, from eight to half-past eight. I fix the time by my husband's finishing work. When I came out of the lodging-house she was opposite.

Coroner: Did you speak to her?

Maxwell: Yes; it was an unusual thing to see her up. She was a young woman who never associated with any one. I spoke across the street, "What, Mary, brings you up so early ?" She said, "Oh, Carrie, I do feel so bad."

Coroner: And yet you say you had only spoken to her twice previously; you knew her name and she knew yours?

Maxwell: Oh, yes; by being about in the lodging-house.

Coroner: What did she say?

Maxwell: She said, "I've had a glass of beer, and I've brought it up again"; and it was in the road. I imagined she had been in the Britannia beer-shop at the corner of the street. I left her, saying that I could pity her feelings. I went to Bishopsgate-street to get my husband's breakfast. Returning I saw her outside the Britannia public-house, talking to a man.

Coroner: This would be about what time?

Maxwell: Between eight and nine o'clock. I was absent about half-an-hour. It was about a quarter to nine.

She reports seeing Mary Jane Kelly at sometime between eight o'clock and half-past eight on the morning of 9th November 1888 at Miller's Court.

Next, Maurice Lewis *(Morning Advertiser, 10th November 1888);*

> There is no direct confirmation of this statement, but a tailor named Lewis says he saw Kelly come out about eight o'clock yesterday morning and go back again to the house.
>
> [...]
>
> Kelly was seen in a public-house known as "Ringers," at the corner of Dorset-street and Commercial-street at about ten o'clock yesterday morning, and that she there met Barnet and had a glass of beer with him. This statement is not substantiated

He saw Mary leave 13 Miller's Court at eight o'clock on the morning of the 9th November 1888, the exact time and place as Caroline Maxwell did – but in this account, *she meets Barnett in the pub* (identified as "Ringers" but judging by geography, certainly The Britannia). Nonetheless, here we go – the last person seen to leave 13 Miller's Court following the murder...is Mary Jane Kelly herself.

The Night of the Murder, and After...

This is the timeline of events as I understand them;

7:30-7:45pm, 8/11/88 - Mary Jane Kelly broke up with Joseph Barnett, who had arrived at Miller's Court empty-handed, and then proceeded to go out drinking with her friend and flatmate Julia.

10pm-11:pm - Daniel Barnett finds her and tries to talk sense into her on behalf of his brother, but fails.

11:45pm – Mary Kelly seen by Mary Ann Cox, drunk, and with a client.

1am-2am 9/11/88 – Mary goes back out and picks up another client, whom she takes to Miller's Court, under the watchful eye of George Hutchinson, who in turn is seen by Sarah Lewis.

2:45am-3am – Mary heads back out of Miller's Court to find Joseph Barnett in The Britannia, asking "Julia" where Mary is. They argue, and Mary storms off – this argument is seen by Mrs Kennedy.

3:30am-3:45am - Joseph takes "Julia" to Miller's Court, and kills her. Cries of "Murder!" are heard by Elizabeth Prater, Sarah Lewis and Mrs Kennedy.

8am – Mary returns to Miller's Court, and finds the body. She vomits in the gutter upon the sight and in shock, tells Caroline Maxwell that she's sick with drink.

10am – Goes to The Britannia to meet Joseph Barnett. She clearly does not suspect him of the murder, and subsequently vanishes, as does he.

I have already suggested one possible explanation for Mary's disappearance from the record books following the murder – the far-fetched notion that she changed her name to Louisa and lived with Barnett for the rest of their lives. I am reluctant to believe this – it again is a little too soap opera for serious consideration. That said, truth can be stranger than fiction, so it like all theories, is worth considering. Playing devil's advocate again, let's explore the reasoning behind this theory a little more.

After finding the body at Miller's Court, and realising that she now needed to hide away to escape the Ripper's attentions, Mary probably believed the situation would allow her to escape the East End as she had wished. However, in her now suicidal and traumatised state, she would have been easily manipulated by Barnett, who managed to convince her to go by a pseudonym and live under his thumb for the remainder of her life. It would have been a huge payoff for such a massive risk – killing a victim in Miller's Court was either an act of reckless abandon or an ice-cold calculation that it would have the

511

maximum impact upon Mary, yet Barnett felt he could deal with the heat it inevitably threw his way. And this is where we deal with one aspect of the Ripper murders that, one way or another, remains to be questioned; was the killer a disorganised offender, dragging women into dark corners on a whim and slaughtering them, or a psychopath with ice for blood who took the calculated risk of exposure and played the odds?

Given that the Ripper appears to select his crime scenes ahead of time, and given that the exact location of each crime can be seen to have rational benefits – such as the spot in Mitre Square sitting in a perfect spot for the killer to notice, and flee, approaching policemen, or his entry and exit timed perfectly to avoid the regular patrols, or his nerves at a street location when he had clearly pre-selected an indoor spot in Buck's Row – we can comfortably say that he was taking the risk. Yes, he risked exposure in many ways, but this was a man who was rolling the dice and gritting his teeth, determined the body he'd so purposefully mutilated and posed for shock value would be found, and therefore selecting locations which carried inherent risk. It is therefore ironic that for a location pegged as "perfect" for the killer to satisfy his urges, the indoor location at Miller's Court actually carried maximum risk of exposure.

Following the murder, Joseph was arrested by Inspector Abberline and held for four hours, but was released without charge. His clothes had been examined for bloodstains and his alibi investigated, and they were satisfied that he had nothing to do with the crime. That all sounds conclusive until you remember that Peter Sutcliffe was questioned at least eight times by police during the many years of the Yorkshire Ripper investigation, and was only eventually identified as the killer by accident, or that

Stephen Port's first victim was found outside his flat and police still didn't make the connection, allowing him to kill three more times – murders the police did not even link together. In this context, one four-hour spell in a police cell and an interview by Abberline looks like small fry, particularly when Barnett was probably expecting it.

So, it fits the overarching argument so far to suggest that Barnett took the risk of assuming total control over Mary by killing this last victim and crossing his fingers that Mary would react like this. However, it is a stretch to believe that Mary, a consistently boisterous and independent figure wearing the trousers in the relationship, would suddenly roll over and become Barnett's doormat for the next half-a-century. It is far more likely that Mary fled as self-protection and took Joseph along only if it suited her. In that observation there lies a potential solution. In the final chapter of this book, I will explain all.

There is one other point of contention in relation to the Ripper murders which no latter-day commentator seems to be able to overcome – why the killer stopped after Miller's Court. It is often said that serial killers cannot and do not stop killing, yet this is another misunderstanding. The Ripper's killing spree came to an end as we know it on 9th November 1888 and many question why this occurred, arguing the killer must have died, been imprisoned, or moved away. In terms of my suspicions around Joseph Barnett, I'd like to point a few things out; Gary Ridgeway, the "Green River Killer," murdered at least 49 victims during his killing spree, 42 of them between 1982-1984. Although he was later connected to murders occurring after this time, the regularity of his crimes petered out until his arrest in 2003. Dennis Rader, the BTK Strangler, murdered 7 of his 10 victims between 1974-1977, committing three more between 1977-1991, and none between them until his arrest in 2004. Peter Tobin, convicted of three murders (two of which were missing people found buried in his former home in Margate, one completely unexpectedly), is repeatedly linked by crime writers and the media to the unsolved Bible John murders in Glasgow in the 1960s. Three women were raped and strangled in the street within 18 months and nobody was ever convicted of the crimes. If Tobin was this killer, and so far, no moves to prosecute him have been made in this regard, then is shows that serial killers can change their *modus operandi* to avoid capture.

In other words, the Ripper may have slowed down, stopped or simply hidden his crimes by changing his MO. If Barnett was partially motivated by his desire to control Mary, having her under his control would be an ideal backdrop for him to be less likely to offend.

In the end, Barnett, if he was the Ripper, won. He evaded justice and was able to keep the focus of his sexual obsession under his control. But my theory rests on several extremely controversial conclusions; that Mary Kelly survived Miller's Court, that Joseph Barnett was the Ripper, and the unlikely possibility that his "wife" Louisa Barnett was in fact Mary living anonymously for the rest of her life. Big and questionable conclusions, I know. However, I feel I have made a case worthy of further consideration...even if by no means did I expect, or wish, to make such conclusions in the first place.

That said, there is room for one last interpretation of the evidence

DANIEL JOHNSON
The Final Conspiracy

By this point you will see that the solution to the Ripper crimes, in my view at least, lies in the final murder. Mary Jane Kelly, Joseph Barnett, 13 Miller's Court and the butchered body on the bed. My conclusions are sound right up until the suggestion that Louisa Barnett was really Mary Jane Kelly hiding away afraid of the killer, and that Barnett had assumed psychological and sexual control over Mary, the object of his obsession. To some, it will sound ridiculous, but to some it will sound like a valid and interesting theory, a neat and tidy explanation which picks up the loose ends and provides a satisfying narrative.

I disagree.

There are a lot of unanswered questions, a lot of room for cold, hard reality to fill in where fancy narratives fail. The above theory is exactly the sort I expect to read in less pragmatic works – the very same sort who suggest the killer was offing witnesses, or harvesting organs, or was some kind of Satanic cultist or Royal henchman. It's a Hollywood ending. After discussing the dangling threads and unanswered questions of the Kelly case with others in the Ripperology community, a new theory emerged – one which offers a surprising twist to the story, and one that stands regardless of whether Joseph Barnett was the killer or not. Allow me to explain.

It is a bit of a mystery how, with such a high income from Barnett's work and Mary's prostitution (not to mention her increased prostitution and Joseph's best-effort daily contributions following his sacking from Billingsgate), Mary was falling in arrears with the rent to the tune of 29 shillings. Rent for 13 Miller's Court was 4/6d (4 shillings and 6 pence) weekly. Joseph Barnett was

515

earning £3 per week[1] (60 shillings) for between four and eight hours work per day – and that was back in 1888. At the time, the average wage for a man of that class was only around £1 per week.. Between April 1887 and August 1888 he was pulling that wage down weekly and we are supposed to believe it was all drunken away? Also, Mary stated her intention to leave London after the Lord Mayor's Show on 9th November 1888, with no further illumination on how she was planning to pay for her trip. It just seems odd that these financial discrepancies exist at all.

A second question to be asked is the nature of Mary's accommodation of her "friends" at Miller's Court. At least two women – "Julia" and Maria Harvey – stayed at 13 Miller's Court much to Barnett's chagrin. Indeed, he gave that as a reason for his decision to leave her (although, he changed his story when asked later, instead suggesting that he was upset at her angry temper). This surely was against the terms of her tenancy at 13 Miller's Court, and would have upset her landlord, John McCarthy. That said, this was a man who was renting most of his lets to known prostitutes whilst apparently turning a blind eye to their activities. This blind eye even seemed to extend to women who were more than a month in rent arrears, despite his knowing full well of their additional income. It seems 9th November 1888 was the first occasion that a determined effort was made to collect rent...immediately after Mary Jane Kelly finds the body on her bed, and meets McCarthy's wife Caroline Maxwell outside the Court! What a coincidence!

McCarthy has himself been touted as a Ripper suspect, and debate was also erupted over whether he

---

[1] Corrected from "hour" in previous edition

was in fact operating as a pimp, with Miller's Court his own personal brothel. However, the better theory to fit the evidence flips this on its head. What if McCarthy was putting rent arrears down on paper for 13 Miller's Court to cover for his "cut" of the income Mary was getting by pimping other women out from that flat?

At the inquest both Thomas Bowyer (who found the body) and John McCarthy state unequivocally that the women on the bed was Mary Jane Kelly, despite her face having been brutally disfigured beyond recognition, as does Barnett. We know from the statement from Maurice Lewis that she was seen with Barnett at the Britannia around 10am on the morning of the discovery of the body, and we know Barnett went immediately to Miller's Court upon hearing of the discovery. We know that the pair's income at 13 Miller's Court was disproportionately high and that given the timeline it was unlikely for her to fall short in rent. And finally, we know that following Barnett's sacking at the fish market, Mary apparently went back to prostitution alongside friends who she was seen with out and about, and whom stayed with her at the flat.

To my eye, it seems there is an obvious explanation. Mary Jane Kelly was a pimp, taking a cut from "Julia," Maria Harvey and possibly others as they worked the streets, operating out of 13 Miller's Court. John McCarthy, a man who knew fine well what was happening at Kelly's flat, was not owed rent at all – in fact, he may have been alerted to the fact that they were keeping up with their rent despite Barnett's unemployment, and inquired, only to learn that Kelly was breaching her tenancy in a new way. Rather than boot her out, he blackmailed her for a cut – which he would explain away to the tax man or to enquiring police officers as rent arrears (pocketing the actual rent she continued to pay him to collect his cut of the earnings from prostitution as the arrears later). Upon Mary's discovery of the body on the bed, she runs into Caroline Maxwell, who certainly told her husband John of her encounter as the body was being discovered. Realising that the body wasn't Mary's, and that he would be investigated for running a brothel if the truth got out, he, Thomas Bowyer and Joseph Barnett (and Mary Jane Kelly) agree to say she was the victim so long as Mary keeps the money she was due to pay John as his cut, so they she could flee London as she planned.

This theory also explains one other odd detail about the statement by Maurice Lewis. From *Morning Advertiser,* 10th November 1888;

> There is no direct confirmation of this statement, but a tailor named Lewis says he saw Kelly come out about eight o'clock yesterday morning and go back again to the house

She left the flat, apparently having found the body, then *goes back inside.* The only possible explanation for her to do so was because she realised she needed to retrieve something there and then because she was certainly never returning. What if she was collecting the money she had stashed away there?

A final point to make is that this theory tallies with the psychological profile of Barnett as the killer. We've established that Mary was the dominant partner, despite Barnett's controlling, if inadequate, nature. After all, she paid the rent for the flat and not him. If she was effectively running a business and earning more than he was, it would have been humiliating and emasculating in precisely the way likely to feed his narcissistic rage. This then would provide an explanation for one aspect of the murder – why he killed his last victim at 13 Miller's Court; t would have been the ultimate retribution, putting Mary Kelly out of business and regaining control over her. She went to him after finding the body, even going to the pub, ordering a drink and sitting openly with him to the point that she was seen there twice by two witnesses. But following Barnett's arrival at 13 Miller's Court (which also followed both Bowyer's discovery of the body and McCarthy learning that Mary was still alive from his wife Caroline Maxwell), suddenly Mary vanishes, and all three men declare unwaveringly that the body is hers. Even though the decision-making and the collusion was between three men with vested interests, it all plays to Barnett's need for control. His inadequate personality would have benefited from the diffusion of responsibility that came with this small conspiracy, allowing him greater leverage with which to control Mary.

Now, the question remains, what happened next? Simply put, for once the absence of information works in our favour. Barnett vanishes from records until 1906. Mary Kelly of course is never seen or heard of again. Mary had stated that she intended to leave London and return to Ireland to her family after the Lord Mayor's Show on the 9th November 1888 anyway. Ergo, that's where she went, possibly with Barnett in tow, at least until 1906, by which time he'd moved back to London and was living with his wife in Shadwell. If Barnett did not follow her, then she could have lived to a ripe old age in Ireland and even had children. If he went with her, she likely died before 1906 when he came back to London. This is speculation – a topic for future research.

This casts Mary Jane Kelly in a particularly poor light – as a manipulative, scheming pimp, using men like

McCarthy and Barnett, and women like "Julia" and Maria Harvey, for her material gain. But that said, she was as human as anyone living and working in a very difficult and brutal time and place. Whether Barnett was the Ripper or not, this angle cannot be easily ignored. After all, the story of Jack the Ripper has always been a story of people.

PART FIVE: Conclusion

JACK THE RIPPER

Conclusion

There is a gaping hole in the heart of Ripperology, and this hole is a yawning chasm that can never be filled...it is the absence of paperwork.

Documents are missing. Lots of them.

The original inquest documents for three of the five victims are lost completely. Original autopsy documents have only begun appearing in the last thirty years or so. Vast gaps exist in Home Office records, police records (including witness statements and notebooks kept by officers carrying out the door-to-door searches after the Annie Chapman murder), and the memoirs of officers from the time carry details that are simply uncorroborated by the evidence due to these gaps.

It does not help that on 6th January 2014, several thick folders full of previously classified Special Branch documents relating to the Ripper case were destroyed, "coincidentally" at the very time as Ripper historian Trevor Marriot was fighting a legal battle for their release to the public. Nor does it help that the entire City of London

Police Archives were burned in the Blitz during WW2. And it is no help at all that files are found to be missing or stolen in the archives we do have access to, no doubt kept by various thoughtless individuals eager for a piece of history to spend eternity gathering dust in their attics.

On the other hand, we have another problem...a mountain of paperwork.

A brief perusal of the casebook.org or jtrforums.com messaging boards will tell you that the field of Ripperology is a rabbit hole, a labyrinth of newspaper articles – many full of errors, or contradictory, or full of uncorroborated details – as well as census records, shipping ledgers, asylum and infirmary records, electoral rolls, you name it.

Between the documents we have, and the documents we lack, one can slap together all kinds of theories and make them stick. Why is Charles Lechmere a suspect? Because there's no documentary evidence either way to suggest the gaps in his story were ever checked out. Why do I suggest Louisa Barnett might possibly have been Mary Kelly? Because no definitive paper trail can be found for Louisa Barnett. At the same time, poor Aaron Kosminski has been dragged through the mud because the presence of some documents (i.e., the Swanson Marginalia and the Macnaghten Memoranda) provides evidence that lacks definitive explanation (i.e., the absence of any independent record of the Seaside Home identification).

This is a 129-year-old case. As far as we know, everything that can exists on the case has been made public, except those now lost Special Branch folders. For nearly a century-and-a-half, the Jack the Ripper murders have been the subject of continual debate, with new theories and new suspects put forward every year. The problem with the Ripper case is that it has become a precious commodity to be traded, a toy to be played with, and an easy form of academia. There are no right answers, and the prize goes to the one with the most shocking or sensational theory. Often, the rules of this game are that new theories mustn't trample on the toes of the traditions of the story. The most popular theories tend to unquestionably include Elizabeth Stride as a Ripper victim. They never question Mary Kelly's victimhood, either, and I suspect my reduction of the final victim's identity to the catch-all title, "the Miller's Court victim" will be treated as nothing short of sacrilege by the Ripperology community. They also tend to go with the idea that both the letters and graffiti are the work of the killer. It is reduced to a child's game, where the grumpiest kids throw a tantrum when someone does something that's against the rules.

I have news for you folks – this isn't a game. It isn't a story. These were real women, murdered by a real man, and he didn't just kill them, he humiliated and butchered them. You can visit their graves, you can visit their murder sites, and you can see their photographs in the pages of this very book. So when I point out the uncomfortable fact that the medical evidence puts the final victim's time of death at around 3:30am, but that two independent witnesses place Mary Jane Kelly, alive, in the same locations at the same times long after this time of death, all I say to you is this – carry on believing it's Mary Jane Kelly lying on the bed if it makes the story in your head play out better, but do not call yourself a Ripperologist, or even an academic, unless you can provide cogent arguments, backed up by legitimate evidence, to disprove my own argument. And if you can – great! We're getting somewhere, you and me. We're back on the academic process. It would then be a case of re-examining the evidence based on our newfound knowledge.

My accusation of Ripperology being easy academia is reinforced when you realise that two things tend to happen when discussing the Ripper; one, that the scientific process goes out of the window, and two, that even educated people suddenly forget how serial killers work. On the first point, let me point you to the almost worthless story of a shawl reportedly from the scene of the Catharine Eddowes murder, which a few years ago was DNA tested to unmask the Ripper once and for all. The results came back and reportedly pointed the finger at Aaron Kosminski. The newspapers went wild, and the Ripperology community went into meltdown...until it became clear to all and sundry that the shawl had no provenance at all, and had been handled by relatives of Catharine Eddowes and left with no environmental protections of any kind. Furthermore, the DNA apparently indicating Kosminski could have matched thousands of people across the UK. The results were worthless and reported by the press in a deeply misleading manner which totally ignored the science involved.

Secondly, as I have noted earlier in this book, the various theories about the Ripper's motivation are often constructed around concepts laypeople can relate to. Picking off a circle of friends to scare someone, or to silence them all and cover up a secret. Murdering them as part of a Satanic or Masonic ritual. Joining the murder scenes to form warped pentagrams or Stars of David. Suggesting the crimes are the work of a man or woman covering up botched abortions or seeking out a specific person and killing the witnesses along the way. Royals gone mad or Jewish lunatics with ritual slaughter knives...the list of theories is endless. But they all have the same things in common; they all assume a rational motive, and that victims are chosen deliberately, their murders fulfil a purpose. Or, the killer is an "other" of some kind, specifically an "other" to a specific audience's "in-group" - the audience being white working-class people in this case, the very people to whom *The Star* newspaper sold its muck-raking rubbish to. The "other" always fall into these categories; Royals, toffs, and immigrants. Dr Barnardo, Arthur Conan Doyle, Prince Albert or Sir William Gull. Poor, harmless Aaron Kosminski.

Royals covering up a conspiracy, toffs acting like perverts, or mad immigrants acting like no Englishman would. This is a shameful pattern that our society repeats, made worse by the fact that such theories inevitably project the prejudices of the audience. Racism, classism, fear and ignorance of mental health, anti-religious bigotry, all can be found in the annals of Ripper theories. But to my eye, with my qualifications in psychology and criminology and a lifelong study of the criminal mind, the most affronting thing is the sheer inability of commentators and theorists to acknowledge that the Ripper was a serial killer, and that he behaved as such.

Even though this book posits that Joseph Barnett is a probable Ripper suspect, I have not trotted out the old, "he killed Mary's friends to scare her off the streets because he loved her so much" story. Instead I have argued his motives from a psychological point of view; I paint a picture of a socially and sexually inadequate man driven by obsession and a pathological need for control, who is acting on deep-seated deviant sexual desires in his murders. And I argue that his crimes are best seen as expressions of anger-retaliatory sexual violence, as seen in cases of rape. His selection of the victims is due to his own familiarity with them as sex workers, possibly because he's patronised their services before, but also likely because he lived and drank in such close proximity to them – not because he and/or Mary Kelly were friends with them. I argue that he was withdrawn, fantasising about his murders at a growing pace, whilst he continued a torturous and unhealthy relationship with Mary. This fantasy lead to him selecting potential murder scenes, victims, even methods, as part of the cycle of fantasy and trolling that he was engaged in all throughout this intensive period of psychological and sexual tension – unemployment in July 1888 all the way to his volatile breakup with Mary in November 1888. And judging by his continued maintenance of this tension – reading Mary the news reports of the Ripper crimes, paying her money directly knowing she was going to drink it away rather than pay her rent, etc. - he was enabling this tense situation whether he consciously realised it or not. Finally, I argue that he took the enormous risk of the Miller's Court murder at least in part to terrify a downtrodden Mary and regain control over the situation, putting her out of business and leaving her dependent upon his support. But the psychological terror angle cannot be downplayed – after all, he'd read her that horrific *Star* article about the Annie Chapman murder, only for her to see it recreated on her own bed on that fateful day at Miller's Court. That was a deliberate act, a piece of theatre which worked perfectly.

It is a theory. One of many. If you can disprove the pillars of my theory as stated above, I implore you to do so. Prove to me without a shadow of a doubt who the Miller's Court victim was. Prove to me that Stride was a Ripper victim. Prove to me that Joseph Barnett is innocent. Prove to me that Mary Kelly wasn't a pimp, that

DANIEL JOHNSON

John McCarthy wasn't faking the rent arrears to cover for his cut – provide me with the evidence! Prove the Ripper wrote all those letters, or even some of them – heck, prove to me either that he wrote or did not write the "From Hell" letter, something I tend to believe but cannot prove! If you can prove all of this, then go ahead and finish the race by proving once and for all who Jack the Ripper really was, because clearly you're a better researcher than anyone else on Earth...but be wary, because the next thing you know, your absolute, definite, unequivocal proof will be shot down in flames by the next book to hit the shelves.

This book is not the last word in the Ripper murders. It is, if anything, yet another new beginning. To finish, I'd like to quote Inspector Abberline first, and Sir Robert Anderson, second;

> Theories! we were lost almost in theories; there were so many of them (Abberline, 28th May 1892, Cassell's Saturday Journal)

> On my return I found the Jack-the-Ripper scare in full swing. When the stolid English go in for a scare they take leave of all moderation and common sense. If nonsense were solid, the nonsense that was talked and written about those murders would sink a Dreadnought (Anderson, *The Lighter Side of My Official Life,* 1910)

References & Bibliography

<u>Inquests</u>

Mary Ann Nichols' Inquest
The Daily Telegraph, 3rd, 4th, 18th, 24th September 1888
Evening News, 3rd September 1888

Annie Chapman's Inquest
The Daily Telegraph, 11th, 13th, 14th, 20th, 27th September 1888

Elizabeth Stride's Inquest
The Daily Telegraph, 2nd, 3rd October 1888

Catharine Eddowes' Inquest
The Daily Telegraph, 5th, 12th October 1888

Mary Jane Kelly's Inquest
The Daily Telegraph, 13th November 1888

<u>Newspaper & Magazine Reports</u>

The Star, 5th, 6th, 8th September 1888, 10th, 12th November 1888, 1st October 1888

The Jewish Chronicle, 3rd March 1910, 11th March 1910

Daily Chronicle, 1st September 1908

Lloyd's Weekly Newspaper, 30th September 1888

Daily News, 12th October 1888

Evening News, 9th October 1888

News of the World, 7th October 1888

The Daily Telegraph, 3rd October 1888, 20th October 1888, 10th November 1888, 18th February 1891

Illustrated Police News, 17th November 1888

Morning Advertiser, 15th October 1888, 10th November 1888

DANIEL JOHNSON

Munster News, 10th November 1888

The Times, 24th November 1888

Pall Mall Gazette, 7th May 1895, 24th March 1903, 31st March 1903

The Daily Mail, 2nd June 1913

Morning Advertiser, 12th November 1888, 30th March 1903, 23rd April 1910

The Sheffield and Rotherham Independent, 1st September 1888

Echo, 16th September 1888, 20th September 1888

Seattle Daily Times, 4th February 1905

Morning Leader, 9th January 1905

City Press, 7th January 1905

Penny Illustrated News, 17th November 1888

The Wheeling Register, 19th November 1888

Standard, 13th November 1888

Cassell's Saturday Journal, 28th May 1892

Crime and Detection (June 1966, Oxford Tallis Press)

Blackwood's Magazine, March 1910

<u>Books</u>

The Crimes, Detection and Death of Jack the Ripper (1987), Martin Fido, Weidenfield Paperbacks, pp. 37-8, 79, 172, 173-4, 212, 213, 223, 231

The Mammoth Book of Jack the Ripper (1999), Maxim Jakubowski and Nathan Braund (eds), Robinson, pp. 173-195, 262

Jack the Ripper: The 21st Century Investigation (2005) Trevor Marriott, John Blake Publishing, pp. 13-14, 165, 182, 183

The Ultimate Jack the Ripper Sourcebook: An Illustrated Encyclopedia (2001) Stewart P. Evans and Keith Skinner, Robinson, pp. 25-7, 213-4, 701

Jack the Ripper: An Encyclopaedia (2010) John J. Eddleston, Metro, pp. 26-7, 86-7, 171, 174

JACK THE RIPPER

The Jack the Ripper A-Z (1991) Paul Begg, Martin Fido and Keith Skinner, Headline, pp. 45-6, 130, 282-90, 489

The Lighter Side of My Official Life (1910) Sir Robert Anderson

Criminals and Crime (1907) Sir Robert Anderson

From Constable to Commissioner (1910) Sir Henry Smith

Days of My Years (1914) Melville Macnaghten

I Caught Crippen (1938) Walter Dew, pp.86, 143-155

Jack the Ripper: Mystery Solved (1991) Paul Harrison

Whoever Fights Monsters (1992) Robert Ressler and Thomas Shachtman, St Martin's Press

Criminal Shadows (1994) David Canter, HarperCollins Publishers

Geographic Profiling (1999) Dr. Kim Rossmo, pp. 239-241

Jack the Ripper: Portrait of a Killer (2003) Patricia Cornwell, Sphere.

The Silence of the Lambs (1989) Thomas Harris, St Martin's Press, p. 339

Official Documents

Dr Brown's Autopsy Report on Catharine Eddowes
Ryder, Stephen P. (Ed.). "Dr Frederick Gordon Brown." Casebook: Jack the Ripper.
Accessed: 16th September 2017 <http://www.casebook.org/witnesses/frederick-gordon-brown.html>

Warren't Report to the Home Secretary
Ryder, Stephen P. (Ed.). "Warren's Report to the Home Secretary." Casebook: Jack the Ripper.
Accessed: 16th September 2017.
<http://www.casebook.org/official_documents/warrenlt.html>

George Hutchinson's Witness Statement
Ryder, Stephen P. (Ed.). "George Hutchinson." Casebook: Jack the Ripper.
Accessed: 16th September 2017.
<http://www.casebook.org/witnesses/w/George_Hutchinson.html>

Estimating Mary Kelly's Time of Death
Ryder, Stephen P. (Ed.). "Estimating Mary Kelly's Time of Death." Casebook:

Jack the Ripper.
Accessed: 16th September 2017.
<http://www.casebook.org/dissertations/ripperoo-todeath.html>

Dr Bond's Postmortem on Mary Kelly
Ryder, Stephen P. (Ed.). "Dr Bond's Postmortem on Mary Kelly." Casebook:
Jack the Ripper.
Accessed: 16th September 2017.
<http://www.casebook.org/official_documents/pm-kelly.html>

FBI Profile of Jack the Ripper, produced by the NCAVC 6th June 1988.
https://vault.fbi.gov/Jack%20the%20Ripper

Other Documents

The Polish Jew Suspect – Jewish Witness Connection: Some Further
Speculations
Ryder, Stephen P. (Ed.). "The Polish Jewish Suspect – Jewish Witness
Connections: Some Further Speculations." Casebook: Jack the Ripper.
Accessed: 16th September 2017.
<http://www.casebook.org/dissertations/rip-polishjew.html>

Rossmo, K. (1995) 'Geographic Profiling: Target Patterns of Serial Murders',
Simon Fraser University

A New Theory on the Jack the Ripper Murders', *True Crime,* April 1982

Joseph Barnett's Porter's License
Ryder, Stephen P. (Ed.). "Hey Joe! Your Porter Story Sounds Fishy!"
Casebook: Jack the Ripper.
Accessed: 16th September 2017.
<http://www.casebook.org/dissertations/dst-barnettporter.html>

Joseph Barnett
Ryder, Stephen P. (Ed.). "Joseph Barnett." Casebook: Jack the Ripper.
Accessed: 16th September 2017.
<http://www.casebook.org/dissertations/barn-art.html>

Amodt (2016) Serial Killer Information Centre; Statistics;
http://maamodt.asp.radford.edu/Serial%20Killer%20Information%20Center/Se
rial%20Killer%20Statistics.pdf

Photographs

All photographs used are in the public domain in the United Kingdom and
were sourced from Wikimedia Commons and Wikipedia.

Other Images

Maps of Whitechapel, showing the locations of the canonical five murders, and the locations of the dwelling places of the victims are sourced from the 1894 Ordinance Survey map of the district. Their use is courtesy of Ordinance Survey.